MAKESHIFT
WORKSHOP SKILLS for
SURVIVAL and SELF-RELIANCE

MAKESHIFT WORKSHOP SKILLS for SURVIVAL and SELF-RELIANCE

Expedient Ways to Make Your Own Tools, Do Your Own Repairs, and Construct Useful Things Out of Raw and Salvaged Materials

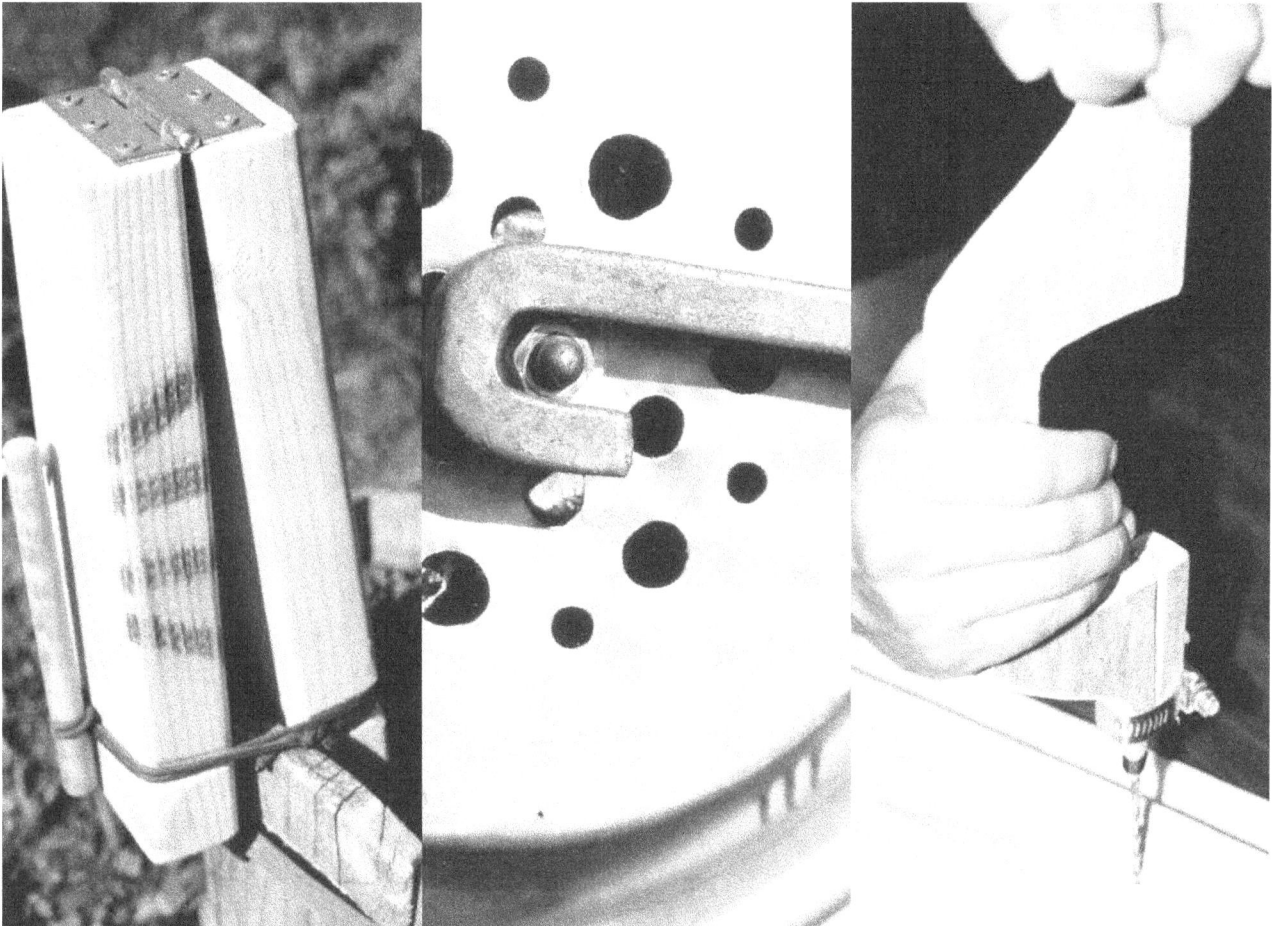

James Ballou

Foreword by Charlie Richie, *Backwoodsman* magazine

Makeshift Workshop Skills for Survival and Self-Reliance: Expedient Ways to Make Your Own Tools, Do Your Own Repairs, and Construct Useful Things Out of Raw and Salvaged Materials

by James Ballou
Copyright © 2009 by James Ballou

ISBN: 978-1-943544-09-7

PrepperPress

Published by Prepper Press
Post-apocalyptic Fiction & Survival Nonfiction

www.PrepperPress.com

Contents

Warning

The information in this book is based on the experiences, research, and beliefs of the author and cannot be duplicated exactly by readers. The author, publisher, and distributors of this book disclaim any liability from any damage or injury of any type that a reader or user of information contained in this book may incur from the use or misuse of said information. This book is *for academic study only*.

Acknowledgments

I dedicate this book to my wife, Alicia, who was very supportive of me throughout this project.

I also owe special thanks to the three very knowledgeable people whom I've been fortunate enough to learn from: John Becker, Vincent Smith, and my dad, Gene Ballou.

Thanks to technical proofreader Don McLean for his helpful ideas and input.

Finally, I wish to thank my patient and insightful editor, Jon Ford, whose skillful, hard work molded the many different elements into the coherent book you are now reading.

Foreword

When the word "makeshift" is broken down, it means anything that is a temporary substitute. It can be something constructed from odds and ends, or something serving in an emergency capacity. Jim Ballou knows how to get the most out of everything. He has an uncanny knack for seeing something that most of us probably wouldn't be able to make into something useful and then improvising it into an item that causes most of us to mutter, "Why didn't I think of that?"

Here at *Backwoodsman* magazine, we've always considered Jim our best writer at improvising alternative methods of doing things. He's the guy who can build a knife from an old pair of scissors, repair a gunstock with rawhide, build a working forge from a barbeque grill, make improvised tools for almost any use, and . . . well, read this book and you will get some idea why I think Jim would be your best buddy on Crusoe's island.

After reading Jim's first book, *Long-Term Survival in The Coming Dark Age*, I thought his approach to assembling supplies, recycling, bartering, and salvaging was a level above what I'd read in other books. His new book, *Makeshift*

Workshop Skills for Survival and Self-Reliance, expounds on the themes of self-sufficiency, adaptability, and practical knowledge he provided in the first book.

I've known Jim for many years, and one of the things I've always appreciated about his work is that it is easy to understand his approach to things. He communicates his methods for accomplishing projects in a straightforward manner we can all understand—no long-winded, confusing sets of plans; just easy-to-follow text, accompanied by clear drawings and photos. His new book is filled with unique and creative ways to turn ordinary items into something useful. He bridges the gap nicely between yesteryear methods of doing things and modern-day techniques for building innovative items basically from scrap. He will capture the interest of any do-it-yourself fan who reads *Makeshift Workshop Skills for Survival and Self-Reliance*.

There are those among us—not necessarily the people who will buy this book, but others—who may ask, "Why do we need to know how to makeshift things? Why can't we just buy another item when the old one breaks?" Try this the next time you are miles from anywhere and you can't just run out and buy a new one. In my case, when I was young I simply didn't have the money to buy new things. Luckily, I've always had a little makeshifter in me, or I would have done without. In our current economic situation, Jim's book is a jewel for those who can't afford to replace essential items or pay to have them repaired.

A survivalist/makeshifter/improviser/back-woodsman is usually a master of a lot of things, and my friend Jim Ballou has indeed mastered many essential skills for those interested in becoming more self-reliant. In the book you are about to read, he enthusiastically shares those skills.

Charlie Richie
Owner/Publisher, *Backwoodsman* magazine

When Improvised Devices Are Necessary

The creative ability to improvise is arguably one of mankind's greatest assets. It has helped the human race adapt to the world's different environments and to ever-changing situations throughout history. It has given birth to invention and, in one way or another, aided the development of virtually every technology ever used by man.

This book is intended to inspire the reader with a kind of "makeshifter's" way of thinking about things. Even when improvised devices aren't absolutely needed, finding new, unconventional ways to devise, adapt, or repair things certainly exercises the creative potential within us and forces us to really use our brains.

Of course, from time to time, we may find ourselves in situations that force us to improvise and adapt to unexpected circumstances—and precisely how we might manage these kinds of situations will be the focus of this book.

To begin, we might ask ourselves this simple question: When would improvised, makeshift devices ever actually be necessary in today's high-tech, civilized world? After all, just about every common human need is easily met these days with sophisticated technologies, quite often requiring no more effort beyond the flip of a switch or the push of a button. The human race has spent thousands of years learning how to make chores easier, and we've certainly come a long way in this regard.

Well, as convenient as so many things are in our time, we still live in an imperfect world. Even the most advanced systems, devices, and technologies in existence are not failsafe. Products and their component parts can break or wear out, batteries can go dead, and infinite types of malfunctions can render the modern conveniences we tend to rely on totally useless. Quick replacements of failed systems or parts may not always be available for a variety of reasons.

Under these circumstances, makeshift technologies could suddenly become very practical. Those of us who possess creative jury-rigging skills might be able to continue functioning much better than those who lack this ability. For this reason, I believe a book that addresses unconventional fabrication and repair methodologies could be an important resource for anyone facing such challenges. Even if the information presented here were never needed, it is still an interesting study in alternative ways of doing things with only a pile of raw or salvaged materials, your hands, and your mind.

CHAPTER 1

Know Your Raw Materials

The makeshifter learns to see almost everything around him as a potential raw material with which to improvise and build things. This stock of potentially useful items includes natural as well as man-made materials of all kinds. In this chapter, we will take a close look at some of the useful materials we might find around the house or in the immediate vicinity outdoors. The better we understand these materials, the more we can do with them.

The most important thing to gain from this chapter is a better sense for selecting the right kind of material for any given application. Ultimately, nothing will be quite as beneficial in this respect as good ole-fashioned, hands-on experience with the different raw materials, with plenty of experimentation.

ROCKS AND MINERALS

Considering the amount of rock on our planet—rocks of various types are found literally everywhere—and the vast possibilities for how the different types of stone might be used in makeshift

Most households contain a vast assortment of building materials for makeshift projects.

projects, it makes sense that it should be at the top of our list of raw materials for consideration in this book.

Rocks can be used as tools for cutting, scraping, sanding, chopping, and pounding, and they can serve as practical building materials for walls and shelters, as primitive weapons, and as art materials. In fact, probably the first truly useful products ever fabricated by humans were stone tools.

Geologists categorize the Earth's rocks into three main categories: igneous rocks, sedimentary rocks, and metamorphic rocks. For our practical purposes, we might divide rocks into just two categories: 1) rocks having a somewhat vitreous (i.e., glasslike) or siliceous nature, like flint, obsidian, chert, agate, jasper, opal, ignimbrite, and others, including most of the other silicates or quartz rocks, which can be knapped into cutting tools, and 2) all other types of rocks, which we might use as sanders, hammers, anvils, scrapers, choppers, throwing stones, weights, or building materials.

Rocks from the first group are very hard, although most of them will also be somewhat brittle, the way man-made glass is hard and brittle. These rocks all share something called the conchoidal fracture characteristic, making them capable of being knapped. (More on this in chapter 4.) With the right break, this group of rocks will produce an extremely sharp edge, making them suitable for a variety of cutting tools, projectile points, and related items.

Obsidian has been called nature's glass, as it most closely simulates the characteristics of man-made glass, although it is typically translucent rather than transparent the way window glass is. Obsidian is formed by rapidly cooling lava flows, and it falls into the volcanic glass category. Because the lava cools at such a rapid rate to form obsidian, the material never forms the kind of crystalline structure common in minerals like quartz. It is therefore capable of possessing an extremely thin, fine edge. Because obsidian is so easily knapped and is capable of producing such a sharp edge, it is often the preferred material for knapping. (In fact, very fine obsidian flakes are still used for micro-surgery, as they are sharper than a man-made edge.) It can be found in several regions of the world having a volcanically active past, including such areas of the western United States as parts of Oregon and the Sierra Nevada Mountains.

Chalcedony is a catch-all term under which various crystalline stones are classified. It includes flint, agate, chert, jasper, onyx, and other quartz rocks of the silica group characterized by their conchoidal fracture behavior. Many of these easily knapped stones were used for tools and weapons during the Stone Age and later by American Indians and other primitive peoples. Varieties of quartz occur naturally throughout the United States and in numerous regions around the world.

Pieces of flint rock chipped from larger pieces I had purchased at a muzzleloader show some years ago.

An interesting and very useful feature of quartz is its ability to produce sparks when struck against carbon steel. This quality was the basis for firearms ignition for nearly 300 years prior to the development of more reliable ignition systems, such as the percussion cap and eventually the metallic cartridge. This ability to create sparks also provided people with an effective fire-lighting method long before the invention of the sulfur match.

In our second category of rocks we have granite, sandstone, greenstone basalt, marble, limestone, and others that have been and can still be useful to humans in one way or another. Grainy rocks like granite and especially sandstone typically have an abrasive quality and might serve as sanders. Granite and other types of sturdy rocks can be put to use as weights and building materials. Limestone is a key ingredient of concrete, and marble, which is a metamorphism of limestone and is composed mainly of calcite, is a common material for building and creating sculptures.

Different types of minerals range from very soft to extremely hard. The Mohs' hardness scale (named after the man who devised it, mineralogist Friedrich Mohs) was a useful early system for testing material hardness. The subject materials were scratched with 10 different stones, starting with the softest and proceeding up the scale until the material could be scratched and its hardness rated. From soft to hard, the 10 stones were: 1) talc, 2) gypsum, 3) calcite, 4) fluorspar, 5) apatite, 6) orthoclase, 7) quartz, 8) topaz, 9) sapphire, and the hardest, 10) diamond.

Let us also consider the importance of precious stones and gemstones to human societies. In art and jewelry, certain rocks are valued for their beauty and rarity. Additionally, diamonds, considered the hardest known material until only recently, are commonly used in dust form in abrasive compounds for certain grinding applications. (A new material called ADNR, for aggregated diamond nanorod, is now the hardest known material.)

CLAY

Clay is another useful raw material found virtually everywhere on Earth. From it, bowls, jars, pots, cups, ladles, jugs, canteens, tiles, pipes, ovens, chimney liners, musical instruments, adobe bricks, statues, tokens, wind chimes, and endless other utilitarian and decorative items can be made.

There are different kinds of clay that might find use in a makeshifter's repertoire, including stoneware, earthenware, terra cotta (a type of earthenware), plasticine, nylon-reinforced clay, polymer clays, kaolin clay (or china clay, which is used in porcelain), and several other variations of what we commonly call clay.

Natural clay is composed of finely grained particles of broken-down igneous rocks that have been compacted in layers of sediments and reduced to a powdery-small grain size over time to form a mud with a plastic consistency that can be molded into useful things. In simple terms, clay is the kind of mud that, when squeezed moist into a clump in the palm of the hand, will stick to itself and more or less hold the shape it's squeezed into. Although malleable in its raw state when moist, it becomes a stiff mass as it dries and is especially hard when baked, or fired. A fired vessel of clay can be wetted without dissolving or returning to its prior malleable state. It will also be much stronger, as dry, unfired clay objects tend to be brittle.

Natural clay can be found in a variety of earth-tone colors, from whitish-gray to brownish-red, and it is abundant in the Earth's surface. Its exact consistency will vary from one geographical source to another.

Working with Clay

In their raw state as collected from the ground, most natural clays will tend to crack as they dry, especially when heated in a fire pit or kiln during the firing process. This is a result of stresses either from shrinkage as moisture leaves the material during drying or from expansion in the heated ceramic materials. It can also be due to excessive pressures created as trapped moisture becomes steam during the firing process.

To keep the material more stable and to minimize cracking and breaking, refractory materials are often added to clay. Called temper or grog, it might consist of pulverized lava rocks; ground-up, once-fired clay shards; fine sand; burned and crushed seashells; or other materials that have previously been super-heated and will therefore be more stable throughout the firing process. You need to add the right amount of temper to the raw clay to achieve acceptable results, and some trial and error is usually involved in determining that amount for each type of clay. Adding temper does tend to stiffen clay somewhat, and adding too much makes it difficult to work, as the temper causes the clay to lose some of its stickiness.

To form a harder, glasslike surface on certain clay pottery and ceramic products, glaze is often added before the final firing process or, in some cases, following an early phase of the firing. There are many different recipes for glaze, but the primary ingredients are silica or boron, commonly in conjunction with a melting agent of either lead or soda, known as a flux. Lead should be avoided for use in glazes applied to vessels intended for food or drink because of the safety hazards associated with it.

One common glaze technique used by aboriginal potters is slip glaze, where you fire the piece once, then coat it with gravy-thickness "slip" made of the same clay and fire it again. The second coat tends to go into the pores of, and seal, the substrate.

Some types of clay, such as stoneware, are fired at high temperature (typically one or two hundred degrees above 2,000°F) and normally vitrify at these higher temperature ranges, i.e., they become nonporous or glassy, and watertight with or without glazing. Stoneware tends to be harder and more durable than earthenware.

Earthenware requires glazing if it will be used for dinner bowls or water vessels, because when unglazed it is porous, even after being fired. Earthenware is known as low-fire clay, often fired at just above 1,700°F because it cannot endure very high temperatures without sustaining damage.

Terra cotta is fired but unglazed earthenware. Normally having an orange-brown color, terra cotta is used extensively in planter pots, where its porous nature is desirable.

As mentioned, it is common for clay products to crack, break, or even explode during firing, but steps can be taken to reduce the chances of damage. Adding temper is one solution, but the wet clay should also be thoroughly kneaded and worked by hand before being molded into its ultimate shape to remove any air pockets that might cause problems during firing. Before firing, the clay should be allowed to dry *thoroughly* to eliminate the problem of trapped moisture in the material. Finally, the clay should be baked *slowly*, with a very gradual increase of the temperature.

The presence of almost microscopic pieces of organic material in clay has been known to cause spalling (mini-explosions in the kiln), so if you are digging your own clay, try to avoid getting roots, grass, bugs, and similar matter in there. I've heard of one potter who would dig the clay and reduce it all to slip, then pour it into large glass fish tanks so it would settle and self-classify. The large chunks of sand and rock would go to the bottom, and he would skim off the organic material that rose to the top of the water. As the clay settled over a few days, he'd decant the water until he had pretty uniform clay, which he would scoop out until he got to the lower layer, where the coarse stuff had settled. Then he'd let the clay dry to the right stiffness and pug-mill it for uniformity.

Some hobbyists, modelers, and sculptors prefer working with synthetic clays, like nylon-reinforced or polymer clay, as these tend to experience less cracking and distortion. Generally these clays aren't suitable for firing, or at least not at any temperature higher than a few hundred degrees Fahrenheit.

Different techniques have been used to shape and form wet clay into usable objects. Products like clay pipes are often formed by squeezing the moist material through presses, and things like bricks and tiles might be pressed into molds.

Forming a clay cup using the coiled rope technique.

The earliest pottery was shaped by hand, without the help of a potter's wheel. Lumps of moist clay were first flattened out and then molded into vessels. A common method, still used today, was to roll a rope of wet clay by hand on a flat surface and coil it to build up the sides of a bowl or cup.

Modern-day potters often use a potter's wheel—essentially a round plate upon which the workpiece sits as it spins—while using their hands and sometimes various scrapers and paddles to sculpt the wet clay into the shape of a vessel. Many potter's wheels are motor driven these days, though human-powered versions are not uncommon.

ANIMAL PRODUCTS

The skins of animals have been used for making clothing, bags, shelters, and other equipment for thousands of years, and antlers, horns, and bones have been used for tools, weapons, containers, and miscellaneous handles for just as long. These items comprise some of nature's most useful raw materials.

Working with Animal Skins

Animal skins vary a great deal in thickness and physical characteristics depending on the size and species of animal, and the resulting products vary in texture to a large extent by the type of tanning process used. Skins left untanned are what we know as rawhide.

Raw animal hides gradually become pliable when thoroughly wet and tend to become stiff and tough when dry. Rawhide is excellent for making expedient repairs to things, and it was used a great deal in this capacity by primitive people wherever wild or domestic animals were accessible. Rawhide is also an excellent material for such things as mallet heads, moccasin soles, snowshoe webbing, knife sheaths, and dog chew toys.

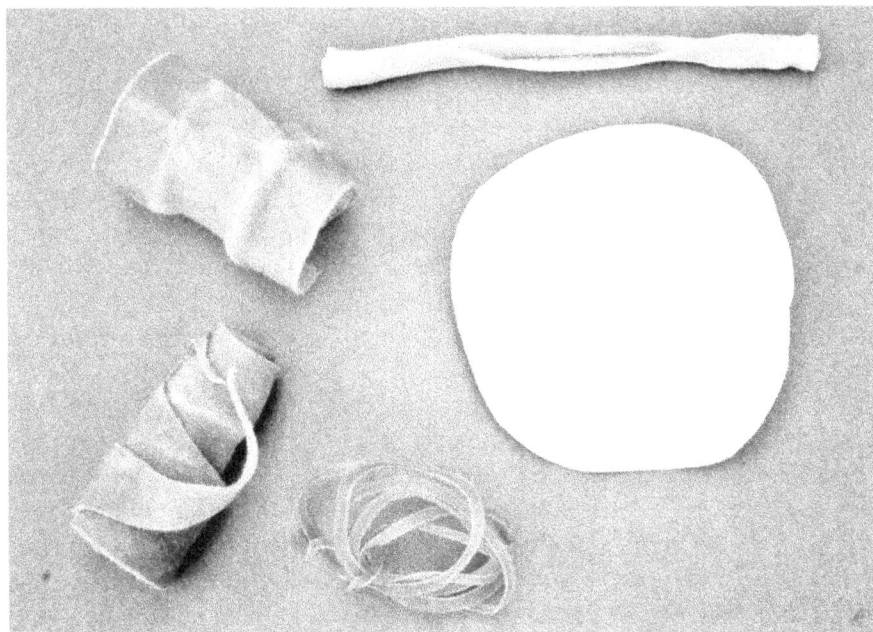

Scraps of dry rawhide waiting to be soaked and formed into useful products.

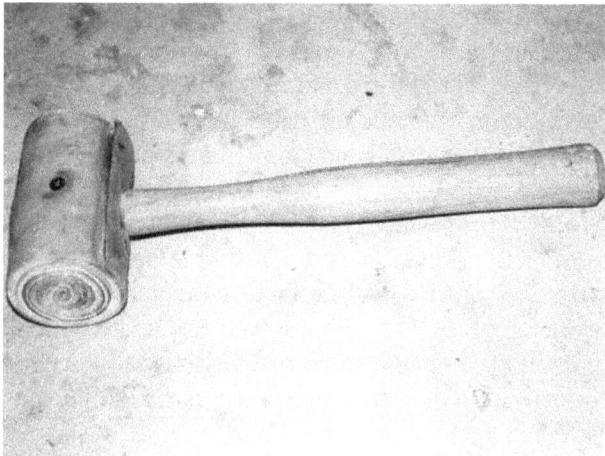

Example of a rawhide mallet.

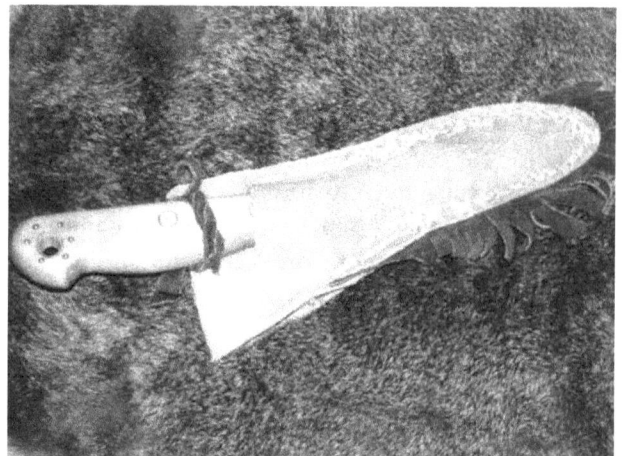

Knife sheath made out of rawhide.

The primary disadvantage to rawhide is that, in its natural state, it loses much of its characteristic rigidity whenever it gets wet. This can be prevented by coating the rawhide with a waterproofing sealer such as resin or varnish.

Tanned hides are preserved in a softer, more pliable state than rawhide. A properly tanned animal skin should resist shrinking, hardening, or deteriorating. Anyone interested in learning how to tan hides should be aware that there are several completely different methods in common use, and they produce leathers, furs, and buckskins that have very different characteristics.

Bark tanning, also known as vegetable tanning, is a very old method that produces high-quality leather ideally suited for tooling and for making holsters, knife sheaths, saddles, handbags, wallets, and similar items. When wetted, the leather is easy to form, and it tends to hold the shapes into which it is molded very well.

Vegetable tanning involves soaking the hide in a solution containing tannic acid (the tannin bath) for a period of time that can be as long as several months for a particularly large animal hide. This extensive time requirement is perhaps the biggest disadvantage to vegetable tanning. The tannic acid, or tannin, can be extracted from tea leaves, leached acorn powder, or the bark of certain trees like walnut, oak, sumac, or hemlock. The source of tannin will affect the resulting color of the tanned leather, but vegetable-tanned leather will be various shades of brown and will typically have a smooth surface, often with a rich sheen.

By contrast, chrome-tanned leather is normally some shade of silvery gray to blue or even greenish in color, and its surface has sort of a grainy roughness to it. If you were to bend a piece of chrome-tanned leather, it would tend to spring back into its original shape when released. Also, chrome-tanned leather is less affected by water than is vegetable-tanned leather. It is generally not as expensive as vegetable-tanned leather because it does not require as much time to make. The potentially negative impact of its waste chemicals on the environment is commonly considered a disadvantage to chrome tanning.

Chrome tanning is accomplished when hides immersed in the chrome bath are completely permeated by a solution of water and chrome crystals (such as chromium sulfate, or chromium potassium sulfate), often in conjunction with other salts. The different chrome-tanning techniques vary in some of the details, but the basic process of saturating an animal hide in a chrome solution remains consistent.

The tanning process commonly called dressing (or alum tanning, "alum" being short for aluminum) is popular with fur skins because, unlike most tanning processes that tend to loosen hair and fur, alum tanning actually helps hold the fur in the skin by shrinking the pores. However, alum tans are not generally considered to be as durable as some of the other types of tans.

The tanning solution for dressing can consist of ammonium alum, aluminum sulfate, or potash (potassium) alum—usually in a mixture with such other ingredients as borax, noniodized salt, club soda, and neatsfoot oil—and used in a two-day immersion bath for small- to medium-sized skins. The solution can also be made into a paste by adding flour or cornmeal, which is then easily applied to the skin. The paste generally works best when left on the skin for a day or two longer than an immersion bath. After the process is complete, the skin is scraped clean and then thoroughly rinsed in water.

Furs and hides that have been tanned with this process can be adversely affected by a prolonged soaking or by dying, as the tanning isn't waterproof. Prolonged soaking can cause the fur to slip.

Another common tanning process is acid tanning (also known as salt-acid tanning, or tawing), although most hide-preserving chemicals are in fact some type of acid. Acid bath recipes usually include sulfuric acid (battery acid), noniodized salt, and water, and some recipes also include saltpeter (potassium nitrate), borax, and sometimes other ingredients as well.

Sulfuric acid is very corrosive and should be handled with care and only while wearing rubber gloves and eye protection. Also, as with most tanning methods involving an immersion bath, wooden or plastic barrels are preferred over metal because of the corrosive nature of the chemicals when they come in contact with metal.

To obtain a quality product, it is crucial to prepare a hide before applying any type of tanning solution. If you don't remove the fatty tissues from the flesh side, the tanning chemicals will probably not penetrate the skin adequately. Likewise, the hair and membrane should be removed from the hair or fur side when tanning any hides except fur skins. Hair, membrane, meat, and fatty tissue can all be scraped off with a hide scraper tool, ideally made of hard steel.

Hair removal is sometimes called graining, while removing fleshy materials is sometimes referred to as membraning. The same scraping tool can perform both tasks when using a dry-scrape method. However, the majority of the fleshy tissue can be scraped off while the hide is still wet, shortly after the animal has been skinned, by scraping the wet hide as clean as possible while it is draped over a log, using either a wooden scraper or a dull drawknife.

The ideal hide scraper for dry scraping is an adze-shaped tool with a sharp beveled edge on a curved steel blade. A good scraper can be made by breaking a section off a flat bastard file and grinding an edge at one end on a radius. The blade can be secured to any sort of solid handle in a configuration resembling an adze. The scraper blade should be curved so that there are no points or corners to catch and rip the skin being scraped.

As suggested, much of the scraping can be done either wet or dry. A deer-sized hide is typically laced to a frame while wet and then scraped on both sides with the dry-scrape method after it dries stiff within the frame. The scraper's edge usually requires periodic sharpening during the process. It is important to completely scrape off the membranes and hair to ensure thorough penetration of the tanning solution. Much of the unwanted matter clinging to a hide can be soaked loose to minimize the scraping chore. A skin can be weighted down in a stream with a heavy rock for a week or longer to soften and loosen it up.

The tanning methods commonly categorized under oil tanning might be viewed as a completely different approach to hide processing and preserving. Considered not a true tanning process by some, oil tanning nevertheless has been used to produce very soft, pliable, and long-lasting products. With this method, skins are permeated with oils that coat and lubricate their fibers.

At some point in time, the American Indians figured out that the natural oils in the brains of animals were perfectly suited for treating hides. Brain tanning is a very effective, though labor-intensive, natural process. Quality pouches, bags, purses, shirts, pants, coats, moccasins, and other products have been made from brain-tanned buckskins.

The various techniques for brain tanning and the exact sequence of steps will differ from one tanner to another, but the four basic phases include:

1. Remove unwanted matter, either by soaking or scraping or a combination of both.
2. Soften the stiff rawhide by twisting, pulling, and working it repeatedly to loosen up the fibers and make the hide more pliable. Extended soaking can also be a useful step of this phase, time permitting.
3. Apply the brains to the skin. The brain of the

animal donating the skin is usually sufficient to tan one hide. The raw or boiled brain matter can be mashed and rubbed into both sides of the skin, or mashed brains can be mixed with warm water and the hide immersed in this bath to soak up the natural oils. Possible substitutions for brains include neatsfoot oil, 10W motor oil, egg yolks, or Ivory soap.

4. Finally, smoke the hide to coat the fibers with pitch. This prevents the fibers from gluing themselves back together, as would happen with untreated or rawhide, and also helps shield the fibers from bacteria to resist decay. The hide can be draped on a framework over a smudge fire that produces heavy smoke, taking care not to heat or burn the hide, and exposing it to thick smoke for 10 to 20 minutes per side.

The most familiar product made of animal skins is, of course, ordinary leather. Leather is produced with different thicknesses, normally measured in ounces. In this system of measuring, each ounce is equal to 1/64 inch of thickness. For example, a hide said to be 4 ounces should be 4/64 of an inch, or 1/16 inch thick.

Leather is widely used commercially to make clothes, shoes, bags, briefcases, holsters, wallets, and all sorts of other products, and makeshift applications for leather are infinite. As just one example, I found that heavy cowhide (something close to 10 ounces) was well suited for making a tool rack in my blacksmith shop. I tacked a series of cowhide loops to a board screwed to the wall, and tool handles of all kinds rest in these loops. (See page 189 for a photo.)

Working with Other Animal Products

Some other animal products you might find ways to use include sinews; antlers from deer, elk, or moose; horns from buffalo, cattle, and rams; the

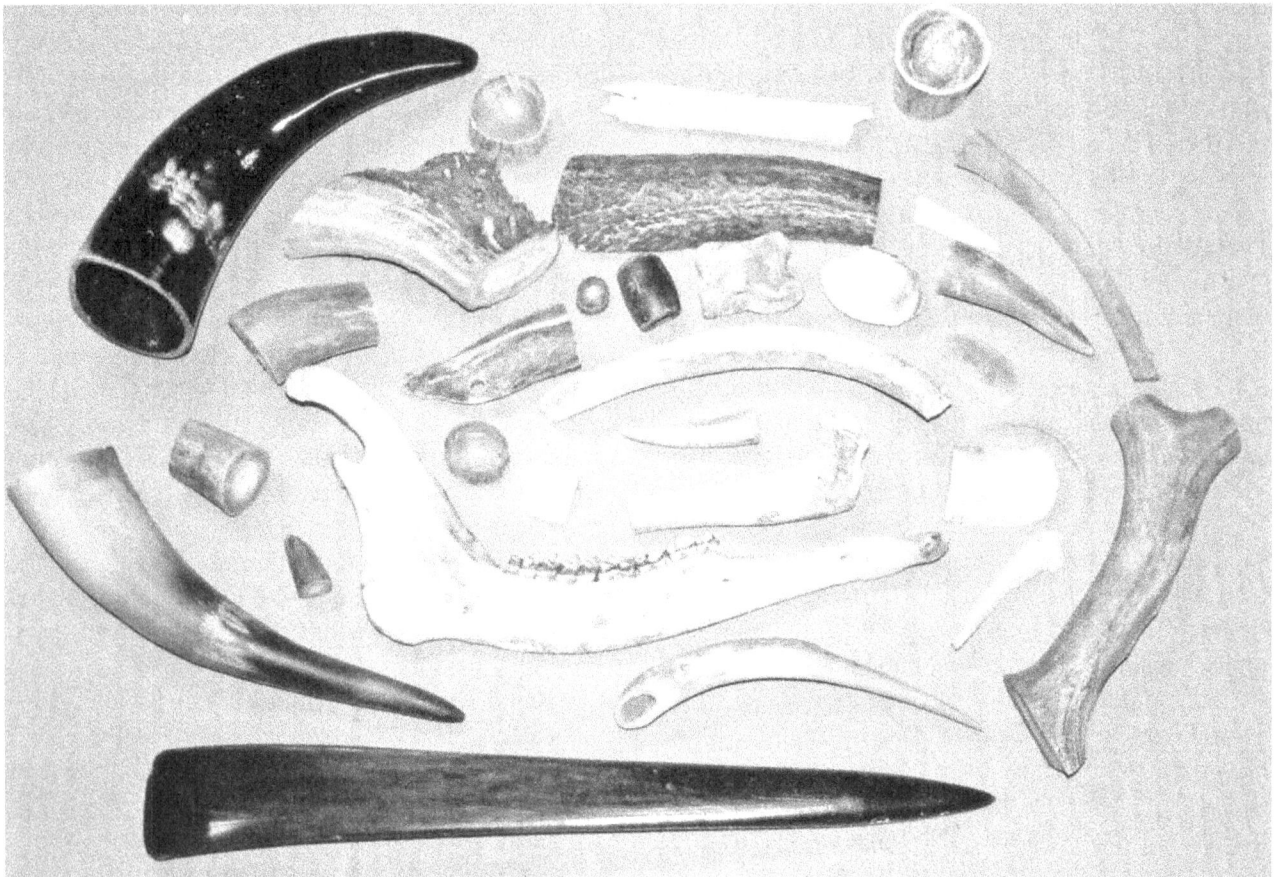

Pieces of horn, antler, and bone provide us with useful raw materials.

bones from any large animal; bird feathers; and the shells of turtles, clams, crabs, and other sea creatures. Some wild animals and birds are now protected by law, so you have to be careful about harvesting and using parts from certain species of wildlife. It is illegal, for example, for anyone but an American Indian to collect and use eagle feathers.

Bones, antlers, and seashells are primarily composed of calcium phosphates and carbonates. Interestingly, calcium is categorized in the periodic table of elements as an alkaline earth metal, atomic number 20. It is no wonder that it forms the rigid structural materials of creatures.

Calcified tissues of the body called dentin form teeth and ivory, the hardest of the animal products. Fibrous structural proteins called keratin form such softer, though still rigid, body parts as hooves, horns, human fingernails and toenails, and the outer layers of bird beaks.

Many of these durable parts of animals can be used as raw materials for both practical and creative purposes. Antlers of all kinds have served as knife handles, gun racks, door handles, lamp stands, hooks, and for numerous other purposes, and bones and horns have been used as containers, tools, and art materials for eons. I find it easy to cut bone, antler, and horn with a coping saw, but you have to be delicate about it to avoid breaking blades. The belt sander and bench grinder are convenient tools for shaping objects of bone, antler, or horn. If you don't have a buffing wheel, you can vigorously rub

bone with a scrap of rough cowhide to obtain a nice-looking sheen on its surface.

Sinew is the tough elastic tendon fibers that connect muscles to bones. American Indians have used it to tie arrowheads onto shafts, back their bows to provide more elasticity and increase strength, and for making sewing thread, bowstrings, and fishing lines, among numerous other applications.

WOOD

The general topic of wood is a vast subject indeed, so we only have room to touch on it here. In general, most types of wood are easy enough to cut, drill, carve, sand, glue together, and stain, but it's helpful to know a little about the characteristics and potential uses of the different varieties.

A whole log or section of a tree will typically reveal three parts having distinctly different characteristics. The outside is covered with bark, and beneath that is the sapwood, which is the living wood in a growing tree and is usually lighter colored than the rest. The darker part in the core of many trees is the heartwood, which is dead wood. In some types of trees, the heartwood is denser and harder than the sapwood, but in others just the opposite is the case.

Wood is commonly categorized as either softwood or hardwood. The soft category includes pine, fir, hemlock, larch or tamarack, yew, redwood,

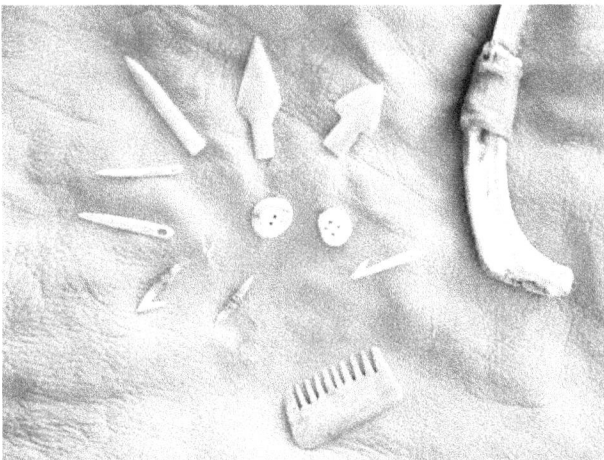

Bones can be made into sewing needles, arrow points, fishhooks, buttons, combs, and tool handles.

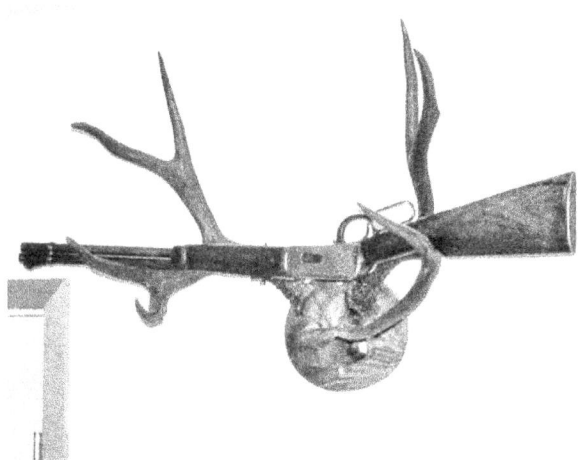

An antler rack can make an excellent rifle rack.

cedar, spruce, and others that are sometimes listed in books as softwood and sometimes as hardwood, depending on the source or context. The hardwood category includes oak, cherry, beech, basswood, birch, boxwood, maple, walnut, mahogany, ebony, rosewood, chestnut, hickory, elm, alder, and a lengthy list of others.

I think it is especially interesting how certain woods that seem comparatively soft, like the poplars and cottonwoods for example, are normally identified as hardwoods. Balsa is the world's softest wood, yet it is in fact classed as a hardwood! In an article on the University of Tennessee's website entitled, "Wood Identification for Hardwood and Softwood Species Native To Tennessee," Brian Bond and Peter Hamner explain this apparent discrepancy succinctly: "The terms softwood and hardwood are used to reference the taxonomical division that separates a species and have little to do with the actual hardness of the wood."

Another category we might make is for the different species of ironwood, often grouped together with the various exotic woods. This describes a group of extremely dense, comparatively heavy hardwoods like lignum vitae, American hornbeam, Osage orange, desert ironwood, and others. Because many of the truly exotic ironwoods have to be imported to the United States, they can be quite expensive and tough to find. Also, the craftsman who works with ironwood will have to sharpen his tools often, because the material tends to be incredibly hard compared to more common types of wood.

In his article "Bow Wood, Part 1" (*Primitive Archer* magazine, Volume 9, Issue 2), Tim Baker provides an interesting discussion about how wood density is measured. He explains that by knowing the specific gravity (SG) of any given type of wood, it will be much easier to understand how the wood will perform (as a bow, in this case) within certain dimensional boundaries.

Specific gravity (also called relative density) is a measure of something's density. The specific gravity of a solid is measured by how heavy it is in relation to the weight of an equal volume of water. It is usually calculated using some method of water displacement. Water has SG of 1; hence, a solid having SG of 2.0 is twice as heavy as water.

Most types of wood fall somewhere between .30 and 1.00, with certain ironwoods like lignum vitae having specific gravity considerably higher than 1. By contrast, balsa will normally have a specific gravity of about .16 or .17. The data can vary slightly from one source to another, but on one website I found, red cedar is shown to have .38 SG, redwood with .45, maple with .75, birch with .67, and pine with .53, just to give you a general reference for comparison.

Using the right wood with the appropriate density is an important consideration for any makeshift wood project. Things like wooden gears, bearings, hinges, or other moving parts need to be as dense and hard as possible to resist wear or fracture, whereas things like cork stoppers should be much softer for their purpose.

Woodworkers also pay a lot of attention to the moisture content of wood, because a piece of wood can change a great deal as it dries out. If you build something using green wood with high moisture content, your final product is likely to be dimensionally different after the wood cures. Shrinkage and warping can also pull or twist pieces

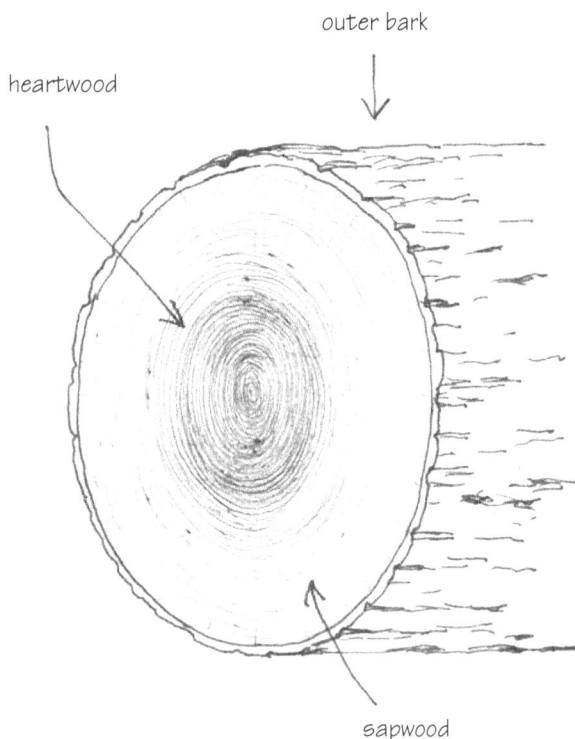

outer bark

heartwood

sapwood

End cut of a log.

apart. To accelerate the curing process, lumber is sometimes kiln-dried.

Many woods are characterized by their natural tendency to crack, split, warp, absorb moisture, and be affected by weather to a greater degree than synthetic materials. However, some of these properties can actually be useful to the craftsman. Oftentimes we can warp or bend a board or strip of wood to conform to a desired configuration by wetting it and clamping it into position until it dries so that it stays as formed. Knots in lumber weaken it, but they can be aesthetically desirable in certain applications where structural integrity is not an issue, such as in rustic flooring, furniture, and indoor wall coverings.

Types of Wood and Their Common Applications

The texture, strength, elasticity, and other properties of different kinds of wood make them each suitable for their own applications. Lignum vitae, for example, being very dense and hard and with high wear resistance, is much better suited for making bearings or certain tools than any of the softer woods. (Even fairly late in the steamship era, shaft bearings were made from lignum vitae, as it was less subject to corrosion than many metals.) Redwood, given its special ability to resist decay, is commonly used for outdoor furniture, wooden fences, decks and outdoor railings, and house siding. Cedar is similarly used for outdoor applications and for boat building, as it also tends to resist decay well. Cedar is also known to have a pleasant aroma, making it popular for building chests and cabinets for storing clothing, although it is rarely relied on for any structural application, being such a soft type of wood.

Lumber from birch trees is used to make hardwood timbers and high-grade plywood. Maple is a popular hardwood for making furniture, musical instruments, and flooring. These two hardwoods have a very light, natural color and sometimes require heavy staining to make their finished products more attractive.

The pines are softer, but they are abundant and less expensive, and some are considered suitable for general construction and for plywood. Larch, or tamarack, is another popular wood for structural framing, as is Douglas fir.

Mahogany is an attractive wood used heavily for decorative trim in expensive homes, for making furniture, and in boats, cabinets, and veneers.

A tough hardwood with a characteristic yellowish tint and distinctive grain, oak is an attractive and popular raw material. Some varieties of oak are fairly common and find wide use in joinery, furniture, flooring, indoor trim, cabinets, and numerous other applications. Because oak is the cheapest hardwood in my area, I routinely use it to make tool handles and other things. I really like the look of oak, although I don't prefer it for detailed carving; the heavy grain tends to interfere with the delicate cuts, in my experience.

Hickory is a very tough, comparatively springy hardwood ideally suited for things like tool handles and wheel spokes. It has also been used widely to make archery equipment. A stick of hickory will be very durable and extremely unlikely to break under normal conditions.

Spruce was a popular wood for masts on sailing ships, building crates, and ladders because it has a degree of resistance to decay and is considered strong enough for those applications. In fact, spruce has one of the greatest strength-to-weight ratios of any wood, which is why it has been used extensively for thin-plywood aircraft skins. (The biggest ever built was Howard Hughes' famous "Spruce Goose.")

The two most popular bow woods have arguably been yew and Osage orange. Yew is a very soft, lightweight softwood conifer with high elasticity. Osage is much denser, being one of the heaviest hardwoods found in North America. It has a very bright, natural orange color. Unlike a yew self bow, a bow made of Osage is not as likely to break if overdrawn.

Most walnut varieties are very attractive, semiporous hardwoods of various shades of brown. Walnut is not extremely hard, but it does make sturdy gunstocks and knife handles. It is easy to carve and shape compared to many other hardwoods. It can be finished to look nice using only linseed oil in some instances, but stain often isn't required, as walnut has its own natural, rich dark brown color. One should wear a facemask when sanding or cutting walnut, because the dust can really mess with the respiratory system.

Ebony is a very dark, richly colored, dense hardwood that has been used to make piano keys, artistic inlays, and other crafts. It can be polished very smooth, and it is a popular wood for knife handles when it's available.

On the other end of the spectrum we find balsa, the lightest of the wood types mentioned here. Because it is so light yet rigid for its weight, balsa is a popular wood for making model airplanes and for floatation devices like buoys and life preservers. It is commonly available in small pieces through hobby and craft stores.

Bamboo is a relatively hard and tough woody plant, but it is actually in the grass family. Bamboo is nevertheless an excellent raw material for making sturdy tubular containers and is also used where it is found for building huts, small bridges, pathways, walls, and numerous other things.

PLASTICS

Plastics are materials that can be shaped when soft and will hold their shape when they harden. We normally think of synthetic (man-made) materials when we think of plastics, but in fact this group includes both synthetic and natural resins, polymers, cellulose derivatives, and casein proteins. We therefore might define the word "plastic" as the capability of a substance to receive form or be molded into a fixed shape.

Synthetic plastics of one type or another have been in use for over a century now. Parkesine, celluloid, and casein plastics were actually developed in the second half of the 19th century, but I would venture to say that the 20th century was the true age of plastics, when their use became widespread.

Materials and products we know as the various plastics include polyethylene, polypropylene, polystyrene, polycarbonate, polyvinyl chloride (PVC), acrylonitrile butadiene styrene (ABS plastic), polyoxymethylene plastic (acetal), nylon, Teflon, phenol-formaldehyde (Bakelite), polyurethane, celluloid, and any of the other polymer materials with plastic characteristics.

The word "polymer" is used to describe a compound of polymer molecules, chiefly composed of the elements carbon, hydrogen, and oxygen. The polymer molecules are the long-chain molecules that link smaller molecules like the carbon and hydrogen ethene molecules to form material with plastic characteristics.

Polymers are popular in the manufacturing of so many different kinds of products because they possess a range of useful properties, from the high corrosion resistance of many plastics to their typically good impact resistance, while being lightweight compared to metals. Some plastics, such as Kydex (thermoplastic acrylic-polyvinyl chloride), are commonly used to make knife sheaths and pistol holsters because they become malleable and easy to form when heated, yet they cool hard to form these sturdy products. Polymers also tend to be much cheaper to produce than the metals they have replaced for numerous applications.

Of course, plastic plays a big role in makeshift work. Whether using a plastic bucket to remove rust from steel tools (see chapter 4), pressing a molded plastic window-blind bracket into service as an improvised brace, or making your own knife sheath out of Kydex, you will find dozens of uses for this universally available material.

Homemade Plastic

We can make our own plastic from ordinary milk that might serve a number of useful special purposes. It doesn't matter whether we use whole milk, powdered milk with water added, or skim or reduced fat milk, because in all cases we will be separating the casein protein from the liquid.

The process is amazingly simple. First, warm some milk in a pan on the stove, then add vinegar, strain the clumps that form, squeeze out as much liquid as you can, mold the doughlike mass into whatever shape you want, and allow it to dry.

Cy Tymony's instructions in his book *Sneaky Uses for Everyday Things* calls for warming 8 ounces of milk in a pan, then adding one tablespoon of vinegar and stirring. I found a video online that shows the same process, but it calls for heating a liter of milk and adding four tablespoons of vinegar. Proportionally, this is about the same milk-to-vinegar ratio as Tymony's recipe, as 8 fluid ounces are very close to a quarter of a liter.

My tendency at first was to accidentally overheat and boil the milk, but it shouldn't be boiled, just heated to about 200°F. Also, I discovered that it takes quite awhile for the plastic mix to completely cure—at least four or five days at room temperature—and even then, the core of a glob the size of a golf ball probably won't be completely dry and hard. I have not yet experimented with baking the material to shorten the curing time.

I found that a ball of this simple milk plastic, after five days of drying, is tough enough to survive a series of throws against a wall without shattering. It is also surprisingly hard on its surface when it dries and can be sanded smooth and painted. Milk plastic might be used to make such things as shirt buttons, temporary knife handles, pistol grips, small gaskets, or plastic spacers.

Not only can you make your own plastic in the kitchen, you can also use a number of ready-made synthetics as raw material for a project. Exact formulas vary by the intended use, but the common denominator is that they are all thermoplastic. In other words, if you heat them, they return to their plastic state and can be reshaped. The ubiquitous 5-gallon bucket would be one example of a source for your raw material. The results are generally not fancy, but it represents a poor-man's Kydex for

Ball composed of milk plastic.

utilitarian items such as ax sheaths or tool holsters. Specific melting temperatures vary, but most items can be softened with a heat gun or even a hair dryer, or you can immerse them in boiling water or hot vegetable oil on the stove and reshape while hot and soft. Common PVC (not CPVC) and ABS pipe are also thermoplastic and can be shaped in hot oil. (If you want to bend a pipe, fill it full of sand or table salt to keep it from collapsing.) Most "recyclable" synthetics, from milk cartons to buckets, can be heat-formed again. This is a broad topic that we might explore further in a future book, but you get the idea.

METAL

This chapter covering the most common raw materials would not be complete without a reasonably comprehensive overview of the metals, considering the importance of metals to human civilization. This also happens to be one of my favorite subjects.

For simplicity, we might categorize all existing metals into one of two basic groups: 1) nonferrous metals, including copper, bronze, brass, tin, nickel, pewter, lead, aluminum, magnesium, titanium, and all of the precious metals like silver, gold, and platinum; and 2) ferrous metals that include iron, steel, and steel alloys. The ferrous metals contain iron and are normally magnetic. (Alloys are materials dissolved in metals in solid solution. In steel, these might include carbon, chromium, molybdenum, vanadium, or other elements or materials that form new steel compositions having different characteristics.)

The term "metallurgy" has been given different definitions by different sources. To me it simply means the study of, or especially the *scientific* study of, metals. In my view, this is one of the most important areas to delve into for anyone who plans to work with metal in their makeshift projects.

Copper

Copper was possibly the first metal to be mined and used by humans. Some sources trace the discovery and exploitation of copper back to more than 10,000 years ago. Its early use is likely owed to the fact that it is an abundant metal that is comparatively easy to mine.

Copper is an element, atomic number 29. It is a ductile, malleable metal having high conductivity of heat and electricity. It has been used to make coins, cookware, vessels and containers of all kinds, art pieces, plumbing pipe, electrical components and wiring, bullet jackets, and musical instruments, among other things. Pure copper has a reddish-brown copper color, very different from most other metals besides gold, which are usually some shade of silver or gray.

Although copper was used in early tools—like the copper ax found several years ago in the Alps with the 5,000-year-old frozen remains of the Ice Man—it is really too soft by itself for practical use in edged tools. Therefore, copper is often combined with other metals to create various metal alloys. Copper combined with tin (or occasionally such other elements as phosphorus or aluminum) produces bronze, which is somewhat harder than copper. Copper and zinc make brass. Small amounts of copper have also been added to certain stainless steel alloys to increase corrosion resistance and, believe it or not, hardenability. Copper melts at 1,981°F and is very close to nickel in weight.

There are numerous ways to use copper in makeshift projects. I have cut sections from heavy copper wire to make rivets for low-stress applications because it is soft and easy to peen with a hammer. It also works well in pressure-flaking tools for flint knapping because it is soft enough to grip the edges of sharp stones or chipped glass. Copper wire is great for tying up shrubs and grape vines; it's soft and not likely to hurt the plant, and the fact that it never rusts away makes it great for this application, as well as all sorts of outdoor repairs.

Aluminum

Aluminum (atomic number 13) is the most abundant metal element in the Earth's crust. It is also one of the most popular metals today for its ability to resist corrosion, its comparatively low cost, its low density (light weight), and because it is easy to machine—all perfect attributes for makeshift projects.

Although aluminum is softer than steel, it is actually quite strong for its weight and is used extensively for certain applications that previously called for steel. Magnesium and titanium exhibit similar and, in some respects, superior properties

and are now used in place of aluminum in certain specialty applications. Aluminum melts at 1,218°F to 1,220°F, and according to Richard Finch's *Welder's Handbook*, a cubic foot of it weighs 166 pounds. By contrast, a cubic foot of mild steel weighs slightly less than 500 pounds, and a cubic foot of lead more than 700 pounds.

The White Metals

Lead, tin, zinc, cadmium, and bismuth are part of the group of soft metals known as white metals. These metals have comparatively low melting temperatures, making them suitable for a wide range of makeshift applications.

Lead, which melts at only 621°F, is a very soft and malleable metal. You can bend a fairly thick lead wire with your fingers. Although we now know how toxic it is, lead is nevertheless very useful for solder and other specialty purposes, and because of its weight it is perfect in things like bullets, tire weights, and fish sinkers. You can melt lead in a steel pot on your kitchen stove for casting your own bullets or fish sinkers; you just don't want to breathe the vapors or allow the molten metal to splatter on you or onto countertops, flooring, or anything flammable.

Tin is another malleable metal that has numerous makeshift applications. In days of old, tinkers and tinsmiths worked with sheets of tin to produce candleholders and candle lanterns, grain scoops, cups, mugs, watering cans, flasks, creamers, candy dishes, containers, milk cans, breadboxes, and various other products for the kitchen and garden. Tin melts at around 450°F.

Early pewter was actually an alloy of lead and tin, although modern pewter is more commonly an alloy of tin, antimony, and copper. Most modern pewter alloys melt at between 420°F and 525°F. I tend to group pewter with the white metals simply because it shares their comparatively low melting temperature, and it is similarly soft and therefore easy to shape.

Gold

Gold and silver are the two best-known precious metals. Gold is an element found in nugget form as well as in ore and veins. Pure gold has a bright yellowish color, and it is the most malleable of all metals. I've heard it said many times that an ounce of gold could be stretched into a wire more than a mile long, but I have yet to try it for myself.

For centuries, gold was minted into coinage and used as a valuation standard. Today it is used in jewelry, decorative art, and plating over other metals because of its beautiful color and luster. It is a good conductor of electricity and heat and finds use in electronic circuitry. It is also superbly corrosion resistant and is used in dentistry. It is considered a rare precious metal that is expensive to mine. It is also very heavy: a cubic foot of pure gold weighs slightly more than 1,200 pounds. Gold melts at 1,945°F.

The karat is the unit of measurement for the amount of gold in the alloy. Used a lot in jewelry, a karat (k) is measured proportionately and not by weight. Thus 14k gold indicates 58.3 percent gold, with the balance being other metals alloyed for strength, 22k is 91.6 percent gold, and 24k is 99.9 percent, considered basically pure gold.

Silver

Silver is also considered a precious metal, although it is not as rare or expensive as gold. It is also very malleable and ductile, but it is harder than gold. It has traditionally been used for many of the same applications as gold, having been minted into coins and used in jewelry and art, and it is used extensively in the photographic film industry. Its melting point is close to 1,750°F.

Silver is soft enough that when it was minted into coins for circulation, it was typically alloyed with other metals to increase its wear resistance. What has been called "coin silver" is actually an alloy of usually 90 percent silver and 10 percent other metals like copper.

Iron and Steel

Civilization as we know it most likely could not have developed without the discovery and exploitation of iron. Without the element iron we would not have steel, and without steel we would not have machines, automobiles, or a wide range of tools needed for numerous tasks in the function of modern societies. Iron is element number 26 on the periodic table, while steel is an alloy consisting of iron and the element carbon, and sometimes other elements or metal alloys.

There are different kinds of steels used for different applications, such as spring steel, tool steel, the various stainless steels, carbon steels, and some steel alloys commonly referred to as alloy steel and low-alloy steel. By far the most common type of steel, and the least expensive, is mild or low-carbon steel. We find it in car bodies, chain link fences, steel cans and containers of all types, the majority of common small steel hardware, and in certain structural applications.

If you will be working with steel, it might be helpful to become familiar with the Unified Numbering System for Metals and Alloys, or UNS, which is a unification of existing numbering systems of alloy designation to minimize confusion between the different systems used in the United States.

The American Iron and Steel Institute (AISI) and Society of Automotive Engineers (SAE) previously standardized the popular four- and five-digit numbering system, wherein the first two-digit number indicates the type of alloy and the last two or three digits indicate the percent of carbon present in the material. For example, a steel designated 1050 indicates plain carbon by the number 10, having .50 percent carbon in the mixture, while 10100 steel would contain 1 percent carbon.

Some of the other alloy designations in the AISI/SAE system indicating various elements added to steels include 13 (manganese); 23 and 25 (nickel); 31, 32, 33, and 34 (nickel-chromium); 40 (molybdenum); 41 (chromium-molybdenum); 50, 51, and 52 (chromium steels); and so on. As an example, 4160 in the AISI/SAE system indicates the steel alloy with at least .50 percent chromium, at least .12 percent molybdenum, and .60 percent carbon, with the balance of nearly 98 percent of the material being iron.

The UNS designations consist of single-prefix letters identifying the family of metals, followed by five numeric digits indicating the composition of the material, similar to the four- and five-digit AISI/SAE system. In the UNS, T indicates tool steels, S indicates stainless steels, G indicates carbon and alloy steels, the F group includes the cast irons, and so on. Steel designated 1020 in the AISI/SAE system would be designated as G10200 in the Unified Numbering System.

There are several types of cast iron, including gray, white, malleable, ductile, and special alloy, each having its own special properties. Cast iron is essentially iron containing small amounts of silicon and more carbon than high-carbon steel, typically 2.0 percent or more. Unlike the carbon in steel, the amount of carbon in cast iron is too high for it to be completely dissolved in the iron (it is no longer in solution). Cast iron is known to be relatively easy to machine and is used for a number of applications, from cooking pots to engine blocks.

The amount of carbon in iron or steel directly affects how hard it can be. Low-carbon steel, or steel having less than .30 percent carbon (often referred to as mild steel), cannot be hardened by normal heat treatment. It can be surface hardened, or case hardened, through a process of carbon absorption where the steel is packed and heated in carbon-rich material for a period of time for its outer surface to absorb the carbon, but its core will remain comparatively soft.

Medium- and high-carbon steels, on the other hand—if we talk about AISI/SAE 1040–1060 as our medium-carbon range, and 1060–10100 for the high-carbon range—can be hardened simply by heating and quenching.

The amounts of carbon and different elements in the material produce other effects as well. It should be noted that *toughness* is not the same as *hardness*. A material can be very hard, as is glass, but not be very tough at all. Hardness relates to deformation resistance, whereas the toughness of a material describes its ability to resist shock. Other important properties when considering the different alloys, besides hardness and toughness, include corrosion resistance, machinability, strength (tensile strength, compression strength, impact strength, fatigue strength, etc.), and ductility, or how much the material will stretch before fracturing.

Consulting a steel alloy chart, like the one listing the elements in alloys and their effects on steel in Daniel A. Brandt's *Metallurgy Fundamentals*, we find the following advantages of the various additives to steel:

- Carbon increases hardness, strength, and wear resistance.
- Chromium increases corrosion resistance and hardenability.
- Molybdenum increases hardenability and high-temperature strength.
- Manganese increases strength and hardenability.
- Phosphorus increases strength.
- Vanadium increases toughness.
- Nickel increases strength and toughness.
- Copper increases corrosion resistance and hardenability.
- Boron increases hardenability.
- Silicon increases deoxidation and hardenability.
- Sulfur or lead improve machinability.

There are tradeoffs to many of these properties. A material that is super hard also tends to be rather brittle and more difficult to cut and machine than a softer material. A softer, more malleable material that is easier to work with may lack sufficient wear resistance for numerous applications, such as gears and other machine parts, or it might bend too easily when the requirement is for a more rigid material. It is because of this that so many different steels and metal alloys exist.

It is also very useful to understand how different heating processes affect steel. For this discussion we will focus on the carbon steels, as these are more common and react predictably to conventional heating and cooling processes.

At room temperature, iron that hasn't been heat-treated or has been heated and cooled very slowly is called ferrite. If we heat a piece of iron or steel in the forge, we can see that it changes colors as it heats up. These colors and shades of colors reveal various stages of structural changes in the material at different temperatures.

Most types of common steel have a melting point somewhere between around 2,500°F and 2,800°F. As this range is approached, the material will eventually be in a semimolten state, and its structure will change. The first phase is when the iron reaches the lower transformation temperature and its structure begins to change; the second is when it finally reaches the upper transformation temperature and the crystal structure has completely changed from ferrite to austenite. In this state, carbon will be dissolved in the iron, the material will be very soft and malleable, and it will no longer be magnetic. This is when it is very easy to shape and forge. The metal will be glowing hot.

Now, if the iron is cooled down very slowly, it will return to its ferrite state. This process of slow cooling is called annealing, and it is a heat-treatment process used to reduce stresses within metal. Annealed material will usually be no harder than it was to start with, and it will be generally easy to cut and machine. You can anneal a piece of hard steel such as a high-carbon file and then be able to cut it or drill into it almost as easily as if it were mild steel.

Interestingly, several of the nonferrous metals like silver are annealed very differently than are the ferrous metals, by quenching and rapid cooling.

Rapidly cooling carbon steel by quenching produces what is called martensite. Medium- and high-carbon steel can be made very hard and brittle this way. The structure of the steel will contain a lot of stress and will likely be prone to cracking and distortion. Martensitic iron can be very difficult to cut or work.

Another important heat-treatment process is known as tempering. This typically involves two stages. First, the steel is heated to its upper transformation temperature and rapidly cooled (quenched), and then it is heated a second time to a lower temperature and kept at that temperature for a period of time before cooling. The purpose of tempering is to preserve as much of the hardness as possible, while at the same time to relieve as much of the internal structural stresses as possible.

Springs are tempered their own way to produce their characteristic elasticity. Springs should be tough, but they don't necessarily have to be very hard. Different alloys used for spring steel would be tempered differently, of course, but using medium-carbon steel to produce a spring, the simplest procedure might entail first heating to bright cherry red (between 1,400°F and 1,500°F) and quenching in oil or water, then reheating to a pale or light blue color (anywhere from around 580°F to over 700°F, depending on whose instructions you follow) and usually following this with a slow cooling.

Blacksmiths, metallurgists, and foundry workers will normally determine, or "read," the temperature ranges of the metal by its different colors and shades. A coating of oxide, called scale, begins to form on iron when it reaches a cherry red

Odd chunks of metal scrap are some of the typical raw materials for makeshift projects.

color, and most forging operations are conducted while the metal is a bright cherry red to orange glow. Forge welding is normally performed while the metal is a bright glowing yellow color, not quite white hot. Carbon steel, especially high-carbon steel, is easily burned and ruined just before it reaches white hot.

There are several different scales or test methods that measure hardness of steel, including Brinell, Vickers, and Rockwell. We already considered the ancient Mohs' hardness scale, which would hardly be practical in our time. Perhaps the simplest method for most of us, and the least sophisticated, is the file test, which entails drawing a file across a sample of steel to see if the tool cuts into it or merely skates over the surface.

Occasionally it might be economical to acquire materials from scrap piles, and the exact type of metal or steel may not be known in some cases. If we are familiar with the products from which our material was salvaged, however, we might have a pretty good idea about the type of alloy.

You might happen to know, for example, that suspension springs used in specific automobiles manufactured during a certain period were made of 5160 chromium steel, or maybe you salvaged an axle that you know, after some research, to be AISI/SAE 4140 or a medium-carbon steel like 1050. You know the type of steel because you know the source. (Author Jim Hrisoulas lists the steel composition of various commonly salvaged items in his books *The Master Bladesmith* and *The Pattern-Welded Blade*. See the Suggested Resources section at the end of this book.)

However, there may be occasions where you won't know the source, and you'll be forced to make an educated guess or perform your own tests to determine the basic composition of what you have. The file test just mentioned can be useful for gaining a rough idea about the material's hardness.

Steel can be salvaged from all sorts of places if you know where to look. Old bed frame rails, for example, consist of a fairly high-carbon steel: it goes from the forming die right into a water bath and comes out very hard and stiff. For this reason, it can be a good source of really cheap, hard steel when you need that shape.

You can also get an idea about carbon content by applying what is called a spark test, where you hold the material to a spinning grinding wheel and observe the generated sparks. Long, dull, red sparks are indicative of cast iron. Long, orange-yellow sparks that explode at the ends are common with mild steel. Brighter, more rapidly exploding sparks generally indicate high carbon, and very heavy and wildly exploding bright sparklers are usual with carbon tool steel.

CHAPTER 2

Making and Using Cord

I view cordage—including nearly every variety and size, from fine thread to heavy rope collectively—as one of our most utilitarian resources available. At some time or another, every human being finds a use for a piece of string, be it garden twine, sewing thread, dental floss, clothesline, a shoelace, or some other cord. In this chapter, we will take a close look at different types of cord, learn how to make our own cordage, and explore a variety of ways to effectively use different kinds of cord for makeshift building and repairs.

TYPES OF CORD

We are fortunate in our time to have access to such a wide range of different types of cord, including fine threads, strings and twines, medium-size cordage, and the heaviest ropes made of a wide variety of natural and synthetic materials. You should have no trouble finding a special type of cord suitable for every application that requires cordage.

Ropes made from natural fibers such as cotton or hemp tend to hold knots well but typically aren't as strong or rot-resistant as ropes made of synthetic, or man-made, fibers. Ropes and cords made of such materials as polyester, nylon, Kevlar, or polypropylene possess certain advantages, but they tend to be somewhat slippery to work with. There is also a wide spectrum of characteristics within the synthetic cord category. For example, nylon has more stretch than polyester, making it more suitable as climbing rope and for certain fishing lines, where a higher percentage of stretch in a line under load is desirable to better sustain the shock of an abrupt tug. Polypropylene rope floats better than the others, making it popular with boaters and water skiers even though it's not as strong as nylon or polyester.

Manufactured rope is available in two forms: twisted and braided. A twisted rope is comprised of fibers, yarns, and three or more strands twisted (laid) together, while a braided rope will have an outer braided sheath or tube covering a core of smaller braided or twisted rope. Twisted rope is easier to manufacture and normally less expensive, easier to splice, and has more stretch and shock-absorbing capability compared to braided rope. On the other hand, braided rope has a smoother outer surface, is softer and more pliable, and is slightly stronger than laid rope.

Cord commonly referred to as string or twine—which might see more use in general than the larger ropes because it is so versatile—can be found in more variations that are suitable for more applications than I will attempt to list here. Cord that has a circumference of less than 1 inch is sometimes referred to as "small stuff."

Likewise, thread also comes in a vast assortment of sizes and compositions. You can buy very fine or very heavy threads suitable for all sorts of applications. Threads are made of silk, cotton, polyester, nylon, linen, animal sinews, and other materials or combinations of materials.

The two most common types of modern fishing line are monofilament nylon—which is single-strand, usually clear line—and braided line, consisting of woven fibers. Braided line tends to be stronger, but it is easier for fish to see in the water. Both types of line are available in a wide range of breaking or tensile strength grades, indicated by their pound-test rating.

A few other fishing line alternatives have become popular in recent years, one example being fluorocarbon line. This is a polymer line often used

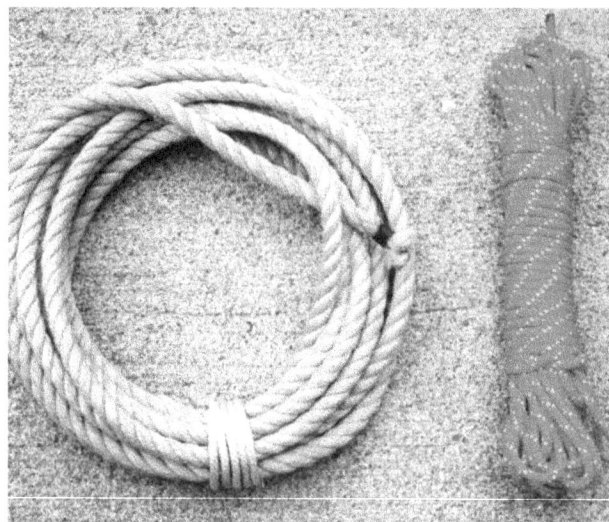

Twisted rope at left, braided rope at right.

as an alternative to monofilament. Although noticeably stiffer than nylon, its main advantage for fishing is that it is virtually invisible in the water.

Two amazingly versatile types of cord worthy of special consideration are dental floss and parachute cord. Probably the majority of my requirements for small- to medium-sized cord could be handled with either of these.

The most common version of dental floss consists of nylon strands bundled together to form a heavy thread-sized cord. You can buy it in both waxed and unwaxed versions. Dental floss is available in every supermarket where they keep the toothpaste, and it is fairly inexpensive.

Waxed dental floss can be used as a sewing thread, especially with leather projects, such as a possible substitute for saddle thread. You might also use it as fishing line. My guess is that the unwaxed variety would be better than waxed as fishing line, although I can't imagine it making a huge difference.

Dental floss can also serve as snare cord for trapping small animals and birds, for wrapping and binding endless kinds of small things, for making lightweight fish nets, and for strands in emergency bowstrings. The nylon variety would certainly not be ideal as bowstring cord, being too stretchy, but enough strands wrapped together might get you by as a temporary expedient with a quickie bow in a survival situation.

Parachute cord, also known as paracord or 550-cord, is small-diameter, general-purpose, medium-sized cord made to military specifications, primarily for parachute rigging. It is about the same diameter as typical braided bootlace cord. The genuine military product comprises a tubular woven nylon sheath that covers usually seven smaller individual twisted nylon cords. It is normally rated with a breaking strength of 550 pounds.

Parachute cord is available in several colors and color combinations, but olive drab, camouflage brown and green, desert tan, and black are the most common. Imitation or artificial parachute cord is widely sold that has softer core material that resembles cotton candy instead of the individual inner cords of real 550. Imitation paracord might work fine as a clothesline, small tent cord, or bootlace, but if your needs call for more strength, you should buy the genuine military-grade parachute cord. It is available through a number of military surplus and outdoor supply dealers.

for bags, and as general-purpose small rope for securing equipment to carry racks, wrapping tool handles, and numerous other purposes. The individual cords inside the sheath can be removed and used by themselves in applications where you need small string or perhaps very heavy thread. They are about the same size as kite string.

Fixes for Frayed Rope

When rope or cord is severed, it often frays or unravels at the cut end. Fortunately, we have several options to prevent this. With most synthetic fibers like nylon, it is often practical to fuse the fibers together at the severed ends by melting them in the flame of a candle or with a cigarette lighter. A stopper knot can be tied near the end of a small-diameter cord to stop the unraveling at that point. Or you might use small stuff or even adhesive tape to "whip" the ends of a rope to hold the strands together.

Whipping/wrapping the end of a rope with tape

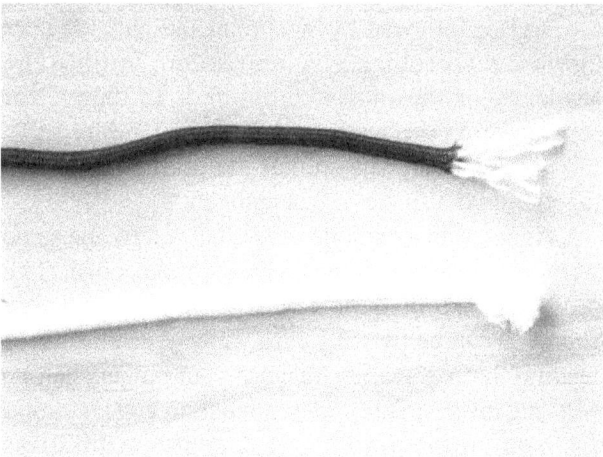

Genuine 550 parachute cord shown at top, with its characteristic seven individual inner cords. The imitation paracord under it is not as strong.

End of a rope whipped with small cord.

Despite its 550-lb. rated breaking strength, parachute cord should never be trusted as a climbing rope. Also, know that nylon cord will melt right through very quickly in applications where a lot of friction is created when one line rubs or wears against another line.

I have found parachute cord to be amazingly useful as bootlaces, guy lines for tents, drawstrings

is the simplest method, although it normally doesn't endure as well as a tight wrapping of small-diameter cord, and some may not consider tape as attractive as a neat whipping of small stuff. Sometimes it can be helpful to wrap a section of rope with tape at a point where the rope is to be cut to impede unraveling and fraying at the ends of both parts. The cut would be made through the center of the taped area.

HOMEMADE CORD

Making usable twine or rope is a simple process, although it can be a tedious and time-consuming task. It gets easier and faster with only a little bit of practice. The basic two-ply twist method, which was probably the most universal technique in primitive societies, has produced usable cord for literally thousands of years.

Various grasses, vines, roots, weeds, and tree barks have supplied natural materials for handmade cordage, as have animal products like sinews, intestines, hair, and hides. Some of the better-known vegetable cord fibers include stinging nettle, dogbane, milkweed, fireweed, flax, cannabis, yucca, sagebrush, cattail, cotton, palm, bamboo, iris, raffia, jute, and the underside of bark from cedar, willow, and juniper trees. I've made cord comparable to garden twine out of an unidentified variety of long grass. There are likely hundreds of other excellent natural cord fibers in different parts of the world. Basically, if a fibrous material can be twisted and bent sharply without splitting or breaking, it can be twisted into cord.

Two-Ply Twist

For instructional purposes, 1/2-inch-wide strips torn or cut from sturdy paper towels will suffice. (Some of the cheaper household paper towels tear too easily to make a tight twist.) The twisting technique would be the same for any material you might use. Strips can be any length from about 6 inches or longer.

Begin the process by pinching a strip at about two-thirds of its length and then rolling about an inch of that area between your fingers into a tubular, string-like segment to simulate a strand of bark or bundle of fibers, then fold a sharp bend in that area. This bend provides two running strands of unequal length to ensure that the twisting process will approach the end of one strand before the end of the other and allow a new strand to be spliced in with the shorter one at that point.

Next, roll into a twist one of the two running strands between your thumb and index finger of one hand (normally your right hand if you are right-handed) while holding the pinched bend with your other hand to keep the work taut. I roll one individual strand—the top strand, as I look at it—

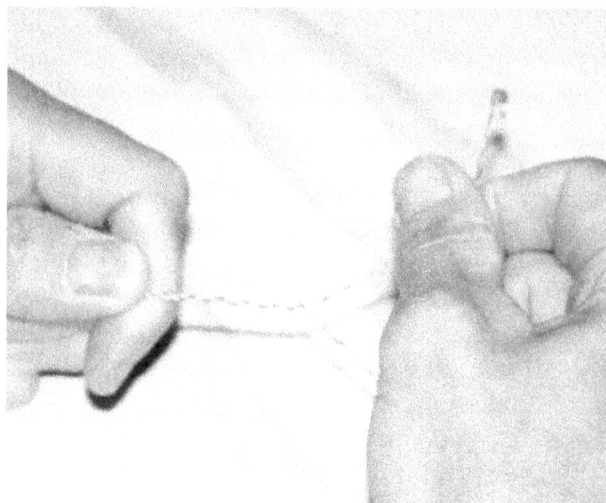

Twisting cord with the right hand while the left hand serves as a vise.

clockwise (away from me) before wrapping the pair of strands together counterclockwise (toward me) about one half to a full turn.

This is then repeated after switching the strands with the fingers, with the next strand in line twisted clockwise, followed by wrapping the pair together again counterclockwise and so on, so that the tendency of the individual strands to unravel or separate from the wrap are blocked by the forces in the reverse twist. The strands are essentially locked together into a string in this manner.

Again, this technique would be exactly the same with any type of fiber used to make cord. The process speeds up quite a bit with practice, and very soon you can be twisting cord while watching TV or reading the newspaper, because your fingers can be working automatically with almost no concentration focused on the activity. It becomes a mindless routine: roll the top strand away from you between two fingers, then rotate/flip the pair of strands 180 degrees toward you, change your finger hold, and repeat. Roll the top strand, flip the pair over, change finger hold, roll the new top strand, flip the pair over, and so on. You only have to think about it when it comes time to splice in a new strand.

When the shorter strand has only about an inch or so of untwisted length remaining, it is time to splice in a new strand. The new piece is simply added in, i.e., married to the ending strand, by overlapping its end with the ending strand and continuing the twisting process, treating the merging strands as one until the ending strand disappears into the twist and becomes the new longer strand. Each time one of the working strands nears its end in the twisting process, a new piece is spliced in as described so that your two-ply cord can be made to any length you want.

A stronger (although slightly bulkier) splice is the elbow splice, which I saw demonstrated some years ago by Jim Riggs in a video about making cordage. This merely entails folding a sharp bend near the end of the new strand being spliced in such a way that it fits into the V-notch where the two working strands wrap/merge together. Each "leg" of the bent new strand is twisted together with each working strand to maximize the interlocking effect of the twisting process.

Incorporating the elbow splice into the two-ply twist method results in stronger overall cord, but usually I end up with a fairly uneven cord containing bulges where the strands were spliced in. This problem can be eliminated to a degree by splicing in strands that have a narrow taper at their starting ends.

There are faster techniques with the basic two-ply twist method than what I have described here,

but this one is very easy to master and will produce a tight, sturdy, usable cord.

Braiding

Another way to intertwine individual strands into a larger diameter cord is to braid them together, using any of the common multiplait braids. Three- and four-plait braids are not at all complicated. Even a five-plait braid is not too hard to manage once you get used to the sequence. Braiding produces a cord with a wider, flatter shape than twisted cords or ropes. This could be a useful feature for making such things as straps, webbing, carry slings, and horse harness.

A braiding sequence can be started only after the individual strands are tied or otherwise secured at one end such that they lie close together and parallel to one another. Three strands can very often be held together and joined with a simple overhand knot near the ends as if the three were a single strand or cord, depending on their thickness. Four strands or more might need to be affixed at the starting end by binding the group together with thread, securing them with adhesive tape, sewing them in position at that point, or possibly locking the ends into some type of clamp. Otherwise, a group of multiple strands eventually becomes too bulky to treat as a single pliable cord with which to form any single knot. For me, it is a lot easier to start a braid sequence when the strands are lying side by side in a row wherever they are attached, as opposed to being bunched together where it is easy to get confused as to which strand is which in the sequence at the start.

To begin the simplest of the braids—the three-plait— either of the two outer strands is first crossed over the middle strand and it then becomes the new middle strand. The other outer strand is then crossed over it to become the new middle strand, and so on. The cords or strands will thus be

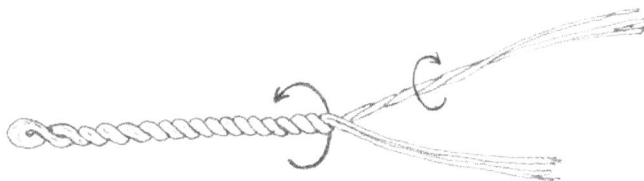

Strands rolled clockwise, then twisted together counterclockwise.

Splicing in new strands and continuing.

Cord making: two-ply twist.

Three-plait braid with round cords.

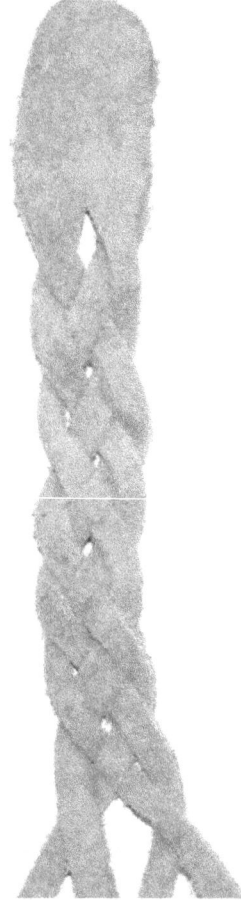

Four-plait braid in leather.

intertwined in alternating fashion. This basic process is the same with more plaits, but the crossover sequence will become more intricate as more plaits are braided.

In my experience, it is much easier to figure out how to braid a particular sequence by following a diagram or by looking at a braid done with different colored cords than to try to follow written instructions. This is one of those "watch and learn" kinds of skills that usually require hands-on practice to master, even though most of the common braid sequences are really quite simple. As with a twisted cord, a braided cord can be made to any desired length by splicing in new strands when needed—just braid the new overlapped strand with the others and continue.

Create a Long Leather Lace
The simplest method I know of for creating a

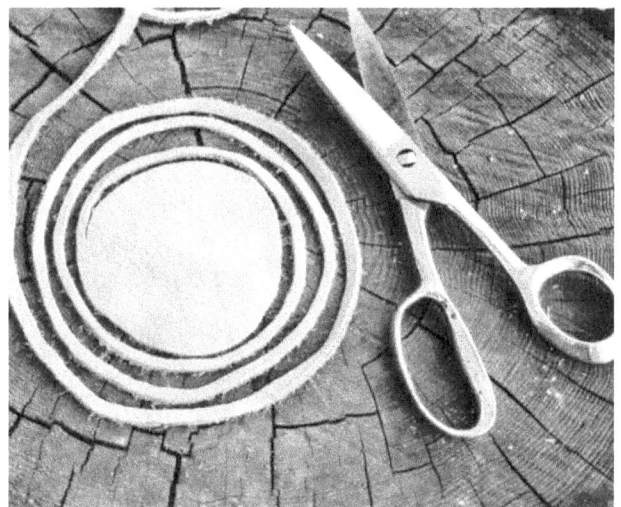

Cutting a long lace out of a circle of leather.

fairly long, even cord is to merely cut one from a scrap of leather or vinyl with scissors or some other sharp cutting tool. The process begins by cutting a roughly round circle in the material, and then cutting a strip inside its border in a gradually progressing spiral to the center, maintaining the desired width of the lace throughout the process. An amazingly long, narrow lace can be cut from a circle of leather that measures just 5 or 6 inches in diameter.

USEFUL KNOTS

Knowing how to produce makeshift cord is beneficial only in conjunction with a working knowledge of how to use it. One's ability to improvise can be enhanced substantially with the knowledge of how to form and use basic knots.

Now is a good time to learn or at least review some basic rope terminology in the context of the formation and application of knots. When we talk about the standing part, we are talking about the part of the rope or cord that is either fixed, under tension, or the source of our working rope. The running end is our working end of rope. A bight is a slack part in the rope, often a loop formed by doubling the rope back on itself.

Knots are often categorized by their basic function. A stopper knot provides bulk in the cord to prevent it from passing through an opening or to stop an end from fraying; hitches are used to secure ropes to objects; bends join ends of ropes together; loops are knots that join rope to itself; shortenings shorten lengths of rope; and so on. Sometimes knots are classified by the activities for which they are most commonly used. Some knots are used a lot in climbing and are often referred to as climbing knots, while others might be grouped together as fishing knots, and still others are typically used in sailing and are called nautical knots. A number of common knots would be considered general purpose, useful for a variety of applications in different activities.

The Bowline Knot

The overhand knot and the square knot are arguably the two most commonly used of all knots, yet the bowline and its variations could well be the most important knot you will ever learn. In his book, *The Klutz Book of Knots*, John Cassidy goes so far as to write this about the bowline: "If you were marooned on a desert island and could only take one knot with you, this would be the one." I like the several bowline knot variations because they are amazingly versatile, easy for me to remember how to tie, and very secure.

It's one thing to master a collection of knots, but remembering to use them where they work best is what really matters most. On more than one occasion, I have encountered a particular application for a special-purpose knot and could not seem to remember the best one to use until later, when the need no longer existed. A bowline knot comes in handy in these kinds of situations because of its versatility.

To form a standard bowline knot, it is often helpful to think of the actions of a ground squirrel. First form a loop in the rope, with the running end

The simple bowline knot.

passing in front of the standing part. Think of this loop as the opening of the squirrel's tunnel in the ground. Now think of the standing part as a pole standing upright just outside the opening of the squirrel's hole on the backside; think of the running end as the squirrel. To form the bowline knot, the squirrel comes up out of his hole, runs around behind the pole, and then jumps back into his hole. Pull the rope taut.

The bowline on a bight might be considered even easier to tie. It forms two loops, making it a popular hoisting and rescue knot. To form it, double the rope and begin the knot with a loop in front of the standing part. The running end will be a bight that forms a loop. After pushing this running loop through the standing loop (again, think of that squirrel coming up out of his hole), the running loop is pulled down in *front* of the rest of the parts, and *they* are pushed through the running loop's eye and pulled taut to complete the knot. With only a bit of practice, the bowline on a bight can be formed in about two or three seconds.

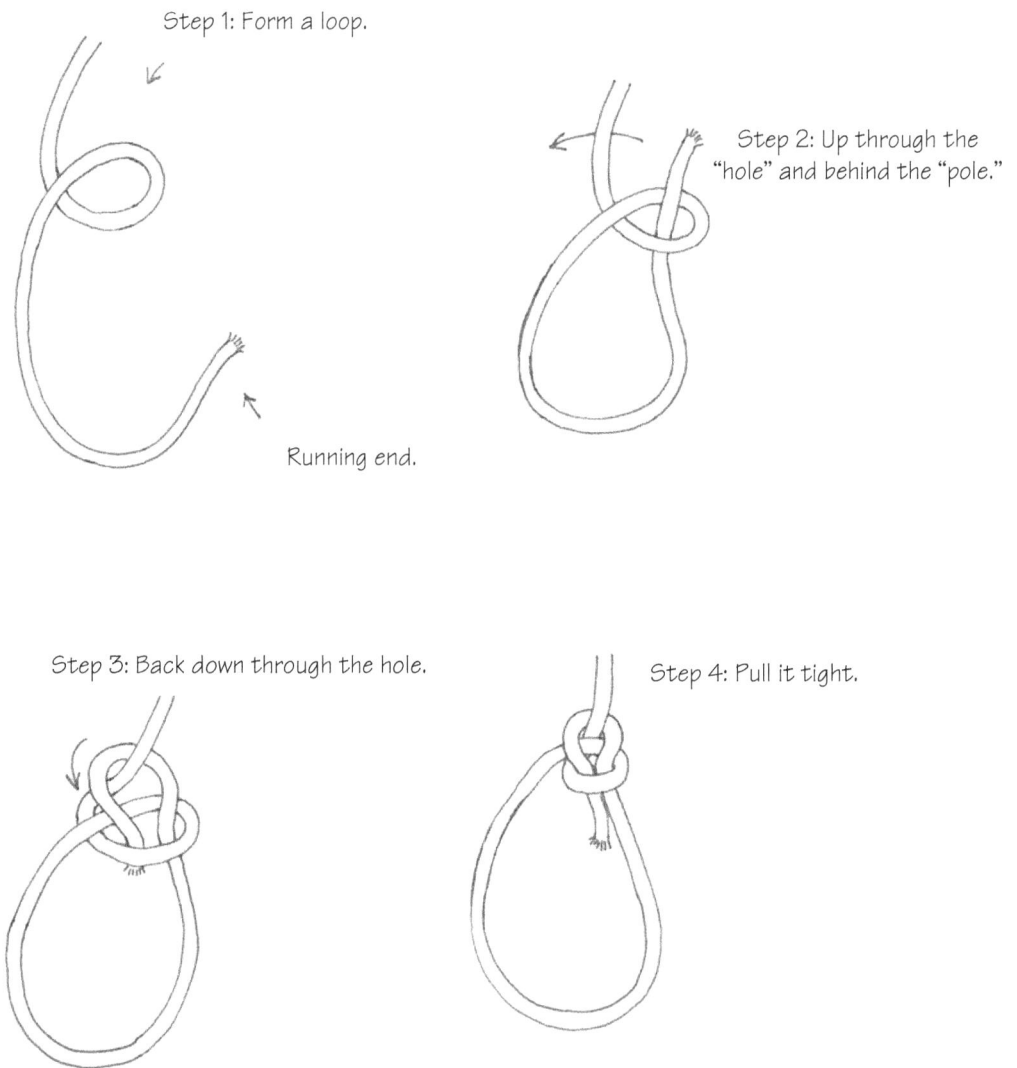

Step 1: Form a loop.

Step 2: Up through the "hole" and behind the "pole."

Running end.

Step 3: Back down through the hole.

Step 4: Pull it tight.

Forming a bowline knot.

1.

B

A

2.

A

B

C

3.

B

A

A

C

4.

A

B

C

.5

C

Pull C taut.

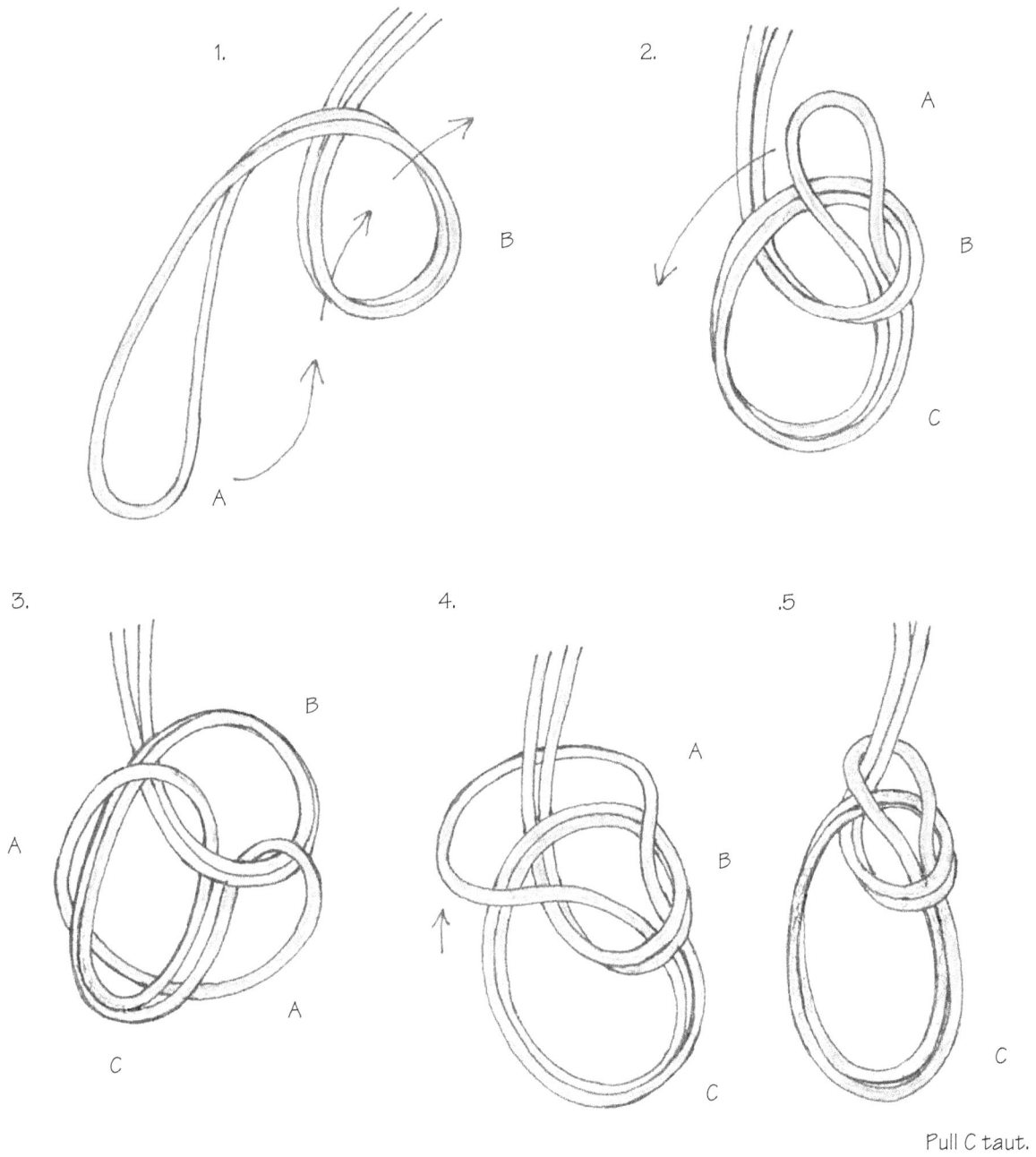

The bowline on a bight.

1.

2.

3.

4.

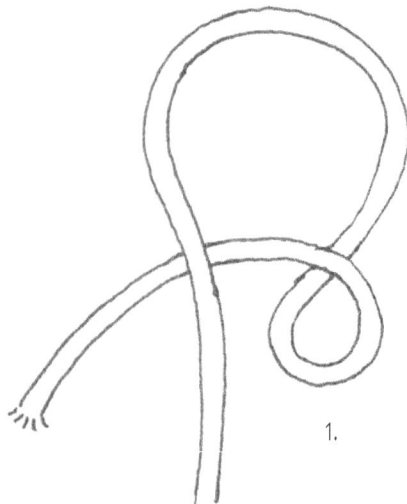

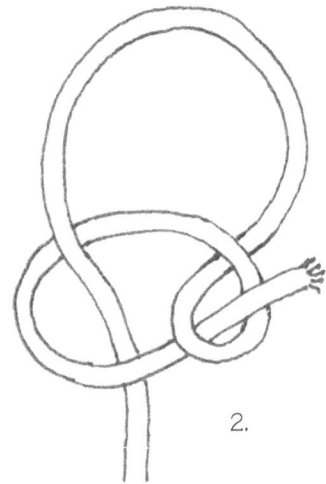

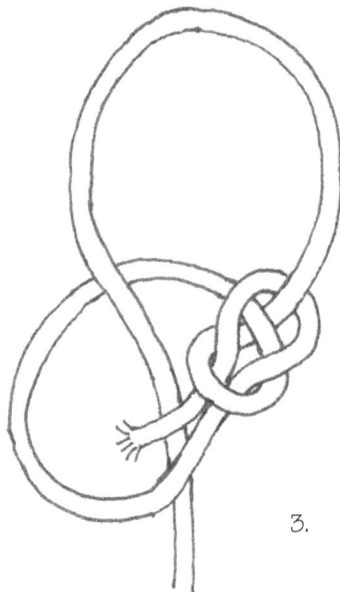

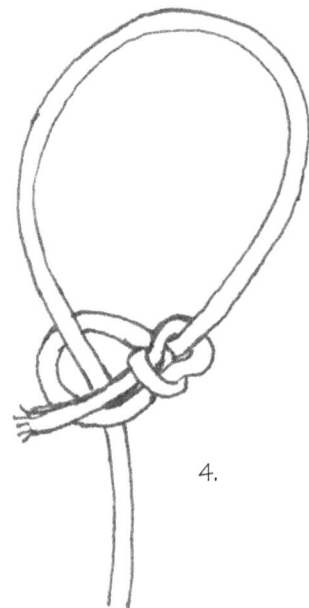

Forming a running bowline.

The running bowline is another useful knot that creates a constricting noose that tightens and loosens easily. For a long time, I thought the running bowline seemed rather confusing until I turned an illustration in a knot book upside-down and saw the standard bowline formation the way I was used to looking at it, except with its loop simply encircling the standing part. The running bowline is really very easy for anyone who knows the standard bowline knot.

Stopper knots.

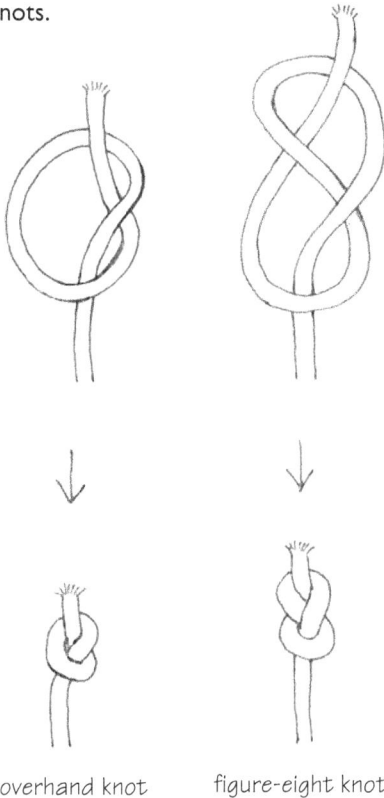

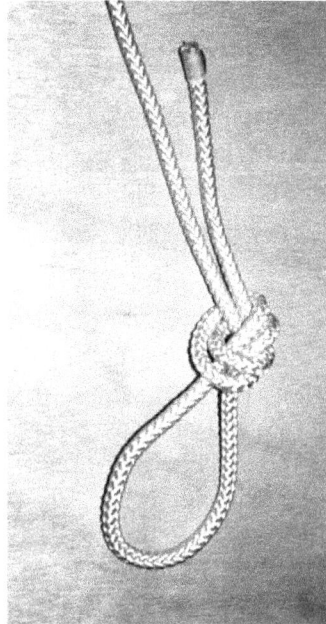

overhand knot   figure-eight knot

The overhand loop.

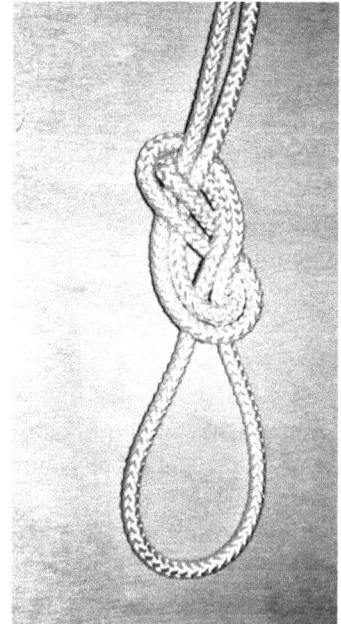

The figure-eight loop.

Stopper Knots

Arguably the most basic and easy to tie of all knots are the simple stopper knots. It's hard to think of anything easier to tie than an overhand knot. Besides being the most common stopper knot, it also happens to be a fundamental component of a number of other more elaborate knots. The overhand knot is simply created by forming a loop and then passing the running end through the loop's eye and pulling it taut.

An overhand loop is merely an overhand knot formed on a bight. It is the easiest way I know of to provide a loop near the end of a cord to which various attachments could be facilitated.

The figure-eight knot is a similarly versatile stopper knot, formed in the configuration resembling the numeral 8. Just as we discovered with the overhand loop, a useful variation of the figure-eight is the figure-eight loop, which is the numeral 8 configuration formed on a bight to create a very secure loop in the rope.

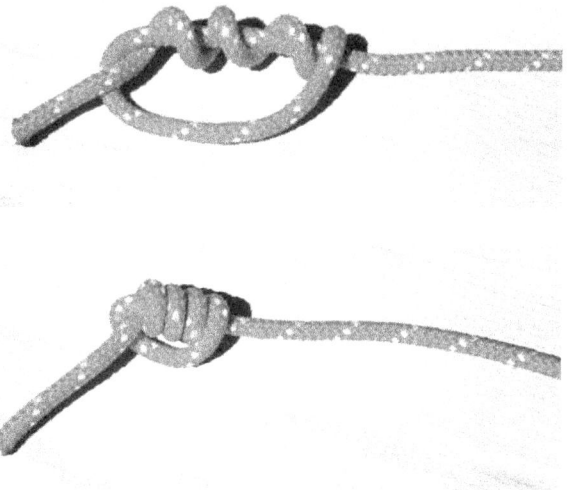

Forming the multiple overhand knot.

When I need a bulkier stopper knot than either a regular overhand or a figure eight, I will occasionally put a few more turns in the overhand to form a multiple overhand knot. It can be somewhat difficult to untie, especially when wet, but it's quick and easy to make, and it serves its intended purpose pretty well.

The heaving line knot is a very good stopper knot that is easy to make and untie. It is created by forming a bight far enough from the end of the rope to allow enough length to work with, wrapping the running end a number of turns around the close end of the resulting loop, and then passing the running end through the eye of the loop and pulling the standing part taut.

The Square Knot

This has to be one of the most famous of all knots and certainly one of the first the average person learning about knots will learn how to tie. It is probably the most popular knot for joining two ropes together. It is easy to tie, easy to remember how to tie, easy to identify quickly, easy to untie, and it will hold fairly well in the right application with ropes or cords of equal diameter.

But the square knot (known to sailors as the reef knot) might actually be overrated whenever included among our most practical knots because there are better, more secure knots to use for some of its purposes. Most knot books recommend against using the square knot with ropes under strain.

Two somewhat similar but even less secure knots that are occasionally mistaken for the square knot are the thief knot and the granny knot. Incorrectly tying the square knot often results in one or the other of these knots, neither of which will hold under any measure of a load. A true square knot consists of two half knots.

To untie the square knot, either of the two ends can be pulled to the side to capsize and loosen the knot.

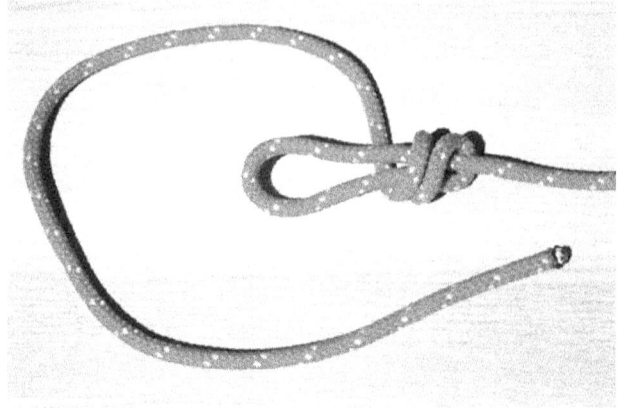

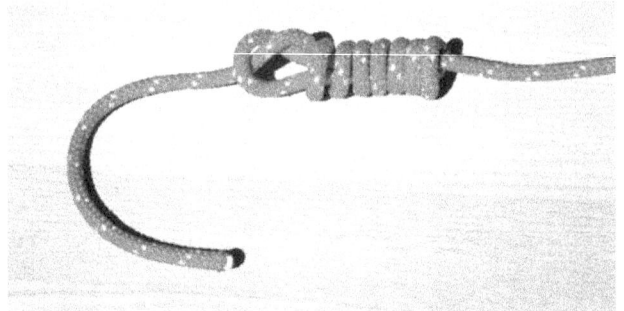

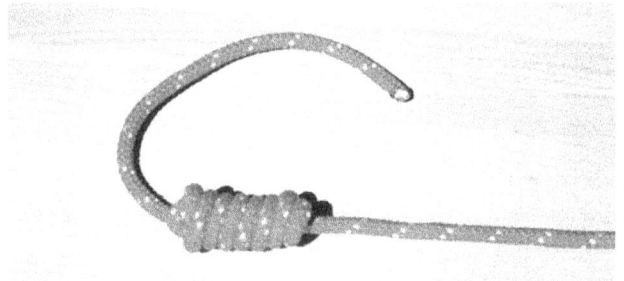

Forming the heaving line knot, from top to bottom.

Joining the ends of a rope with a square knot.

Thief knot.

Granny knot.

34

Sheet Bend

The sheet bend and the double sheet bend are two very practical knots for joining ropes, and their biggest advantage is that they can successfully join two ropes of different diameters. The sheet bend is generally considered a strong knot, and it is very easy to remember how to tie. The small cord is fed through, around, and then under its own standing part in the bight formed in the larger rope. The double sheet bend is formed by wrapping the cord's running end twice around the larger rope's bight before passing it under its own standing part. For added security with either knot, tie the ends with half hitches to their respective standing parts.

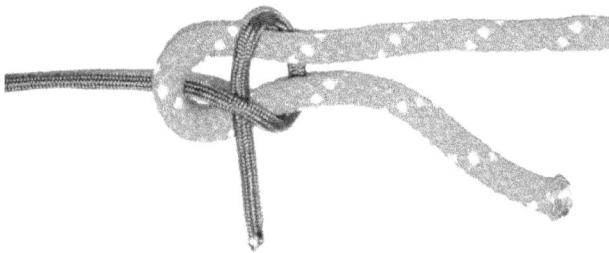

Cords of different sizes joined with the sheet bend.

The double sheet bend.

Sheepshank

If you need to shorten the length of a rope without cutting it, the logical approach is to use a knot that secures a doubled-up section. The most popular shortening knot is the sheepshank, which is easy to tie in the middle of a rope, easy to untie, and holds itself together very well as long as there is constant tension on both ends of the line. This knot could also be useful if there happened to be a weak spot in the rope one wished to bypass, especially if there is going to be any strain put on the rope.

The sheepshank is easy to form by doubling the rope on itself like a zigzag wherever desired and then forming loops in the standing parts near each end of the zigzag such that its ends can be pushed through the loops. Any tension on the line constricts the loops to secure the knot. The knot will come undone quickly with any slack in the line, making it a very temporary device.

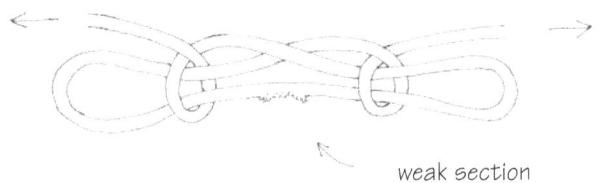

weak section

Sheepshank

A more permanent variation of the sheepshank is the knotted sheepshank. This one is started with a simple running knot or slip noose (running end doubles back on itself and an overhand knot is formed, through which the standing part passes). The standing part—the part that freely slides through the overhand knot—now becomes the new running end, and it doubles back on itself and is formed into an overhand knot that catches the end of the loop. Now both ends of the zigzag are knotted, and the shortening won't come undone merely with slack in the rope.

Forming the knotted sheepshank.

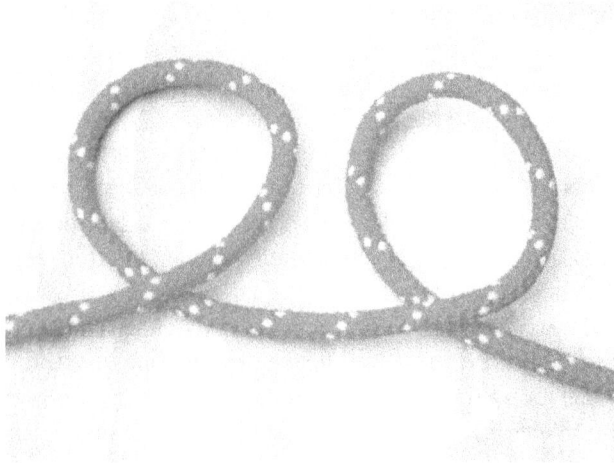

The clove hitch can be started by forming two loops side by side.

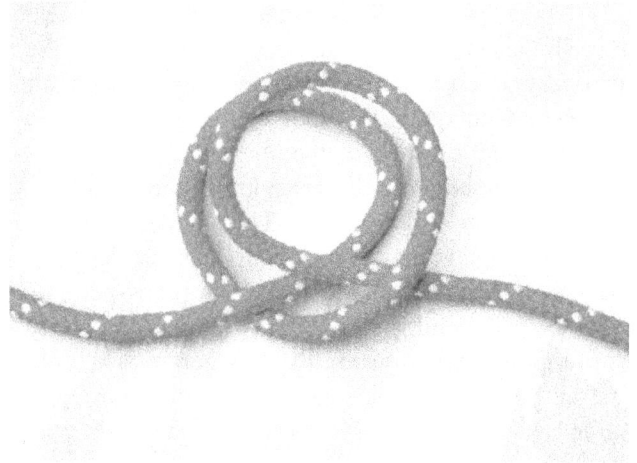

Pull the bottom coil over the top.

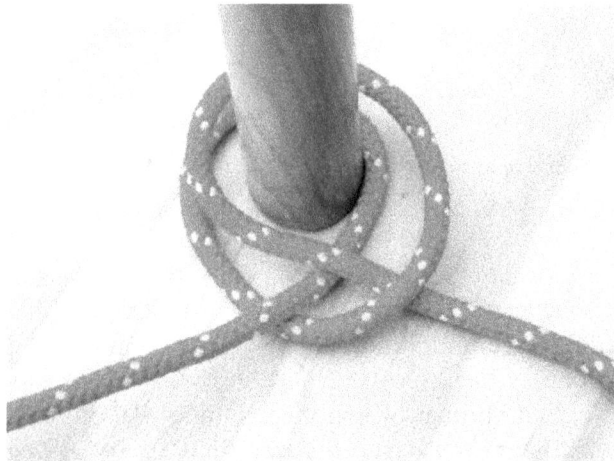

Cast the loops over a post.

A clove hitch on a round bar.

Hitches

The three hitches I encounter the most are the clove hitch, the timber hitch, and the round turn with two half hitches. I believe they are the most important hitches to learn how to tie for a makeshifter's purposes.

The clove hitch is a well-known temporary mooring hitch. It is easy to tie and untie, and it works well for temporarily attaching a medium-sized rope to a round post. A fast way to make it is to form two loops side by side and simply pull the bottom loop or coil over the top coil so that together they form a single O that can be dropped over the top of a post. The clove hitch is not the most secure hitch, however, as it can work itself loose with uneven strain.

The timber hitch is an excellent general-purpose hitch in my view, as it is very easy to tie and capable of holding more securely than might be expected by the looks of it, as long as it is under a constant strain. It is described by Tim Baker in *The Traditional Bowyer's Bible, Volume 2* as a potentially useful knot for attaching a bowstring to the nock of a bow because when it is tightened, the string tension keeps it from slipping, and it is easy to adjust once the tension is relaxed.

Timber hitch.

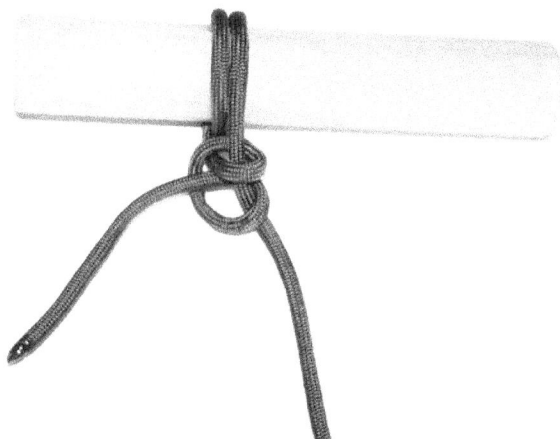

The round turn and two half hitches.

Possibly the best of the popular hitches is the two half hitches, or a round turn and two half hitches. It is not difficult to tie (or for me to remember how to tie), and it is a strong hitch. It might be considered more secure than either of the

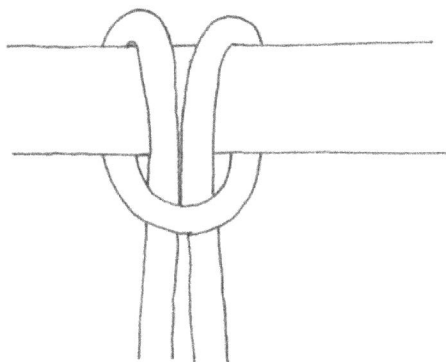

Cow hitch.

other two hitches mentioned here because it doesn't tend to loosen quite as easily when tension on the rope is relaxed. The hitch is formed by passing the rope's running end one or several turns around a post or other fixture and securing it with half hitches tied around the standing part.

The cow hitch and the Prusik knot are worth knowing. The cow hitch (or lanyard hitch) consists of two single hitches. It is not a particularly secure hitch by any means, but it is very simple and easy to form, and it might serve as a temporary attachment to a ring or a post.

The Prusik knot is started like a cow hitch, but then the ropes are passed around the post or object a second time and through the loop again. This knot is well known to modern mountain climbers—by using a Prusik knot to join a loop in medium rope to the middle of a heavy main climbing rope, a climber can attach step loops at intervals that grip the main rope firmly with sideways tension, such as when he steps into the loop with his weight, yet can also be slid up or down on the main rope for adjustment after the tension on the loop is relaxed. (For an entertaining example of a Prusik knot in action, see the James Bond film *For Your Eyes Only*.)

The Prusik knot.

To form an artillery loop, start with a simple loop, with one part crossed over the middle to divide it in half.

The top part of the loop is lifted over and pushed through the bottom half as shown here.

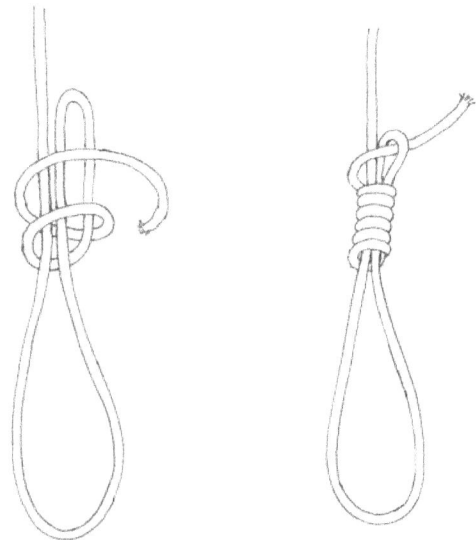

The completed artillery loop.

Forming the hangman's knot.

Artillery Loop

The artillery loop (at least one book I know of refers to this knot as the harness loop) is a handy trick for creating a loop in the middle of a rope to which other ropes can be tied, especially when you can't use the ends of the rope for this purpose. It is very easy to form by starting with a loop that has one part crossing over in front to divide it into two halves, and then one half of the loop is pulled over and pushed through the other half. The accompanying photos illustrate the idea better than I can explain it.

Hangman's Knot

Sometimes referred to as the hangman's noose or executioner's knot, this one forms a robust, strong constricting noose. It is formed by making a loop and doubling the running end back to form another loop facing the standing part, with enough working length to make at least seven turns around the standing part and smaller loop. Before the turns completely bury the smaller loop, the running end is passed through the eye and it is then cinched up to secure the running end.

Useful Fishing Knots

Two very good knots for attaching fish line to the eyes of hooks are the improved clinch knot and the uni-knot. The best way to visualize how to tie these knots is to study the accompanying sketches and then practice them over and over again.

The knot known as the fisherman's knot (or sometimes the waterman's knot, not to be confused with the fisherman's bend) is an excellent knot to know for joining two fish lines together. Basically, I would describe it as two lines overlapping one another, each with an overhand knot that ties around the other line such that the two overhand knots jam together when the lines are pulled in opposite directions.

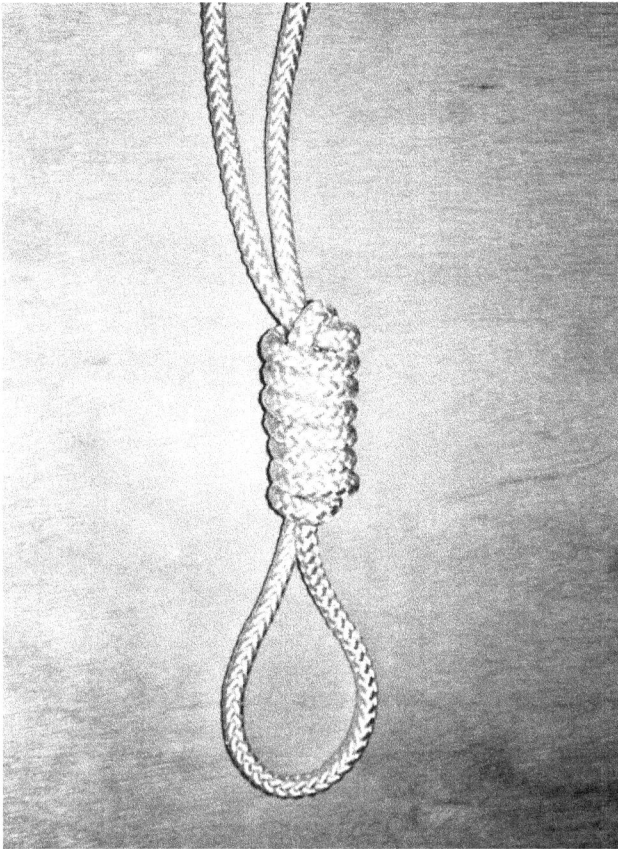

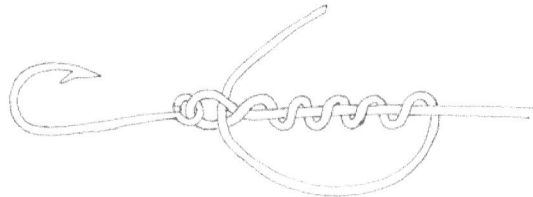

The hangman's knot completed.

The hangman's knot is a running knot, but although it will slide on its standing part to either constrict or loosen the noose, it doesn't slide very easily. However, when the noose is tightened around an object, the knot will hold very securely.

Improved clinch knot.

Uni-knot.

The fisherman's knot is formed with two overhand knots that tie around the attaching line.

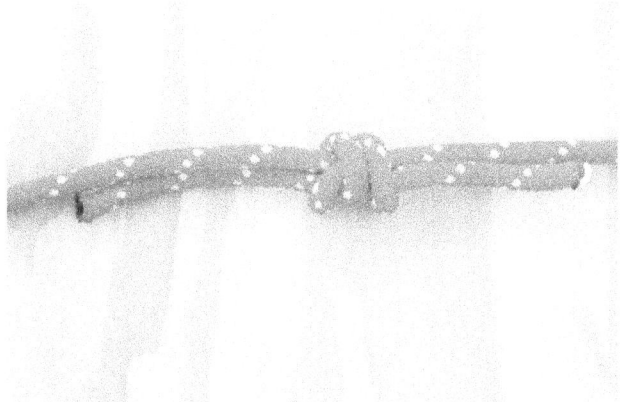

The fisherman's knot jammed together.

NET MAKING

The utility value of nets for fishing, animal trapping, or suspending and securing gear makes them worthy of our attention in this chapter. We will take a look at two different methods for creating nets.

The first thing to consider before starting any kind of homemade net is that, regardless of what method is used to construct it, a net of any practical size larger than a shopping bag requires a substantial amount of cord compared to most other projects that call for cordage.

The first method we will look at, and probably the most conventional for weaving the mesh of a net, starts with a long, continuous cord. With the help of a netting shuttle that holds the running supply of cord, the net maker works across each row of mesh by tying the individual knots wherever needed. These knots connect the mesh at intervals to create the desired openings, or cells. Some type of simple measuring gauge is useful to keep the mesh openings all close to a uniform size.

The process begins by tying a framework or headline, which would normally consist of small rope or heavier cord than the mesh cord. The common procedure for starting the first row is to work from left to right, so you would secure the standing part of the mesh cord to the upper left corner or left end of the headline, then attach the beginning mesh loops at evenly spaced intervals across this heavier cord, ideally using clove hitches.

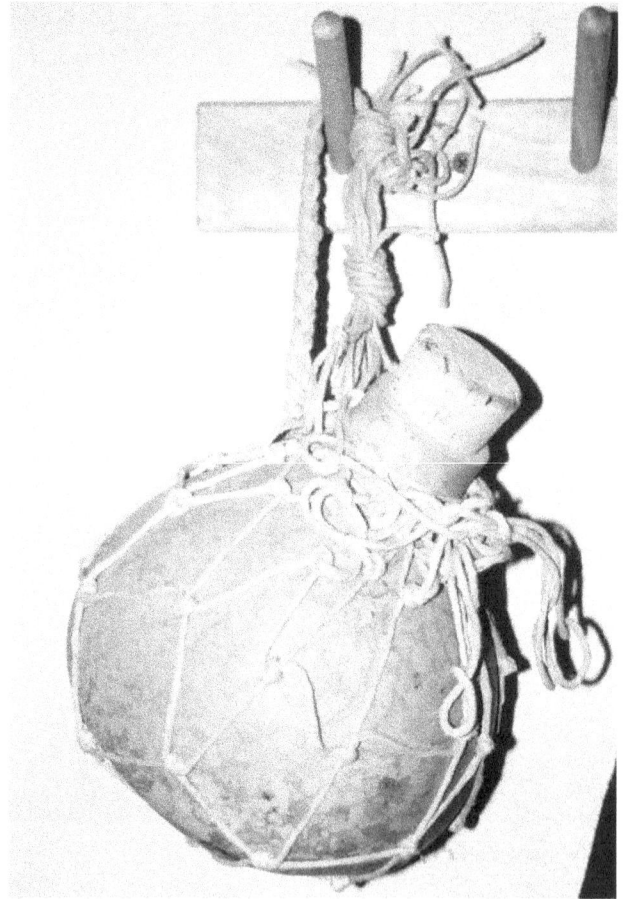

This gourd canteen is supported in a homemade net carrier.

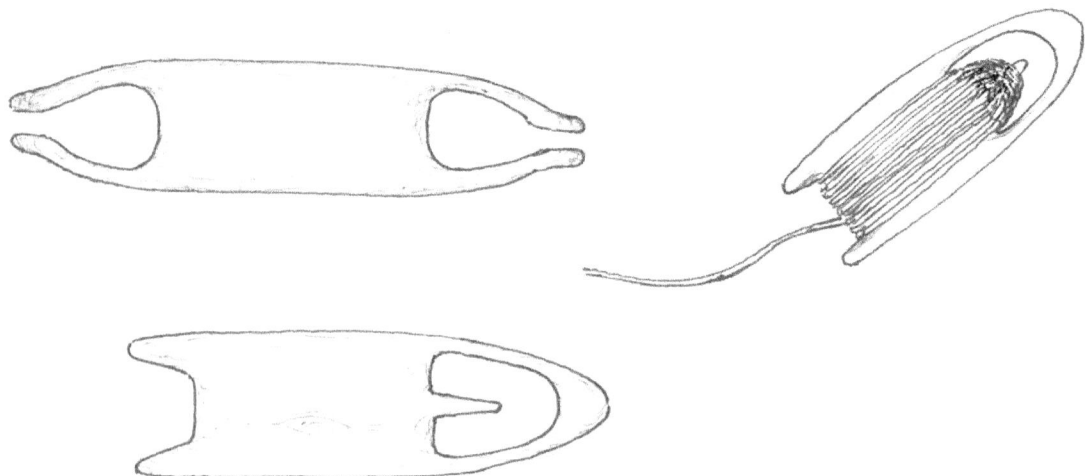

Shuttles, also known as netting needles, from which to unwind cord as you work.

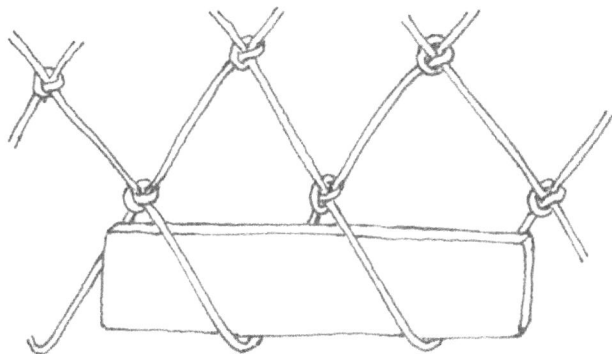

Using a netting gauge, or mesh stick, as a reference for creating a uniform size for the openings.

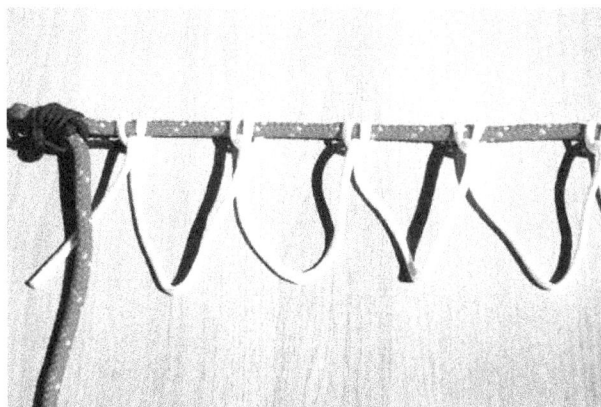

Forming the beginning loops of the net mesh along the top from left to right, attaching to the headline with clove hitches.

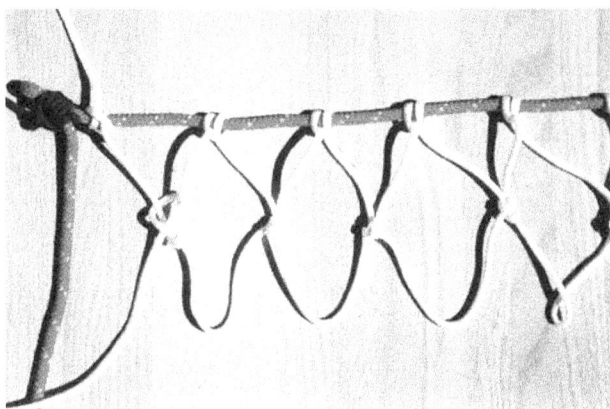

Working back across to form mesh cells, tying to the bottoms of the loops with sheet bend knots.

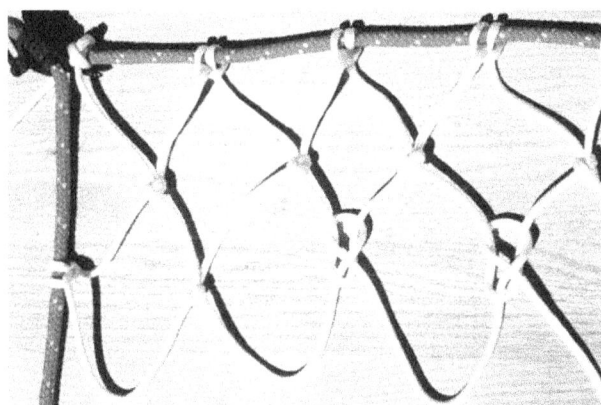

Continuing the process to form a net.

As you work your way back across, pass the netting shuttle (sometimes referred to as a netting needle) through the mesh loops you've created while unrolling enough cord to work with as you go. Tie to the bottom center of each loop with the running mesh cord, preferably using sheet bend knots (although several other knots could be used as alternatives), after pinching the bottom of each loop to make the knotting easier.

This process is continued as described, working one row at a time horizontally and then coming back across, repeatedly attaching the running cord to the bottoms of the loops to create complete mesh cells. As noted, the mesh size is easy to keep consistent by working in conjunction with a gauge (also called a mesh stick), which can be almost any piece of wood

or flat material of desired dimensions that can slide through the mesh as you work.

The other method for creating a net with cord involves attaching separate doubled lengths of the mesh-sized cord to a horizontally suspended, heavier headline at the desired intervals, most conveniently with Prusik knots, and working with these pairs of cord rather than with a continuous running cord. With this method, individual legs of the separate, vertically hanging pairs are connected to legs of the neighboring pairs in order to create the mesh cells. The cords are paired in alternating sequence and knotted together easily with overhand knots, as can be seen in the illustrations. One advantage of this method is that it does not necessitate the use of a netting shuttle.

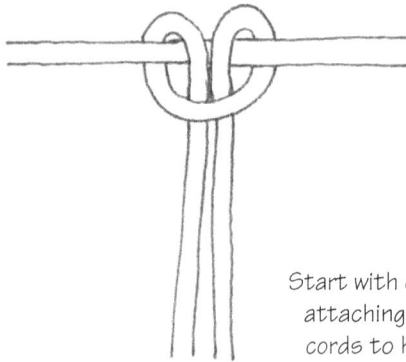

Start with cow hitch, attaching doubled cords to headline.

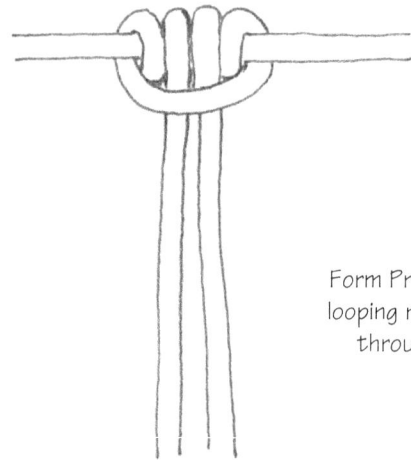

Form Prusik knot by looping running ends through again.

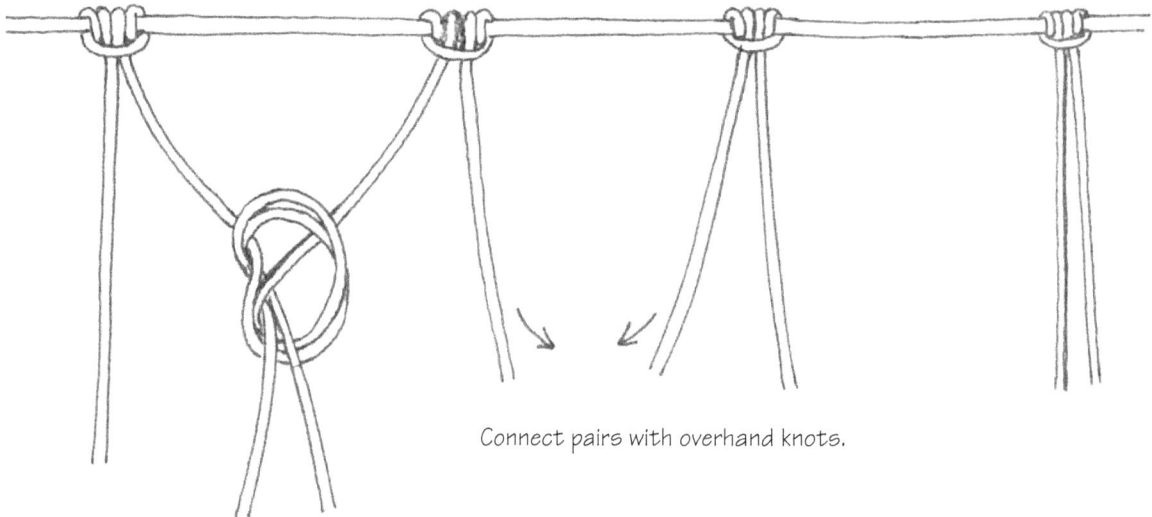

Connect pairs with overhand knots.

Net making: connecting pairs of cord.

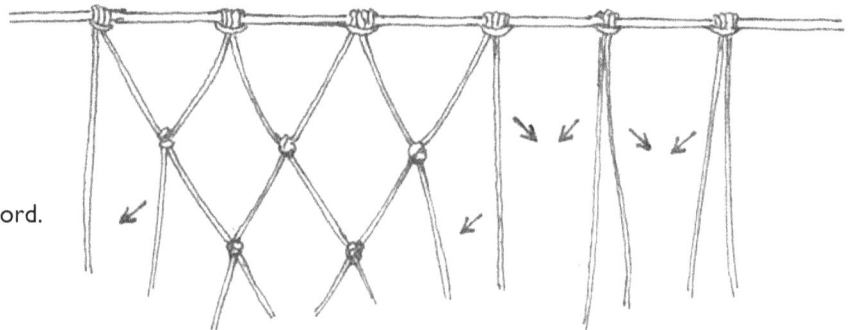

Continue process to form complete net.

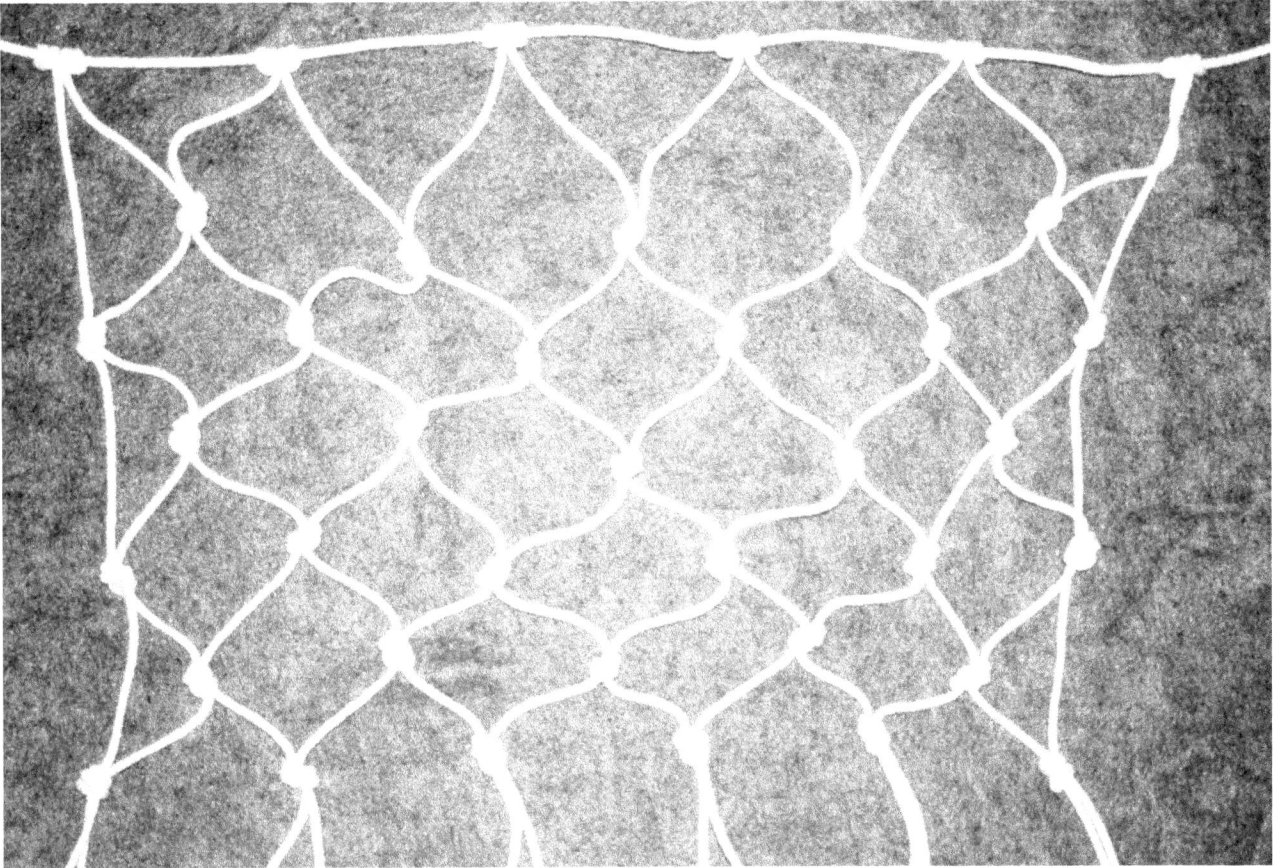

Small net made by tying the legs of pairs of cords that hang from the headline, using overhand knots at intervals to form the mesh cells.

CHAPTER 3

Makeshift Metalworking

Human civilization really began to advance appreciably in technology only after the dawn of the Iron Age. Iron tools facilitated the efficient cutting and shaping of wood for building things like structures, furniture, and ships on a large scale, and countless human activities—from cooking and gardening to chopping firewood and butchering animals—were improved dramatically with iron tools.

One does not have to spend years as an apprentice to a master blacksmith before being able to successfully create functional tools and other items by heating and manipulating metal, and the basic task does not normally require sophisticated or special tools. A myriad of serviceable tools and hardware can be created with very low-tech methods and makeshift equipment. The beauty of the forge is that it can essentially serve as the "factory" for the production of nearly every sort of common metal item we might find a need for.

The four essentials needed to commence blacksmithing are a forge or other heat source, some sort of anvil, a hammer, and tongs (or other device for safely picking up and gripping the hot metal).

A selection of handmade metal implements.

With just these four basic things and a bit of practice, a tremendous amount of small-scale manufacturing can be accomplished. Of course, a full complement of metalworking tools would typically also include a heavy vise; a water bucket for quenching; a swage block; an assortment of hardies, mandrels, chisels, and punches; a hacksaw; a wire brush; miscellaneous metal files; and protective clothing.

THE FORGE

In its most basic form, a forge is simply a bowl or basin to hold fuel (typically hot coals or charcoal, if we omit modern gas-fired forge designs at this stage), with an air duct piped into it through which air is blown for raising the temperature of the burning fuel. In a makeshift environment, a small pit in the ground with some type of simple bellows to push air through a pipe into it might suffice as a functional forge for heating metal. Small forges can

Three of the four essentials of blacksmithing: anvil, hammer, and tongs.

also be made out of vehicle brake drums, water heater cores, barbecues, and numerous other discarded products containing some type of basin.

Single-lung bellows attached to a makeshift side-draft forge.

Side view of a single-lung bellows.

THE FORGE AIR SUPPLY

For thousands of years, people have known that fires burn much hotter with a blast of air. Human lungs, blowpipes, draft tunnels, bellows bags, and fan blowers of every configuration have provided air to forges. In a situation involving the need to improvise, one has several possibilities for pumping air into a forge.

The Blacksmith's Bellows

A bellows is basically a bag that forces out air in a controlled fashion when squeezed. Bellows work by taking in air when the bag is expanded and pushing the air through a nozzle when it is compressed. This action is facilitated by intake holes that allow air into the bag, with soft flaps covering the holes on the *inside* of the bag to create one-way valves. These flaps (typically made of leather) are forced flat over the holes during compression to block the air from escaping and are lifted up by suction to open the holes to take in air when the bag is expanded.

I constructed a single-lung (or single-chamber) bellows for a makeshift forge several years ago as an experiment (discussed in my first book for Paladin Press, *Long-Term Survival in the Coming Dark Age*). This bellows did indeed pump air into the bowl of the forge as intended, but the contraption was certainly not efficient. It required not only some trial-and-error adjustments before it would work at all but continuous, rapid pumping on the operating lever to keep the air moving in fairly short bursts. A more desirable sustained, even flow of air was simply not possible with this setup.

A more effective forge bellows would either be a traditional double-lung, double-action bellows or a pair of single-diaphragm bellows working in an alternating sequence to keep a steadier flow of air blowing onto the coals.

The traditional double-lung bellows is an ingenious system designed such that one chamber is always being compressed during operation and pushing air through the nozzle, even while the bellows is taking in air. This creates a more even and sustained flow of air than is possible with a simple single-lung bellows.

Bellows typically are constructed of wooden flaps with hinges or wooden frame pieces to support the shape of everything and control the bags. The soft portions of the bags are usually made from animal skins, cotton canvas, or some other flexible cloth with a tight weave that will hold air. In Volume #10 of Ron and Karen Hoods' *Woodsmaster* DVD video series (check out their website at www.survival.com), a

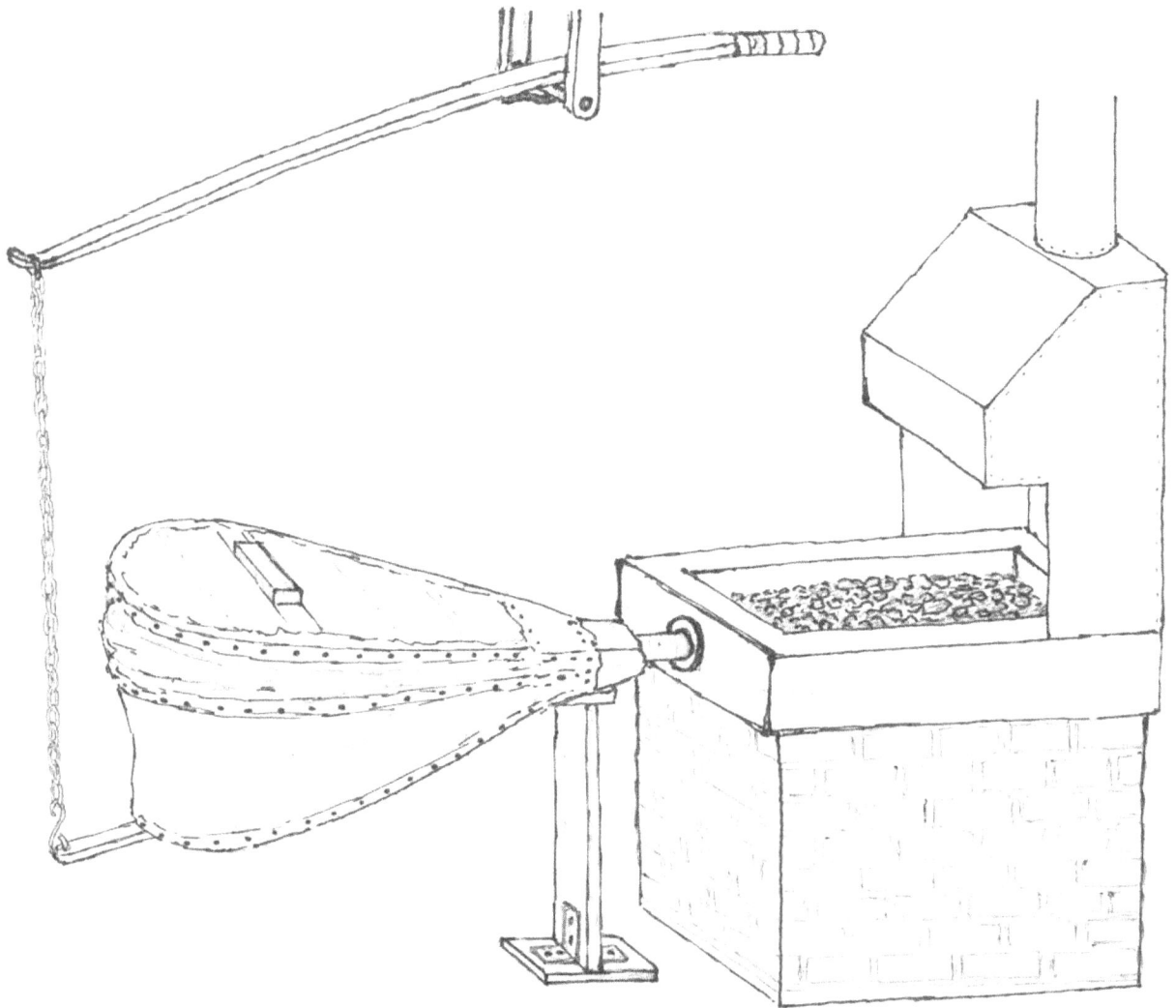

Masonry forge with double-action bellows.

operating handle

weight

hinged leaves

forge

Air flow represented by arrows.

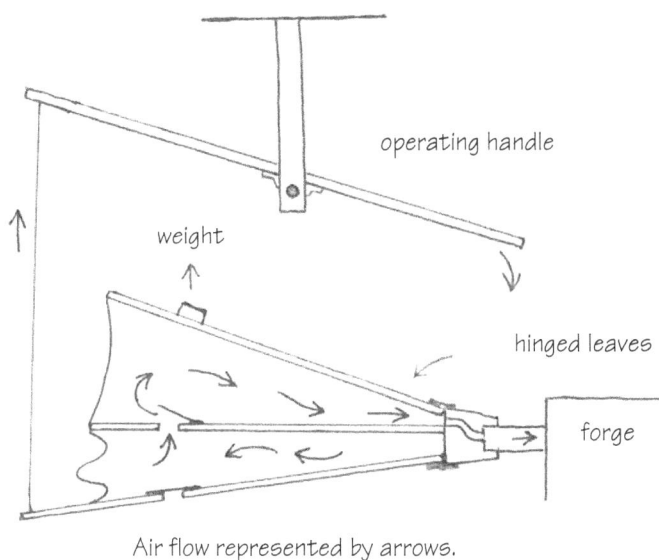

1) Handle pulled down—Top lung takes in air, as air pressure from bottom lung forces weight up.

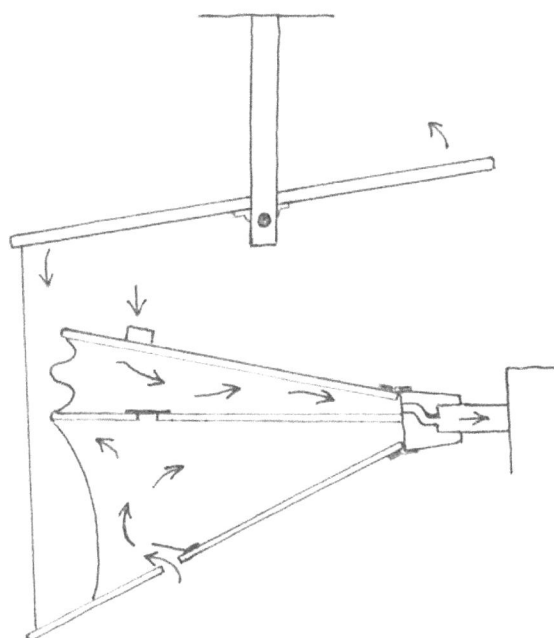

2) Handle released/raised—Bottom lung takes in air, and weight compresses top lung. Air is pushed through nozzle to forge during both stages of operation.

Double-action bellows in two stages.

field demonstration of a campfire forge shows a heavy-duty plastic trash bag converted to a makeshift bellows to provide the air blast.

Rotary Fans and Forge Blowers

A hundred years ago, hand-cranked forge blowers were very popular with blacksmiths, being compact, easy to control, and capable of providing a more easily sustained, even flow of air than most bellows were capable of. By simply turning a crank, the blacksmith was able to spin an impeller that pushed air through a duct to the forge. A system of gears made the manual cranking efficient. More recently, electrically powered blowers have become popular for use with coal forges among a lot of modern blacksmiths.

The old hand-crank blowers are still my favorite way to provide air to the forge. They are simple, easy to use, typically function very effectively, need little maintenance, and don't require electricity. They can still be found from time to time at farm auctions, flea markets, and antique stores.

I have seen numerous variations of the rotary fan blower principle described in books and magazine articles over the years that offered suggestions for adapting such things as electric hair

An old Champion hand-crank forge blower.

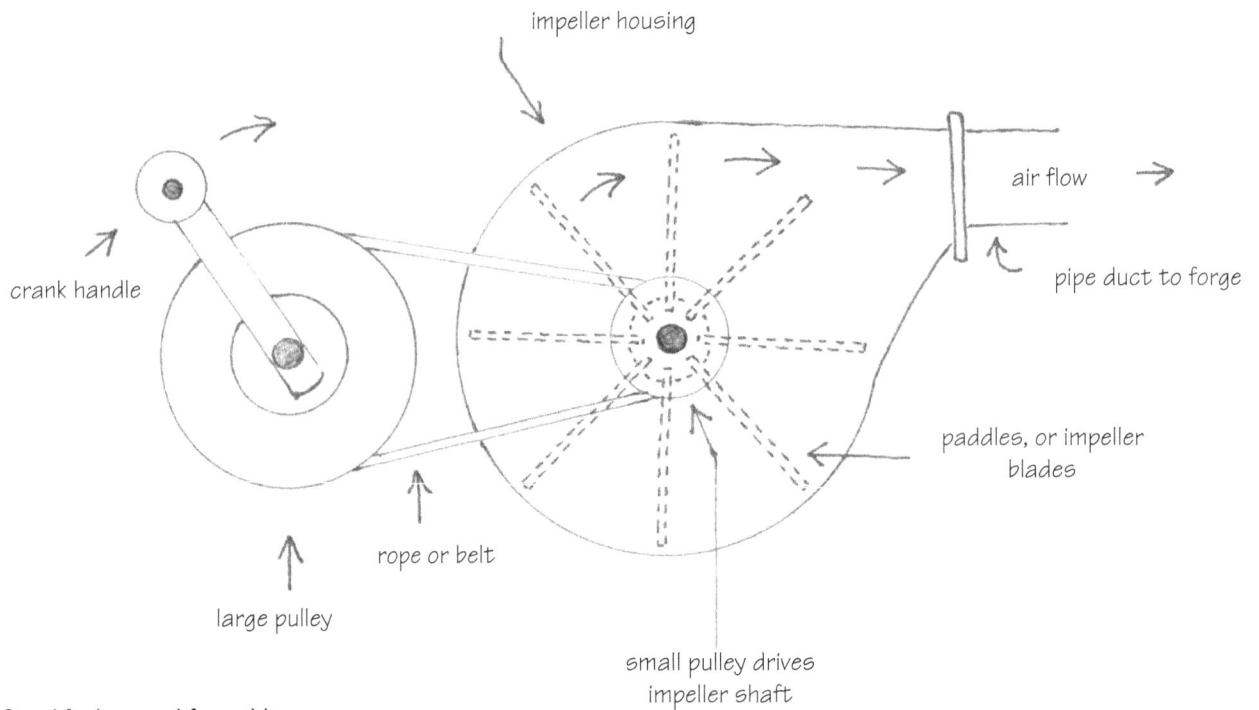

impeller housing

crank handle

air flow

pipe duct to forge

rope or belt

large pulley

paddles, or impeller blades

small pulley drives impeller shaft

Simplified manual forge blower.

dryers and vacuum cleaners for use with makeshift forges. I've experimented with some of these ideas (see the photos of my vacuum cleaner device), but the possibilities are indeed numerous.

FORGE FUEL

A lot of modern blacksmiths have taken to using gas to heat their metal, mainly because of the convenience and cleaner nature of gas compared to

Air blast to forge provided by an old vacuum cleaner.

other fuels. While I do use a gas torch for soldering, brazing, and forging small metal objects, I still normally use forging coal for most of my blacksmith activities.

It is easiest for me to obtain the hottest fires with forging coal, sometimes called bituminous soft coal. It's filthy and smoky and produces clinkers (impurities that melt out of the burning coal and solidify into a hard mass) that should be removed from the bottom of the forge periodically before they clog it up, but it also turns into coke as it burns. Coke is the lighter, mostly carbon remains of the coal after the impurities have melted out of it, and it is the preferred fuel for blacksmithing because it burns cleaner and with very little smoke. Feed and farm stores in rural areas sometimes sell forge coal, mainly because some farriers still use it. It is also available through blacksmith supply stores. Coal that contains anthracite (hard coal) is probably the best for this purpose, whenever it's available.

Perhaps the longest-used forge fuel has been charcoal, which is nothing more than charred wood.

A lot of serious bladesmiths still prefer burning pure charcoal instead of forging coal because it imparts fewer impurities onto the hot steel. Small chunks of wood can be charred in an enclosed steel canister (having only a small opening for gases to escape) set in a campfire. When flames start to shoot out of the gas vent like a torch, the canister can be removed from the fire and allowed to cool. The wood will have been charred in this oxygen-starved environment and will retain its structure rather than being merely burned into ashes. The charred coals in a campfire might also be doused with water and saved for later use in a makeshift forge, after being allowed to dry. The biggest advantage to using charcoal as opposed to other fuels, in my view, is that charcoal can be produced anywhere trees grow or wherever wood is available.

If a coal forge is to be set up indoors or under a roof, some type of forge hood and chimney system is essential to clear away the smoke and soot. While charred wood/charcoal doesn't produce nearly as much filthy soot as coal, it does tend to generate

Heating metal with forge coal.

hundreds of tiny embers that float all over everything, so the potential fire hazard of forging with charcoal in any wooded or dry brush area should be carefully considered.

HOMEMADE FORGE AND FORGE BLOWER PROJECT

Building an 18th century-style bellows system is certainly achievable by any do-it-yourselfer with a minimum of such materials as wood, canvas or leather, and glue or metal tacks. However, I was especially curious to learn how someone might fabricate a rotary hand-crank blower while on a tight budget and without access to a lot of specialty products or uncommon materials. I have an antique portable forge and blower in my blacksmith shop that I normally use, but the following is a detailed description of my experiments with a makeshift forge and blower that I constructed entirely from common, locally scrounged materials.

Building the Forge

First, I adapted a small, inexpensive barbecue bowl for the forge basin. To the existing vent hole in the bottom center of the bowl, I bolted a pipe flange and connected pipe sections with a T-fitting so that I could pipe air in from my makeshift blower.

The size of barbecue bowl I used was really too

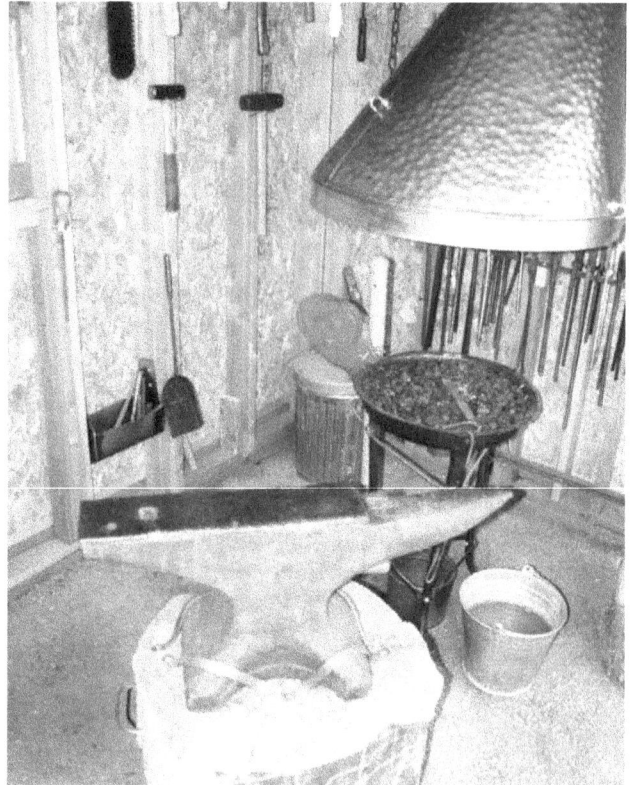

A chimney hood over the forge is essential in an indoor shop to allow smoke and soot an open escape. Mine is simply a funnel and tube made out of sheet metal. To give it that old-world appearance, it was dinged all over with a ball-peen hammer.

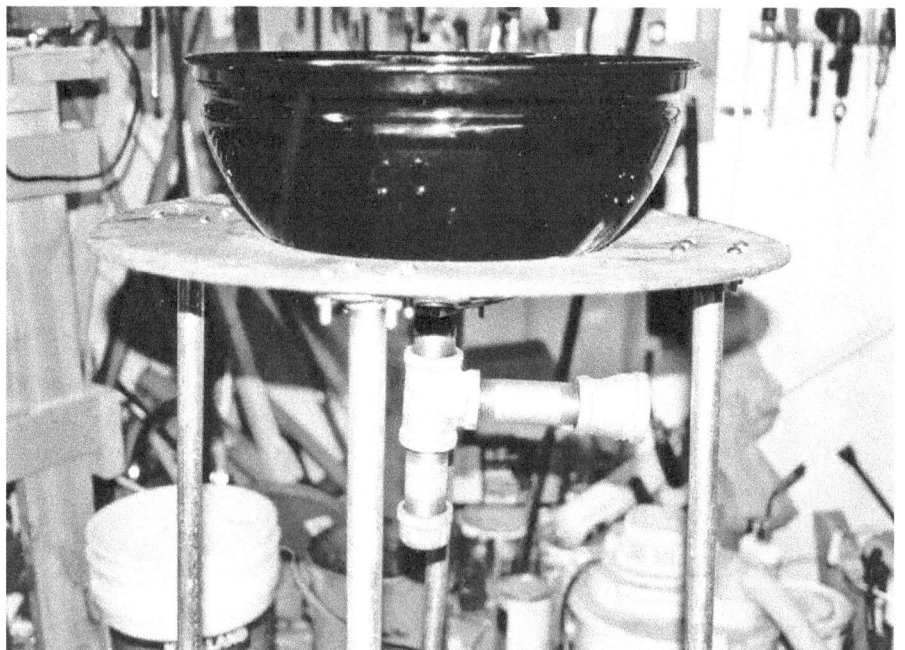

This small, homemade forge starts life as a little barbecue bowl with pipe fittings attached to the bottom for the air supply.

small in diameter and too deep to be practical for my purposes, so I cut a U-shaped area out of one side and connected a section of strap iron to the top (after bending it to match the contour) to cover the thin edge of the bowl where it was cut. With some trial and error, I secured this top strap into position by brazing. This also serves as a kind of small tray or hearth for metal stock heated in the forge.

Inexpensive barbecues have bowls constructed of very thin metal coated with some type of heat-resistant enamel. Anyone attempting to drill, cut, or bend this material should wear safety glasses, because the coating chips into tiny pieces and flips up from the area being worked. Also, because the bowl is so thin, the inside should be lined with something like clay or cement to sustain the higher forge heat. I lined mine with modeling clay, but I later discovered that fire or furnace cement is much better for this purpose, as it handles the heat better and cracks less.

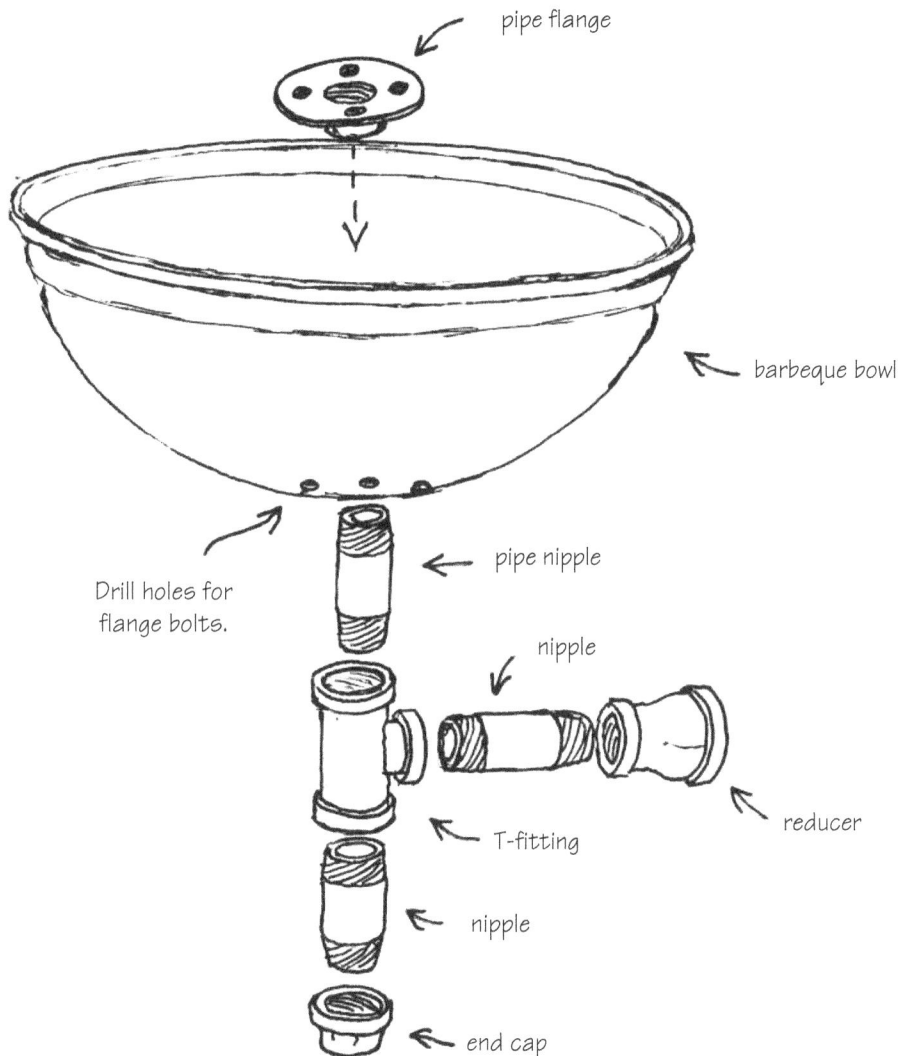

pipe flange

barbeque bowl

Drill holes for flange bolts.

pipe nipple

nipple

T-fitting

reducer

nipple

end cap

Parts for makeshift forge from local hardware store.

The bowl could be supported by the legs that come with the barbecue unit, but this option seemed too rickety in my view, so I built a more robust stand out of pipe fittings and scrap metal.

A cast-iron drain or small grate would have been ideal for covering the air opening in the bottom of the bowl (technically called the tuyere), but I didn't happen to find anything like that, so I drilled a cluster of holes through a 1/2-inch-thick steel plate that I found in one of my junk boxes and positioned it over the opening. This helps prevent the coals and fire from dropping down the pipe.

Barbecue bowl with hearth brazed to the cutout area in the side, vent to cover hole in bottom, and clay lining the inside.

Building the Blower

My idea for a blower was to connect paddles to a revolving axle to create an impeller and house this inside a makeshift container that directed the fanned air into a section of pipe, simulating a traditional forge blower. For the hand-crank mechanism, I used the foot pedals, sprocket, and chain from a kid's bike that I found at a yard sale for $5. I imagine that a larger, multiple-gear bike sprocket assembly would work better than what I used, but my contraption is nevertheless functional.

I silver-soldered eight 2 x 4 x 1/8-inch-thick steel makeshift paddles perpendicular to the bicycle's rear axle after removing the wheel's spokes and rim. My housing for the impeller mechanism was made from the bottom of a metal 5-gallon bucket to cover most of the action, coupled with an aluminum pie tin to cover the open side. These were bolted to the

The pedal mechanism from a kid's bicycle is adapted to power the makeshift blower.

bicycle frame to keep them in position. I cut holes in both housing pieces to create openings around the axle area where I expected the fan to draw in air.

I cut an opening out of the housing and attached a short, 2-inch-diameter pipe nipple for the air duct. This allows air to be funneled from the blower to the

Steel paddles were soldered to the rear axle, and the bottom section of a metal bucket was used as the major part of the housing.

Flaps of soft leather were glued to the faces of the paddles to help the device circulate more air.

forge. Any sort of temporary tubing can be pipe clamped or duct taped in place to connect the blower to the forge when it's all set up.

Initial testing of the blower made it clear that, while the paddles were circulating some air during vigorous pedaling/cranking, a generous clearance around the paddles inside the housing limited the amount of air being pushed. My remedy was to attach larger flaps of soft leather to the faces of the steel paddles with J.B. Weld glue. This modification made a huge difference in the blower's performance.

Unfortunately with my design, there is an excessive amount of open area where the bicycle frame and chain enter the back of the housing. A good deal of fanned air is lost through that area, making the device less efficient, I believe, than one that's more enclosed around the circumference of the housing where the air is fanned. A functionally superior blower, such as the next one I plan to build, will have a more enclosed outer periphery, perhaps in conjunction with larger air intake holes.

The makeshift forge and blower detailed here looks pretty weird, I must admit, but it does work moderately well. It represents one way to get set up with very low investment.

Makeshift blower with the aluminum cover plate secured in position. The apparatus is bolted to a stand.

Makeshift forge and blower set up and operational.

Using the makeshift forge.

MAKESHIFT ANVILS

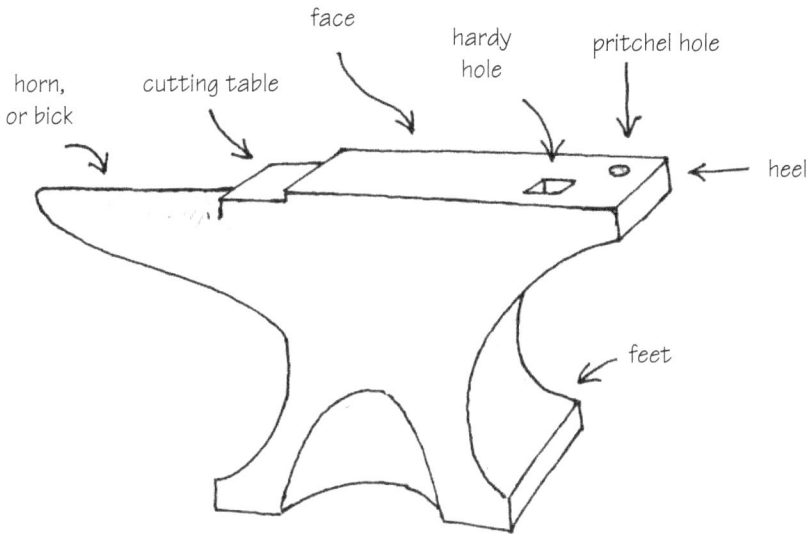

face

hardy
hole

pritchel hole

horn,
or bick

cutting table

heel

feet

Traditional London-pattern anvil.

For most metalsmiths, something solid upon which to hammer the hot metal is as essential as an effective heat source. Quality blacksmith anvils can be quite expensive new, and used older anvils in good condition can be fairly difficult to find. Some makeshift alternative is often a viable option.

Almost any large block of steel can serve as a functional anvil. The first anvils used for working metal were probably large rocks. A sturdy, heavy rock with a relatively flat surface might still serve as such in a makeshift situation. The important consideration here would be the possibility of flying rock chips from a shattering rock. Eye protection would be essential under such working conditions.

Miscellaneous improvised anvils, clockwise from left: section of railroad rail, length of steel round stock (such as part of an axle), small homemade rivet anvil mounted on 2 x 4 base, section of I-beam, flat steel bar, forming dolly.

Other makeshift anvils might be adapted from parts of heavy machinery or engine blocks, sections of railroad rail, heavy I-beams, or other heavy steel scrap. I have a small, makeshift double-horned anvil that I adapted from a large steel nautical cleat.

The anvil should be securely mounted atop a solid base at a comfortable working height. Tree stumps have been popular anvil bases for eons, but it is not difficult to build a robust, stable, wooden or metal stand for a medium-sized anvil. You could even press an existing item into service as a base, such as a solid butcher block. The legs could be cut down to make it the proper working height if necessary.

ADDITIONAL MAKESHIFT FORGE TOOLS

Now that we have our makeshift forge and anvil, we need a few other tools. As I mentioned, the fundamental four items needed to work hot metal include the heat source, the anvil, tongs or pliers, and some sort of hammer.

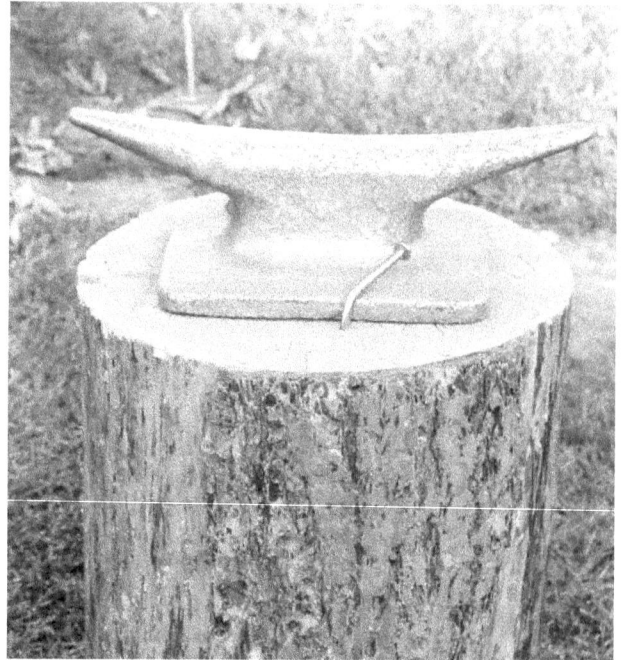

A large steel nautical cleat serves as a makeshift double-horn anvil.

Anvil stands made from assorted lumber (left) and an old tree stump.

Various homemade tongs and pliers.

Blacksmith tongs are easily made from rebar.

Tongs and Pliers

In my experience, blacksmith tongs are simple and easy to make from sticks of rebar or other steel round bars of roughly 1/2-inch diameter. Two pieces must be pinned at the pivot point like scissors and then shaped at the business end to form gripping jaws. The best part about making your own tongs is that you can heat and shape the jaws to fit your own unique requirements. Smaller pliers can be created in exactly the same way.

To create the pivot joint, simply hammer a somewhat flat section in each bar where they will pivot against each other, punch the holes, and then bolt, pin, or rivet them together at that point so that the working ends will overlap enough to allow jaws to be formed in alignment. If your riveted joint tightly locks the two pieces together initially, it is no problem to loosen the joint with hammer persuasion at the jaws or handles.

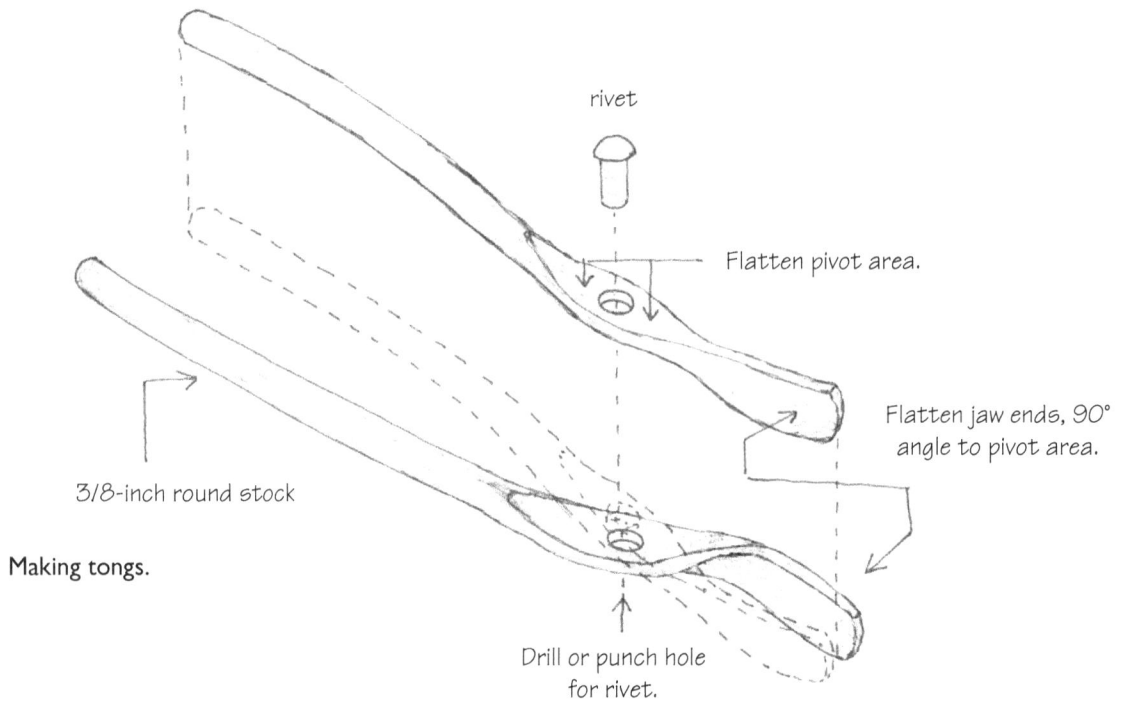

rivet

Flatten pivot area.

Flatten jaw ends, 90° angle to pivot area.

3/8-inch round stock

Making tongs.

Drill or punch hole for rivet.

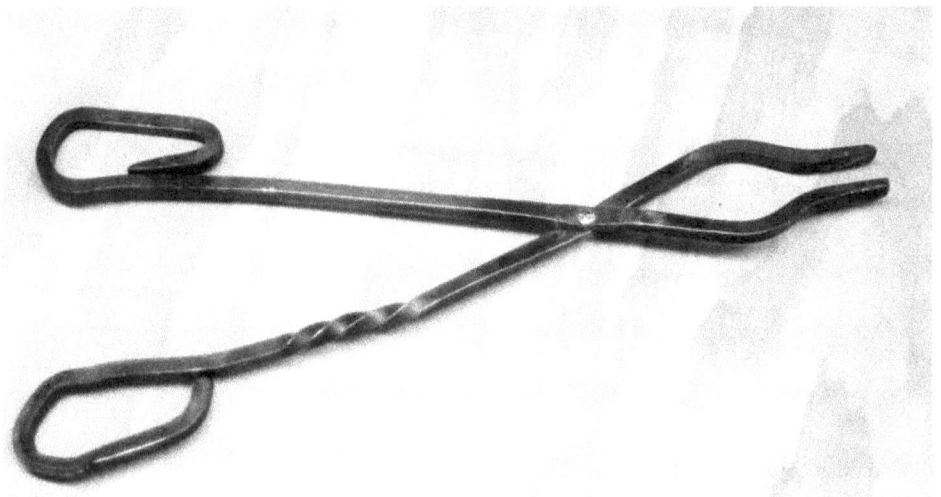

Lightweight campfire tongs made from 1/4-inch square stock.

Very simple tongs made from strap iron with a bolt through the pivot point.

Hammers

Almost any steel-headed hammer of sufficient weight can be used effectively to hammer hot metal over an anvil. Different metalsmiths indeed prefer different sizes and styles of hammers. In a remote area with very limited materials available, a hefty rock might be used as a hammer, but again, gloves and goggles should be worn in case it shatters.

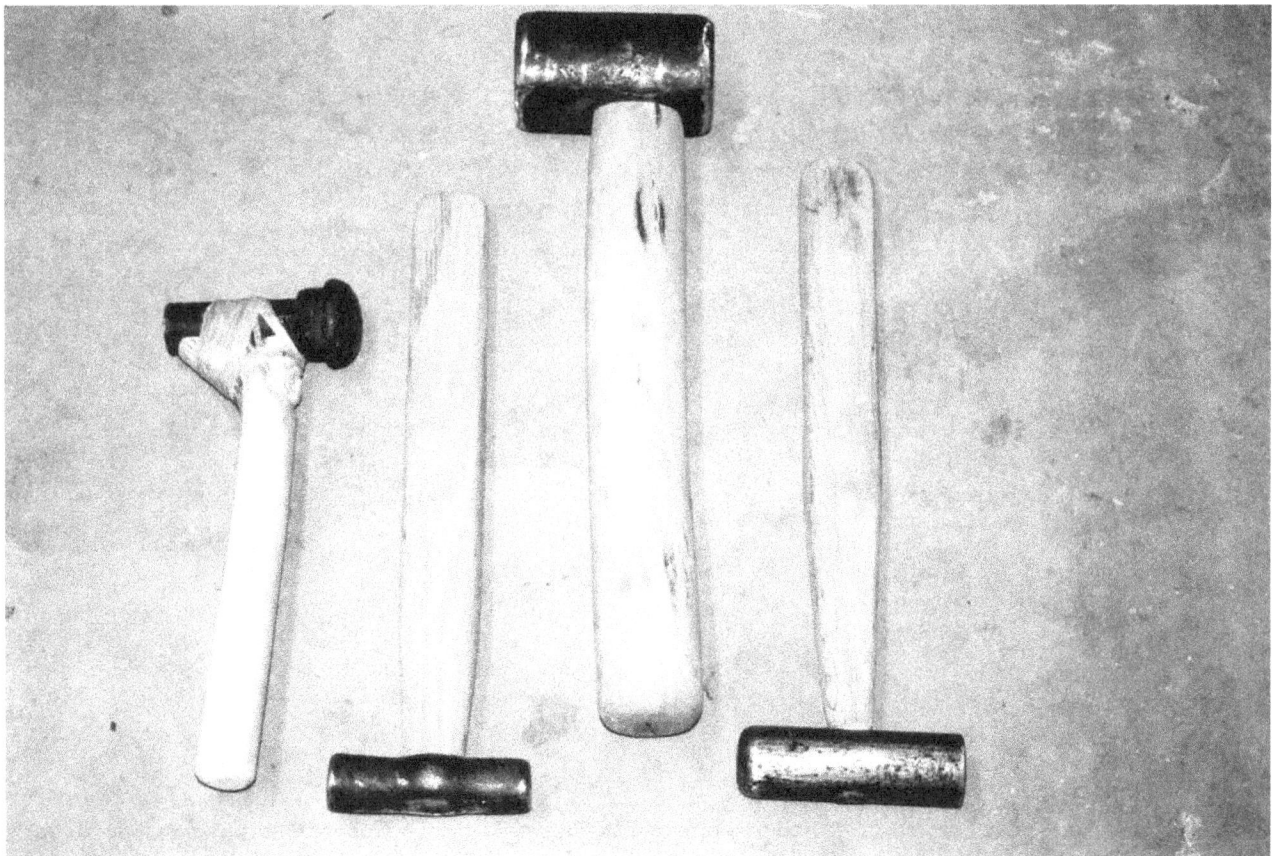

Homemade hammers.

Hammers can be fabricated in several different ways. I made one lightweight hammer by sawing off a section of 1 1/4-inch-diameter steel round stock, drilling a hole crossways through the middle for the eye, elongating the eye hole with a rattail file, and fitting a wooden handle into the eye in the conventional manner. I made another hammer by pounding a small block of steel into the basic shape for the head and then hot punching the hole for the eye. I created yet another functional hammer by cutting a huge bolt to the desired length with a hacksaw for my hammerhead, filing tie-on grooves into one side, and then attaching it with tight wrappings of heavy thread to a sturdy handle cut from a tree branch. All of these homemade hammers work well.

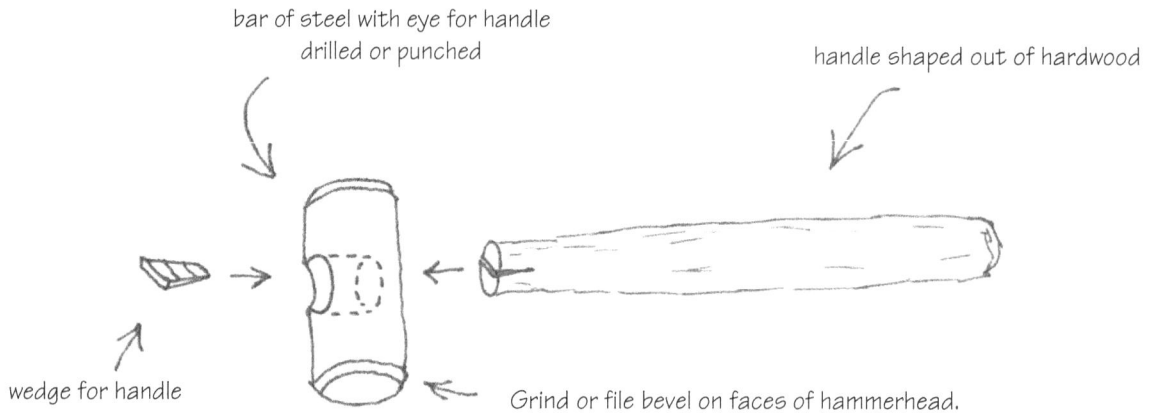

bar of steel with eye for handle
drilled or punched

handle shaped out of hardwood

wedge for handle

Grind or file bevel on faces of hammerhead.

Components of a homemade hammer.

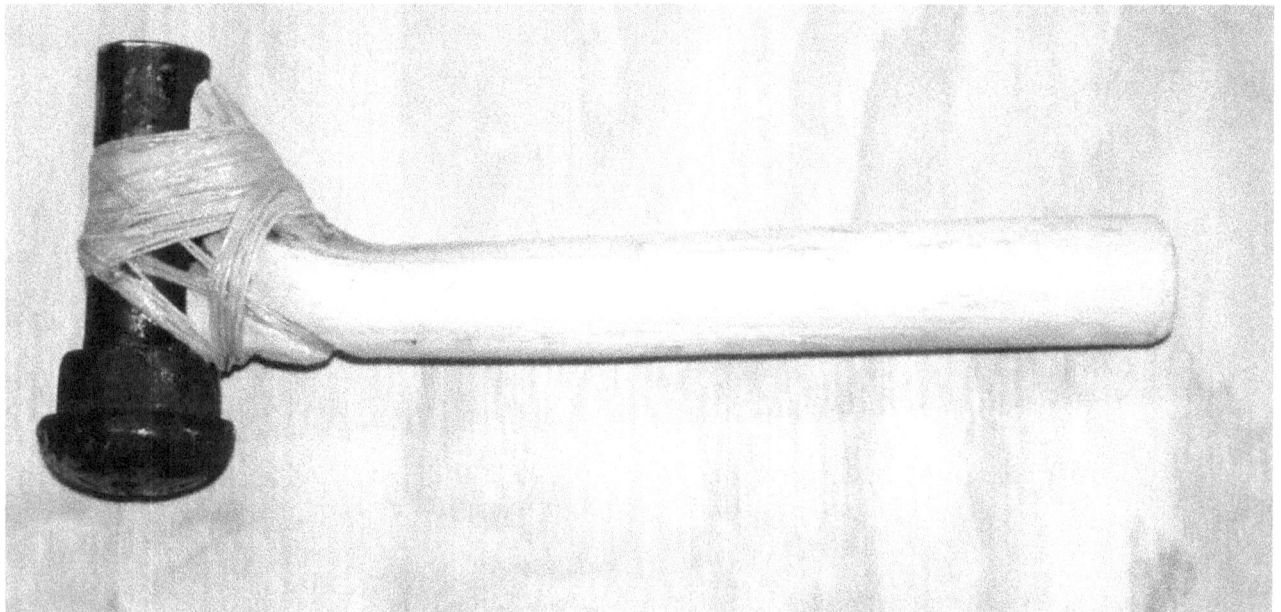

This hammer is made from a large bolt secured to a tree branch with heavy thread. Copper "motor rewind" wire could also be used to attach the head, as it bends almost as easily as thread or string but is more enduring, and it can be twisted up incredibly tight (as we'll see in chapter 5). If you scrub off the shellac coating on the copper wire, you can even solder the loose ends. The wire comes in sizes from thread to #10 or so.

Miscellaneous punches and pritchels I use in my blacksmith shop for hot punching.

Other Useful Blacksmith Tools

Blacksmiths often use an assortment of specialty tools, such as chisels, punches, swage blocks, and miscellaneous forming tools, stakes, and hardies. Any of these can be fabricated by the blacksmith himself or adapted from other existing tools.

Hardies are useful blacksmith tools that have a square-shaped shank designed to set into the square hole of a traditional anvil. Variations include fuller hardies for lengthening or stretching steel, chisel or cutting hardies, cone-shaped hardies for forming rings or dome-shaped curves, and forked hardies for bending, to name just a few. Several of the hardies in my collection were adapted from things like cold chisels and ax heads.

Anvil hardy used for cutting. This one was made from an old, handled chisel.

BASIC BLACKSMITHING PROCESSES

You already know how steel can be heated in a small forge to the degree that it becomes soft, malleable, and easy to manipulate and form into a variety of useful products. The following are some useful things to remember when working with hot metal.

First, think ahead and set up your metal shop with the tools and equipment within arm's reach of the forge wherever possible. This will save time spent moving the workpiece from the fire to the anvil or reaching for needed tools while the piece is quickly losing its usable heat.

Most hot metal work is typically accomplished with the steel heated to the temperature range where it glows from a light cherry red to a bright orange, usually between about 1,400°F and 1,750°F. Forge welding will require higher heat, normally around 2,000°F or even hotter (buttery yellow glow to almost white hot), depending on the type of steel. A small coal forge can heat small pieces of steel to well above 2,000°F. (We'll talk more about forge welding in chapter 6.)

Scale forms on the surface of the steel while it is cherry red, normally around 1,600°F, and begins to flake off at around 1,700°F. Scale is the accumulation of oxides that form when the hot steel is exposed to air. This won't interfere with most forge applications except forge welding, when it must be cleaned away before pieces of hot steel start

Bending hot metal using a turning fork and vise.

Thinning the edge, or drawing out the hot steel, with hammer strikes.

to stick together. Removing scale is normally accomplished by introducing flux to the surfaces to be welded as soon as the scale forms. Flux acts like a solvent to melt away the scale. Borax is commonly used as flux.

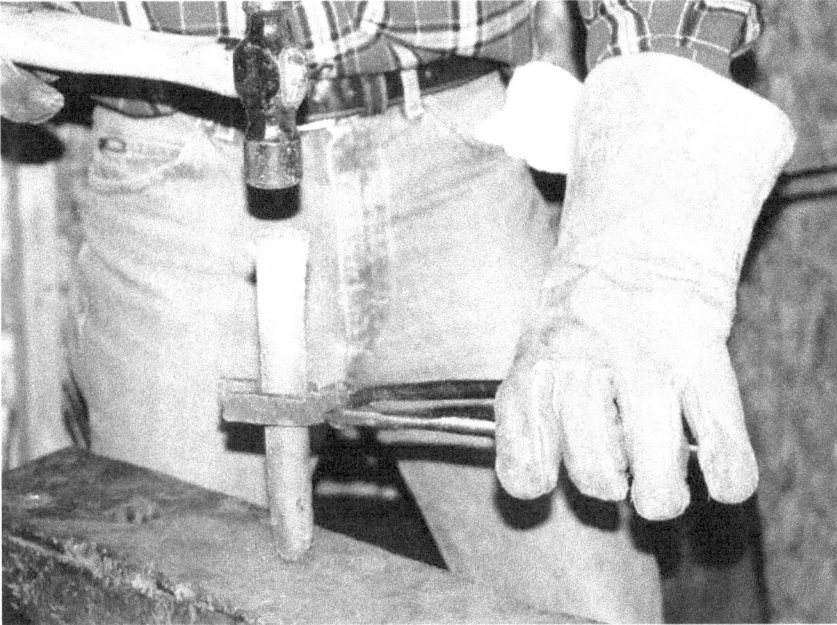

Upsetting—making the hot end shorter and thicker.

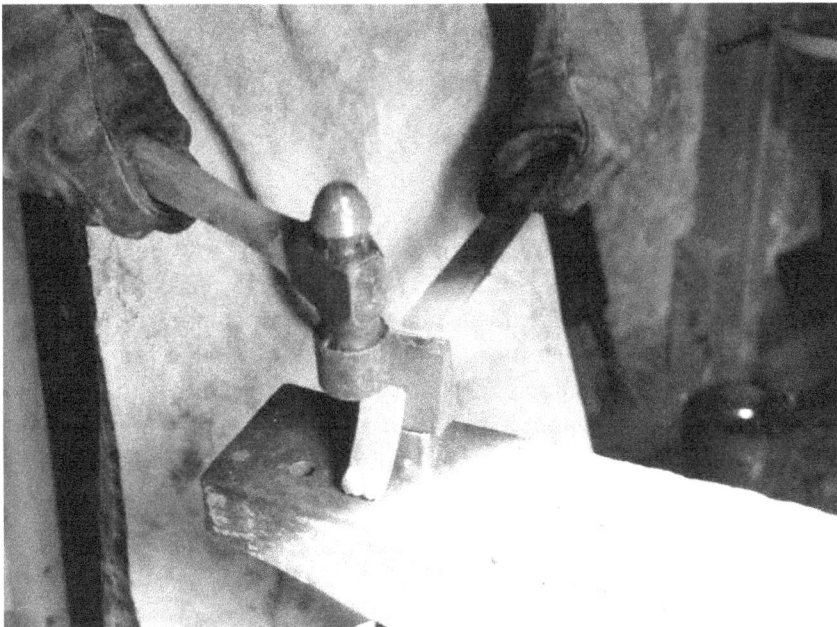

Shearing hot steel over the cutting hardy.

surface and the steel hisses.

Drawing out steel means to stretch it by making it longer or wider. This is often done either by regular, direct hammer blows to the hot steel or by using some type of fuller to progressively groove the work in order to better control the drawing-out direction. A fuller is simply a tool designed for grooving hot steel.

The opposite of drawing out is upsetting. Upsetting means making the workpiece—typically a short rod or cylindrical bar—shorter and thicker. Upsetting is accomplished by hammering the object on its ends. This is the process used in riveting.

In addition to these techniques, hot steel can also be cut or sheared over a cutting hardy or with a hammer and chisel. It can be bent and twisted by applying leverage. It can be flattened out into a thinner dimension with direct hammer blows or with a flatter tool and hammer. And it can be perforated with a hammer and punch.

Remember from chapter 1 that the higher the percentage of carbon in a piece of steel, the harder it can become. Mild steel with very low carbon content cannot be thoroughly hardened with normal heat-treatment processes. Mild steel is comparatively soft and easy to cut, drill, or file cold, but it has very low wear resistance. A knife blade made of low-carbon steel would not hold a sharp edge. Most cutting tools are best made of harder material.

Plain high-carbon steel, on the other hand, becomes very hard and brittle when sufficiently

When heated too hot, usually somewhere above 2,000°F with small- to medium-sized pieces of steel, the material will actually burn and become damaged beyond recovery. You'll know this is occurring when sparklers start erupting from the

Punching a hole through hot steel.

heated and quenched in water or oil for rapid cooling. This creates a lot of stress in the steel's molecular structure. This stress can be relieved greatly and the material softened by the process known as annealing. Steel can be annealed by heating it to a high heat and then allowing it to cool very slowly, such as while buried in the gradually cooling ashes of a dying campfire.

Tempering is a process of relieving stress in high-carbon steel to prevent unwanted cracking and brittleness, while maintaining as much of the steel's strength and hardness as possible. Tempering is accomplished by first heating to a high heat and quenching, then re-heating to a much lower temperature and allowing the workpiece to air cool.

CHAPTER 4

Improvised Tools

Because we are humans, we use tools in conjunction with nearly all our routine chores. The nature of our existence virtually demands the use of tools, and our ability to invent, make, and use tools is one of the things that sets us apart from most animals.

In the previous chapter we looked at ways to make our own hammers and pliers. In this chapter we will learn how to make more of the tools we will need to accomplish basic makeshift projects. It's one thing to build and repair things using the latest store-bought tools, but a greater challenge lies in building and repairing things with homemade or improvised implements. Hopefully, this chapter will inspire your imagination and get you to think of new ideas for fashioning your own tools.

THE FIRST TOOLS

The first effective tools built by human hands were likely made of stone. Even in modern times, certain rocks can be modified to accomplish a myriad of common chores. In chapter 1 we examined different types of rocks and various ways

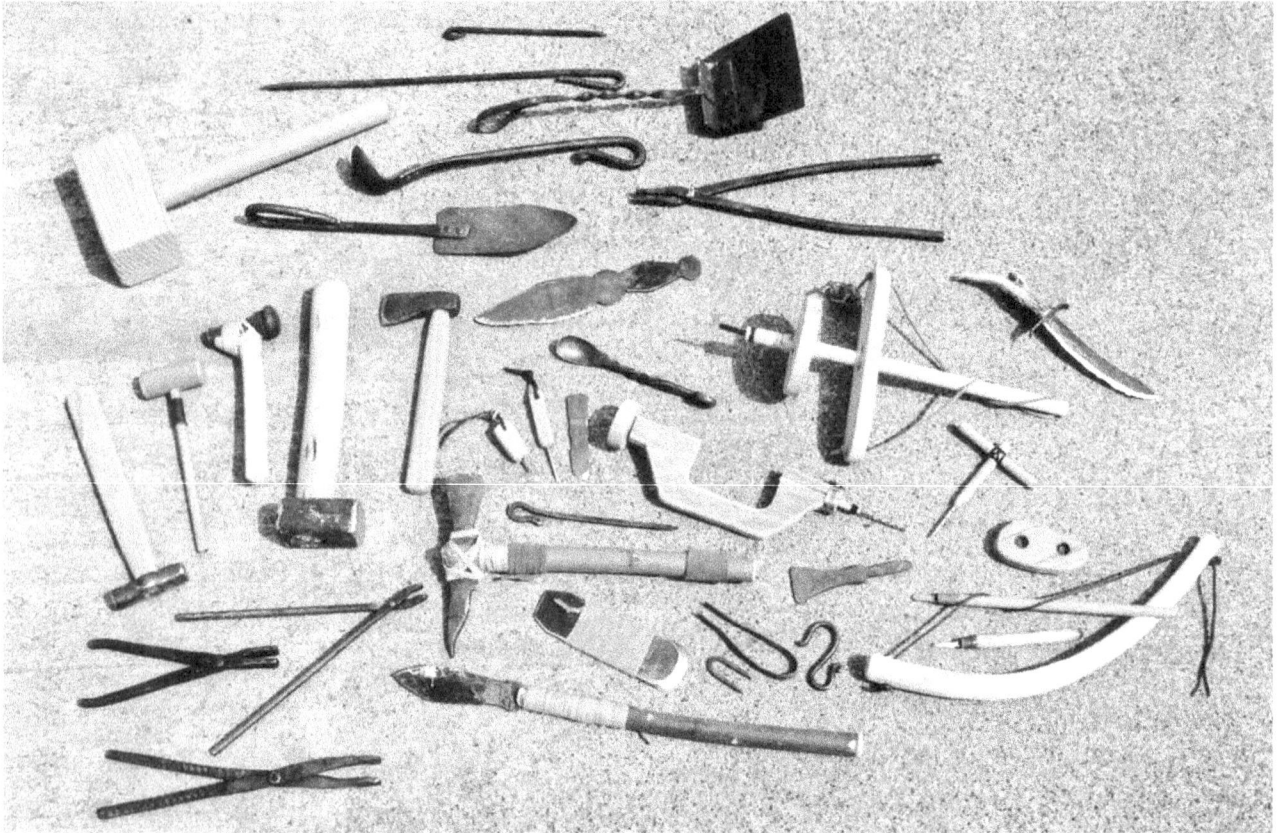

Assorted improvised tools.

in which we might use them. Here we will explore the ancient techniques for converting natural rocks into functional tools. This is known as lithic technology.

Flint Knapping

Flint knapping is a skill that has helped primitive people survive for thousands of years. It might be described simply as the various techniques for breaking or chipping rocks to create sharp edges, particularly rocks that exhibit the characteristics of conchoidal fracture. Conchoidal fracture can be defined as the way certain brittle materials break with smooth fracture lines that follow a cone shape expanding away from the point of impact. A typical example of conchoidal fracture is those chips that commonly occur in car windshields when struck by gravel or other tiny, hard objects.

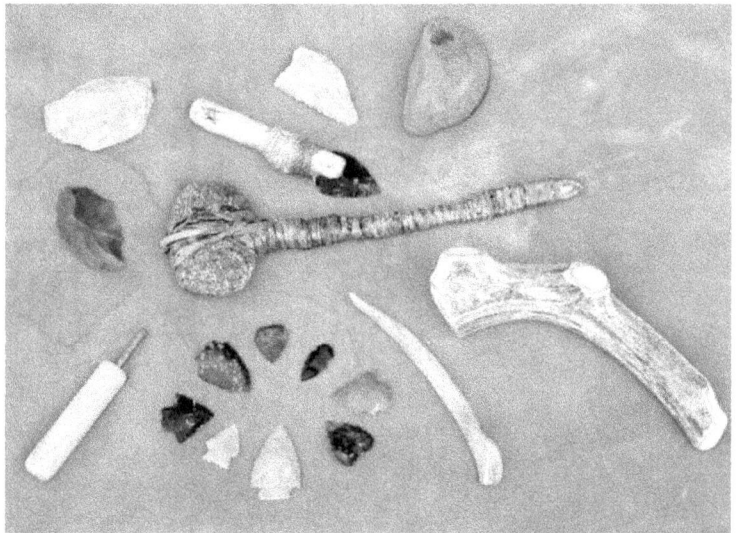

Stone Age tools.

Flint knapping is generally divided into two basic techniques: 1) percussion flaking, which entails striking blows to the material with a hammer stone or antler billet to detach flakes or blades, and

leather palm protector

abrader

goggles

antler hammer

antler and copper flakers

pieces of flint

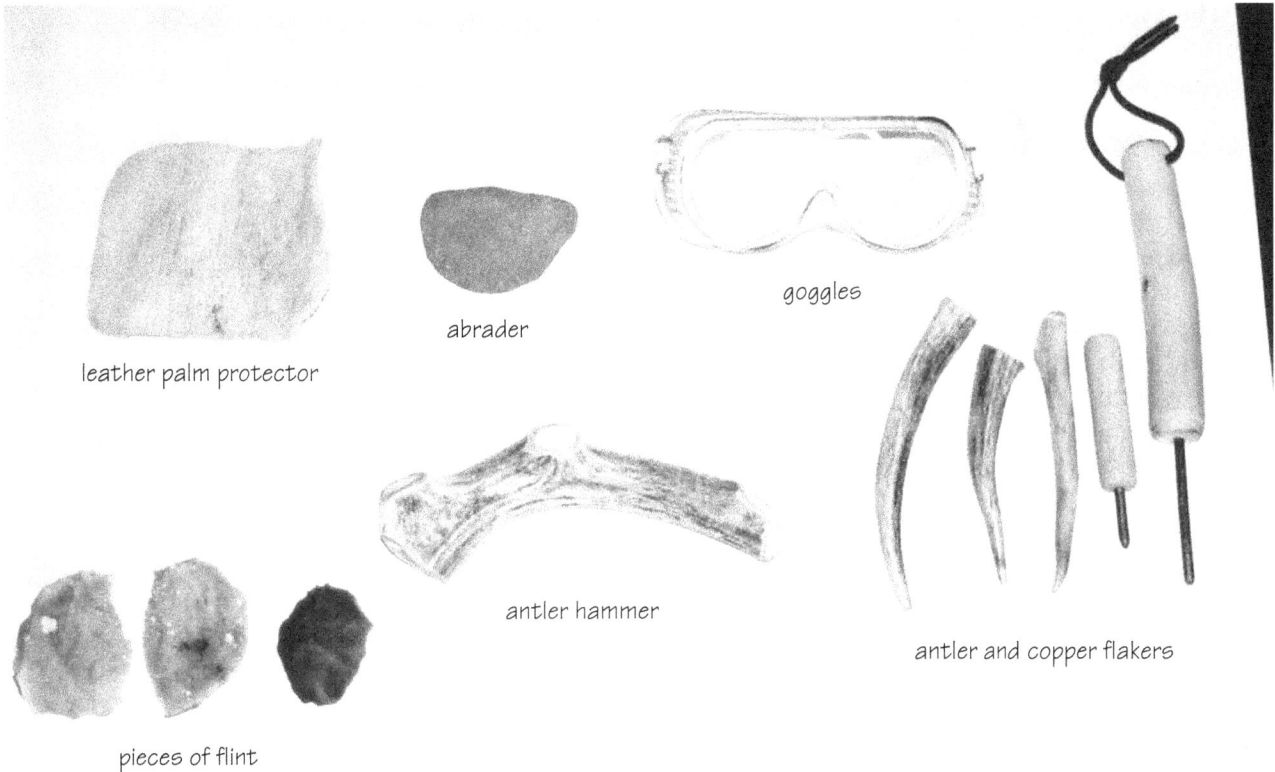

Flint knapping tools.

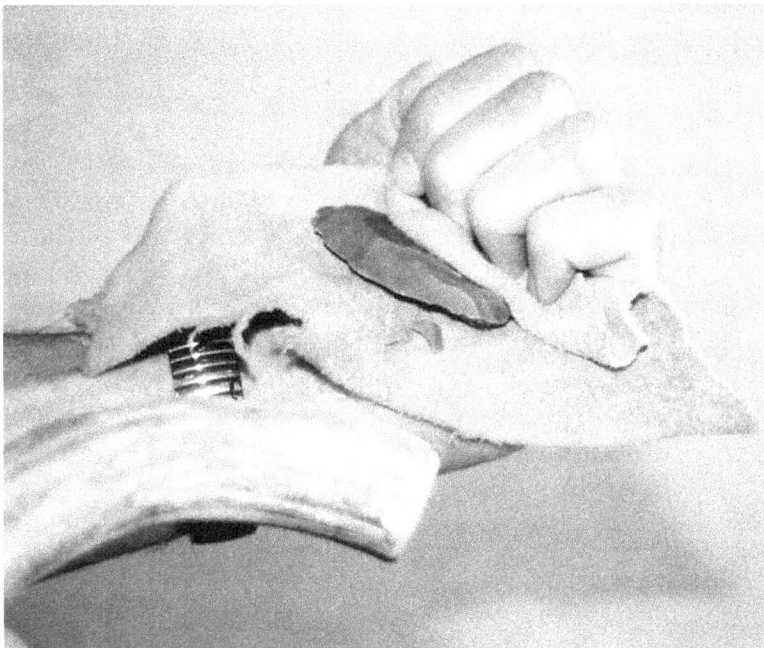

2) pressure flaking, which entails pressing flakes from the material using any of the various pointed flaking tools, such as a tapered copper rod set into a handle or an antler tine. Indirect percussion entails using a hammer stone in conjunction with a punch, usually made of antler.

The best knapping techniques may vary from one kind of rock to another. Typically, large rocks are reduced first with percussion, and then the edges are further refined with pressure flake techniques. In some instances, however, only one or the other technique would be used exclusively to create a tool or weapon.

Percussion flaking with an antler hammer.

The kinds of rocks that were typically knapped into weapons or cutting tools included flint, obsidian, chert, agate, and other varieties of quartz and glassy rocks. In the absence of good natural material to work with, knapping techniques can be applied to most types of man-made glass.

The first thing you should do before breaking sharp rocks is protect your eyes and hands. Tiny rock chips invariably fly about while knapping, and some sort of goggles or protective eyeglasses are important, as those small pieces are like slivers of glass. Thick leather gloves or a leather pad should also be used to minimize cuts to the palm and fingers. (I keep a box of bandages handy when working with sharp rocks, as I almost invariably need some.) A canvas or leather apron draped over the lap is useful for keeping most of the tiny flakes off your clothes, and the flakes should be disposed of just as one would dispose of broken glass. Some who do a lot of flint knapping also wear a respirator while working to limit the amount of silica dust getting into the lungs, which can cause silicosis over an extended period of exposure.

The key to success with knapping is to understand angles of fracture and to develop a feel for snapping off pieces of the desired size and shape. With practice, a knapper learns how conchoidal fracture can be applied to achieve controlled material reduction and thus create the desired shapes and sizes of the rock pieces and form the desired cutting edges.

Materials like antler and copper are the most common for hammers and flaking tools because they are soft enough to properly grip the

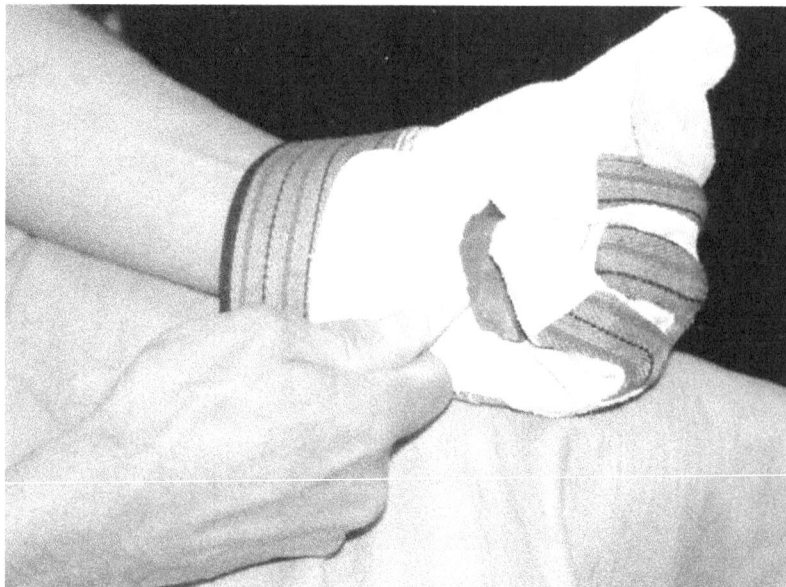

Pressure flaking with an antler tine.

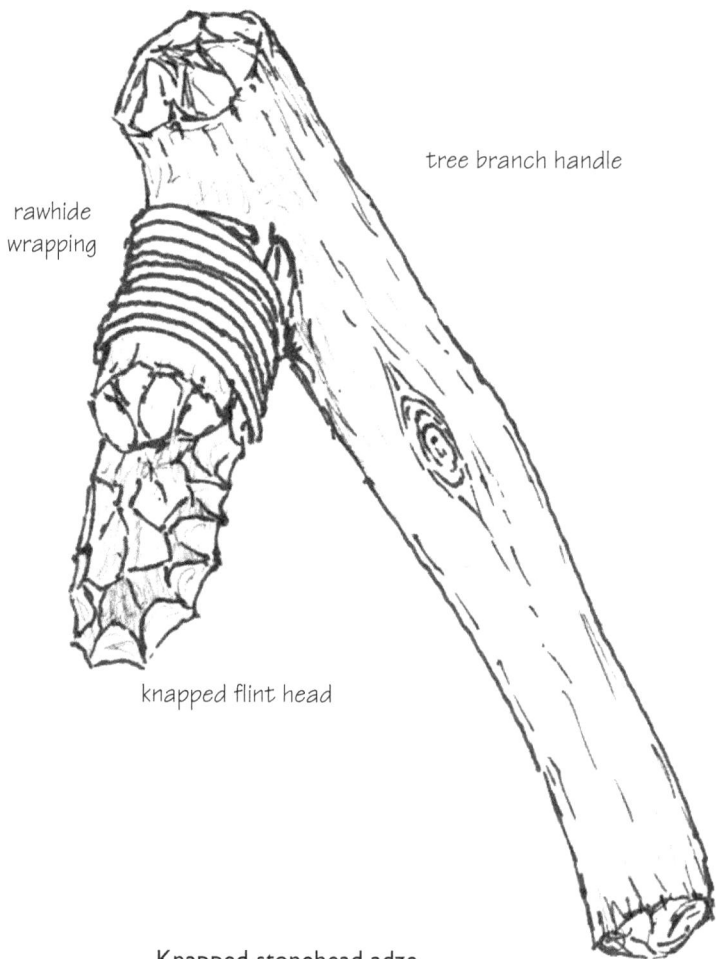

tree branch handle

rawhide wrapping

knapped flint head

Knapped stonehead adze.

70

Start with flint nodule.

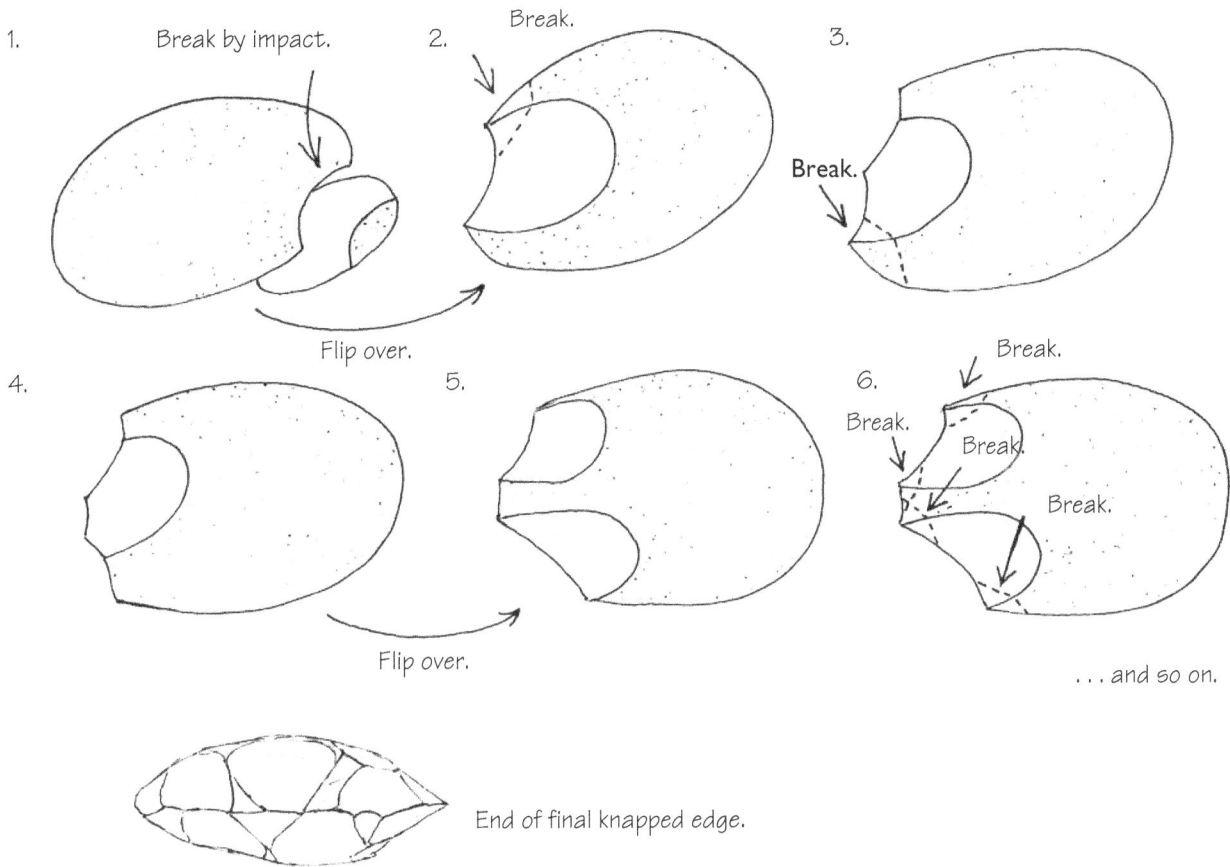

1. Break by impact.

2. Break.

3. Break.

Flip over.

4.

5.

6. Break. Break. Break. Break.

Flip over.

. . . and so on.

End of final knapped edge.

Stone reduction.

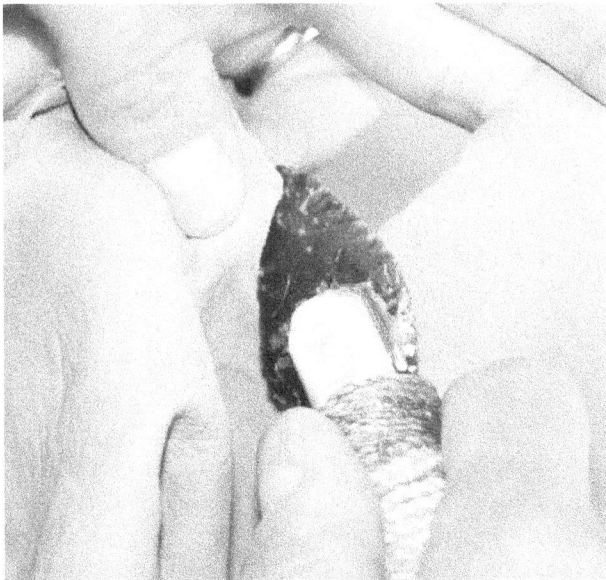

Cutting elk hide with a flint knife.

edge of the hard stone being reduced, yet solid enough to impart the force required to detach flakes. A steel hammer tends to transmit the impact energy too quickly through the rock, causing it to shatter rather than break into the desired larger pieces. Hard steel also lacks the "bite" characteristic of the softer tools that keep them from sliding off the workpiece.

A working edge of stone will crumble or become too sharp to facilitate good contact with the flaking tool from time to time. In such cases, it can be prepared, or abraded periodically with an abrasive rock such as a piece of sandstone to improve tool purchase on the edge.

Heat-Treating Flint

Such rocks as agate can be quite tough and difficult to knap. Evidence suggests that Stone Age people sometimes heat-treated their rocks to make them easier to knap. There are several theories about what exactly occurs in the rock during the heat-treating process, but the result is that it makes the material better suited to knapping.

Modern-day knappers have used various heat-treating methods that have included pottery kilns and even kitchen ovens for their convenience. Primitive people built fire pits in the ground and layered their lithic materials in the earth so that a high temperature (anywhere from about 400°F to 800°F, depending on the type of rock) could be sustained in the rocks for many hours, followed by gradual cooling that normally took several days to complete. A lengthy study of the thermal treatment of rocks is found in D.C. Waldorf's excellent book, *The Art of Flint Knapping* (see Suggested Resources for Further Study, page 203). Some very brittle materials—such as man-made glass, obsidian, and certain varieties of chert—require no heat-treating at all for easy knapping.

Other Stone Reduction Methods

Aside from knapping, or chipping off flakes from the main workpiece, rocks like basalt, granite, and others can be shaped or modified using either of two other material-reduction methods. The first is

Using a rock as a sharpening stone.

called abrading, which is simply grinding away material as needed to obtain the desired shape. This was traditionally accomplished using another rock with an abrasive surface; in modern times, grinding wheels are commonly employed to achieve the same result. A modern makeshift example of the abrading principle is using an abrasive rock in place of an oilstone to sharpen a steel knife blade.

The second method of material reduction is called pecking, and it entails repeatedly striking the surface of the workpiece with a pointed hard rock or other hard material in order to crumble away layers as needed to obtain the desired shape. Both abrading and pecking were used to create such implements as hammer stones, grooved ax heads, celts, and mortars and pestles.

IMPROVISED DRILLS

Considering how often we need to put holes in materials for various purposes, we should always have the capability to drill under any circumstances. Makeshift drilling machines and improvised drill bits are not as difficult to build as might be expected. Remember that holes were drilled through things thousands of years before electric drills and power drill presses were invented.

The T-Handle Drill

Perhaps the simplest makeshift way to make a tool for drilling holes entails merely tightening a small drill bit into a pin vise. An improvised pin vise that can accommodate larger bits can be fashioned out of a dowel, with a T-handle attached for easier turning. It is slowly turned by hand to bore a hole, just as one would turn a manual screwdriver. Very early drills made from stone employed the T-handle design.

The Bow Drill

Probably the most widely used of the primitive manual drill machines was the bow drill. Commonly depicted in drawings of ancient craftsmen, the system consists of a short hand bow with its bowstring wrapped one turn around a shaft that functions as the spindle that holds a boring bit. A top socket facilitates downward hand pressure on the vertically stabilized spindle such that a horizontal sawing motion with the bow produces

The slow but functional makeshift T-handle drill, using a regular twist bit.

rotation at the spindle, and thus the bit is able to bore a hole into an object secured under it.

Functional top sockets have been made of hard wood, bone, antler, polished stone, steel, and even glass. Normally, the denser the material, the less friction it will generate at that contact point. The socket must have an adequate depression into which the spindle will fit.

A simple version of the bow drill system has been used as a method for creating fire by friction, where a tapered wooden spindle is rotated in a notched hole of a wooden fireboard to generate the friction. The basic technique is the same in either case. As long as the spindle holds a properly shaped and secured drill bit constructed of sufficiently hard material, this method is quite effective as a means for drilling small holes.

Some key factors that affect the operation of the bow drill include:

1. Having the right design and material of the top socket. You want to minimize the friction at that top contact point.

Drilling with a bow drill.

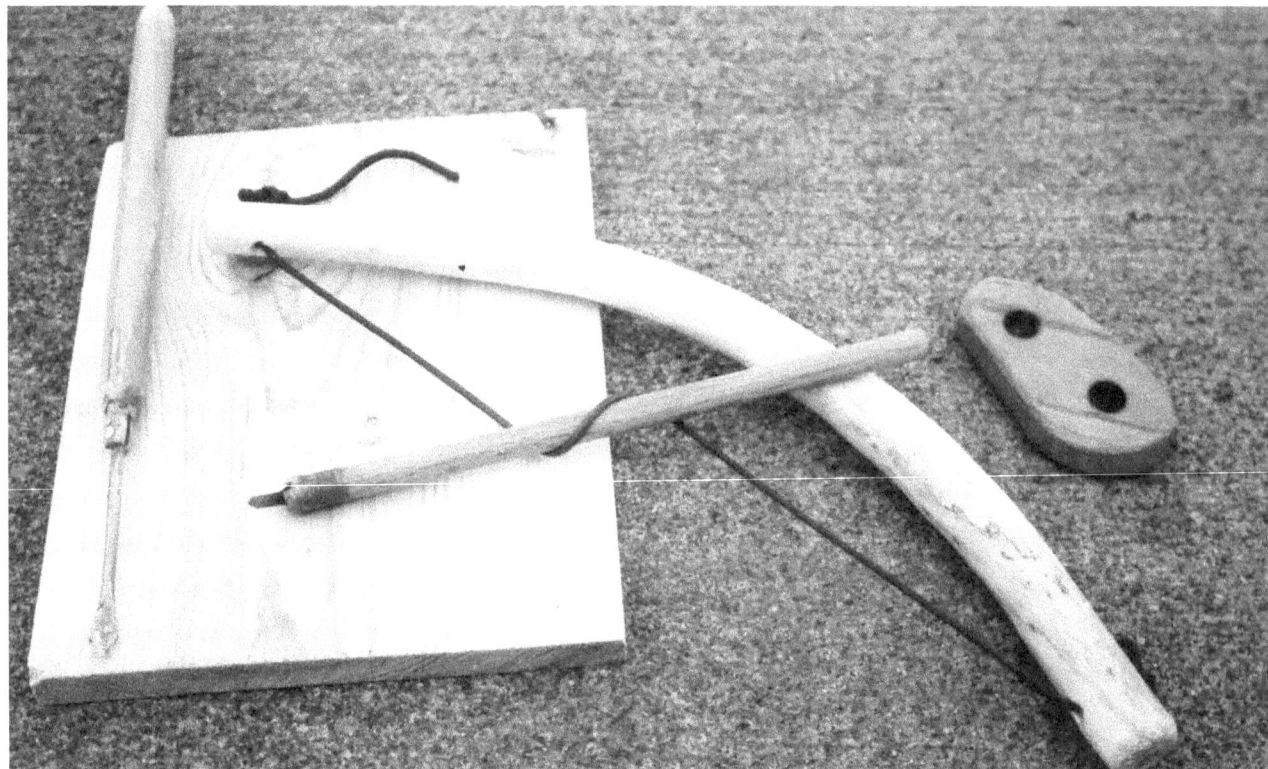

The bow drill with two different bit options. The bit at left is a makeshift spade-type bit created by hammering flat the tip of a large nail and sharpening it. Its shank is set into a hole in the wooden spindle and cross-pinned. The other bit is made from a small piece of metal broken off a thin flat file, set into the slot of its spindle, and secured with wrappings of cord and glue.

2. Maintaining a consistent sawing motion. It should be even and controlled, in conjunction with gradual downward pressure on the top socket.

3. Attaining proper tension on the bowstring wrapped around the spindle. A string that is too loose will slip and fail to continue rotating the shaft. A string that is too tight will generate excess friction and interfere with a smooth, fluid rotation of the spindle.

4. Maintaining upright stabilization of the spindle during operation.

5. Choosing the right design and material of the bit. It should be harder than the material being drilled; straight, centered, and well secured in the spindle; with a properly shaped and sharpened tip, of the proper diameter to achieve the desired hole size.

The Indian Pump Drill

Another ancient drilling machine is what is sometimes called the Indian pump drill, as it was a popular tool with such Native American groups as the Eskimos for boring small holes in things like wood, bone, horn, ivory, and seashells.

The system consists of a shaft, or spindle that holds the bit, with a simple wooden flywheel mounted low, where its weight provides rotational inertia. A pump platform slides over the spindle and is suspended in a horizontal position by a cord attached at each end and to the top of the spindle. The cord is wrapped around the spindle so it lifts the platform with the last phase of the rotation in one direction; a downward push on the platform unwinds the cord and produces rotation in the opposite direction. The flywheel, which is simply a wooden disk that fits over the spindle, helps sustain the rotational force needed to wind the cord back up each time and lift the platform. The process is repeated with every downward push on the platform that forces the cord to unwind.

An efficient pump drill will have a flywheel of sufficient thickness and diameter for mass, a wide pump platform with an oversized hole through which

The Indian pump drill. Note the removable bit section, making this a versatile drilling machine.

the spindle loosely fits so it will not bind or produce excess friction, and a long, straight shaft of proportional diameter that holds the appropriate boring bit securely and centered at the bottom end. The device is actually very simple to build and operate, as can be seen in the photos. I built the example shown with a removable bit section so I could change bits for different drilling tasks. This bit section is attached to the shaft with an extended tongue that fits into a slot in the shaft and is cross-pinned in place with a wooden dowel.

The Brace and Bit

One of the simplest manual drill machines is the traditional brace and bit. This type of tool is still in production and can be found in most hardware stores. The system consists of either an auger-type or spade bit chucked into a simple brace that forms a crank handle. You almost feel as if you are cranking to start an early automobile when turning the brace to bore a hole. The brace and bit works especially well when drilling large holes through soft wood.

A makeshift brace can be fabricated in a number of ways. I built a very crude example, mainly from wood, that employs a small, factory-made twist bit (see photos on the next page). I ground the shank of the bit flat so it would fit into a slot in the makeshift chuck and then secured it in position with tight wrappings of cord. The hose clamp helps secure the bit holder firmly in its fixed position so it can be turned by the brace handle. It might not look like much, but the device actually works.

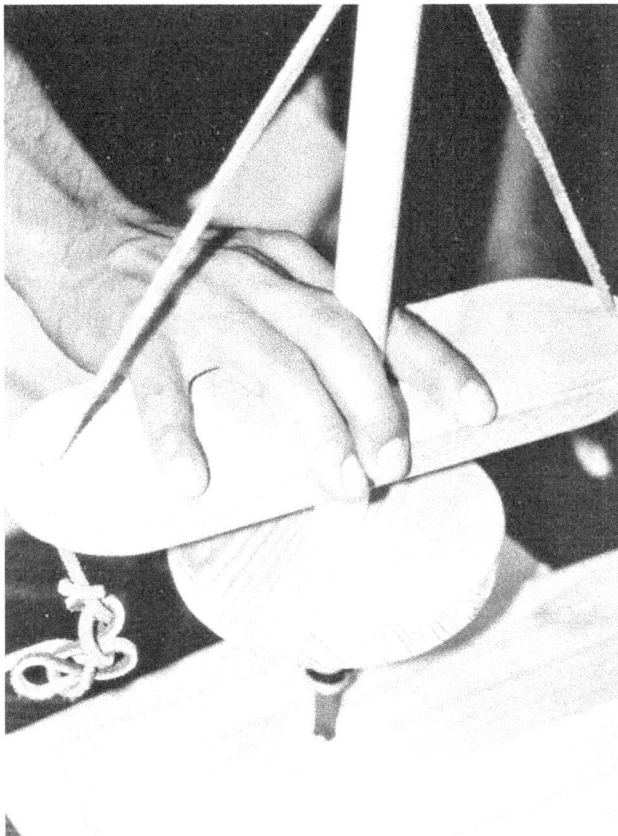

Drilling with the Indian pump drill.

The key elements of a successful drill brace are:

1. A free-turning head, or top spindle, that allows one to apply downward pressure on the tool while turning the handle. It can be a simple palm-sized hardwood disk that freely rotates on a center nail, for example.

2. Alignment of the top and bottom vertical sections of the brace handle with the center drilling axis.

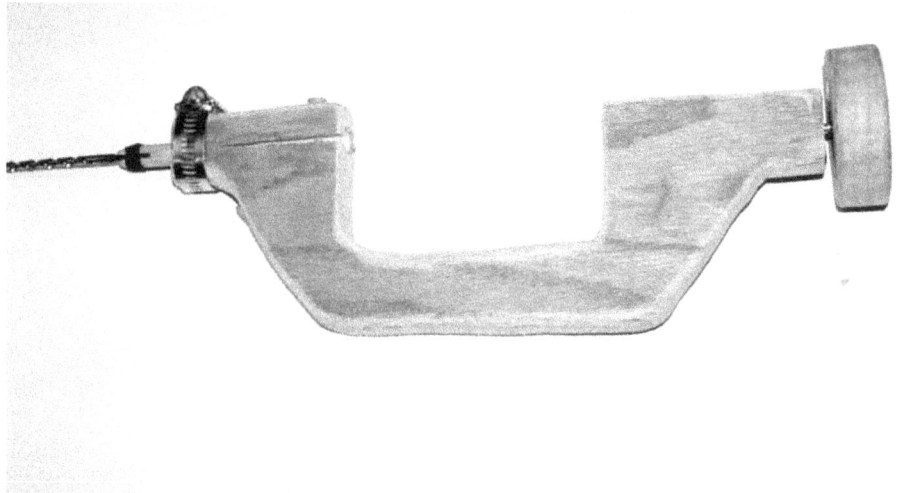

A very crude but functional homemade brace drill.

3. Some type of device like a jaw chuck that will hold a drill bit securely and centered during drilling.

Larger augers for boring into the ground or through ice also have a brace-type handle attached as a fixed unit to the bit. The principle of manual operation is the same with these as with the standard brace-and-bit system.

Eggbeater Drill Machines

Through an arrangement of gears, the manually powered eggbeater-type drills are capable of applying greater mechanical advantages than most other manual drill machines. (We'll discuss mechanical advantages more in chapter 9.) Quality new and used eggbeater drills in a wide range of sizes are fairly easy to find even today, and the basic design lends itself well to adaptation to a manual drill-press arrangement. You just need some type of makeshift apparatus that holds the tool vertically and allows it to be lowered gradually during the drilling process.

A blacksmith friend of mine, Ron Washburn, created the manual drill press shown in the illustration on page 77. The frame consists of a vertical post welded to a baseplate and two arms that pivot on bolts, allowing them to swing up and down freely. He is able to apply downward pressure on the turning bit as he cranks the handle by stepping into an iron loop on the end of a chain suspended from the top arm.

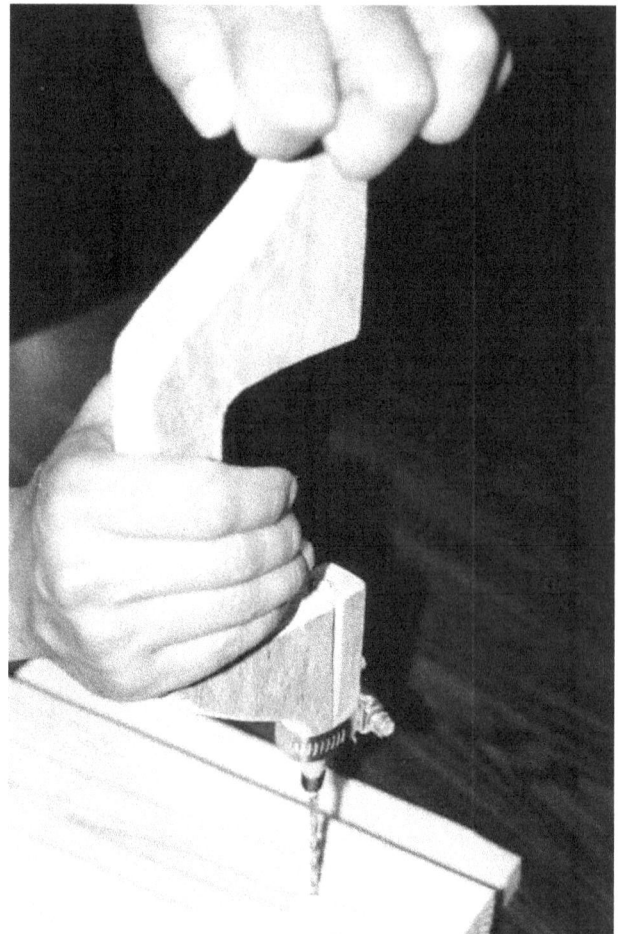

Using the makeshift brace drill.

Drill Bits

There are many different designs of drill bits used for different applications. A highly skilled metal worker might be able to fashion effective twist bits and auger bits, but less complicated bit designs can be made with makeshift methods. A simple variation of the flat spade-type drill bit, for example, is a fairly easy item to fabricate from scrap steel, as seen in the illustration below.

For certain applications, I have found that small pieces of files lend themselves well as makeshift drill bits because they're hard and, properly ground, will cut through most common materials quite well. The biggest drawback to file steel is that it tends to be somewhat brittle because it is so hard. Heavy torque applied to a bit made from file steel is likely to break it. I learned by trial and error that the thinnest files are to be avoided for drill bit stock.

Also, it is usually advantageous to design a drill bit with a cutting surface of larger diameter than the diameter of the bit's shank. This will allow you to bore holes with sufficient clearance for the shank to minimize friction and stress on the bit during the drilling process.

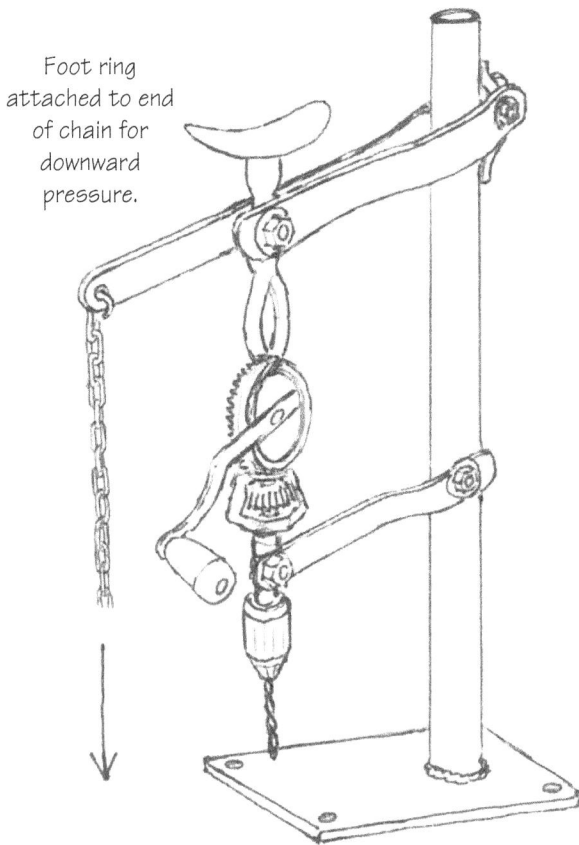

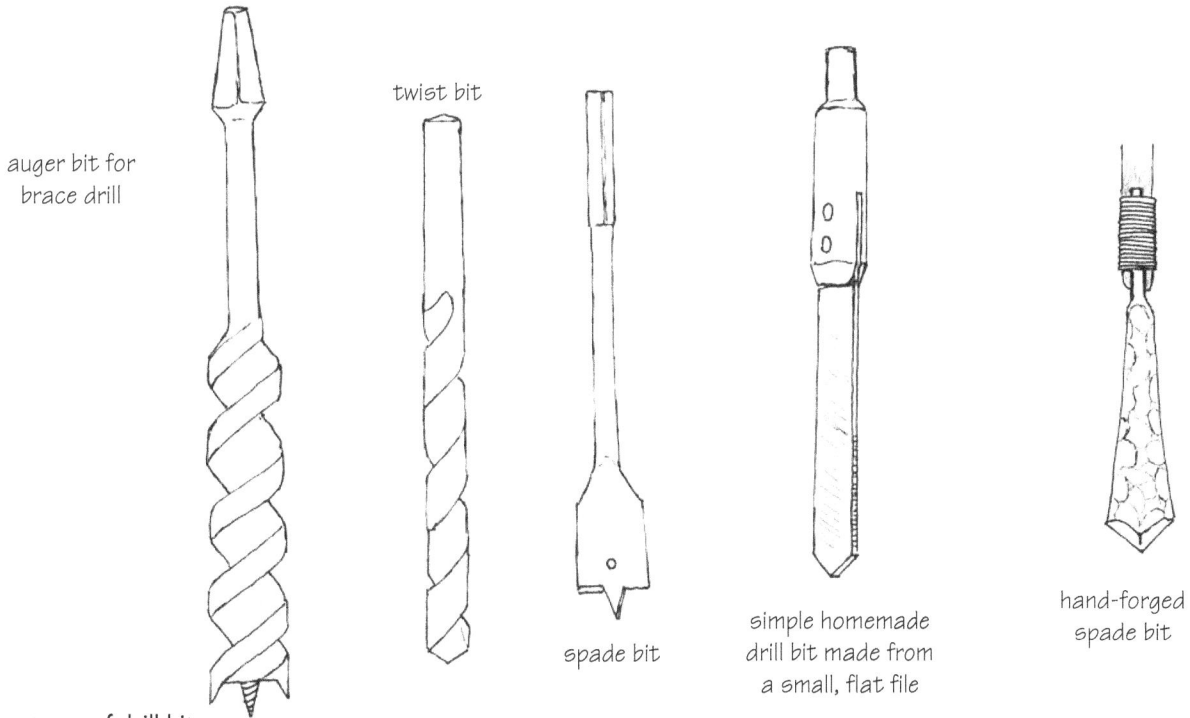

Foot ring attached to end of chain for downward pressure.

A breast drill connected to a vertical post to create a drill press.

auger bit for brace drill

twist bit

spade bit

simple homemade drill bit made from a small, flat file

hand-forged spade bit

Various types of drill bits.

MAKESHIFT SAWS

If you already have plenty of good files and saw blades of every variety, making numerous other kinds of hand tools is not usually a problem. But have you ever tried to create an effective saw blade from scrap? This objective nagged me as an irresistible challenge until I built some experimental saws and tested them. In this section I will share the results of my research and experimentation with makeshift saws.

The first homemade handsaw with blade taller than practical.

To start, it's important to understand exactly how saw teeth cut. Whereas a knife blade uses the very gradual wedge shape of its tapered edge to separate material in the cutting or slicing process, saw teeth actually act like a series of tiny chisels in a row, each chiseling off small bits of material during the sawing. In other words, a knife blade essentially wedges material apart at a microscopic level, while a saw chews or chisels out material. Hence, you wouldn't want your saw teeth to taper along the sides like the edge of a knife blade.

The crude homemade handsaw will actually cut soft wood.

If you look closely at a lot of common saw blades, you can see that in many cases the teeth are offset from center in both directions in an alternating sequence. This is to ensure that they will chisel out a larger slot in the material being sawn than the thickness of the blade, giving the blade adequate clearance to move back and forth in the deepening cut without binding. It also sets those tiny chisels in position to bite off more material during every pass.

Improvised saw blades might be fabricated in a number of ways, depending upon the tools and materials available to work with and the specific sawing tasks at hand. I created some functional saws for rough-cutting wood using mild steel for the blades. The soft, mild steel was easy for me to work but obviously was not the best material for saw teeth, as it probably won't stay sharp very long during prolonged use. Even so, my makeshift saws proved to be surprisingly effective during my sawing experiments.

The catch to my method was that I needed one saw to make another, because my makeshift teeth were created with a hacksaw. Without access to a hacksaw, functional saw teeth could still be created with a sharp chisel and a forge, by hot cutting the metal over a cutting block or anvil. We should keep in mind that the first saw blade made of metal had to have been made entirely without sawing out the teeth.

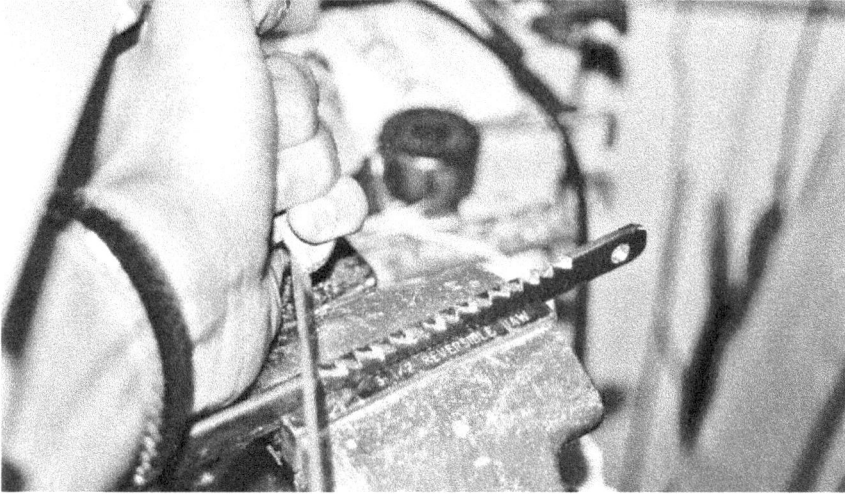

Cutting teeth into the second, narrow blade. I'm using a hacksaw here, but a narrow corner file might also do the job.

Note the alternating angles of the teeth to help them chisel through wood.

The improved makeshift saw blade secured to its frame.

A thin saw blade should be made of spring steel, or at least properly tempered steel, to allow some degree of flex and avoid crumpling or breaking under stress. Steel that is too hard to cut or file easily can be softened by annealing and, after the work is completed, rehardened.

My first homemade saw blade was not a very good design. The thickness of the teeth was the same as the body of the blade, and the blade was thicker and taller than it needed to be for the smoothest sawing action. Nor were the shape of the teeth ideal.

I made a close inspection of the teeth of a large crosscut saw to get an idea about how I should shape the teeth on my second homemade saw blade. Based on my observations, I cut the teeth with alternating angles for superior chiseling action, and I made the body of the blade narrower, allowing it to pass through the cut with less bind or friction. Still plenty of room for improvement, but this second homemade saw chewed through a couple of thick tree branches without any trouble.

Handy Bucksaws and Bow Saws

Nearly any straight saw blade can be mounted into a bucksaw configuration of one variation or another, and this usually creates a fairly rigid frame that makes the blade easy to handle and use. The basic concept involves two vertical bars that serve as handles, to which the blade is secured on its ends at the bottoms. The handles pivot over a horizontal bar and are pulled toward the frame's center at their tops in order to create the tension that keeps the whole unit rigid.

The frame can be made of hardwood dowels, tree branches, narrow flat boards, or metal pipe or tubing. The tops of the handles can be drawn toward the center with rope, strong twine, or even cables or metal wire in conjunction with turnbuckles, just as one might tighten up a fence gate. The simple system shown in the photos and sketch includes thin rope looped through the tops of the handles and twisted tight with the tourniquet method, using a short, sturdy dowel through the loop.

Sawing with the improved homemade saw.

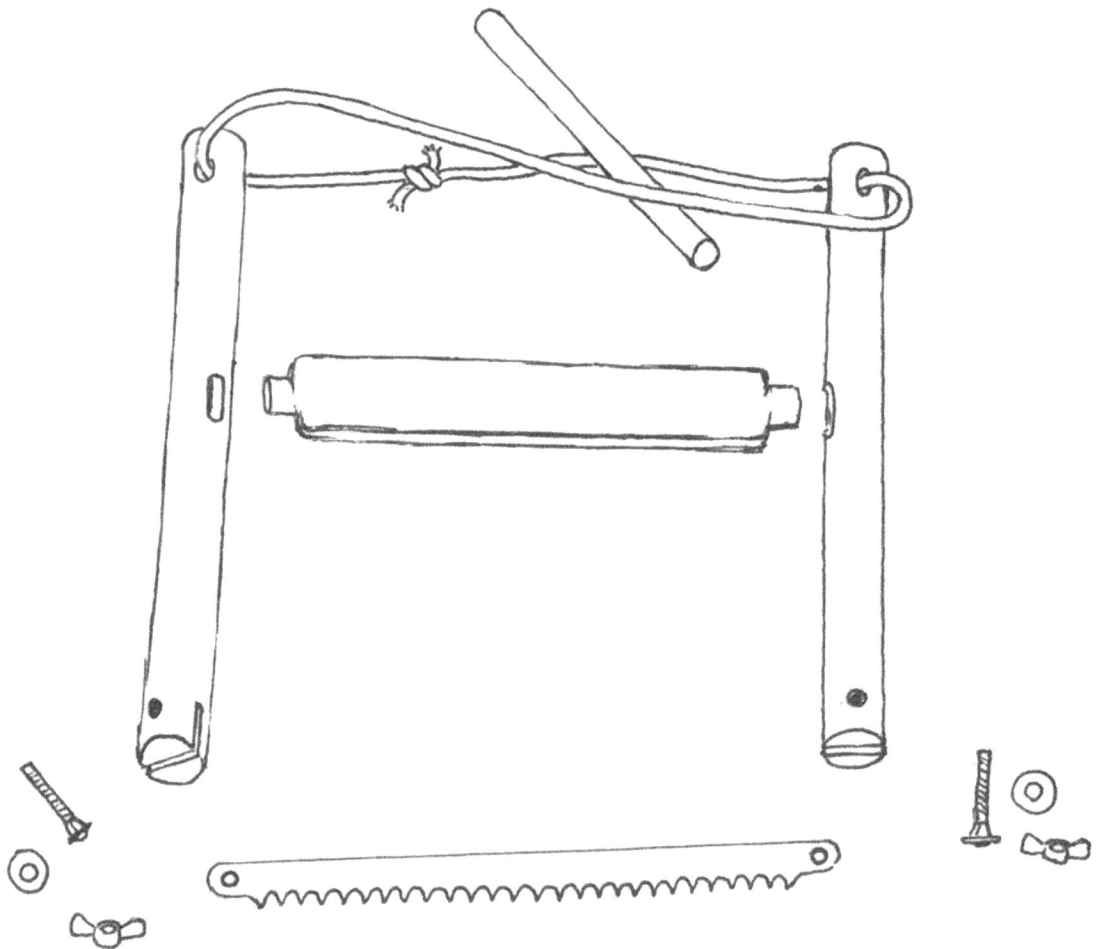

Components of a homemade bucksaw.

The homemade bucksaw assembled.

The dowel is braced against the horizontal bar with the tension of the twisted cord to prevent untwisting.

Besides being easy to assemble, the neat thing about a bucksaw like this is that it can be disassembled easily for stowing in a pack. Disassembled, it takes up less space than a typical bow saw or almost any similar saw that is ready to use. It is also very easy to change blades, and its tension is adjustable.

A bow saw is a similar yet simpler configuration. It is simply a bow of one form or another that has a saw blade mounted on the ends of its limbs. The bow keeps the blade rigid and forms a handle. It is not as versatile as a bucksaw, because it won't collapse as small for packing, and blade tension is not as easily adjusted. However, in some instances a simple bow saw might be quicker and easier to build in the field than a typical bucksaw.

Camping and outdoor supply stores usually carry those handy little wire saws that coil up nicely

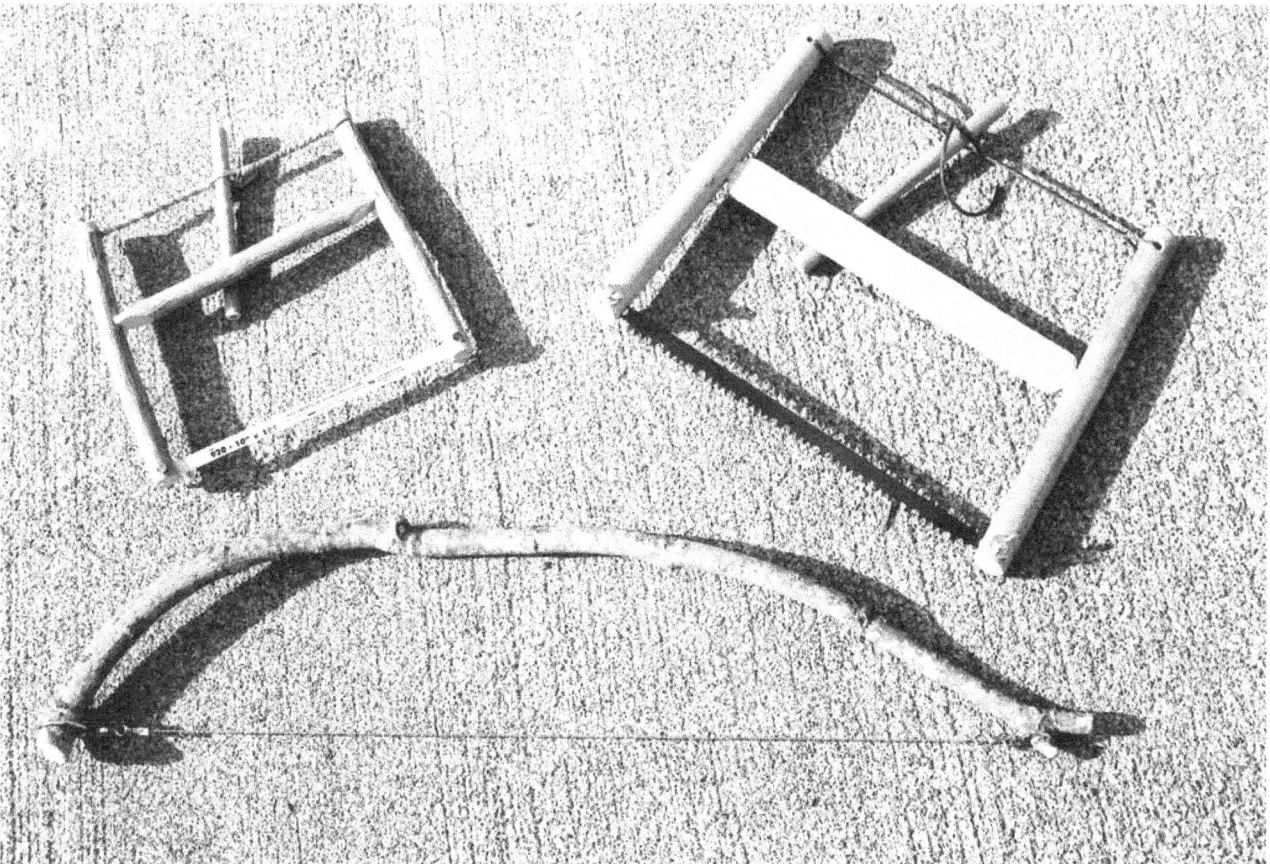

An improvised bow saw compared to two sizes of bucksaw.

in a pocket or survival kit. One of these can be quickly hooked onto a bent branch to create an expedient bow saw in the woods. In my experience, these cut through green wood quite efficiently.

Before leaving our discussion of makeshift saws, I should at least mention the construction of manually powered sawing machines. Some interesting devices have been made over the years, as detailed in a number of books that describe traditional woodcraft techniques. In his book *The Woodwright's Shop*, for example, author Roy Underhill describes the foot-operated reciprocating band saw in his shop, which employs the power of a spring pole to lift the blade between each downward cutting motion made by stepping on the foot pedal.

MAKESHIFT FILES AND RASPS

After reading Alexander Weygers' discussion about making files and rasps by hand in his book, *The Complete Modern Blacksmith*, I could not resist trying some of my own experiments in this area. He explained that homemade files cannot compete with machine-made examples, being comparatively crude. My attempts were no exception to this, but I did discover just how well a crude file can perform on wood, if not so great on harder materials.

The basic method for making a file by hand entails firmly mounting a blank piece of annealed high-carbon steel to a block of wood and then

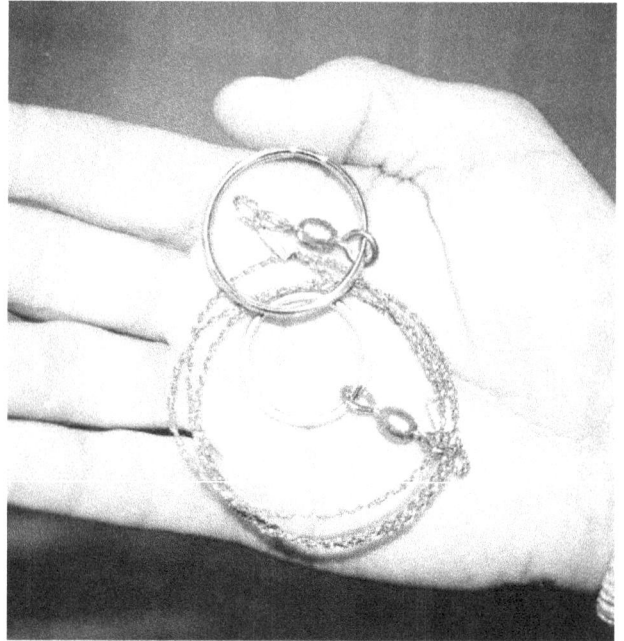

A coiled wire saw, ready to be stowed in a pocket. These are available in most sporting goods stores and work great as quickie bow saw blades.

securing the block in the jaws of a bench vise. By striking a sharp cold chisel with a hammer, the steel can be raised in rows by the wedge action of the chisel's edge as it digs into the surface. When all the desired rows of teeth have been created, the soft annealed carbon steel can then be rehardened by heating and quenching so it will be capable of

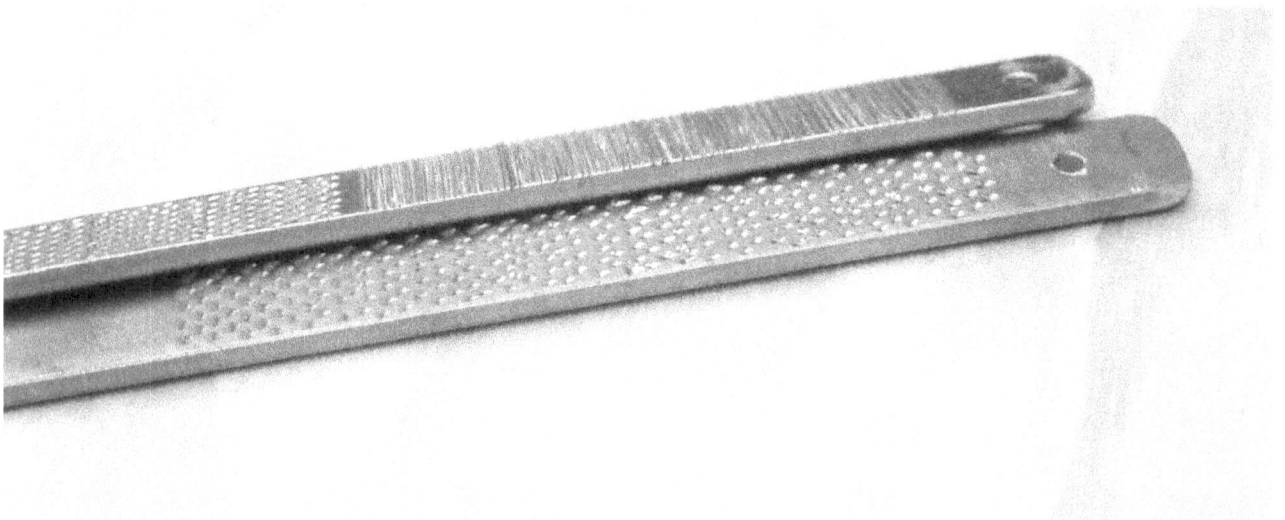

Homemade rasp and file.

Making file teeth by striking a sharp homemade chisel with a hammer. Hammer not shown.

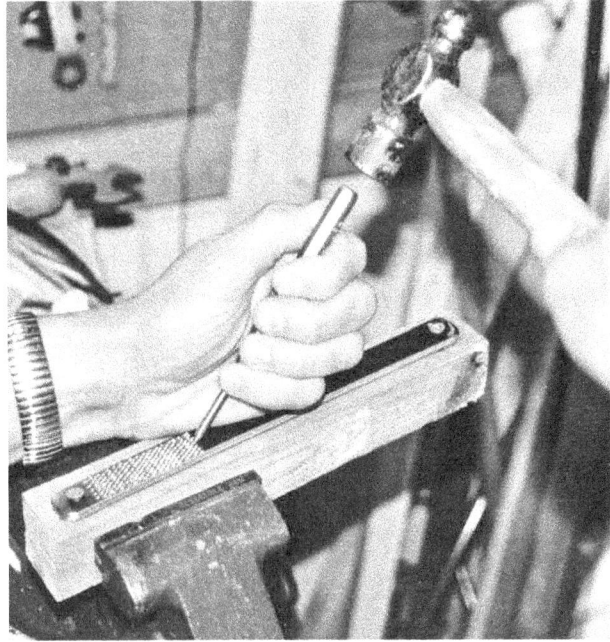

A pointed punch is used to form teeth in a homemade wood rasp.

Close-up of the alternating pattern of the rasp teeth.

Shaping wood with the homemade rasp.

Wooden knobs added to this homemade rasp to provide handles.

cutting material that is not as hard. Low-carbon steel can in fact be used, as Mr. Weygers points out; the surface just needs to be hardened by applying case-hardening compound over the toothed surface.

Wood rasps are easy to make with the same basic technique, except that a pointed, hard steel punch is used instead of a chisel. I ground a pointed taper on the end of a 3/16-inch drift punch for this purpose. A pointed round punch does an excellent job of raising small burrs that serve as the cutting teeth of your rasp. I discovered that rasps can be made of soft steel and left unhardened for cutting soft wood. The several rasps I created seem to perform about as well as factory-made versions, and after a moderate amount of use they still have not become noticeably dull.

HOMEMADE KNIVES

Making quality custom knives normally requires a skill level acquired only after a substantial amount of practice and experience working with steel. The best products also take a good deal of time to create from start to finish.

Less refined, yet functional edged tools can be made by almost anyone fairly quickly. Any sharp piece of steel or broken glass can serve as a functional knife to slice, scrape, shave, or chop through a variety of materials under emergency conditions. In certain situations, a simple wrapping of cord or rawhide along the grip area might provide a serviceable handle to prevent the blade's cutting edge from slicing the hand.

Steel suitable for homemade knife blades might be found in leaf springs, saw blades, garden tools, lawn mower blades, or in various other old or worn tools made of hard steel.

A lot of very good knives have been fashioned from file steel. Files are by necessity very hard, and therefore they produce blades that will hold their edge extremely well as compared with many other types of steel. The downside to making knives out

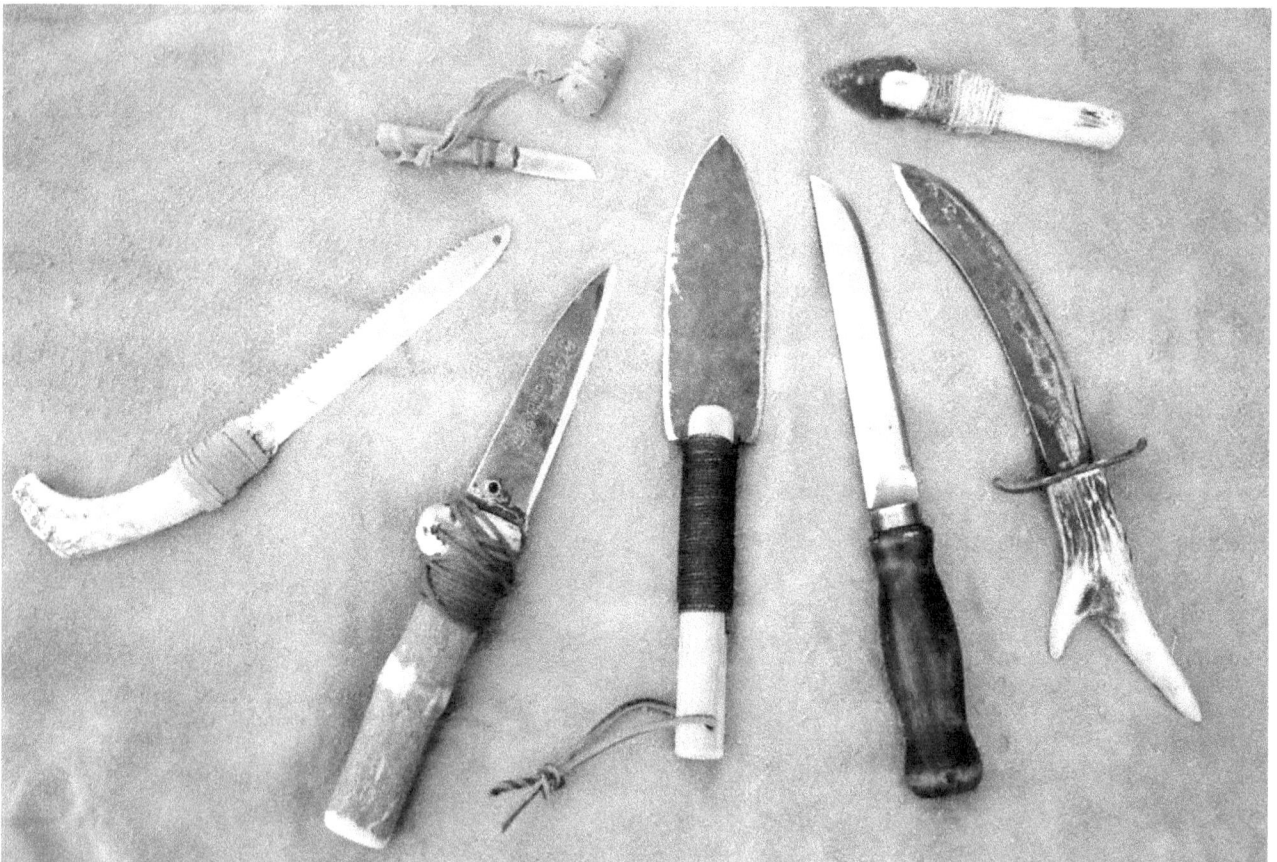

Various makeshift knives.

This knife blade was made from a file.

of files is that the material is so very hard, it is actually brittle. If you attempt to pry with a file blade, it is apt to snap eventually because it essentially has no flex to it. This is quite different from a knife made from a leaf spring, which has a lot of flex. (It is also why nail pullers and pry bars are best made of thick spring steel that won't snap under leverage pressure.)

There are several different methods to create knives. Hammer forging, as we explored in chapter 3, is mainly a process of material displacement. The hammering pushes the heated steel in various directions to achieve the desired shape. Grinding or cutting the blade out of steel stock is known as stock removal, or material removal. In this case, the material is not reshaped but merely cut down from a larger piece to the desired shape of a knife or other product. Often a combination of these two methods will be applied to produce a finished knife.

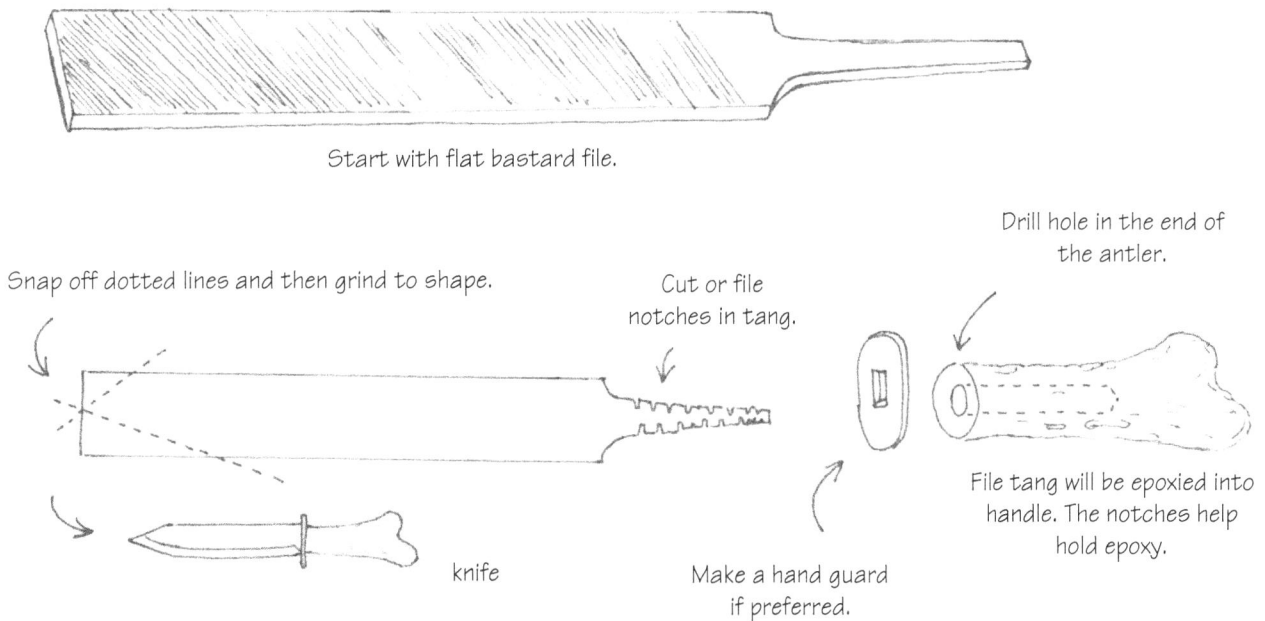

Start with flat bastard file.

Snap off dotted lines and then grind to shape.

Cut or file notches in tang.

Drill hole in the end of the antler.

knife

Make a hand guard if preferred.

File tang will be epoxied into handle. The notches help hold epoxy.

Making a knife out of a file.

Whenever using a high-speed grinding wheel to grind a piece of steel, care should be taken not to burn the workpiece. As noted in chapter 3, steel will burn. Especially small pieces or thin areas of the steel are prone to damage during the grinding process, because an enormous amount of friction heat is generated. When the steel starts turning blue or brown, it is overheated and usually ruined at that point. This can be avoided by periodically dipping the workpiece in a can of water to keep it cool, by progressing slowly with the grinding, and by taking care not to apply excessive pressure against the grinding wheel.

Every knife, or even sharp or pointed tools that will be carried around, should have some type of sheath or blade cover to protect its edge and prevent it from cutting other things unintentionally.

Improvised sheaths can be fashioned quite simply from cardboard and tape, cowhide or rawhide sewn or laced together, molded plastic, panels of wood riveted or screwed together, or, for very small points, a cork stopper.

CHISELS, PUNCHES, AND SCREWDRIVERS

Chisels, punches, and flat screwdrivers are simple tools and easy to make with the heating and hammering process or by grinding other broken tools into the desired shape. (Punches of every variety, for example, can be ground out of broken drill bits, rattail files, or other tools.) The main objective in either case will be to form the proper taper at one end of the piece.

The key here is selecting the right steel. If the

Makeshift knife sheaths, from left to right: 1) sewn rawhide, 2) riveted leather, 3) duct-taped cardboard, 4) wrapped leather, 5) slotted cork. To prevent misplacing it, the small cork blade cover is attached to the knife handle with a leather thong.

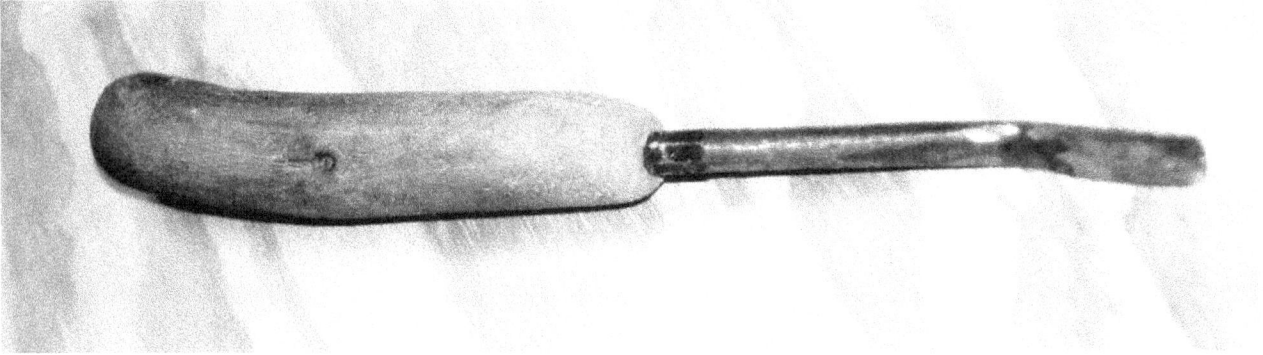

Gouge chisel ground out of another tool and fitted with a wooden handle.

Simply grind chisel bevel on end of file.

Regular file handle is ideal for chisel.

A file/chisel combo.

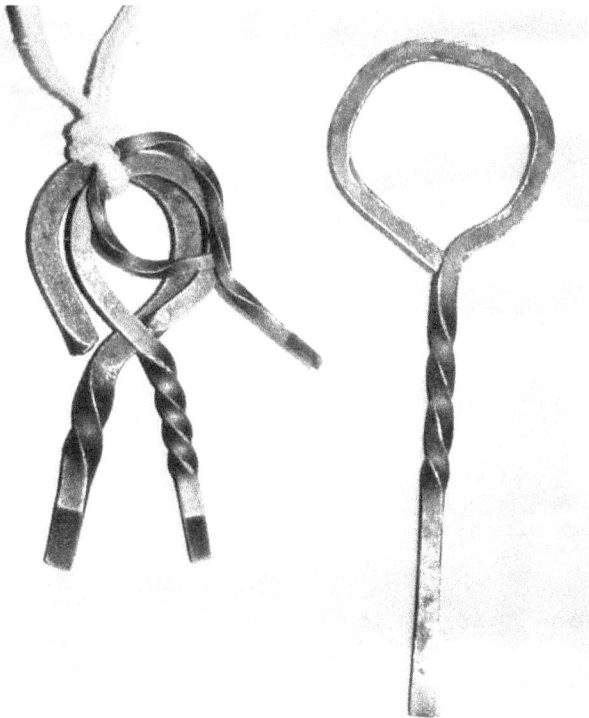

Hand-forged flathead screwdrivers.

material is too soft, such as low-carbon steel, then the tool won't endure very much service, as it will be subject to excessive deformation under the strain of torque while turning tight-fitting screws, or under the force of chiseling or punching action. If the material is too hard, it will be prone to chipping, cracking, or snapping apart under pressure. Using the right steel when a source is available is clearly advantageous. Proper tempering of carbon steel is also helpful in producing tools like this.

MAKESHIFT AXES

The ax is perhaps second only to the knife in terms of its recognized utility value as a simple tool. For felling trees, notching poles, carving dugout boats, trimming branches off logs, chopping and splitting firewood, or hacking through the heavy bones of large animals, the various styles of axes and hatchets really have no equal among the numerous hand tools used by man.

Three makeshift hatchets.

We will explore three different makeshift ax head designs here. The first example is merely a 4-inch section of steel that was hacksawed off a log-splitter wedge. The head was grooved around its circumference with a half-round file to receive the primitive-style wraparound handle. The handle consists of a thinned tree branch that was pliable when green, which was folded around the groove in the ax head and secured with strips of rawhide and glue. Despite the fairly soft steel of the wedge, this little hand ax functions surprisingly well. I've used it as a camp hatchet and as a small hammer.

Our next example is a more contemporary design consisting of a hammer-forged, wedge-shaped hatchet head with a punched hole, or eye, through which the wooden handle fits. The handle is held tight by means of a tiny steel wedge driven into the top of the eye in the conventional manner. This head was shaped from a short section of 1-inch-diameter square stock. It makes a handy little belt ax.

The last example is a forged and tapered flat bar of steel set into the end of a split branch and secured in position with strips of rawhide in the same manner as a lot of early stone ax heads were affixed to their handles. This system is perhaps the least secure of the three mentioned here, but I've chopped

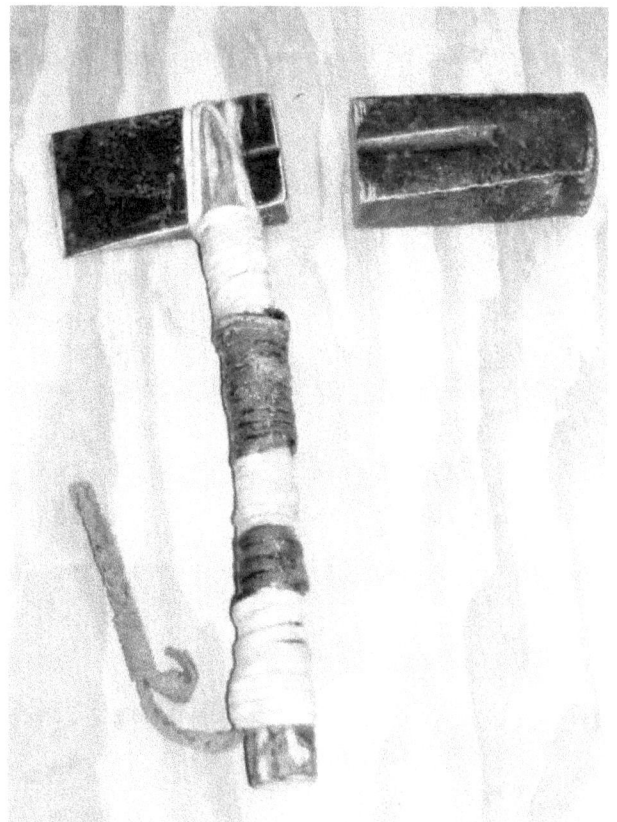

Hatchet head made out of a log-splitter wedge.

Forging a punched-eye hatchet head.

Chopping wood with a primitive-style axe.

through some branches and small logs with it and so far the head has not worked itself loose.

This discussion about makeshift axes brings to mind the ice skate lashed to a stick that was used as an improvised ax by Tom Hanks' character in the movie *Cast Away*. There are numerous such ways in which improvised axes could be fashioned in an emergency, using just a little imagination.

IMPROVISED WRENCHES

The most basic wrench design is extremely simple—a tool comprised of a bar, plate of steel, or other tough material having a slot or hole through which a workpiece can be gripped and torque can be applied in order to turn a bolt, bend material, or perform whatever task is at hand for which a wrench is suited.

You could create a wrench by filing a slot into a thick piece of steel of the desired size to fit the intended workpiece, or you might hot bend a hook in the end of a sturdy bar that can fit over a workpiece. A primitive wrench for straightening arrow shafts can be created simply by boring a hole through a piece of hardwood.

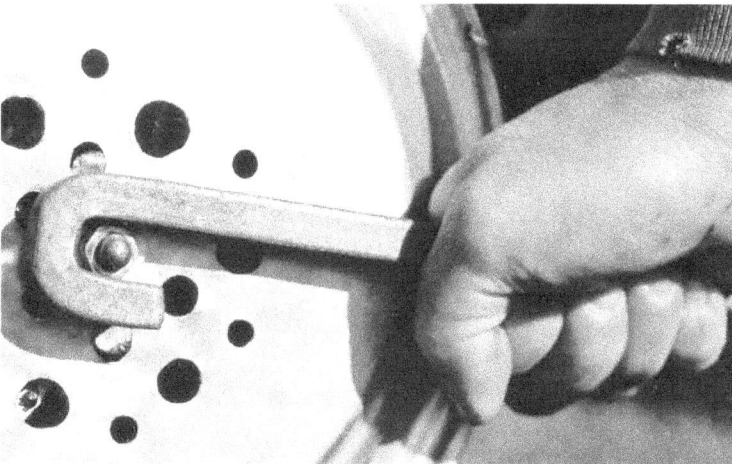

A steel square bar bent into a hook is used here as a wrench to loosen a nut.

Straightening an arrow shaft with a wooden arrow wrench.

THREAD-CUTTING TOOLS

Using a forge or some other method to heat metal in conjunction with a few other tools, numerous steel implements are fairly easy to make, even without the help of an anvil in some cases. One example is a thread-cutting die or screw plate, which can be fabricated from a thick, flat file. I discovered this is successfully accomplished as follows.

First, know that the file steel as it comes from the hardware store is way too hard to cut or machine with other tools. You have to soften the material by annealing it before you do anything else. Heat the file in your forge until it glows orange, and then allow it to cool gradually while buried under the coals with the dying fire in the forge. Hours later, after the heat has left the steel, it can be drilled—ideally using a drill press—with the correct diameter bit for the size die you want. After you have the hole drilled, you can easily cut threads into the file with the appropriate tap. Several different diameter holes with different threads might even be cut into one file to make a multiple screw plate.

Once the threads are cut, cut three or four slots, equally spaced around the hole, using a very small square file. This is the time-consuming part. Care must be taken to leave sharply defined edges on both sides of each slot, as this will help facilitate the thread cutting for which the finished tool is intended. These cutout areas will also provide channels for the displacement of the metal chips and shavings cut from any shaft being threaded.

After all the machine work has been accomplished to create a threading die, it should be reheated and quenched in oil or water to restore the original hardness. Like a very hard file, any tool intended to cut steel, such as a die, needs to be harder than most other steel.

Alex W. Bealer describes a device called a jamb plate in his book, *The Art of Blacksmithing*. It essentially is a simple type of die that forces the thread groove into a steel shaft rather than cutting it in the conventional manner, as there are no cutting edges on the jamb plate's threads. Steel shafts are likely threaded hot with such a method.

Threading dies, also called screw plates, made out of files. Note the three slots in the bottom hole; these facilitate removal of metal chips and shavings during the threading process.

A homemade barrel vise comprised of two thick blocks of oak, each with a groove that conforms to the contour of a typical octagon or round gun barrel, sandwiched by heavy steel plates. The plates serve as the rigid platforms against which the bolts and nuts tighten the two oak halves around the barrel. The unit is mounted securely to the workbench.

Using a gun-action wrench in conjunction with the homemade barrel vise.

VISES AND CLAMPS

Have you ever found yourself trying to cut with a saw or drill through an object that wasn't held firmly or secured into a fixed position somehow? Trying to hold an object with one hand while operating a tool with the other can be enormously frustrating and, in certain situations, a safety hazard. For this reason, among others, I believe clamps and vises of all kinds are some of the most important tools ever invented.

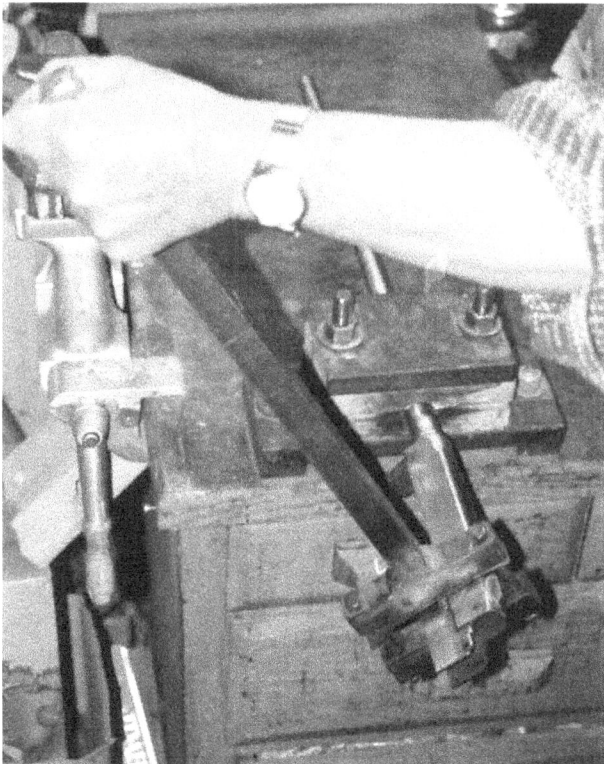

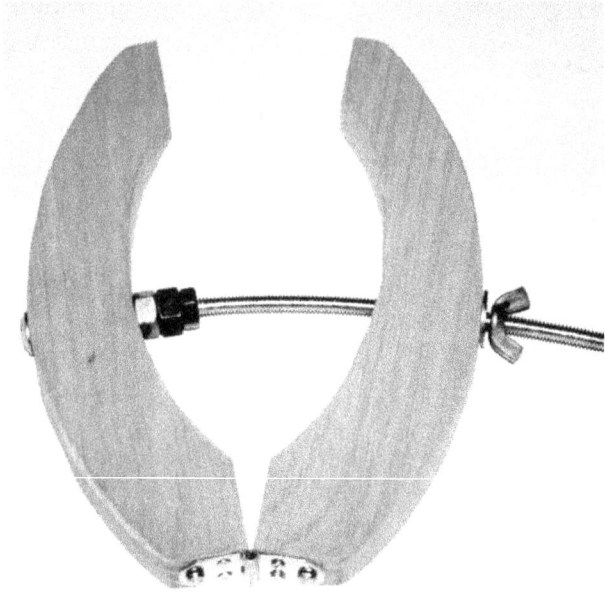

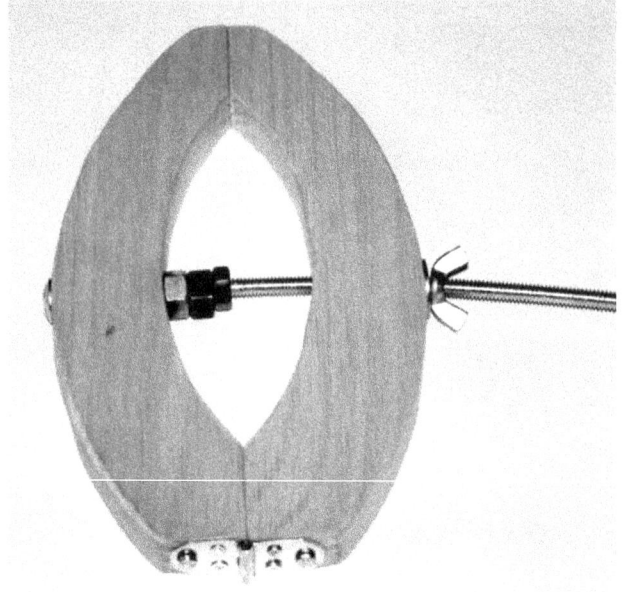

A makeshift wooden C-clamp, shown with jaws open and locked closed.

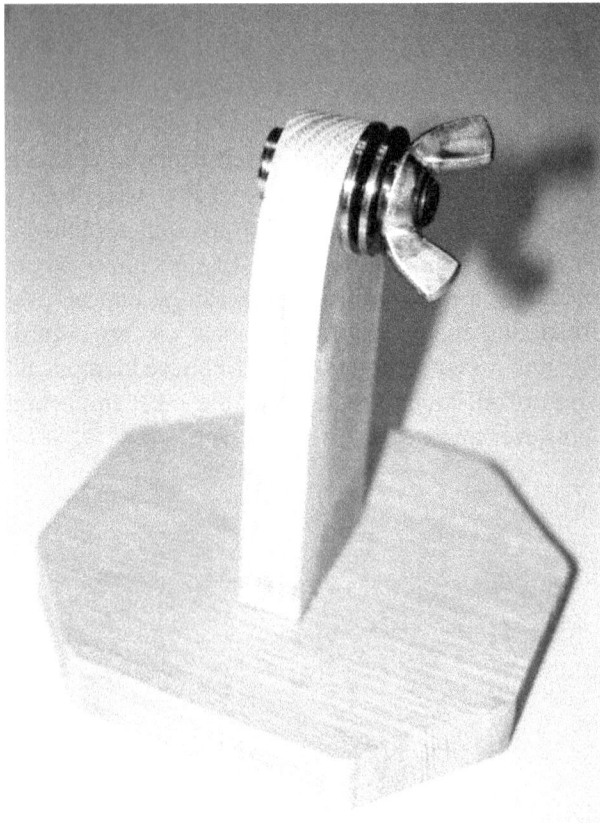

The wing nut and washer vise, useful for small applications such as fly tying.

A parallel-jaw clamp employing 3/8-inch carriage bolts, washers, wing nuts, and two blocks of hardwood.

As far as I can tell, there are six basic types of clamping systems (if we don't include such gripping tools as pliers or tongs) that make use of leverage. The first type, and the strongest of them all, uses the screw principle to apply compression. This includes typical modern bench vises, hose clamps, pipe clamps, and common C-clamps whose gripping components are tightened or loosened by turning a threaded shaft, or screw. Using long bolts or threaded steel rod in conjunction with washers and wing nuts of appropriate size, a variety of different, interesting, and functional makeshift clamps can be devised, as can be seen in the accompanying photos.

Next we find the popular spring clamps that employ the power of a spring to provide clamping action. This group includes everything from store-bought spring clamps to alligator clips to ordinary clothespins. In some cases, an elastic band might be substituted for a spring in a makeshift clamp.

Miscellaneous small clamping devices suitable for all sorts of light-duty makeshift tasks. All but the top C-clamp utilize a spring in some fashion to provide the clamping action.

Kitchen tongs and a rubber band are combined to create an effective makeshift clamp.

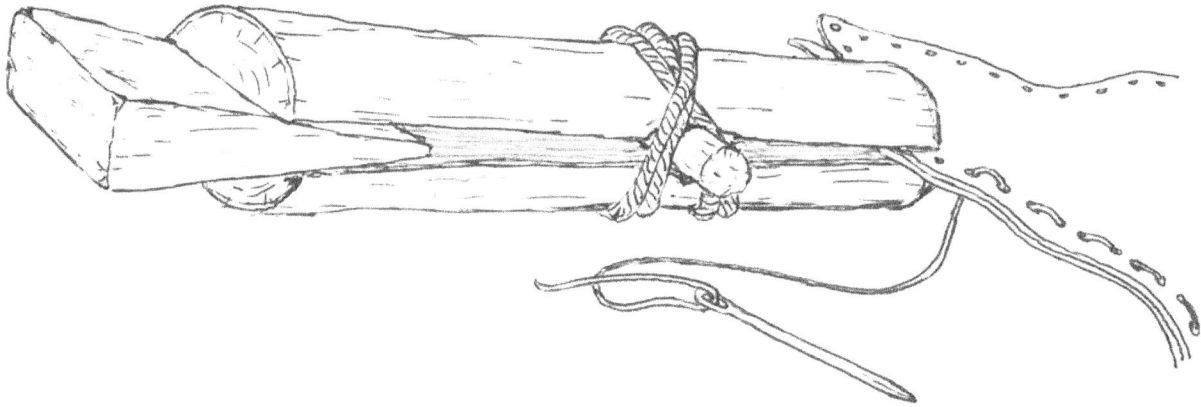

Wedge clamp made out of a split branch, a dowel spacer, and cordage.

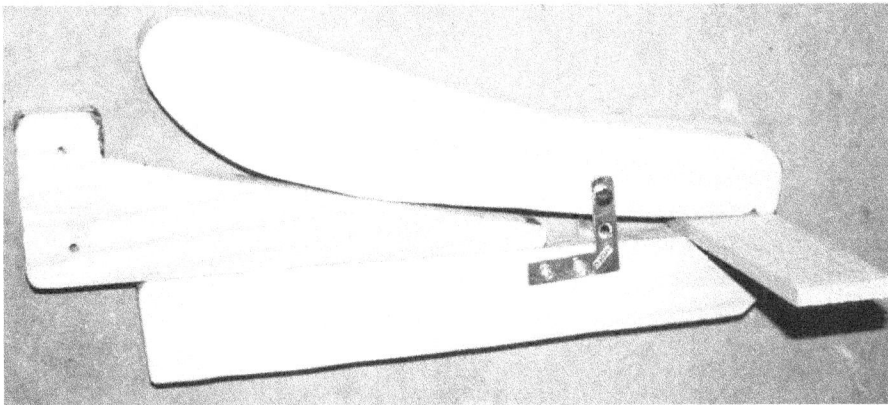

A simple wooden clamp that uses a wedge to compress the workpiece.

The third type of clamp employs a wedge to hold the workpiece. By driving a wedge between two objects loosely held together and thereby forcing them apart at one end as far as they will go, it creates pinching pressure at the opposite end, which can be used as clamping jaws.

An even simpler use of a wedge has the object to be secured placed within an oversized band or loop of metal, with the wedge forced into the loose space along one side of the object to hold it firmly. The wedge can normally be driven loose with a mallet to open the clamp and free the workpiece. This conveniently simple and surprisingly effective clamping method was especially popular during the Colonial period in early America.

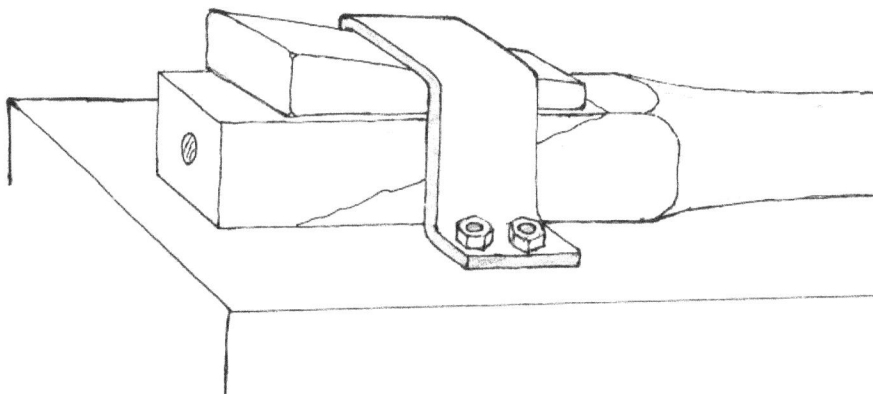

Broken chair leg clamped together with steel strap and wedge while glue sets.

A fourth method for creating a vise or clamp utilizes the constricting power of twisted rope. Using a metal rod, sturdy stick, or hardwood dowel to twist a loop of rope or cord like a tourniquet, the hinged jaws of a clamp can be tightened to grip a workpiece quite firmly. The tourniquet stick can be stopped from untwisting by almost any kind of fixed obstruction or makeshift catch, be it an anchored large nail, peg, or pin as a stop or a loop of cord over one end of the stick to secure it. I mounted such a vise to my workbench, and it actually works quite well.

Right: A 2 x 4 tourniquet clamp made out of two hinged pieces of 2 x 4, some leather cord, and a peg catch.

Bottom left: A 2 x 4 tourniquet vise mounted to my workbench. This one uses a small rope as the tourniquet and a nail as the catch to prevent the rope from untwisting.

Bottom right: Sawing through a large nail held in the makeshift vise, using makeshift bucksaw with a hacksaw blade.

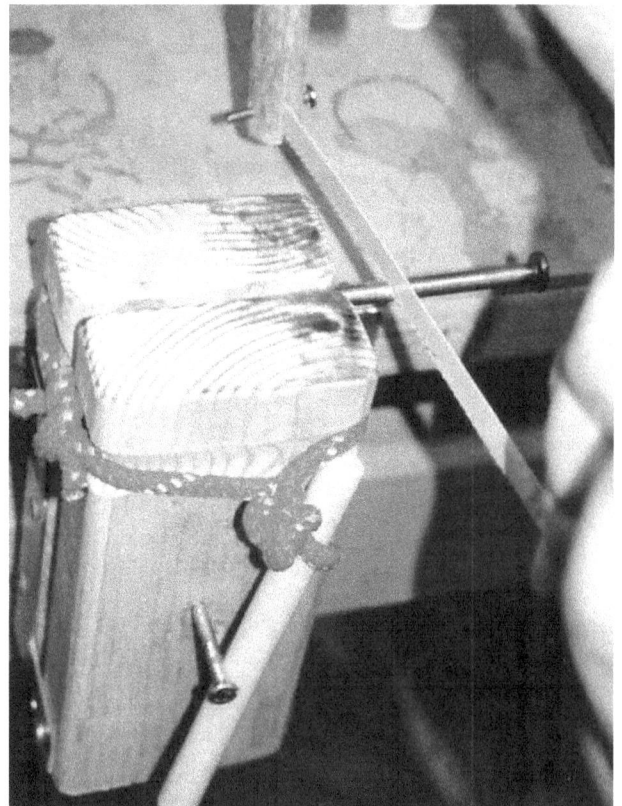

Several years ago while building a shed in my backyard, I found myself in need of a long, powerful clamp to draw two vertical frame posts toward each other. None of the pipe clamps I had on hand would reach both posts, so I decided to loop a heavy rope around them and start twisting it up with the handle of my hammer. This simple makeshift method proved very successful in that situation.

A lot of very effective clamps designed in recent years employ a system of mechanical linkages that utilize levers and pivots to create their powerful mechanical advantage. Sometimes called a toggle clamp, variations of this system can be seen in locking pliers like the well-known Vise-Grip brand, some ratcheting-bar clamp designs, and various hold-down clamps for tables and bench tops. This technology actually involves some fairly sophisticated engineering.

The last type of vise we will look at was commonly used in Colonial-era shaving horses. These rely on manual force—in this case, leg power—to apply downward pressure on an arm with a jaw (referred to as a dumbhead by Roy Underhill in his book, *The Woodwright's Shop*) to hold a workpiece in position. This system is still used in shaving horses for bow making and in early American-style wooden furniture handwork.

The shaving horse represents a type of vise. The craftsman applies foot pressure to the vertical arm to hold the workpiece in place.

MEASURING AND MARKING AIDS

Accurate measuring can be achieved when a known quantity is available as a point of reference for gauging other quantities. With linear measurement, the tools for determining distance include such devices as rulers, measuring tapes, micrometers, calipers, and range finders. Any instrument designed to measure a straight-line distance between two points would fall into this category. Likewise, a variety of other instruments are used to plot angles, draw circles, and weigh things.

In a makeshift situation, precision tools for measuring and marking might not be readily available, but functional improvised substitutions are possible. Homemade versions will tend to be inferior to manufactured tools, but in many instances they can still fulfill their intended purposes.

The key requirement for accurate measuring, as previously mentioned, is having some known quantity that can serve as a point of reference. For example, if you knew for certain that your thumb measured 1 inch across at its widest area, then you would always have a fast and reliable reference for inches, which could then be used to calculate feet and yards. If you knew that the buttons on your shirt were exactly half an inch in diameter, then you could use them as your point of reference to measure other things, and so on.

As it turns out, we have quite a variety of good points of reference in our world that are suitable for miscellaneous measurements. Standard-size notebook or computer printer paper measures 8 1/2 x 11 inches. Standard-size business cards are 2 x 3 1/2 inches. United States paper currency normally measures a hair over 6 1/8 inches in length by about 2 5/8 inches wide. Quarters are roughly 15/16 inch in diameter, nickels are 13/16 inch, pennies are 3/4 inch, and dimes are 11/16 inch.

It might be practical for us to create our own gauging tools in certain situations. A length of cord, for example, could be marked at inch intervals (or at centimeter intervals for a metric rule) to make a handy measuring line. Measurement markings could also be scratched or engraved on the back of a knife blade to create a quick reference in the field.

For measuring the weight of small objects, you could build a makeshift balancing scale that

A penny makes an ideal reference for a 3/4-inch hole.

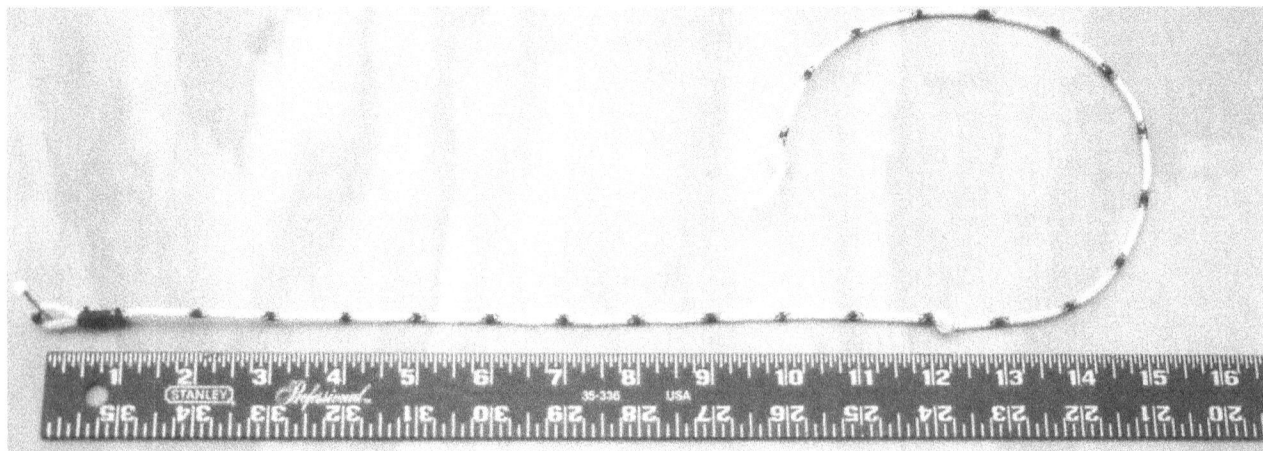

A 2-foot measuring cord with inch designations marked with a permanent marker and feet gauged by knots. Very useful for measuring straight lines or circumference.

suspends two paper cups (or some other type of little trays) of equal weight from both ends of a dowel that is set up to pivot at its center. If the empty suspended cups, together with their hanger wire or string, keep the pivoting horizontal dowel level, then you can use the apparatus as a reliable scale. All you would need is something of a known weight as a reference to balance against. According to my hand-loading scale, a pellet of #8 lead birdshot weighs almost exactly, or certainly very close to, 1 grain. There *may* be variances in weight from different shot makers, so individual testing and confirming weight equivalents is advised.

Let's assume that a single pellet of #8 lead birdshot weighs the equivalent of 1 grain. With the object to be weighed sitting in the cup on one side, you would add a quantity of shot to the other cup. When the scale balances level, simply count the number of shot to find the object's weight in grains. (It takes 437.5 grains to equal 1 ounce, so again, this system would only be practical when weighing small objects.)

Recording measurements will require some method for marking. If you don't have access to pencil or paper, notations can be scratched on a metal plate or carved into a piece of wood. That lead shot used in our makeshift scale above can be inlet

into the end of a stick and employed as a crude writing device. I found that by charring the tip of a pointed wooden dowel with a flame, I was able to create an expedient marker that can be used like a pencil. This method of charcoal writing has its limitations. The markings can't be expected to endure as well as permanent markings (depending to some degree on the surface being marked), and the wood requires repeated burning to keep the tip freshly charred and capable of scrawling a legible mark. Even so, if you don't have a regular pencil or ink pen with which to write, this method does work.

Many different recipes have been used in the past to make ink for writing and printing. Ink might be produced in a makeshift situation by soaking or boiling organic materials such as red berries, certain roots, crushed walnut shells, or tree bark. Soot from a candle (lamp black) has been used in conjunction with egg yolks (some recipes call for egg whites) and honey to create usable writing ink. If you use oak bark or other tannic acid product in an iron container, it makes an old form of ink called iron gall ink. The Constitution was penned with this kind of ink, and it still reads as well today as when it was written.

WOODEN TOOLS

This chapter would be considered incomplete without some discussion of hand tools made entirely of wood. The simplest example of a useful wooden tool might be merely a sturdy tree branch sharpened at one end and used as a digging stick.

Wooden mallets are normally easy enough to make, and they can be very useful for rapping on certain things to which blows from a steel hammer would be too destructive. Any hammer-shaped configuration utilizing hardwood for the head might serve as a functional wooden mallet, such as a croquet mallet, judge's gavel, shillelagh, or toddler's toy hammer.

Gun ramrods and bullet starters for muzzleloaders are also commonly made of wood. Wooden wedges,

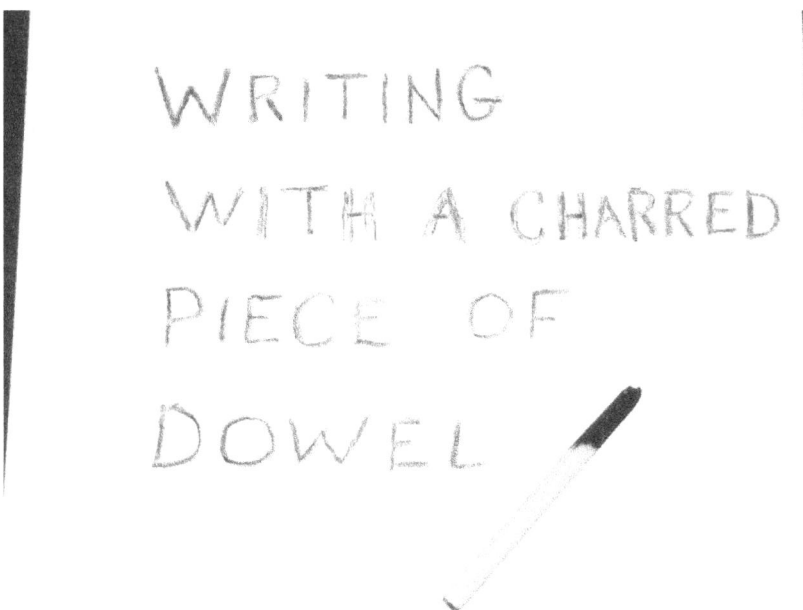

Although it has its limitations, writing with a charred dowel does work.

Homemade wooden mallets, left to right: 1) section of 4 x 4 lumber with length of broom handle inserted, 2) hardwood, ball-shaped drawer knob with dowel handle inserted, 3) section of hardwood dowel cross-pinned to a dowel handle, 4) T-section cut from a wooden chair leg, and 5) another hardwood dowel head with dowel handle.

Cord keeps tongs aligned.

Thinned section to facilitate sharp bend.

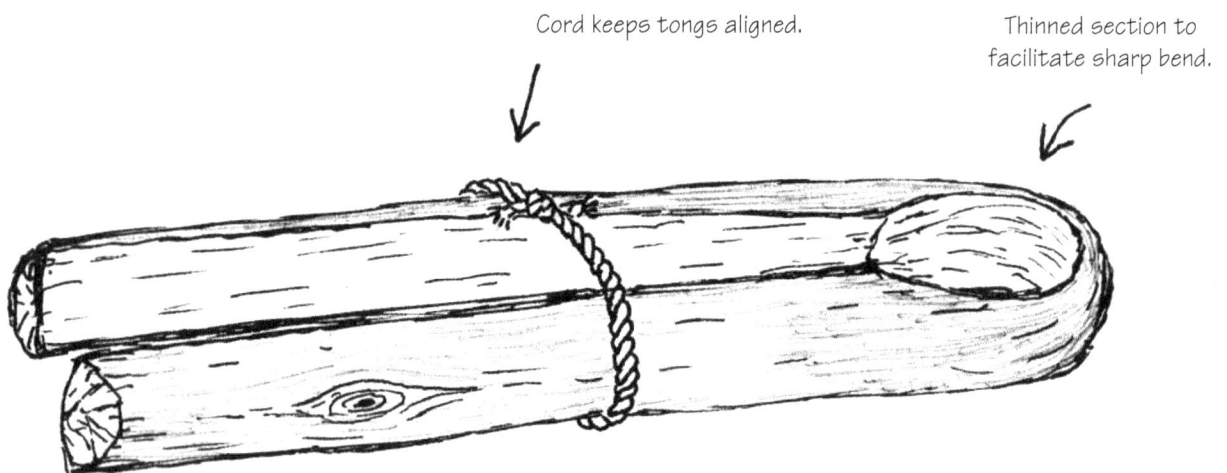

Improvised wooden tongs made from split green tree branch. This tool might be useful at the campfire.

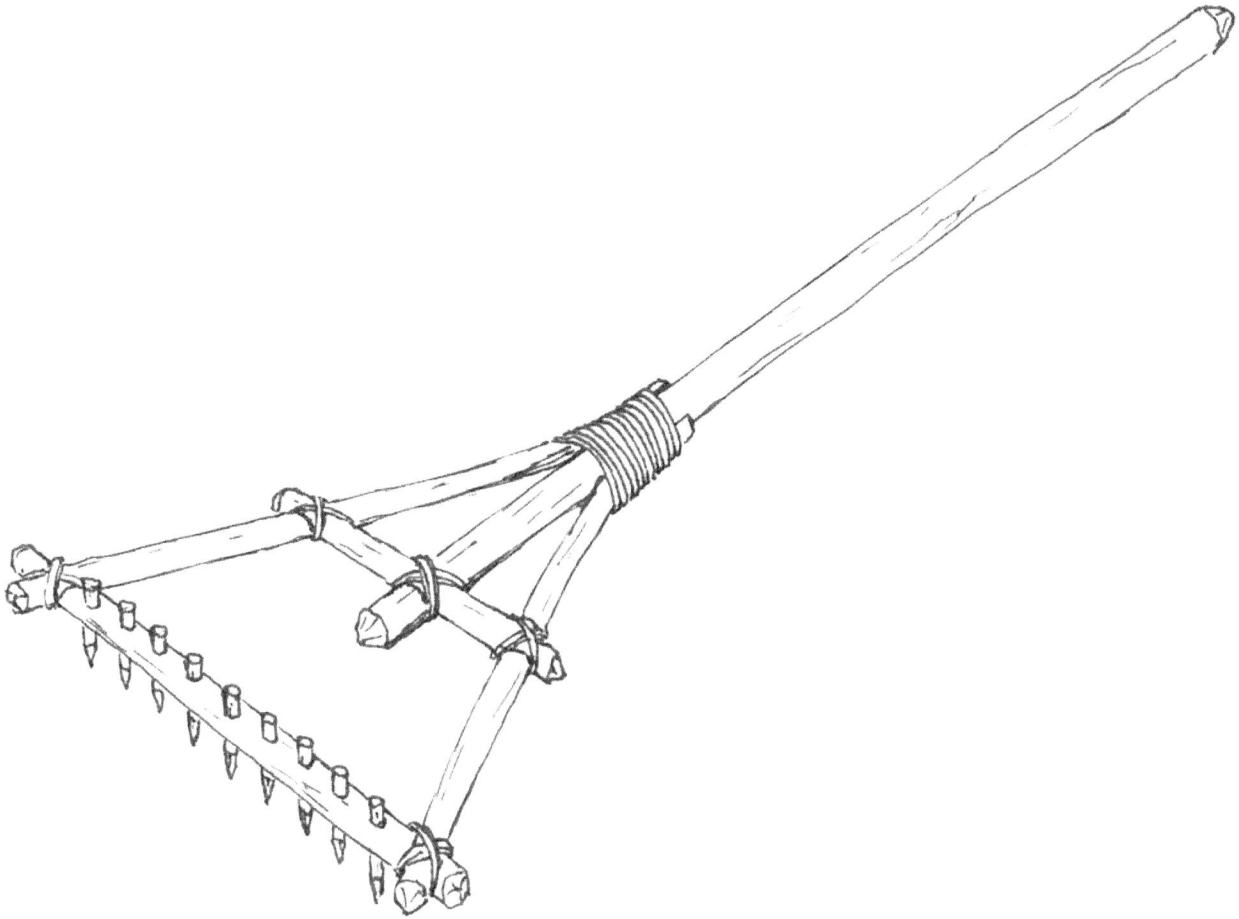

Leaf rake made from tree branches for the handle and frame and whittled sticks for the tines.

roller pins, salad tongs, and old wagon axles and wheel bearings have all been made of wood, to list just a few handy tools. A leaf rake made entirely from tree branches bound together with cord might also find purpose around the yard.

CHAPTER 5

Expedient Repair Methods

T hings break or fail from time to time, and new replacements or parts are not always readily available. If we want more service from certain products or devices, we sometimes have to get creative with functional repair methods.

While a lot of common fixes involve the usual methods and techniques, many of the repairs I routinely make to things around my house are simply one of a kind. Very often I have to devise a unique approach to a unique project. Finding the best method might take a bit of research or some experimentation before the appropriate repair is made.

The key ingredient to all good repairs is to approach each situation methodically. Each project will present its own challenges, but careful planning and execution will save a lot of headaches.

We will explore some interesting and often very effective repair methods in this chapter. They aren't always pretty, but good repairs do serve their intended purpose.

Grind new bevel on hammer end.

Tighten up head by driving wedge into eye.

Cracked handle tightly wrapped with strong cord or rawhide.

Sharpen bit on grinding wheel.

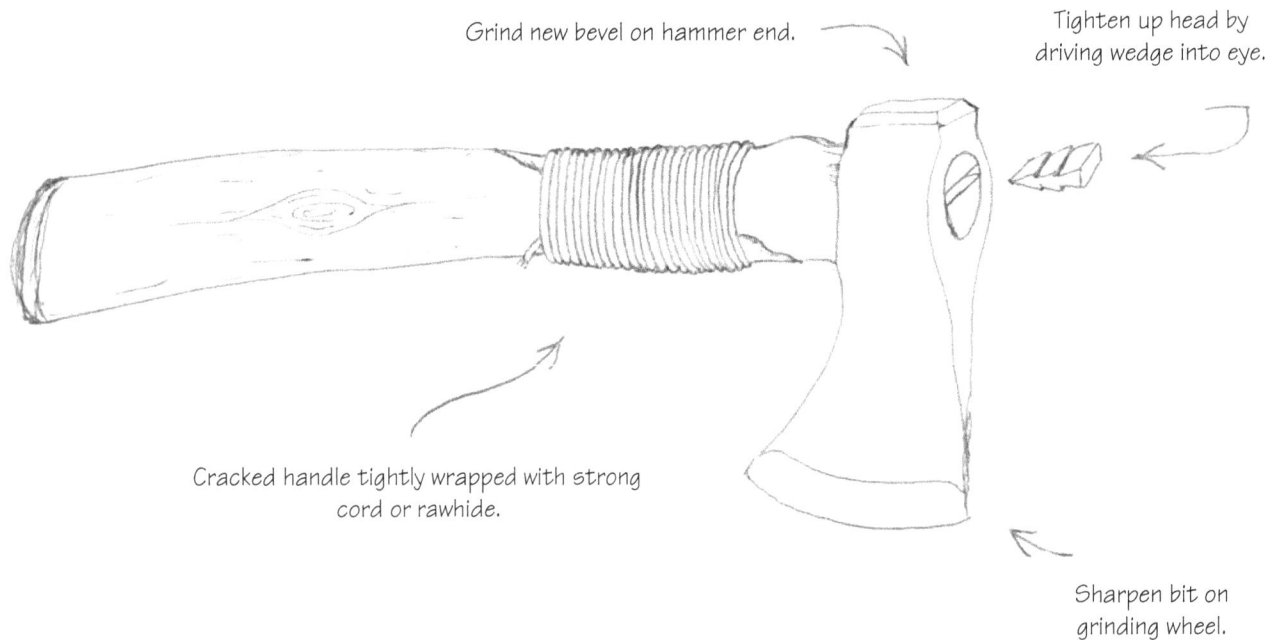

Miscellaneous home workshop repairs to a hatchet.

REPAIRING WITH GLUE

One of the first methods of repair that typically comes to mind when common things break is simply gluing the broken pieces back together. When done properly using the appropriate product, gluing can be very effective.

In primitive societies, tree sap (sometimes called pitch resin), boiled animal sinews and hides, fish products, and other natural sticky substances were relied upon for joining objects. Most of us learned as kids how sticky and hard-drying a paste made from flour and water can be. Some of these old, simple methods served their intended functions effectively and might still be used for certain applications.

Today there are numerous types of glues and epoxies on the market for bonding different materials, and it is useful to know which ones work for bonding which kinds of materials. Some products appear to be marketed as all-purpose

miracle glues, but I have experimented with a wide variety of adhesives over the years, and every product I have ever tested would more accurately be described as "special purpose." Here we will take a look at some of the common glue types and how they work.

Hide Glue

Several manufacturers have marketed their own variations of hide glue, from powders that require mixing or special preparation before use to ready-to-use liquid glues. Genuine hide glue can actually be processed at home exactly the way some Indians did it—by shaving natural, untanned animal skins into fine strips and boiling these down into sticky glue. The messy, stinky process takes hours to complete, but it has provided people with effective glue under primitive circumstances.

Hide glue tends to bond with very good strength in the appropriate application, and I have used the liquid version for a wide variety of tasks with excellent results. The main advantage to hide glue over some adhesives is its ability to sustain shock. When cured, it forms a tough, almost rubbery texture that resists shattering, as might occur with a lot of dried resins. For this reason it is a popular product for gluing points and nocks on the ends of arrows, or the tips on the ends of cue sticks that are used for knocking billiard or pool balls around. Because it forms incredibly strong bonds with wood, it is used a lot in the furniture manufacturing industry as well.

The main disadvantage to hide glue (as is the case with sinew and nearly all raw animal products) is that it softens and loses its strength when it gets wet. If you need a waterproof outdoor adhesive, hide glue is probably not a good choice unless some type of waterproof coating is added after it cures.

Polyurethane Glue

Some of the strongest adhesives I have ever used are the polyurethane glues, marketed under such brand names such as Elmer's Ultimate Glue, PL Premium Wood Glue, ProBond, Gorilla Glue, and Loctite Sumo Glue. This type of glue is known for bonding a wide variety of materials, for being waterproof, and for creating extremely strong bonds.

Polyurethane glues react with moisture from the air or from the materials being joined in order to complete the curing process. Some of the application instructions actually advise wiping the surfaces to be joined with a damp cloth prior to adding the glue. Pieces being joined should be tightly clamped during the curing because the glue swells as it hardens, tending to push the separate pieces apart.

Excess drips of curing polyurethane glue form into a sort of soft, plastic, foamy glob or film. This is usually not difficult to remove from the surface area around the repair with a sharp knife or scraper after the glue dries, at least in my

An assortment of commercial glue products.

Curing polyurethane glue. Notice how it oozes from the crack.

experience, leading one to marvel at how it could possibly bond anything with any degree of strength.

Because of the foamy nature of dried polyurethane glue, I wouldn't recommend it as a filler material for holes or cavities in any material. Epoxy resins or filler putties would be better for that purpose. Most polyurethane adhesives also have a comparatively long curing time. I normally leave repairs clamped together at room temperature for 12 to 24 hours to allow the glue to cure completely.

Epoxy Resin

Epoxy resin calls for mixing two parts, the resin and the hardener, which causes a chemical reaction that creates heat in the mixture that aids the curing process. The most common two-part epoxy products sold today, such as those marketed under the brand name Devcon, form a type of hard plastic when cured.

When used according to the directions, the various epoxies typically have good strength with the prescribed materials, but in my experience most of them will not bond as well as polyurethane glue with a surface connection. I have also noticed that some epoxy resins tend to dry somewhat hard and brittle, and they are sometimes prone to breaking or shattering, especially along thin edges. They can, however, be useful for filling holes or embedding certain objects in resin. I have used epoxies successfully when setting tangs of knife blades into antler handles, where there was space to be filled around the tang in the hole drilled into the antler.

Some epoxy resin products tend to have a fairly short curing time. Devcon, in fact, markets a "5-minute" epoxy, and you can find even faster drying versions. I learned from trial and error to select a product specifically advertised as waterproof, as some of them are not.

One of my favorite two-part adhesives, especially wherever metals must be joined and soldering or welding might be impractical for whatever reason, is the popular J.B. Weld product from the J.B. Weld Company. This adhesive cures hard and is very easy to use. If I were forced to choose only one multipurpose type of glue, J.B. Weld would be a versatile candidate. I have used it successfully in numerous applications where I was initially skeptical about the practicality of using any kind of glue, and to the best of my recollection this product has never failed me.

Super Glue

Products like Elmer's Krazy Glue, Loctite QuickTite, Super Glue, and other generic products marketed as "super glue" are one-part, quick-drying, general-purpose household glues that have found a place in first-aid kits as adhesives for closing wounds, as well as enjoying a degree of popularity among such hobbyists as model airplane builders. This popular group of adhesives is sometimes referred to as acrylic resin or CA glue, having cyanoacrylate as a primary ingredient.

Leg was broken at the knee on this plastic horse. Repaired successfully with Super Glue.

CA glues typically dry very quickly—often almost instantly upon application, making them tricky to use sometimes. They are most commonly applied as a thin, clear, sticky liquid or gel, and are notorious for bonding skin, eyelids, and fingers together, demanding special care in their application. Even so, they have a reputation for high-strength bonding when completely cured, and they work especially well for such tasks as gluing broken or chipped glass or ceramic pieces together. Although often advertised as being able to bond almost any kind of material, CA glues seem to be more effective with nonporous materials than with porous materials like wood.

PVA Glue

Polyvinyl acetate (PVA) is a nonacidic, generally nontoxic synthetic polymer. According to glue manufacturer Franklin International, PVA glues include the common white glues and the yellow aliphatic resins (AR glues, such as carpenter's glue). Collectively, PVA glues are possibly the best-selling type of glue in America. These have been the traditional adhesives for gluing paper or wood for many years, although the advantages of such other adhesives as hide glue and the polyurethane glues for joining wood have become better known in recent years.

PVA glues only adhere to porous materials like wood, paper, cardboard, leather, and cloth, and traditionally none of the popular PVA products were completely waterproof, though some have been advertised as being water-resistant. When properly applied to clean surfaces with the right material, securely clamped during curing, and given adequate curing time at the optimum temperature, PVA glues (especially the yellow carpenter's glues) normally bond very well.

Rubber Cement

A somewhat different kind of adhesive from any discussed above falls under the rubber cement category. This group includes such brands as Shoe GOO, Barge, Studio Gum, some of the products marketed as Amazing GOOP by Eclectic Products, Inc. (not to be confused with the Goop waterless hand cleaner found in many workshops), and a range of similar adhesives sold by various companies. These are the rubbery, gummy, contact adhesives ideally suited to joining two pieces of rubberlike material. A typical application for rubber cement would be gluing the rubber sole onto a shoe or boot.

Rubber cement doesn't dry hard like resin but instead remains rubbery. This makes it suitable in situations where a product needs a degree of elasticity, such as when something will be subjected to a lot of movement or shock. I have not experienced great success with most rubber cements I have used over the years. However, I did find a Shoe GOO product to be an effective adhesive for a quickie repair I made to a synthetic rifle sling several years ago, and the glued connection still seems to be holding together quite well as of this writing.

Ceramic Tile Mastic

The word "mastic" originally referred to a small tree in the pistachio family that grows in the Mediterranean. The tree produces a commercially exploited resin that has found use in certain varnish products and as a spice and a natural chewing gum.

Special adhesives for setting tile are sometimes referred to generically as mastic, or more specifically, ceramic tile mastic, and different manufacturers produce very different specialty products under this name. RLA Polymers, for example, advertises its own acrylic-based Acrylbond Mastic, described on the company's website as a premixed mastic tile adhesive designed for bonding all types of porous ceramic, stone, or mosaic tiles except green marble.

Besides its primary role as an adhesive for laying tile, mastic has been used for such tasks as sealing leaky cracks at the joints of home-heating ductwork.

Homemade Glue

Now that I have discussed some of the commercial glues on the market today and the special applications for the different products, let's consider making our own adhesives.

Probably the easiest gluelike substance anyone can make is the simple wheat flour and water mixture, which creates a sticky, obviously nontoxic paste that will dry fairly hard yet remain water-soluble. This could be an effective adhesive with cardboard or paper, but it clearly has a very limited application. Hot oatmeal might also be used this way, as it also makes a sticky slurry that dries hard. The important thing with these homemade glues is to allow adequate drying/curing time and not to expect too much from them.

Another popular homemade glue requires only milk, vinegar, water, and baking soda for its ingredients. Milk glue is sometimes referred to as casein glue, because the casein protein is precipitated out of the milk by the vinegar (which is an acid), and this casein acts as the bonding agent. As described in chapter 1, milk plastic is made in a similar way, except without the baking soda.

Cy Tymony explains his method for making milk glue in his book *Sneaky Uses for Everyday Things*, which calls for warming (but not boiling) 8 ounces of cow milk to 250°F, adding a tablespoon of vinegar, and stirring until the mixture forms clumps. You then strain the clumpy mix and squeeze out as much of the liquid as possible before throwing it

Everything needed for making milk glue.

back into the pot and adding 1/4 cup of water and a tablespoon of baking soda. When it stops bubbling, the mixture is ready to be used as glue. I came across several similar recipes during my research that called for nonfat powdered milk instead of regular whole milk.

I found that this concoction does work. In spite of my repeated tendency to unintentionally boil the milk, I did manage to use my resulting mixture to stick two small, flat strips of oak together that required a surprising amount of force to separate in my own unscientific adhesion-strength test. I can see where this could potentially be a useful homemade adhesive.

In my own experiments, I found it easy to produce stronger bonding makeshift glue by simply boiling a small amount of water with unflavored gelatin stirred into it. This gels into sticky lumps that, while still soft and warm, can be rubbed onto whatever surfaces are to be joined.

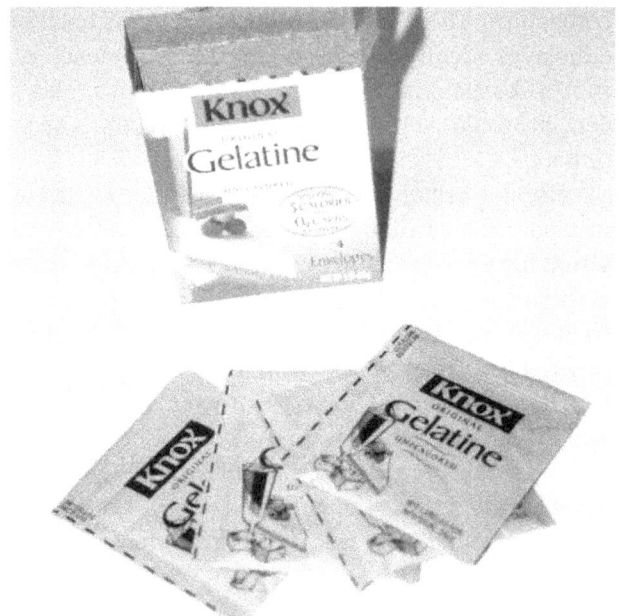

Powdered glue—just add water!

Gelatin is composed of protein obtained by partially dissolving animal connective tissue (called collagen) in water. You can usually find it in the baking supply section of your local supermarket—it comes as a powder in small packets and is used for making Jell-O. Gelatin glue would be useful for the same applications where one would use hide glue. I discovered that gelatin bonds wood with amazing strength.

Another ad hoc glue for some applications can be paint. (Don't think so? Try opening a window after it's been painted shut.) Several coats might serve as a laminate to hold items together and would be a great use of all that old, half-dried paint you may have stowed in the basement.

Finally, I suggested earlier that you could boil down shavings of raw animal hides or sinews into a sticky mass, and this could produce some excellent wood glue if you have the stomach for a project like this. The reality is that most glue products are smelly and messy.

Useful Gluing Techniques

Once you've obtained or mixed up a batch of what you believe is the right kind of glue for your purpose, you should then give serious consideration to the application process. How you prepare the surfaces to be glued and how the glue is applied will often be crucial to the success of the bond.

When I get everything ready for a gluing job, I like to think ahead about the mess and cleanup. Clearing an adequate work area on a table or workbench is always helpful, and you'll want to put down a protective layer of newspaper or some kind of drop cloth to keep messy spills off your tabletop. I have also found that wearing latex gloves saves the hands from a considerable mess with most activities involving glue.

You will want everything you might use close at hand, such as clamps, an X-Acto knife or nail to pierce the nozzle on the tube of glue, applicator stick or brush, extra latex gloves, and wipe-up cloth or paper towels. It can be rather inconvenient having to search for a needed item after the gluing project is already underway. Think ahead and have everything ready if you want to save yourself a lot of frustration.

There sometimes are safety concerns as well when using certain glue products. It's always a good idea to protect your eyes and keep a

This handy repair kit contains miscellaneous tools and useful gear for a multitude of small repair jobs, including a bottle of polyurethane glue.

circulation of fresh air around the work area. Whenever using any type of glue with toxic fumes, either wear a respirator or at least work outdoors during warm, dry weather and away from pets or other people, just like you would if you were spray painting. I recommend reading and heeding the warning labels on the products' containers.

Surfaces to be glued should be prepared before applying the adhesive. This could mean simply cleaning them, or at least ensuring they are free of dirt, sawdust, or grease that could interfere with the process. With certain materials, preparing surfaces for gluing might entail roughing them up with sandpaper or a file to eliminate areas that would be too smooth for the glue to adhere properly. In some wood repair jobs, the task of getting the pieces of wood to fit together tightly can be aided by wetting them with water before gluing and clamping them. Damp wood is softer than dry wood, and on its surface it will have more give to it, allowing the separate pieces to better conform and mold to one another. As mentioned earlier, some of the polyurethane glues require a light application of water to activate the adhesive's ingredients, so wetting the pieces before gluing and clamping them would serve two useful purposes.

I have used the point of an X-Acto knife on occasion to stab numerous tiny slits in tight-grained hardwood before applying certain adhesives that work best with porous surfaces. This gives the glue spaces to seep and lock into. Similarly, before setting the tang of a knife blade into an antler handle with epoxy, I will usually make notches in the steel tang with a hacksaw to give the resin more spaces to fill and harden into.

The conventional wisdom about gluing two objects together recommends that the glue be applied to *both* surfaces to ensure adequate adhesion. Applying the glue to only one of two surfaces to be joined allows for potentially incomplete coverage of the adhesive. It is always important to use enough glue for the job and to spread it evenly across the surface for maximum coverage.

Whenever attempting to glue a crack where access to the bonding surfaces inside the crack is limited, it might be necessary to pry the pieces apart enough to get the needed quantity of glue between them before clamping everything up. This can be a challenge sometimes, but you need to insert enough glue for a strong bond.

After the glue is applied and the parts fit together, they should be firmly clamped whenever possible. Where the use of C-clamps or spring clamps may not be practical due to space limitations,

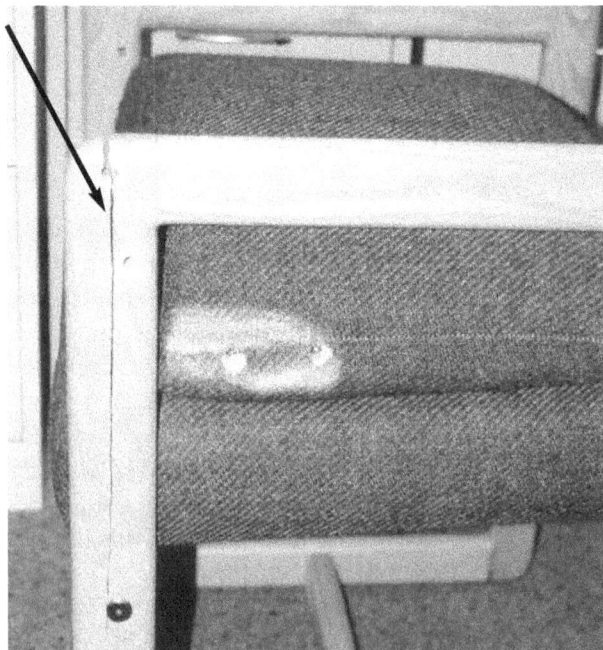

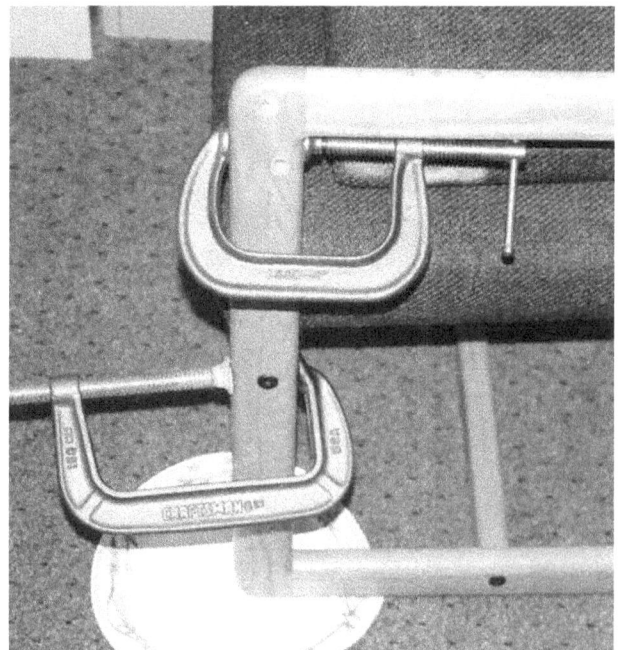

The broken arm of this chair is glued and clamped together until the glue dries.

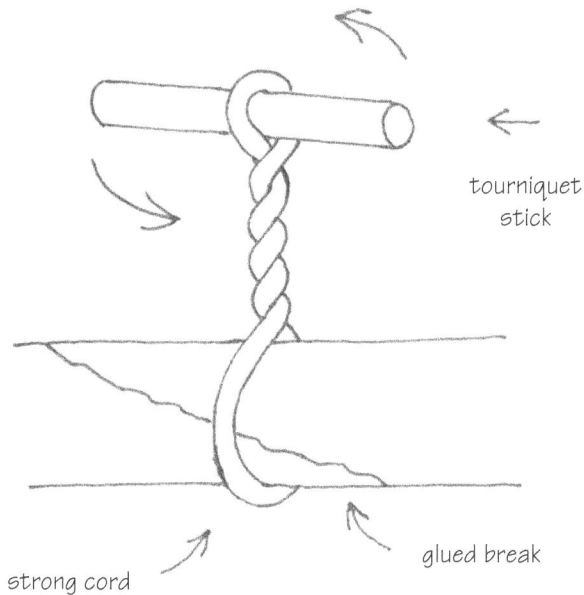

Twisted-rope clamping.

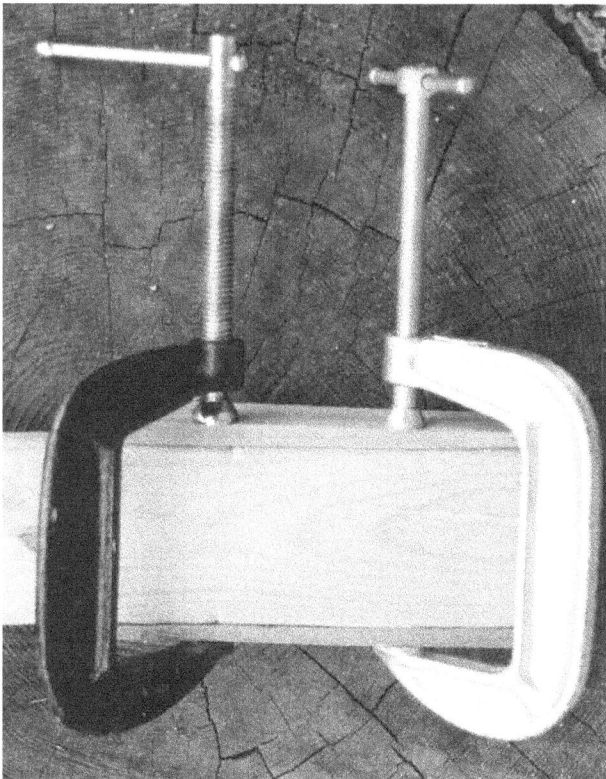

The work is protected from the jaws of the clamps with small, flat pieces of wood.

a simple loop of twisted cord with a tourniquet stick that can be secured in position might serve well, just like the twisted-rope clamps discussed in chapter 4. Rubber bands can also be employed to temporarily hold parts together for gluing.

Some kinds of projects are held together more practically in a bench vise or with C-clamps or locking pliers until the glue dries. When doing so, it can be beneficial to sandwich the parts being glued between thin strips of hardwood or something similar to prevent the jaws from marring the outer surfaces of the item being repaired, as well as to distribute the clamping pressure more evenly.

After the glue has been applied and the parts secured in position, the bottle or tube of glue should be capped or closed as soon as possible to keep it from hardening. I don't know how many bottles of glue I've wasted over the years by leaving the caps off too long or failing to completely seal the opening after the first use. Conserve your glue by closing up the bottle right away and making sure it is completely and firmly capped.

Excess globs, spills, and drips are usually easier to clean up immediately after clamping the parts together than later on when the glue begins to harden. When using polyurethane glue, it might be necessary to remove globs of glue at different stages of curing, since it continues oozing as it dries. With some projects, solvents or alcohol-saturated cloth might help clean away excess glue, depending on the type of glue being used. Most of the time I find that a simple damp rag is fine for wiping up most of a glue mess before it starts to harden.

Finally, it is essential that the glue be allowed to set up or cure completely before putting the repaired item back into service. As previously noted, different glue products have different time requirements for hardening. I prefer to leave most of my projects set in the clamps in a warm, dry place for a couple of days whenever possible, just to be on the safe side. (Room temperature is normally fine.) Ultimately, I don't believe there is such a thing as allowing too much time for any glue to cure.

ADHESIVE TAPE REPAIRS

Glue is not the only general class of adhesive finding widescale use in our modern world. Adhesive tape is another important basic product for certain makeshift repairs or projects, as it is so easy to use, inexpensive, practical for a wide range of applications, and available at grocery stores, convenience stores, or hardware stores. And, just as there are different types of glue for different purposes, there are also different types of adhesive tape for different purposes. Wikipedia lists four main classes of tape: pressure-sensitive tape (PSA), water-activated tape, heat-activated tape, and drywall tape. In this section we will focus on the first category, the familiar pressure-sensitive adhesive tapes.

A key application difference between tape and glue, generally speaking, is that tape should be considered more as a temporary adhesive. We would normally tape something up to hold it together only until it is practical to apply a more permanent method of repair. An exception to this might be a book with loose, torn, or tattered pages that could be permanently repaired with clear tape to extend its life.

There seem to be adhesive tape products for just about every conceivable need. When the hard plastic cover for one of my car's blinker lights was shattered recently, I found some durable, transparent, amber tape at the local auto parts store specifically intended for such expedient repairs. The tape is designed to protect the blinker bulb from rain and mud until the correct new cover is installed. And when I needed to connect custom ducting from a replacement blower to my coal forge recently, I found the perfect heat-resistant metal-foil tape at the local hardware store, which I used for wrapping the connection in order to minimize air leaks. These are just a couple examples of specialty tape products available to us.

However, keep in mind that most adhesive tapes considered to be "special purpose" possess a degree of versatility beyond their intended applications.

A few common types of adhesive tape, clockwise from left: 1) masking tape, 2) duct tape, 3) camouflage duct tape, 4) clear Scotch tape, 5) vinyl electrical tape, 6) amber headlight repair tape, and 7) cloth electrician's tape.

This broken broom handle is repaired with a combination of glue and adhesive tape.

One example that comes to mind is vinyl electrical tape, used primarily to wrap electrical connections and wires. I have used this product to create makeshift fins for crossbow bolts and darts, to wrap the ends of rope to prevent fraying, and to make numerous small, expedient repairs. Heat-shrink tape is another handy specialty tape used by electricians that could serve all sorts of makeshift repair purposes (though I've yet to try it). It's like vinyl electrical tape, but it's thicker and comes in wider sizes. Once it's in place, you heat it and it shrinks to conform to irregular workpieces (like a bulky electrical connection, for which it was designed).

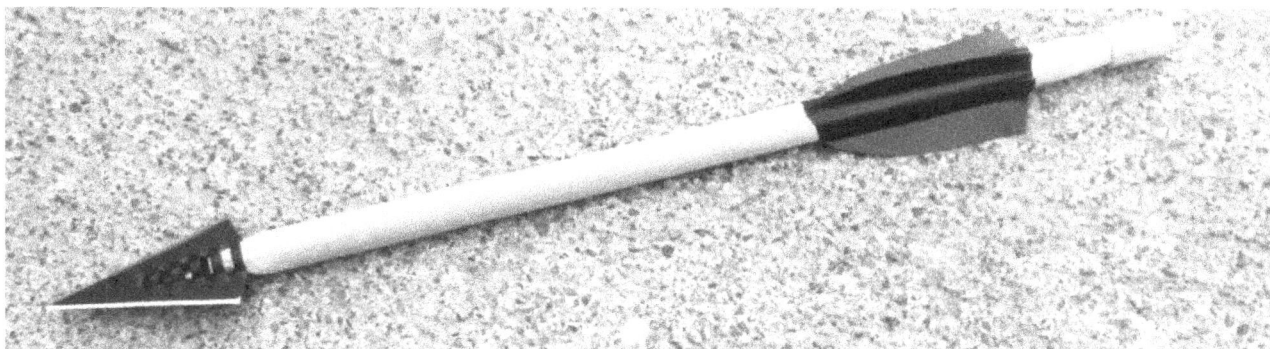

The fins for this dart are fashioned from vinyl electrical tape.

When we think of a common type of general-purpose or multipurpose tape, most of us automatically think of duct tape. Known to military personnel as "hundred mile an hour tape," duct tape is fabric-reinforced vinyl adhesive tape that comes in various colors (most commonly silvery gray) and is sold under different brand names. It is normally very easy to tear by hand, and it sticks to a wide range of surfaces fairly well. A list of potential uses for duct tape could alone fill a lengthy book, and in fact there are a number of books devoted entirely to the myriad uses for this product, including those by "the Duct Tape Guys," Jim Berg and Tim Nyberg, who have their own website: DuctTapeGuys.com.

I've seen plenty of broken windows held together by duct tape, as well as countless hose connections. I would be reluctant to use duct tape where a lot of strength is critical in a repair, but for expedient repairs on torn backpacks, tarps, tents, coats, boots, inflatable rafts, curtains, duffel bags, notebooks, knife sheaths, vinyl furniture, and plenty of other gear, duct tape inevitably finds a use, and often with good success. I have even found duct tape suitable for making expedient arrow fletching.

Friction tape is another versatile product, which for a time was commonly used by electricians before plastic or vinyl electrical tape became popular. It is a cloth tape impregnated

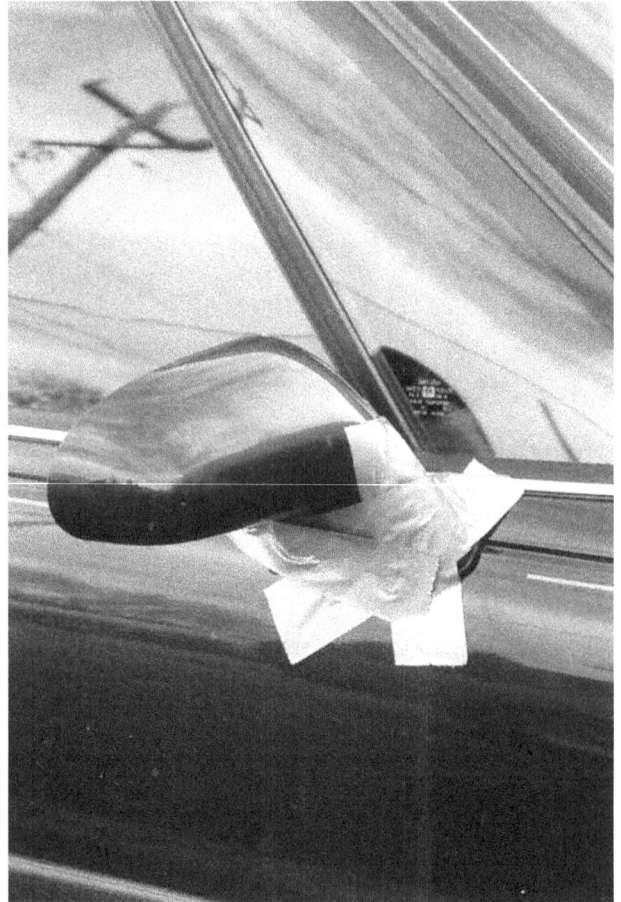

Side mirror on car is temporarily duct-taped in place until it can be replaced

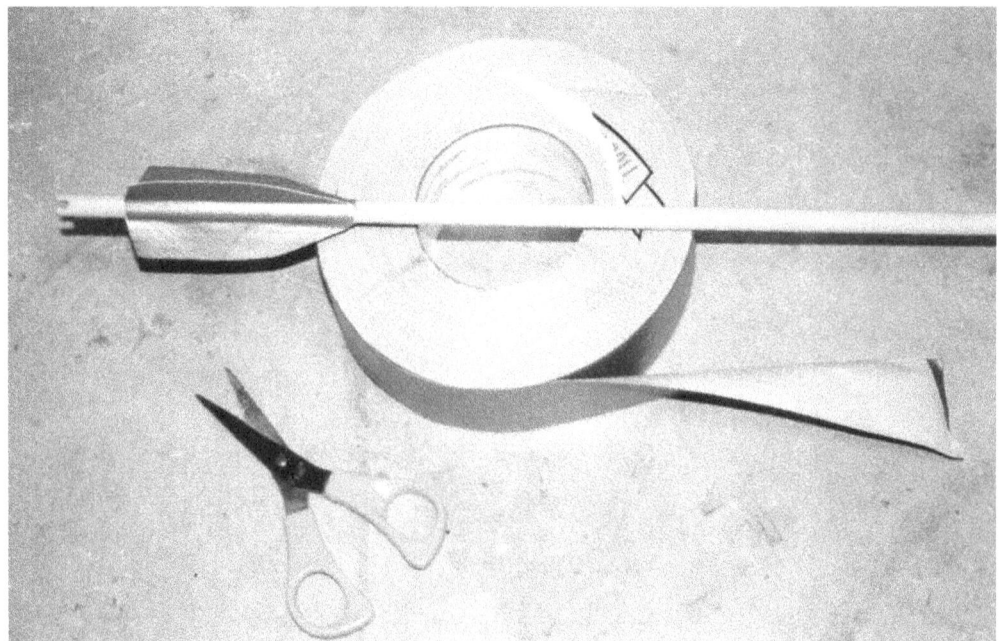

Arrow fletching made from duct tape.

with adhesive that makes it sticky on both sides. It has also been used for years as a handle wrapping for sledgehammers and baseball bats, to provide an improved gripping surface and a softer hold for the hand.

Filament-reinforced strapping tape is another product I've found very useful for makeshift repairs, being ideal for strapping bags and boxes that need reinforcing. Strapping tape sticks to most surfaces well, and it seems to stay in place better than most adhesive tapes I have used. Available in different widths, it is tough enough that it usually requires a cutting edge to sever it, as opposed to duct tape, which can be torn by hand.

One drawback to most adhesive tapes, at least as far as temporary repairs go, is that they tend to leave behind a sticky, dirt-attracting film on the repaired

surfaces after being removed. It can be a hassle to clean off the gummy, sticky mess.

REPAIRS WITH CORD, WIRE, AND TIES

How many things throughout your lifetime have you tied together with string or bound with wire? You've probably had to do that more times than you can remember, right? I know I have, and I've learned a few useful tricks along the way that I will share with you here.

Sometimes a tight wrapping of strong cord is sufficient to securely bind two objects together, and this is one of the simplest and cleanest kinds of repairs you can make. The best way to keep the wrap tight and avoid bulky knots is to form a loop, or bight, in the cord and lay it along the surface of

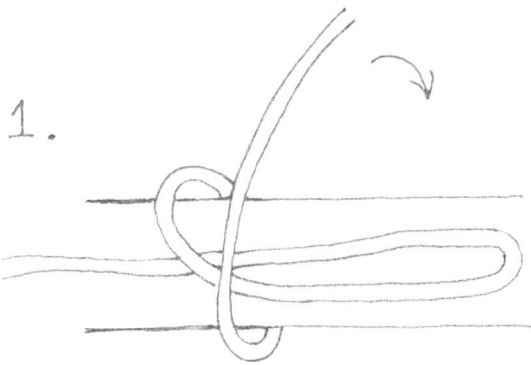

1.

Make bight and begin wrapping working end around.

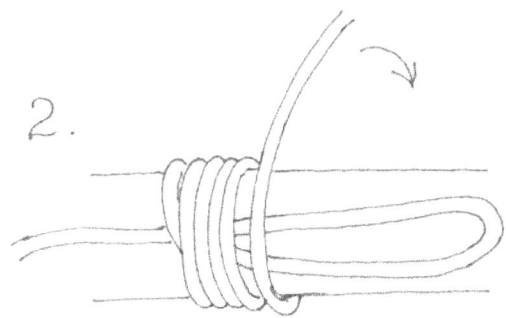

2.

Continue wrapping working end, keeping the coils close and the cord taut.

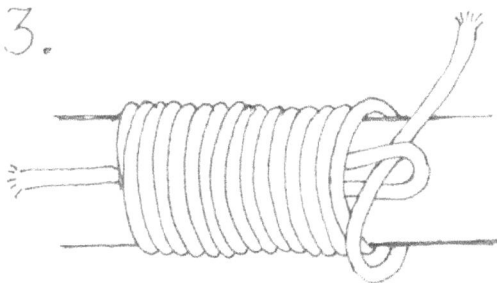

3.

Pass working end through bight loop.

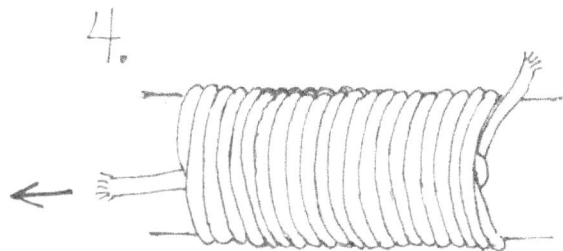

4.

Pull other end of cord to snug loop and working end under the wrapping.

Cord binding without knots.

whatever is to be wrapped; then proceed to wind the working end tightly around the bight and object or objects to be bound. Keep the coil wraps close together and the cord taut while wrapping. Just before completely wrapping over the end of the loop, pass the working end through the opening and pull the other end of the cord, drawing the loop and working end under the wrapping and securing everything neatly and firmly. No knots are needed with this method. Exposed ends of cord can be trimmed off after the wrap is completed for a neater appearance.

This method is often used for whipping the ends of heavy rope with small-diameter cord to prevent the rope ends from fraying. When done properly, it is a more secure and permanent (as well as neater looking) whipping method than simply wrapping the rope ends with adhesive tape.

Binding things with metal wire is another common method of repair, especially when fixing broken sections in wooden fences, because it is fast and easy when using the right tools, and it normally holds securely with wire of heavy enough gauge.

The tools you will want for bending and handling wire include large wire cutters, pliers, and leather gloves to protect your hands. Electrician's pliers with their robust noses and built-in wire cutters work well for managing most gauges of hand wire. For securing fence boards, heavy steel hand wire or hay-baling wire usually works well. A popular tool for managing metal wire is the traditional fence pliers—the multifunction tool that can bend and cut wire and also pull and hammer staples.

Metal wire is easily joined, and a loop or coil of it can be used to bind things firmly by twisting both

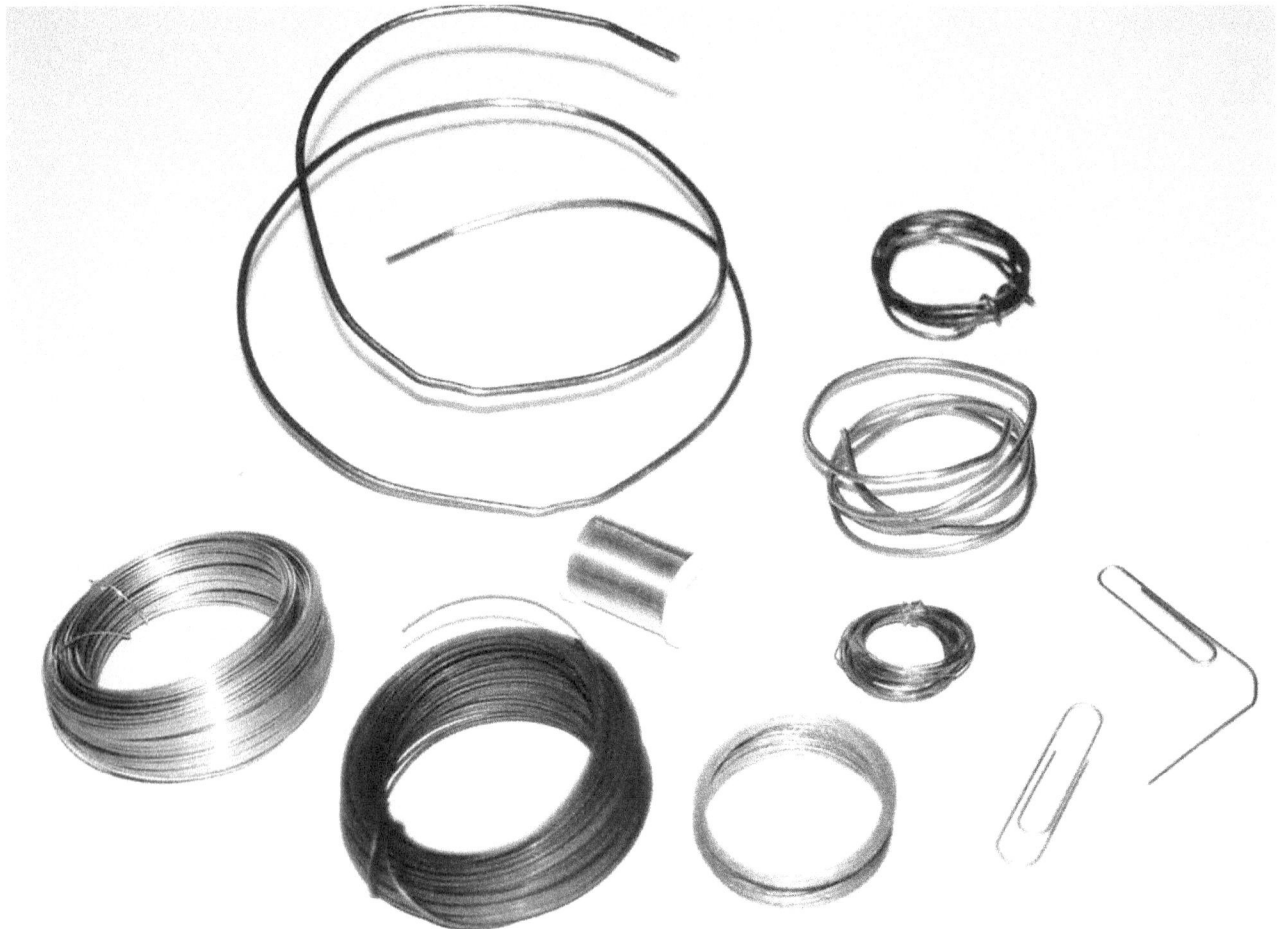

Miscellaneous sizes of metal wire are infinitely utilitarian.

ends together for a number of turns with pliers. The ends will wrap themselves together and tighten up the loop with amazing constriction power. The neat thing about this method is that the pliable wire will not unwind itself; the ends remain twisted together.

Binding two boards together with coat hanger wire.

Old fence held together with steel wire. Not pretty, but it holds.

Ends of metal wire can be sharp, and two ends twisted together grow into a fairly rigid, twisted section that should be bent down and out of the way or tucked under something to prevent dangerous snags and cuts to people or livestock. Also, the wire will tend to cut or dig into very soft or weathered boards. A strip of thin sheet metal can be placed under a binding of heavy-gauge steel wire in certain situations to prevent such damage.

A repair to a fence or anything else with a binding of metal wire may not look very pretty, but if done well it will normally hold for a long time. It is preferable to keep both ends of the wire twisting together equally, as opposed to one part simply wrapping around the other, which wouldn't hold as securely. It is also important to use heavy enough wire. I once made several frustrating attempts to repair a fence with this method, only to have my thin wire break each time I went to twist it up. I then obtained a thicker gauge of wire and the problem disappeared.

A variety of flat metal and synthetic fiber bands, plus the tools for cinching and connecting them, are available for strapping or binding all sorts of wooden and cardboard boxes and crates. Many of these products are popular in the moving and shipping industries but are also well suited for a variety of expedient repairs, like tightening up a wooden chest whose sides might be coming apart, or banding up a loose wooden barrel, for example.

Locking plastic cable ties can be incredibly handy for binding certain items together because they are quick and easy

Fishing reel secured to makeshift pole using cable ties.

to use, lightweight, compact, and inexpensive, and they possess an amazing degree of holding strength. I always try to keep several cable ties in my repair kits, and they find use from time to time. You'll find various lengths and colors in the electrical supply section of the hardware store.

Another handy product for the repair kit is a hose clamp. Hose clamps are thin metal bands with rows of slots that are engaged by the threads of a screw mounted on one end so that turning the screw in one direction constricts the band, and turning it in the opposite direction opens the band and loosens the clamp. Hose clamps come in an assortment of sizes, and for their intended purpose they have no equal. If you need to cut and remove a split or damaged portion of a rubber hose in your car's engine and then attach a replacement section, hose clamps are usually the answer. I've used hose clamps to repair a broken lawn mower handle, a broken snow shovel handle, and for numerous other makeshift purposes.

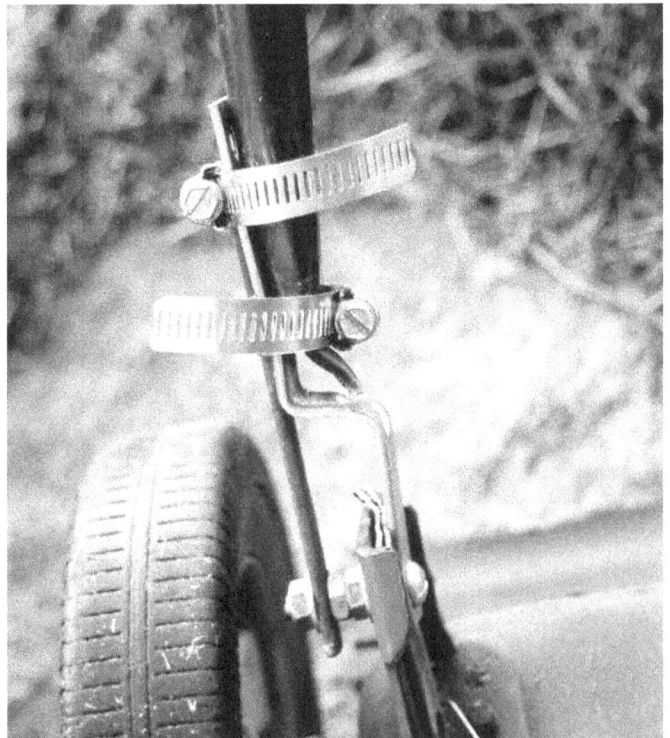

Lawn mower handle repaired with steel strap and hose clamps.

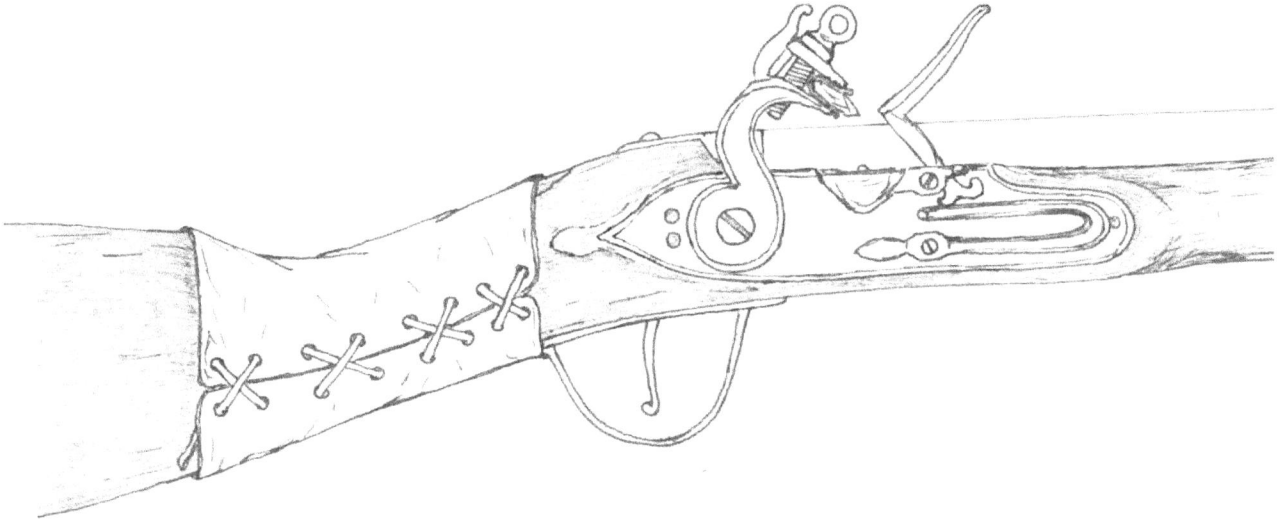

Rawhide wrapped around gunstock to repair crack.

RAWHIDE REPAIRS

The American Indians used raw animal hides for repairs to their tools, weapons, and other gear for thousands of years, much like we use duct tape for seemingly infinite purposes today. Raw (i.e., untanned) skins of mammals possess some particularly useful qualities. Pliable when thoroughly wet, rawhide becomes rigid when dry, somewhat like hard rubber or plastic. This is because it contains its own natural glue, and the glue bonds the skin fibers together during the drying process.

These characteristics make rawhide especially useful for a myriad of expedient repairs. A cracked rifle stock or an ax handle might be wrapped with strips of wet rawhide in order to hold the parts together quite firmly when the hide dries and hardens. A rawhide lace can be used just like any other cord to bind something up, or a wider rawhide band can be wrapped around a cracked section of something, with its opposite edges drawn together by lacing through holes punched with an awl. I have tightly wrapped nylon cord over the top of a band of wet rawhide for added reinforcement on a repair of an ax handle. The hide more or less conformed to the contour of the handle.

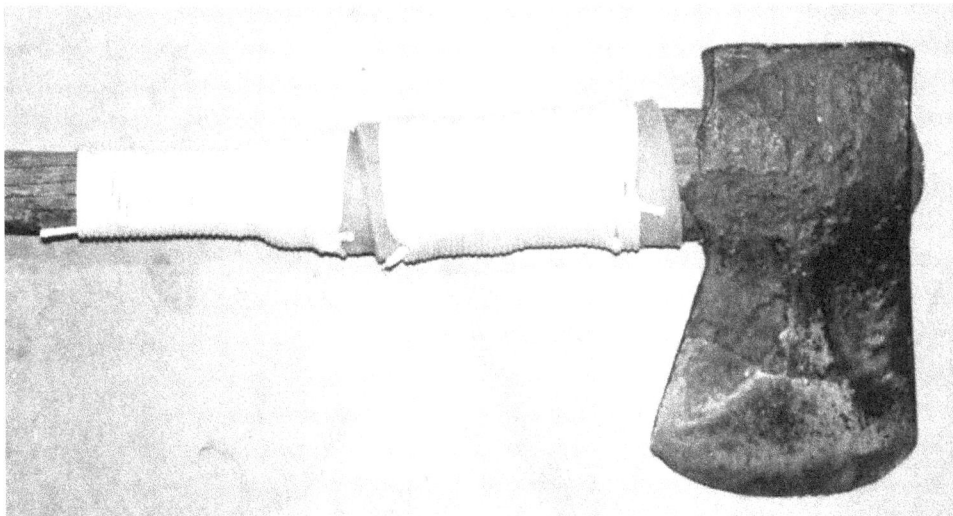

Broken ax handle wrapped with rawhide and nylon cord.

Another way to use thick rawhide (or even heavy tanned cowhide, for that matter) in a makeshift repair is as an expedient hinge. Straps of thick hide can be tacked or screwed to a lightweight door or box lid and its frame, allowing the door or lid to swing open and closed, the same as if metal hinges were used. This is worth remembering for the day you find yourself up in the mountains with limited hardware and in need of expedient hinges.

Improvised box hinge made of heavy cowhide. A section of rawhide would work equally well.

Rawhide has been used for replacement soles on boots and shoes, and it has long been a common sole material for moccasins. I have even made expedient replacement buttons for wilderness clothing out of small pieces of rawhide. These are very easy to make—I just cut out the disks from a single layer of sturdy rawhide and drill the tiny holes for the thread—and they work as well as plastic or wooden buttons.

Natural, unprocessed rawhide will have all the desirable qualities of a good repair material, tending to shrink as it hardens. I have also experimented quite a bit with the various factory-processed rawhide materials used in chew toys for dogs found in the pet supplies section of my local supermarket, with mixed results. This stiff rawhide requires thorough soaking in warm water before it can be pliable enough to shape and mold to fit the project.

PINS, PEGS, AND DOWEL REPAIRS

An ax I have used for a number of winters to split small logs into fire starter kindling began developing a hairline crack in the wooden handle, starting near the head and angling lengthwise halfway through the handle, nearly a foot in length.

My initial effort to halt the cracking consisted of tightly wrapping the compromised section with nylon cord to bind it up. This worked well for a while, but after extended heavy use, the crack progressed further up and eventually all the way through the handle. This crack, although not easily noticed at first glance, began to actually pinch the palm of my hand whenever I chopped kindling without wearing leather gloves.

Eventually, the split ax handle began separating into two pieces—only the head of the ax held it together. The time had come for a more secure and permanent repair. I decided to use dowel pegs in conjunction with polyurethane glue.

I clamped the handle to hold it together and drilled three 5/16-inch-diameter holes well spaced along the length of the crack, perpendicular to it and centered through the handle. I then cut three 5/16-inch hardwood dowel sections to length of the width of the handle and sanded a slight bevel on each end of the pegs to make them easier to hammer into the holes.

I wanted to get as much glue as possible into the crack to bond the splitting surfaces together, so after the holes were drilled I removed the clamps, pried the crack open as far as I could without completely separating the handle, and allowed the glue to ooze deep down between the pieces. I then clamped the handle back together and applied glue to the dowel pegs before tapping them into the holes. I chose polyurethane glue for this job because of its great bonding strength and because it is waterproof. After the glue dried, I sanded the surface of the handle to clean it up. The resulting repair appears to be stronger than any section of the handle ever was before the crack. In fact, this handle, though appearing well used, is actually much stronger than a new one.

Dowel pins were used to repair this cracked ax handle.

This is an example of how a very strong, permanent repair can easily be made to a broken wooden handle or anything else with the cross-pinning method—in this case, using hardwood dowels with glue to pin the two broken pieces together. Broken parts of things that were previously only glued can in some instances be drilled and pinned for additional security. It is very rare when two parts that have been carefully doweled or pinned together will not remain together as one piece.

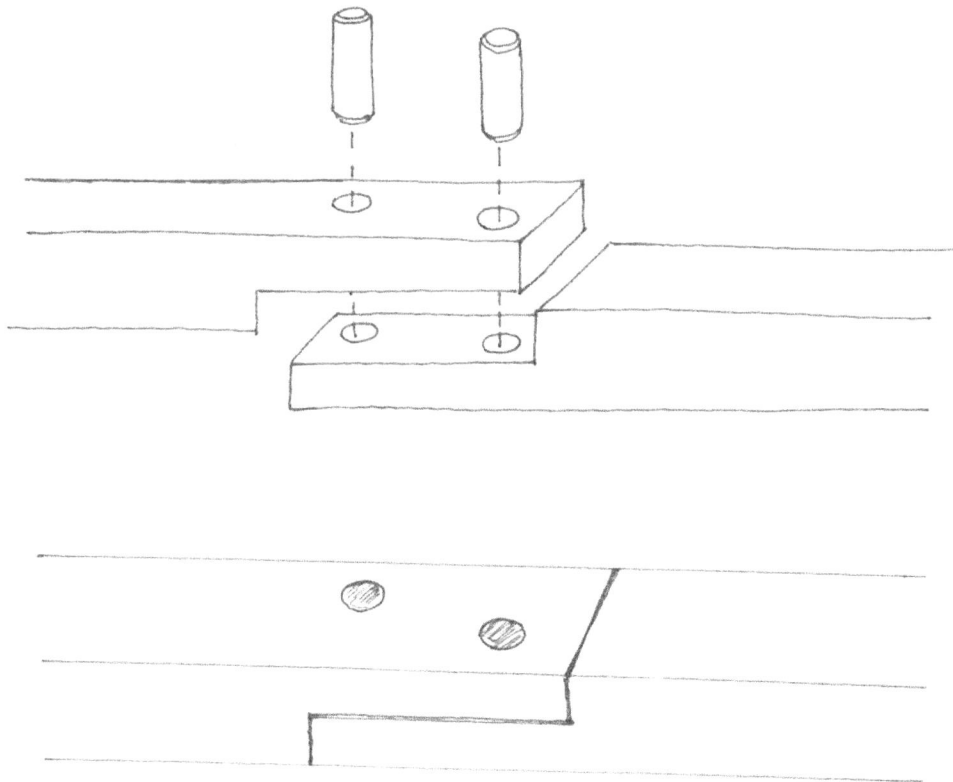

Doweled, lapped connection.

Pins and dowels used in this way provide the same basic function as nails, except nails can be merely hammered into the wood or other material without predrilling holes. Miscellaneous nails and spikes are practical for certain fastening tasks, especially with larger projects involving rough carpentry, where the aesthetics of visible nail heads, hammer marks in the wood, and the occasional bent-over nail or splits in the large frame boards from the nails aren't as critical as with smaller repair projects. Nails have the advantage of being quick and simple to use, requiring just a few swings of a hammer. However, simply nailing things together with smooth, straight, metal nails rarely provides a connection as secure as one done with glue and pins, and the resulting appearance of the latter repair will usually be nicer.

Driving a square peg into a round hole is a neat trick that is rarely practiced these days in conventional building and crafts, but back in the age of sailing ships, nearly all wooden sailing vessels were held together by square pegs in round holes. This

mallet

It is normally easier to drive a peg with beveled ends.

top view

Driving a square peg into a round hole.

would be a useful method where a rustic appearance is desirable, such as pinning door and window frames into log cabins. The square shape of a peg creates a very snug fit when forced into a round hole in wood of slightly less diameter, producing substantial holding power. No glue would be necessary with this method.

Of course, one must drill holes before inserting blunt pins or wooden dowels, either round or square, into something being assembled or repaired. Any pins or dowel pegs should have a tight enough fit

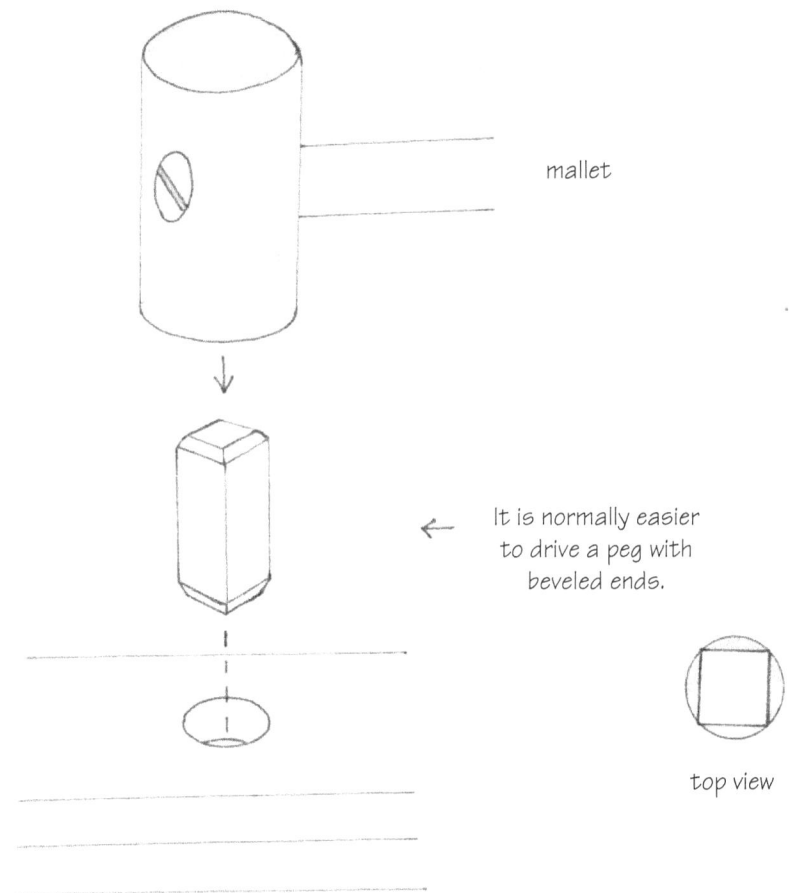

within their respective holes to hold firmly. The corresponding bit size to drill the pilot hole should always be chosen carefully to ensure this.

Also remember that whenever you drill holes into something, it tends to affect the structural integrity of the object being drilled. The diameter of the holes you create in order to pin parts together should be considered carefully in relation to the size of the parts. If you have to remove an excess of material in order to make your repair, it could be defeating the whole purpose.

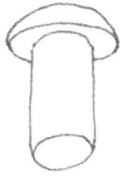

Solid rivet with head.

Blind "pop" rivet.

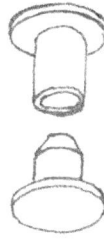

Two-part harness rivet.

Solid metal pin that
would be peened on both
ends to form a rivet.

Several types of rivets.

An assortment of rivets.

RIVETED CONNECTIONS

Riveting is one of the oldest and simplest methods for permanently joining pieces of metal and other things. Wikipedia defines a rivet as a mechanical fastener, and it lists at least eight different types of rivets. I would loosely define a rivet as a cylindrical metal pin that fits into a hole and is locked in place with expanded ends. You can get solid rivets with heads, blind (pop) rivets that can be inserted through a hole and expanded on the opposite side with a rivet gun, various hollow rivets, split rivets, and two-part rivets for joining pieces of leather.

It seems to me that there is a fine line between what defines the simplest type of rivet and a cross pin in a knife handle, for example. There are similarities between the two: their basic purpose of holding the handle together is the same, and it can be difficult to distinguish the difference on a finished knife handle, where rivet heads are often ground flat, flush with the surface of the handle.

The basis for a rivet's function is the expanded

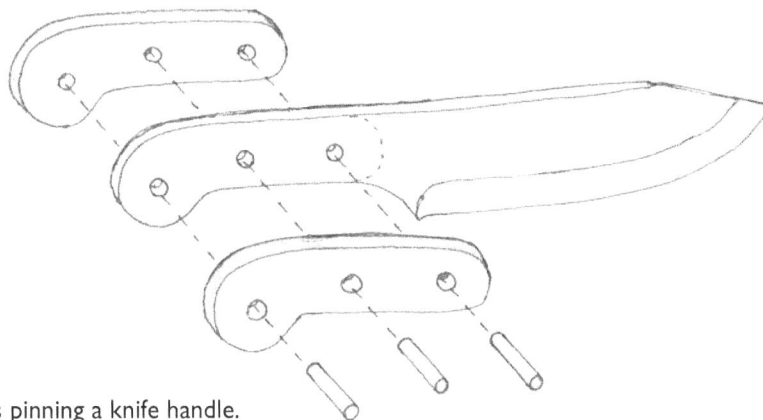

Cross pinning a knife handle.

flat-faced
hammer

ball-peen (also ball-pein)
hammer

anvil

Center the solid pin in
the rivet hole and
support against anvil.

Hammer top of pin to
upset it.

Hammer/peen top end
into a dome-shaped
head. Opposite end
begins upsetting.

Flip work and repeat to
set rivet.

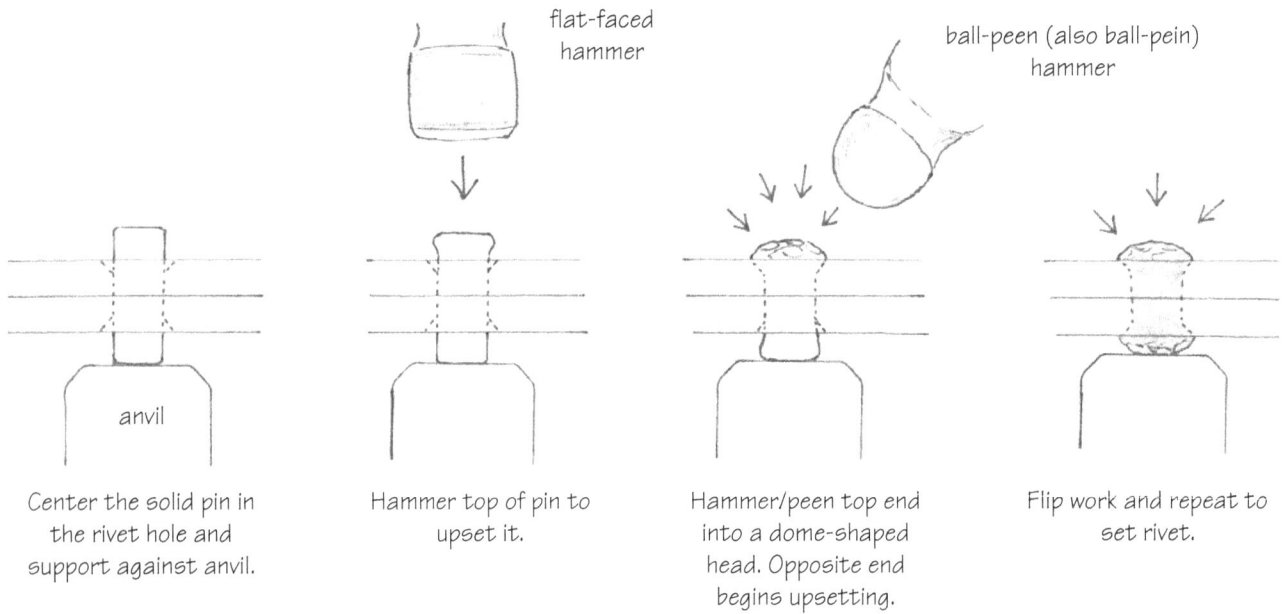

Setting a solid rivet (work shown in cross section). Note that the hole's openings are beveled. The set rivet is smashed down to fill the space.

portion on both its ends that lock it into position in the hole to which it is fitted. Expanding the metal rod at one or both ends after it is fitted into the hole is simply a matter of upsetting (i.e., thickening the diameter) of the rod to lock it in place. This is done by hammering it on each end while the opposite end is supported against a solid anvil of some sort, like a bucking bar. An upset portion of a rivet exerts a significant amount of outward pressure within the hole it fills.

While steel bridge builders traditionally used hot rivets in the past, most small connections are more easily fastened with cold rivets, or rivets that can be upset cold. A cold solid rivet should be a soft, malleable metal, such as copper or mild steel, which will easily yield to light hammer blows without cracking, shearing, or chipping. The ends of a soft metal rod are essentially mushroomed to form the heads of the rivet.

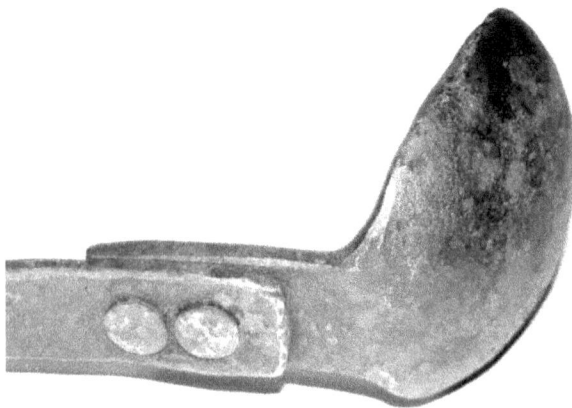

Solid steel rivets hold this ladle dipper to its handle.

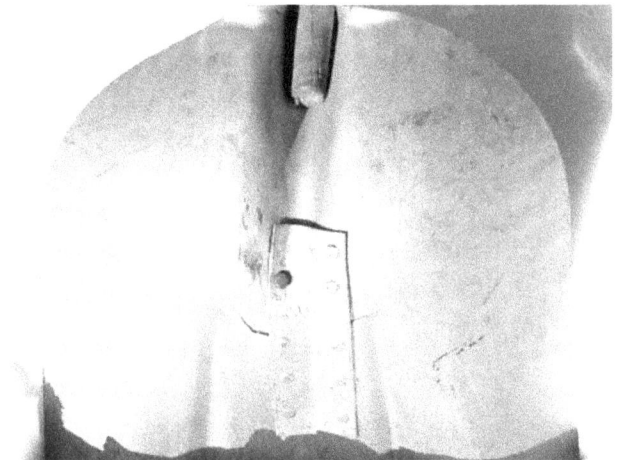

Shovel blade repaired with rivets and sheet metal.

You can easily make your own rivets for most typical applications. Any short length of cylindrical metal rod has the potential to serve as a simple rivet, or you can cut your own from heavy gauge wire, mild steel rod, or nails. The steel in a common nail is typically soft and works well. Cut it into sections the same as if you were making cross pins. You can use the end of a nail with the head on it for a quick rivet in certain applications where you don't care whether or not the heads on both sides look the same. You will want the length of your rivets to be longer than the full depth of the hole they are to fill, to allow enough material on both ends to form the heads. Also, the ends of the rivet pins should be cut or filed off flat and at a 90-degree angle to the sides prior to hammering them to minimize the tendency of the rivet to collapse sideways like a bent-over nail, especially when riveting soft materials like leather or wood.

Small-diameter copper tubing can be cut to make good little hollow rivets. You set them with a cone-shaped tool like a punch. The tubing will usually split around the annulus; then you just hammer that flat. This method works well for soft material like knife sheaths, as opposed to hard material like a tin bucket.

Whenever joining soft materials such as leather, wood, bone, plastic, or horn with solid rivets, experience has taught me that it is normally a good idea to place appropriately sized flat washers under the rivet heads to better support the expanding heads. This also minimizes cracking with materials like wood or bone.

When riveting solid metal parts together, or when riveting things like slabs on custom knife handles, where the more refined aesthetics of the final product are important, it is sometimes beneficial to bevel the rims of the holes at the surface or on the surface-side openings of the washers if they're thick enough. This should be done carefully by drilling into the mouth of the hole with an oversized drill bit to a shallow depth to create a slight funnel shape at the entrance of the hole, in the same way you would countersink screw holes to sink screw heads below the surface. This gives the rivet's head room to expand below the surface. With a deep enough bevel, the domes of the rivet heads can be ground off flush with the surface for a neater appearance.

Properly riveted connections can be considered fairly strong, especially with solid rivets. The neat thing about this method is its simplicity and the unsophisticated nature of the few required tools, as opposed to welded connections (covered in the next

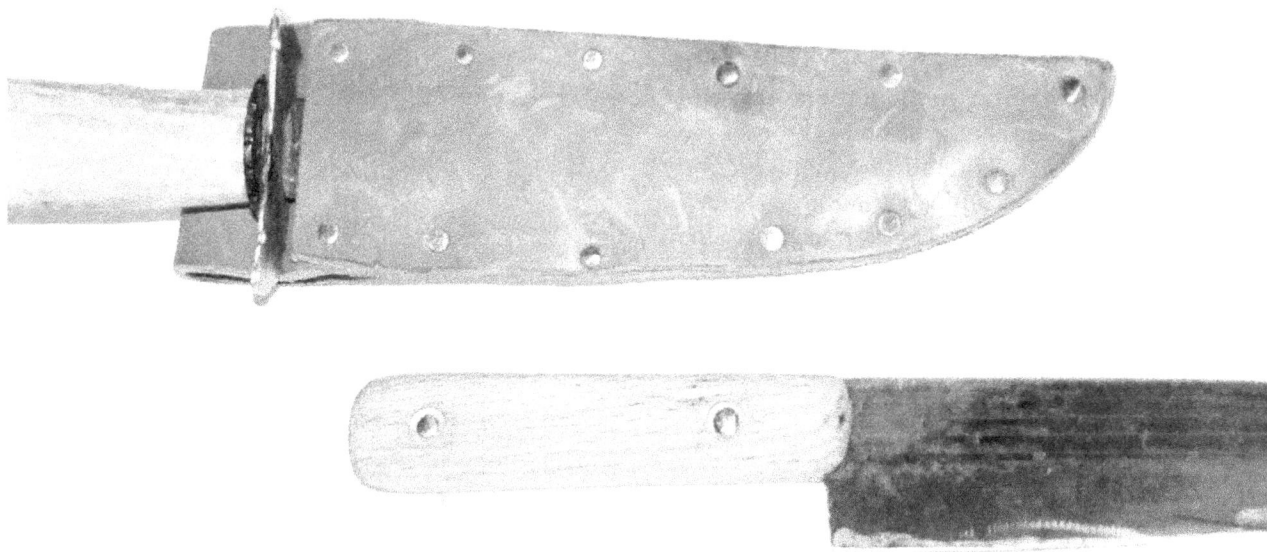

This leather sheath was riveted together with sections of copper wire. The knife handle below it was riveted together with steel rivets made from nails. The rivet ends are supported with washers.

chapter). Perhaps the hardest part is drilling and aligning the holes for the rivets.

When a project entails connecting pieces of sheet metal or other pieces of flat, rigid materials, where access to the side opposite the working side might be awkward or restricted, using blind rivets in conjunction with a rivet gun might be practical.

A rivet gun, also known as a pop riveter, is an easy and, for me, fun tool to use, and it can be indispensable around the house for riveting rain gutters, aluminum screen door frames, trailer canopies, and things like that. This tool is only practical for permanent connections that won't be taken apart later. Although a properly welded or brazed seam would generally be considered stronger where applicable, pop-riveted connections are much easier to accomplish with a very low skill level, and they do hold with considerable tenacity.

A pop rivet, more correctly referred to as a blind rivet, either of steel or aluminum, consists of a tubular body, a headed mandrel housed within the body for setting the rivet, a base flange or head, and the stem that fits into the nozzle of the tool. To use a blind rivet with the rivet gun, insert the stem into the nozzle and guide the rivet body through the hole in the pieces you intend to attach. As you operate the handles much like you would do with a pair of pliers, the mandrel gets drawn back into the rivet body to set it, expanding the end on the far side to lock the workpieces together. As you continue operating the handles, the stem eventually breaks off, leaving just the expanded rivet body set in the hole.

Rivets of any type should not be used in conjunction with or to supplement other fasteners, such as screws or bolts in a given connection, because the fitting tightness and load-bearing capacities of the two systems are different, and combining them could cause one to jeopardize the integrity of the other.

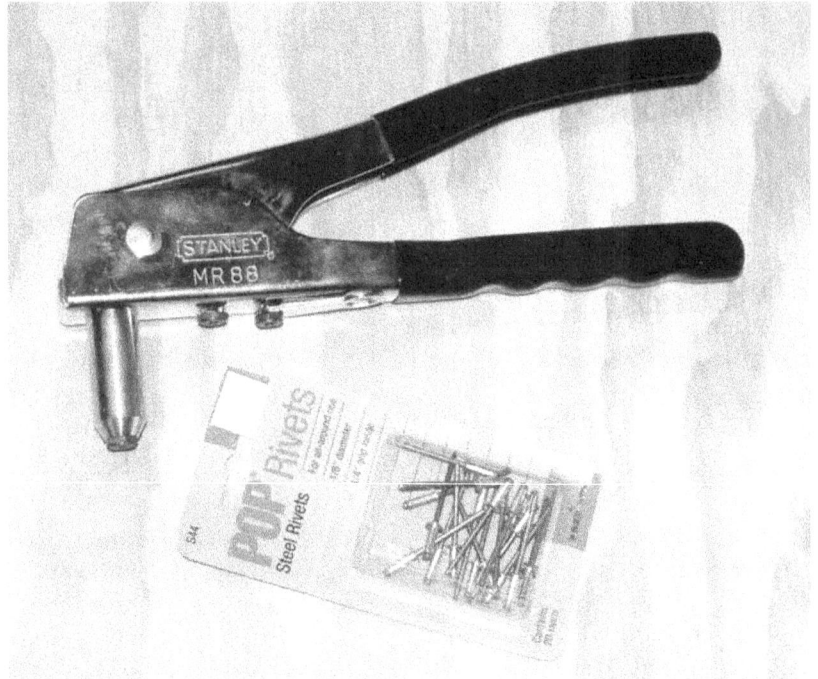

A rivet gun, also known as a pop riveter.

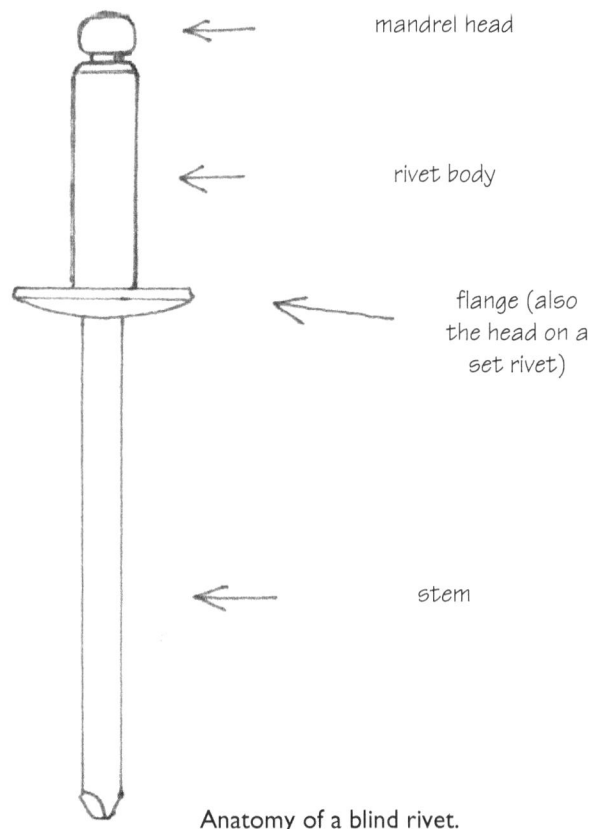

Anatomy of a blind rivet.

mandrel head

rivet body

flange (also the head on a set rivet)

stem

riveter tool

Insert rivet body into hole using tool.

Activate rivet tool; stem is drawn into tool.

Rivet body expands.

Rivet is set and stem breaks free.

Cross section of panels being connected.

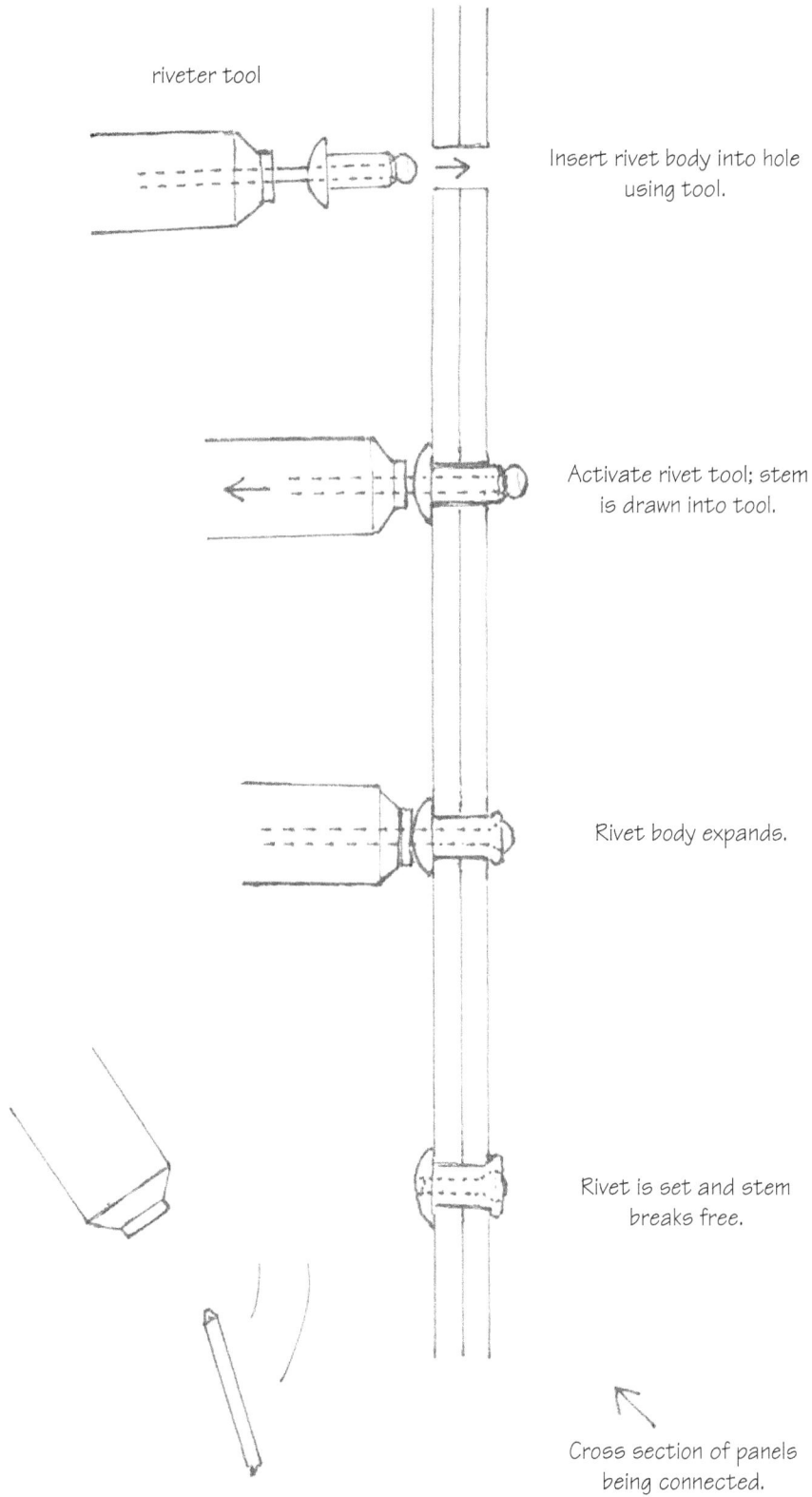

Setting a blind rivet.

WORKING WITH SCREWS AND BOLTS

Threaded screws and bolts are important fasteners for numerous applications. Although typically slower to install than common nails or staples, screws and bolts tend to hold more securely due to the threads on their shafts. The basic difference between a screw and a bolt is that a screw is tightened by turning a head; a bolt is tightened by turning on a nut.

The screw (or a threaded bolt) represents a type of simple machine, which is a device that multiplies or redirects applied force to provide some type of mechanical advantage. The mechanical advantage of a screw (or more specifically, the theoretical mechanical advantage, discounting any loss to friction) can be calculated with a simple formula: circumference of the screw (diameter x 3.1416)—or the circumference of the circle of applied force if we use a tool to turn the screw—divided by the pitch of the screw's threads. (Calculating the actual mechanical advantage that factors in friction would be applicable to such tasks as lifting a weight with a screw jack or tightening the jaws of a bench vise.)

The basis for a screw's various functions is the inclined plane of its threads (i.e., its ridges and grooves) that spiral around its shaft. A measurement of the distance from a point on a thread to the same point on the next thread above or below it is called the screw's pitch. We can see that if we were to rotate a screw in its hole one full turn (360 degrees), it will have been raised or lowered the distance of one pitch. This rotational motion that provides vertical up or down linear motion (on the inclined plane of the wraparound thread) is an example of a simple machine redirecting applied force.

We could determine the advantages of a screw for one mechanical operation or another, but for our purpose here we will focus on the essence of what makes a screw or a threaded bolt an efficient fastener for joining things. For this we consider the role the threads play in locking individual parts together. The shorter the pitch of the thread, the greater the screw's holding ability, because it provides more friction under load than you would have with a thread having a sharply inclined plane, such as is seen, for example, on the old pump-type Yankee screwdriver that was designed to rotate on its thread more easily.

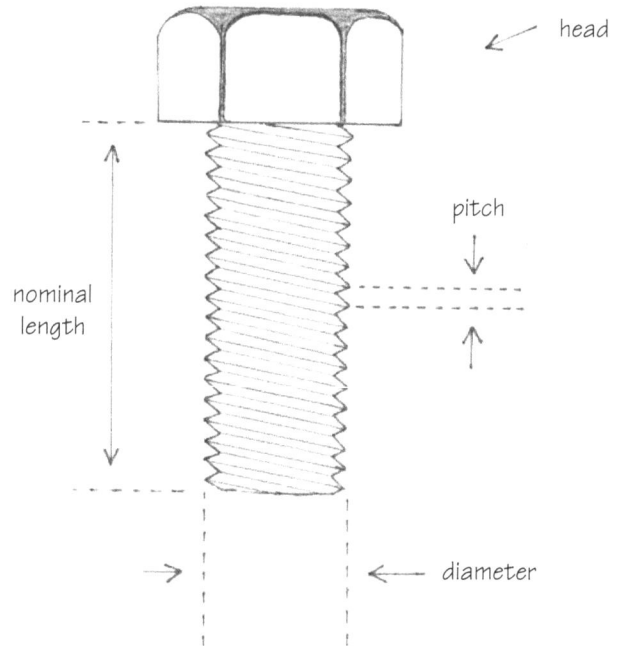

Threaded bolt.

A number of variables will affect the amount of friction at play with the threaded screw's operation. Thread pitch in relation to the screw's shaft diameter, the dimensional shape of the threads, material composition of the fasteners as well as of the adjacent contact surfaces, and the forces of the load will all have some bearing on the screw's performance.

The fastening capability of a screw with its threaded shaft, as compared to a common nail with a smooth, straight shaft, is somewhat analogous to that of a ringed nail. With the threaded screw and the ringed nail, more surface area will be in contact with the board or parts being fastened than would exist between a smooth nail and the same board or parts. Hence more friction will be present with the threaded fastener or ringed nail, and it will lock the parts together more securely. The obvious advantage of the screw over the ringed nail (or any nail or rivet) is its ability to be easily backed out of its hole by reverse rotation if the parts must later be disassembled. Good luck ever removing a ringed nail without tearing up the work.

One example of the advantage of screws over

smooth nails was impressed upon me when I needed to repair the wooden slats in the fence that encloses my backyard. The builder of the fence (before I bought the house) used framing nails to secure the vertical slats to the horizontal fence boards. As the aging fence boards began to weather and warp, the nails began popping out here and there and the slats were falling away from the fence. Every few months I found myself tacking the slats back into position using nails, in the same way the rest of the fence was held together. It didn't take very long for me to figure out that screws would handle the job more permanently. I then installed weather-resistant coated deck screws into much of the fence, and now, even after several years, none of the slats screwed into place have yet fallen off the fence. The screws I used were comparatively expensive, but they hold!

A handy tool for this kind of task is a battery-powered screwdriver or cordless drill. I recommend any of the 18-volt models for their power. In the example above, I did not predrill the fence boards, as they were made of relatively soft cedar. The screws went into the boards easily, with negligible splitting. In most cases, however, especially when working with woodscrews, screw holes should be predrilled to avoid splitting the work. (There are self-drilling screws for use with sheet metal.) Drill pilot holes with a bit having a diameter the same as or slightly less than the screw's shaft, rather than the outside thread diameter, so the threads will have solid material to screw into.

Whenever assembling or disassembling anything fastened with screws, it is important to use a screwdriver tip of a size and shape that most closely matches the screw head whenever possible. An oversized or undersized tip can really mess up a screw head or make turning the screw a challenge. Some tips are designed better than others. Gunsmith screwdrivers have precision tips with a parallel profile to help keep them from slipping out of screw slots.

Nuts and bolts also rely on the forces of friction provided by their threads to fasten things together. A nut turning on the threaded shaft of a bolt functions very similarly to the screw in a C-clamp or bench vise that tightens against the resistance of an object in the jaws. Without getting too much into the science of it, it is useful to understand that substantial forces are at play when a nut is tightened on a bolt that locks several parts together. The tension on the bolt provided by the tightened nut, known as preload, produces considerable friction in the threads. The direction of the nut is therefore not automatically reversed on its threads to relieve its compression action. Hence nuts and bolts can be very powerful fasteners.

precision gunsmith-type screwdriver tip

standard flathead (sometimes called "slotted" or "square-bar") screwdriver tip

Select the tip that best fits the screw head. Compare the taper in the standard tip to the parallel profile of the precision tip.

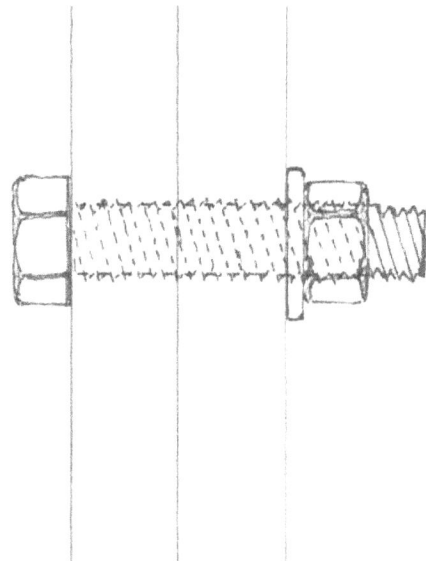

Typical bolted connection in cross section.

Common types of bolts include carriage bolts, stove bolts, lag bolts, hanger bolts, eyebolts, machine bolts, stud bolts, and expansion bolts. In the United States, bolts are typically identified by their specific type, length in inches, and diameter in addition to the number of threads per inch. For example, a machine bolt with a length of 2 1/2 inches, 3/4 inch in diameter, and 20 threads per inch would be referred to as a "two and a half inch three-quarter twenty machine bolt." By contrast, metric screws and bolts are designated by their diameter in millimeters and the pitch of their threads in millimeters. Hence, a metric bolt designated as M10 x 1.5 would indicate a bolt with a diameter of 10 millimeters and having a thread pitch of 1 1/2 millimeters.

The various bolt types all have their advantages for certain applications. For example, a carriage bolt is ideal for joining large wooden components because it can be secured in its hole by turning the nut on only one end—the base of the head is automatically drawn into the wood when the nut is tightened, and its squared shape tends to prevent the bolt from turning with the nut. I will often select a carriage bolt that is longer than needed and then saw off the protruding excess with a hacksaw after the nut has been tightened adequately. The rough edge from the saw cut on the end of the bolt can be smoothed up with just a few swipes of a fine-cut flat bastard file.

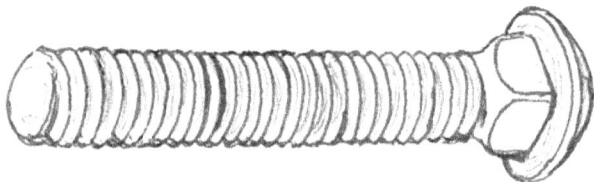

Carriage bolt.

Carriage bolts came in handy for a recent repair I made to a section of wooden fence that was blown down by wind. I firmly planted two new, treated, 4 x 4-inch wooden posts vertically, several feet into the ground, alongside the temporarily propped up broken posts, which were partially rotted at ground

New treated post set in the ground and bolted to broken fence post.

level. Using two 10-inch-long 3/8-inch carriage bolts with the corresponding washers and nuts for each new post, I bolted the new posts to what remained of the old posts (after drilling 3/8-inch holes through both posts using a 12-inch-long drill bit). This repair is very solid, and I imagine it will take quite a wind to blow it down again.

A washer provides a specific platform over which a nut can be tightened. Different types of washers are appropriate for different applications. Flat washers are used primarily to distribute the load over a greater surface than is possible with the nut alone, as well as to provide a smoother bearing surface for the nut to turn on. Fender washers are large-diameter flat washers designed to spread the load in fenders or other sheet metal, though they also work well for the same purpose in leather, rubber, or heavy canvas. A split lock washer (also known as a helical spring lock washer) acts as a spring that is compressed by the tightening of the

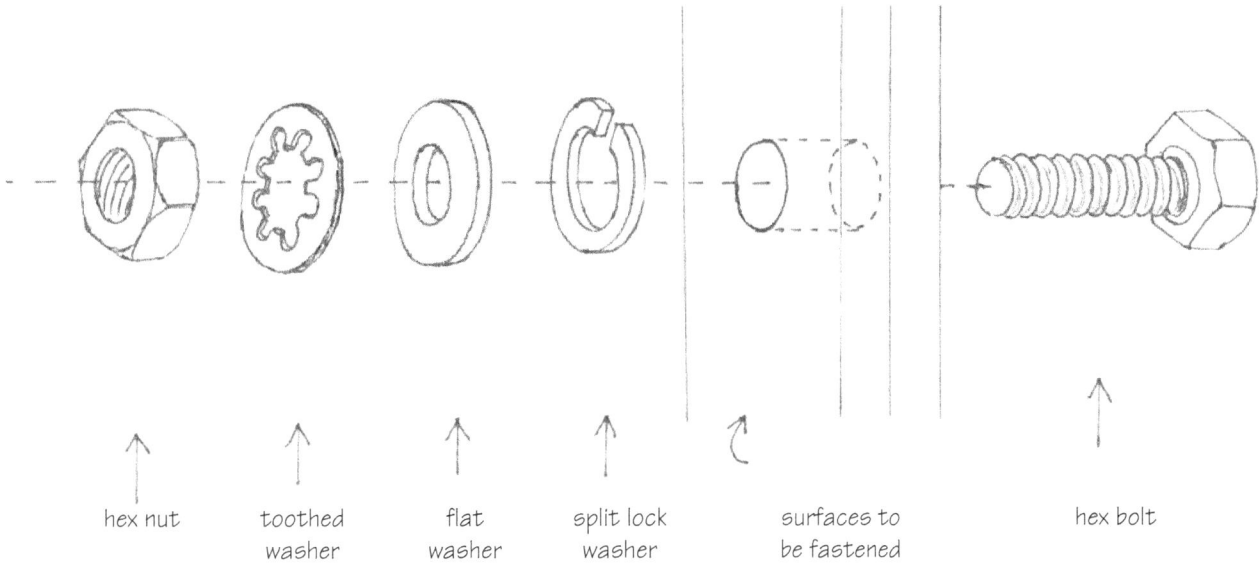

Miscellaneous washers. In practice, only one or two types of washers would be practical for a single application.

nut, thereby creating added tension in the threads that helps the nut resist being loosened by repeated vibration. Toothed washers also help prevent nuts and bolts from backing out.

PREPARING THE WORK BEFORE REPAIRS

Properly preparing a damaged item for a repair might include first cleaning or removing a bad part, sanding or degreasing surfaces before gluing or welding, or positioning supports wherever needed before repairing or replacing structural beams in building restorations and remodels. Let's look at a handful of typical preparation tasks.

Removing Bad Parts

Occasionally, a repair will first require removing old, rusty, corroded, or otherwise damaged parts, sections, or fasteners before new materials can be installed. This might entail prying, sawing, filing, chiseling, or grinding away the bad area or old hardware. Depending on how badly rusted or damaged something is, as well as how accessible it is, this work can be a challenge. Have you ever tried to remove a bolt from an old faucet that had a nut rusted and stuck on its threads under the sink? Or how about trying to turn a screw whose slot was

deformed or eroded to the degree that it could no longer be engaged by a screwdriver?

Situations like these call for special tools. It may be awkward at best, and next to impossible in the tightest places, to work a wrench, pry bar, or handsaw effectively, so a special tool might be needed that can operate in close quarters and either securely grip or cut through pretty much anything. This is where a small, high-speed, rotary tool can save the day.

Handheld rotary power tools—like the little Dremel Moto-Tool and the similar but heavier tools from RotoZip that look like different versions of a small, router-type tool—can be indispensable in a wide variety of specialty applications. These machines spin special bits, cutters, grinders, and rotary files at very high revolutions per minute (rpm) and can be used to drill, sand, grind, sculpt, carve, and cut a wide range of materials. I encounter situations quite often where the versatile little Dremel seems to be the only tool that will get the job done. It makes me wonder how I ever got along without one.

Grinding through a rusted bolt in an awkward space is usually achievable with a rotary tool, where most other tools simply won't work. I recommend the heavy cutting wheels/disks for a job like this,

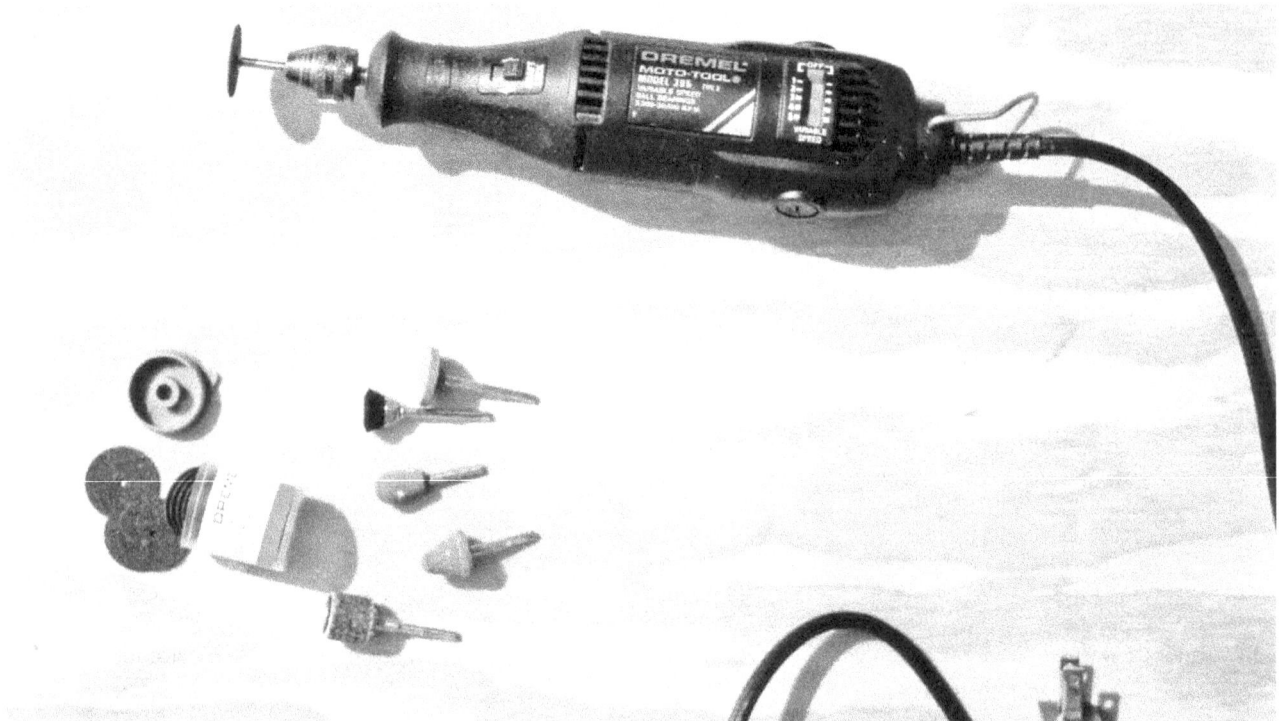

Dremel Moto-Tool with several different types of bits and cutters.

because the thin disks just fly apart after only a few seconds when used to cut steel. I should also mention the importance of wearing eye protection whenever using one of these tools, given the flinging grinding dust and the frequent shattered disks or grinder bits.

Not long ago I installed a two-way pet door in the metal door between our family room and garage. My first plan was to drill the four corner holes to outline the opening, as shown in the instructions for installation in a wooden door, and then simply saw the four border lines with a hand hacksaw. Drilling the corner holes was the easy part. However, a metal door like this is made of two sheet-metal outer skins that sandwich a core of foam insulation. Getting any hacksaw blade to cut both skins simultaneously turned out to be next to impossible with the tools I had, and there wasn't enough space between the two to saw only one side at a time. A big saber saw would've handled it, but I didn't happen to have one at the time.

My next not-so-great idea was to use tin snips to shear the sheet metal along the pencil lines I had drawn, envisioning a process something like cutting the side of an aluminum pop can with scissors. Again, the method proved frustratingly impractical.

Eventually the light bulb in my head lit up and I decided to employ the Dremel. With heavy cutoff disks, this tool made the task of neatly cutting out the opening on each side fast and easy. This is just one example of how a rotary tool can be used as an expedient cutting device for a typical household project.

The larger RotoZip tools that were originally developed for cutting sheetrock are well suited to cutting thicker and heavier material. One of these tools would be ideal for cutting various shapes out of plywood boards, with perhaps cleaner cuts than one would expect to get with a jigsaw or saber saw.

Occasionally, you might encounter a screw that is broken off in its hole or otherwise difficult or impossible to remove with a regular screwdriver, where cutting or grinding it out may not be the most practical solution. In such instances, an impact screwdriver can be used to force a stubborn screw to turn in its hole. Screw extractors, often loosely referred to as easy-outs, provide another possible solution to the problem. Sold in sets of assorted

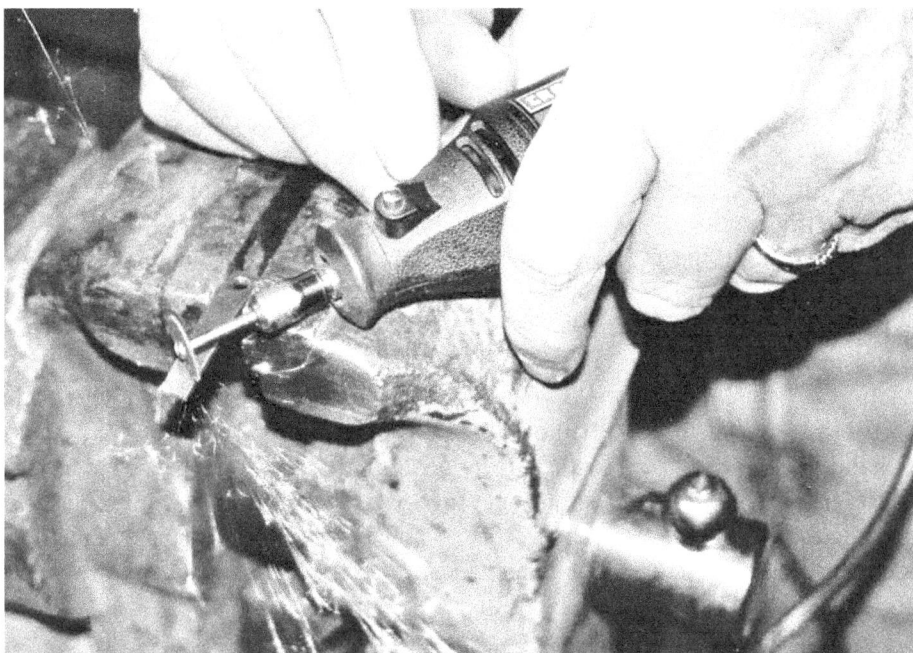

Grinding through spring steel with a small rotary tool.

The key with this type of repair is proceeding slowly and carefully with sharp tools and fine sandpaper, and periodically checking the fit. Very often there is a temptation to cut faster and hurry the job, but keep in mind that it is always much easier to cut a little more material off than to try to add any back on.

Over the last 30-some years, my dad has done a considerable amount of restoration on antique guns as a hobby, including shaping and fitting more gunstocks than I can count. During that time, he has learned some very effective methods for obtaining the desirable, tight wood-to-metal fit, as well as set some near perfect inlays in wood. The secret to his best work, besides his many years of experience, is his use of pattern ink. Whenever he fits anything in wood where a somewhat refined final result is important, he will remove only small amounts of wood at a time and repeatedly check how the pieces fit together. During this process, he applies either pattern ink or charcoal to the surfaces

sizes, screw extractors are hard steel tools designed to help back screws out on their threads. Normally, you will need to drill a small hole into the head or whatever remains of the screw to provide a space that the tapered tool can grab before it can twist the screw out of the hole. A dose of penetrating oil helps the process. (We'll discuss another trick for handling stuck, damaged, or stubborn screws in chapter 8.)

Prepping
Damaged Wood

Preparing the work for repairs to broken furniture, old gunstocks, or other wooden products may occasionally involve cutting away sections of rotted or splintered wood before adding new pieces. In cases where the appearance of the repaired item is important, special care must be taken to first clean or remove the bad section before gluing and inserting a new piece into the space. In typical wood restoration projects, the bad section is chiseled out carefully, followed by precise measuring, marking, and cutting the fill-in piece to fit in the opened area. The goal is a sturdy repair that is not easy to notice at a glance, enhancing the overall visual appearance of the repaired piece.

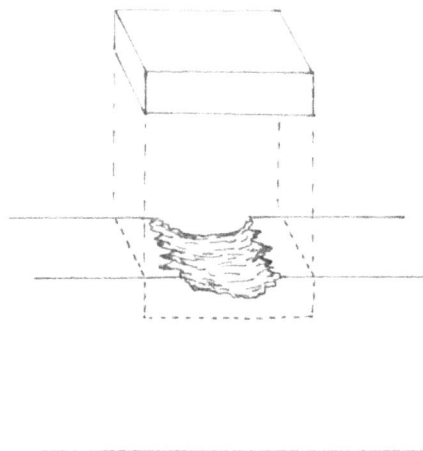

When repairing a damaged wood item, cut around damaged area and insert new section with glue.

to see where they touch. This shows him where the high spots are that can be sanded or filed a bit more until the separate pieces finally fit together as perfectly as possible.

Dealing with a Hole in a Wall

Another example of where cutting away a section around the damaged area before making the repair would be an appropriate strategy is with the following method for repairing a hole in a wall. The standard approach to fixing a hole in a plaster or sheetrock wall is to secure a section of screen or chicken wire in the hole and then fill the space with plaster. I recently watched a demonstration on television of an easier and better method for repairing holes ranging from about half-dollar size on up to the diameter of a cantaloupe that I think is worth explaining here.

For this method, you will need a spare scrap of sheetrock larger than the diameter of the hole, some sheetrock joint compound (commonly called "mud"), a pencil, drywall saw (or steak knife in a pinch), box cutter or utility knife, and a putty knife. Here's how you do it:

1. Cut a square hole in the wall around the damaged area.
2. Cut a piece out of the scrap to create a patch that will more than cover the square hole you've cut in the wall. The patch should be considerably larger than the square hole. Its general shape doesn't matter.
3. In pencil, draw on the backside of the patch a square shape that roughly matches the hole you've cut in the wall. The drawn square can be slightly smaller than the square hole in the wall, but it should be close in size and shape, as it will soon fit into the hole like a plug. It should be roughly centered in the back of the patch.
4. Using your box cutter, score four grid lines across the entire back of the patch that outline your pencil marks, taking care *not* to cut completely through the patch of sheetrock, as you'll want to keep the face paper of the patch intact. The face paper will hold the plug in position when you fit it into the wall.
5. Peel back along the score lines and remove the material surrounding the square on the back of the patch so you end up with the square plug of

sheetrock attached to the backside of the larger section of face paper.
6. Fit the plug into the hole in the wall and spread some watered-down mud over the face paper (now flat against the wall covering the hole) with the putty knife and smooth it out. Let it set up overnight before painting the wall.

CLOTHING REPAIRS

Everyone wears clothing, so in my view, everyone should know a few basic clothing repair methods. A lot of clothing repairs are easy to make with just a needle and thread. Running the simple in-and-out stitch is about the simplest thing anyone can ever learn how to do, and this general method has connected a lot of pieces of cloth fabric since

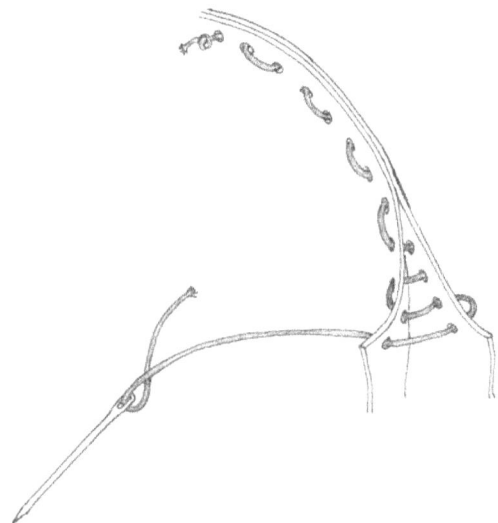

The simplest type of running in-and-out stitch. Tie off both ends and you're done.

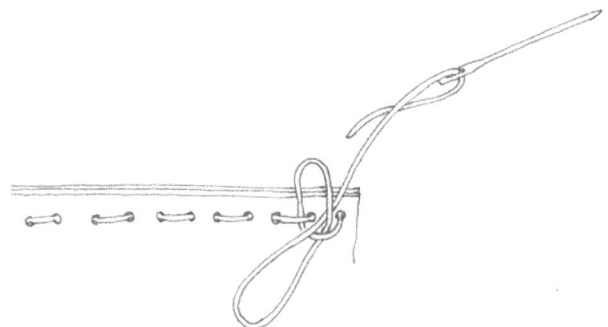

One method for tying off the end of a stitch.

134

the advent of woven cloth, and even long before that with animal skins.

You can assemble a basic sewing kit with just a selection of needles, threads, and buttons; a small pair of scissors; pins and a pin cushion; a thimble; and a flexible tape measure. You can buy a little, inexpensive stitch-puller hook wherever sewing supplies are sold, but I've found X-Acto knives very handy for cutting stitches between seams for removal.

Holes in pants pockets are a common nuisance, but they are usually quick and easy to fix. Where the original stitches in a pocket seam have simply come undone, the hole can be mended by hand-sewing the seam closed again. Occasionally, however, the inside of a pocket will have holes created by extensive wear from heavy key rings, pocket knives, or coins, and sometimes the pocket liner or pouch material will be worn so thin that it won't hold stitches.

I discovered an effective way to close holes in pocket liners where sewing isn't a viable solution. All you have to do is pinch or twist the torn portion into a small wad of cloth and tightly bind this section with wraps of strong thread or rubber bands.

A hole in the corner of this pocket liner is closed with a rubber band.

This is a slightly bulkier repair than neatly sewn seams, but it's quick and easy to make, and it does prevent your key chain from working its way down the leg of your pants or loose change from dribbling wherever you go. I would consider this only a temporary repair, not intended to last very long or survive the washing machine. Amazingly, though, I used this method to bind the worn-through corners of one pair of pants, and it is *still* holding after at least two years and through numerous washings! I never would have believed this makeshift repair would have lasted even half that long.

Buttons on shirts can eventually pop loose when the thread holding them on wears and breaks. Whenever I replace a button on an article of clothing, I try to use the strongest thread I can find to prevent losing the button again. Also, stretched-out buttonholes is a common occurrence with cotton shirts. Adding a few extra stitches at both ends of the slot-shaped buttonholes can help prevent the hole from stretching and keep the buttons from slipping out. To replace missing buttons, don't forget the expedient method I mentioned earlier in this chapter—fashioning replacements out of cut and drilled circles of rawhide.

The elbows in shirtsleeves and the knees in trouser legs typically sustain greater wear than most other parts of clothing, especially with kids' clothes, and holes occasionally wear through in these areas. The functional life of an article of clothing can be extended by sewing on cloth patches to cover the tears and stop them from spreading, or just to provide added protection to these high-wear areas. If one patch fails to provide sufficient reinforcement to a badly torn or worn area, it might be practical to sew patches on both sides to sandwich the damaged area between them.

In a pinch, fabric can be rejoined with a stapler or dots of polyurethane. Hot-melt glue works well, too, as it's ready to use instantly. Don't overlook the several types of fabric glue that are available specifically for bonding fabric, either temporarily or permanently.

Repairs to Leather

Stitch repairs to leather products can be easy to make with a few additional tools. A sharp awl for punching the holes before running the needle is essential. With stiff, heavy cowhide, it might be practical to drill the stitch holes with a drill press and a tiny drill bit. Saddle makers and leather workers often use this method. Larger holes are required for lacing, and for that a rotary leather punch is a useful tool. (Quick tip: You can stop a short rip from spreading in leather simply by drilling or punching a hole at each end of the rip. The same technique works with materials like vinyl, paper, or even thin sheet aluminum.)

A thimble is a handy item to help push the needle through the material, and a palm thimble is very easy to make. You just cut its shape out of a scrap of heavy cowhide or tough rawhide, and then create a hole at one end that loops over your thumb to keep it in your palm while you sew. It's just a thick piece of hide that helps you push on the back of the needle. I always keep a small pair of duckbill pliers at hand when sewing leather, as I often use it to pull on the front of the needle to help it through the stitch holes.

For most of my leather sewing projects, I like to use waxed linen saddle thread and the largest size of glovers' needles. Small spring clamps can be used to keep separate pieces together and properly aligned until they are sewn up. Some leather crafters also glue the pieces together before they sew the seams.

CHAPTER 6

Doing Your Own Soldering, Brazing, and Welding

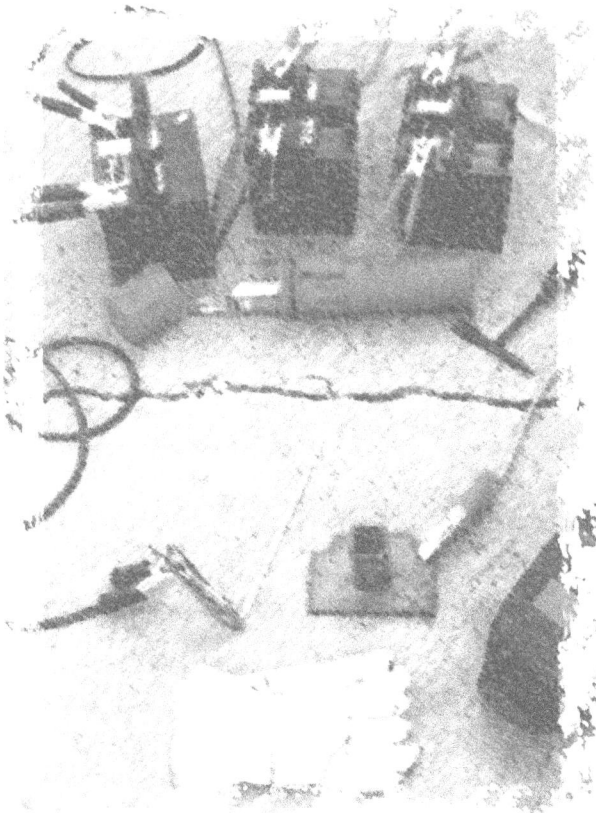

We have seen how the ability to connect things together is essential to numerous repair tasks, but acquiring the ability to solidly and permanently join two pieces of metal really opens up a lot of doors for the makeshifter. It not only provides the most practical method for repairing broken metal products in many situations, it also allows for the fabrication of certain metal items that might be extremely difficult to produce by other means.

Some people who have never worked with hot metal might tend to shy away from soldering or welding activities, but this need not be so. The keys to safely soldering or welding are (as with every other potentially dangerous activity): 1) thoroughly understanding the process and all the potential hazards, 2) creating a controlled work environment with due consideration to the first item, and 3) paying close attention to the details. Adhere to this methodology and you should enjoy a safe and successful future with these activities.

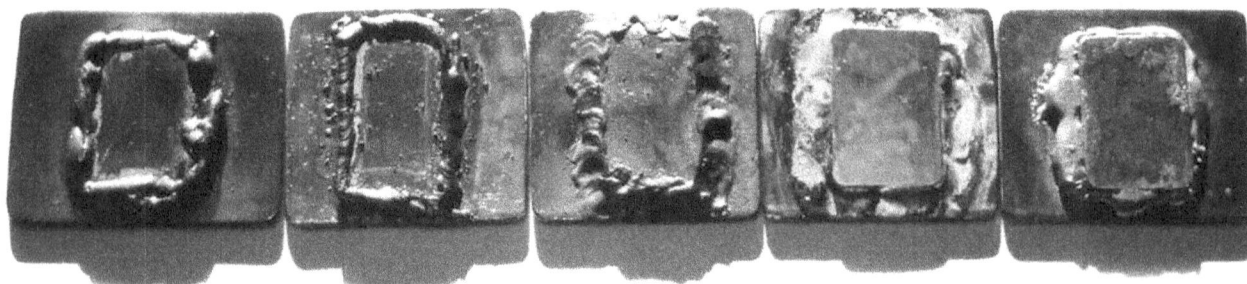

| MIG-welded connection | stick-welded connection | gas-welded connection | brazed connection | soldered connection |

Several different connection samples with small steel plates.

SOLDERING AND BRAZING

Soldering and brazing are similar processes in that with both methods, molten metal is introduced like an adhesive to separate metal parts to bond them together, in this case by capillary action. The metal parts (the base metals) are not themselves melted—only the solder or braze filler metal is melted. An analogy would be applying glue to boards to stick them together; in soldering or brazing, the molten filler metal can be likened to glue that sticks the metal parts together.

By contrast, welding involves the actual melting and fusing together of the base metals where they are joined. One of the biggest differences between the methods is the temperature range wherein each is accomplished. Soldering is performed at much lower temperature than what is required with any of the various welding methods. (We'll get into welding in more detail below.)

Soft solder (so called because it is composed of soft metal alloys) commonly comes as coiled wire, whereas hard solder (i.e., alloys with 70 percent or more silver) is available as wire, strips, or sheets. Most lead/tin and other alloys of soft-metal solders melt at a temperature somewhere between 300°F and 600°F. Hard solder melts in the 1,200°F to 1,400°F range.

I divide soldering into two basic categories: 1) soldering with a soldering gun or a soldering iron, which is practical for electronic circuitry connections and other low-heat applications, and 2) soldering with the flame of a torch, which works well where a larger volume of heat is appropriate,

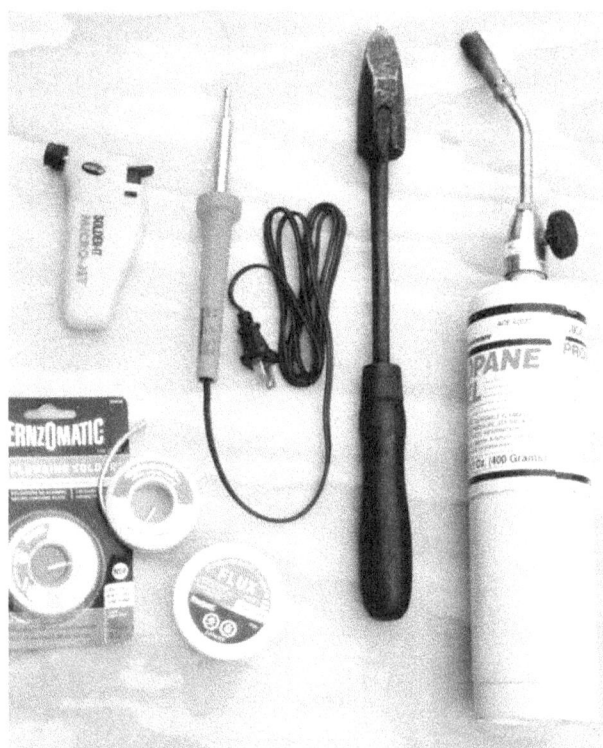

A few examples of different soldering tools, left to right: 1) compact butane soldering torch, 2) hobby electronics soldering iron, 3) old-time soldering iron, and 4) propane gas torch. At bottom left are typical packages of wire solder and a container of flux.

such as with pipe connections, jewelry crafts, and such tasks as attaching sight blades onto gun barrels.

Molten metal will not normally adhere to oxidized surfaces, so an oxide-removing agent known as a flux is commonly used in soldering, brazing, and some types of welding. With soldering, the two basic types of fluxes are rosin and acid. The acid-based fluxes tend to be more effective but are also more corrosive and caustic than rosin flux. Rosin is therefore preferable with things like electronic circuits, where it would be difficult to clean the work after the soldering is complete.

Fluxes are available in paste and liquid form, and some special solders come with flux in their cores, making them simpler to use because they don't require the extra step of fluxing the work before applying the solder. Likewise, some braze rods come with a coating of flux on the outside of the rod, and these have become very popular for their ease of use.

Soldering irons and guns rely on the transfer of heat from the tip of the tool to the work in order to melt the solder. The solder is not applied directly to the tip of the iron (which is usually made of copper) but to the work surface that has been heated by the iron. Tinning, however, is the process of coating the tip of the iron with a thin layer of solder to improve its ability to transfer the heat. Tinning is sometimes also done to the surfaces of the base metals to enhance adhesion, especially when heating with a flame.

The old traditional soldering irons were externally heated by either a gas flame or in a special oven for this purpose. Today, soldering irons and guns are most often electrically heated with their own heating elements

Since solder often contains lead, crafters should understand and be mindful of the potential health hazards associated with lead (although lead-free solders are pretty common these days). Besides the usual safety measures when working with high heat (fire extinguisher, eye protection, work gloves, etc.), care should be exercised in the handling of the gun or iron with its hot tip, which should never come in contact with a flammable surface for any duration.

The process of soldering or brazing consists of four basic steps: 1) cleaning and preparing the surfaces to be joined, 2) heating the base metals, after tinning the tip of the iron if using a soldering iron, 3) adding flux to the base metals or filler metal, and 4) adding the molten solder or braze filler to join the base metals. As already noted, you can skip step 3 if you use solder with a flux core or flux-coated braze rod.

Soldering with a flame is easily done with most wire solders using a small, inexpensive propane torch. For best results, remember to use the flame to heat the base metals and not the solder directly. One of the most common problems encountered by beginning crafters when soldering or brazing is failing to heat the base metals sufficiently. The base metals should be hot enough to allow the solder or braze filler to completely liquefy and easily flow to wherever it is needed.

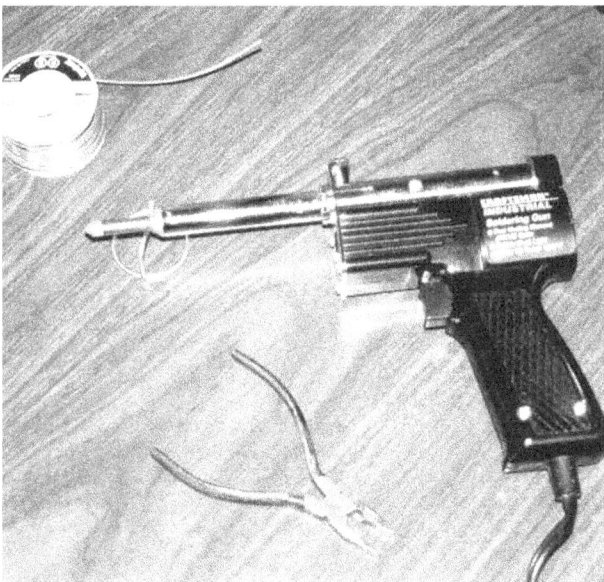

Typical soldering gun.

Soldering with an electric soldering gun.

Soldering with a road flare. Note that the flame is directed to the backside of the work surface to minimize contamination.

I discovered that in a pinch, it is possible to solder using an emergency road flare for the heat source. Road flares provide a fairly hot, steady flame that will burn for up to 15 minutes, which is more than enough time to accomplish most soft solder tasks that can be done with a torch. The biggest challenge with the road flare is its dirty flame, which leaves sulfur-white residue on everything heated by it. I found that by directing the flame to the backside of the work, the surfaces to be joined are kept reasonably uncontaminated. Soldering with a flare would only be an option where proper ventilation is available, preferably in the outdoors, and where the potential fire hazard is easily contained.

Brazing requires more heat than what is required for most soldering operations. Braze rods consisting of alloys of brass, bronze, nickel, silver, or aluminum all have considerably higher melting temperatures, typically 1,150°F to 1,750°F. A little propane torch used for thawing frozen water pipes,

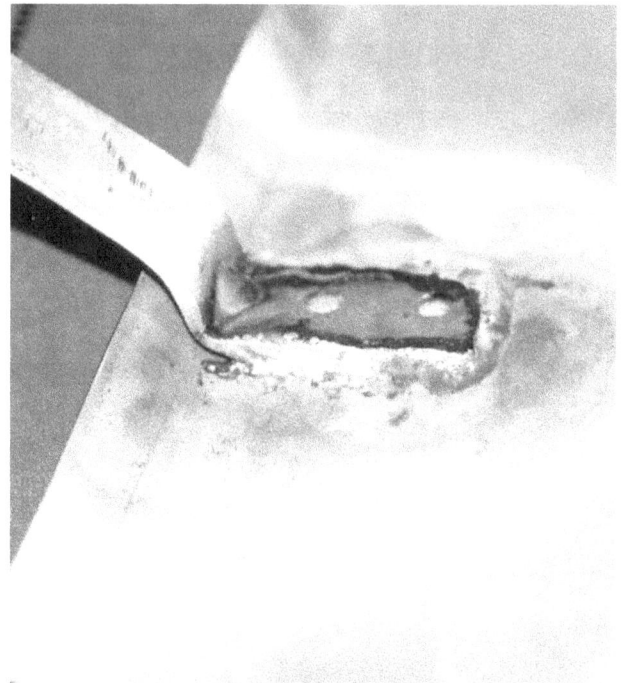

A typical brazed connection.

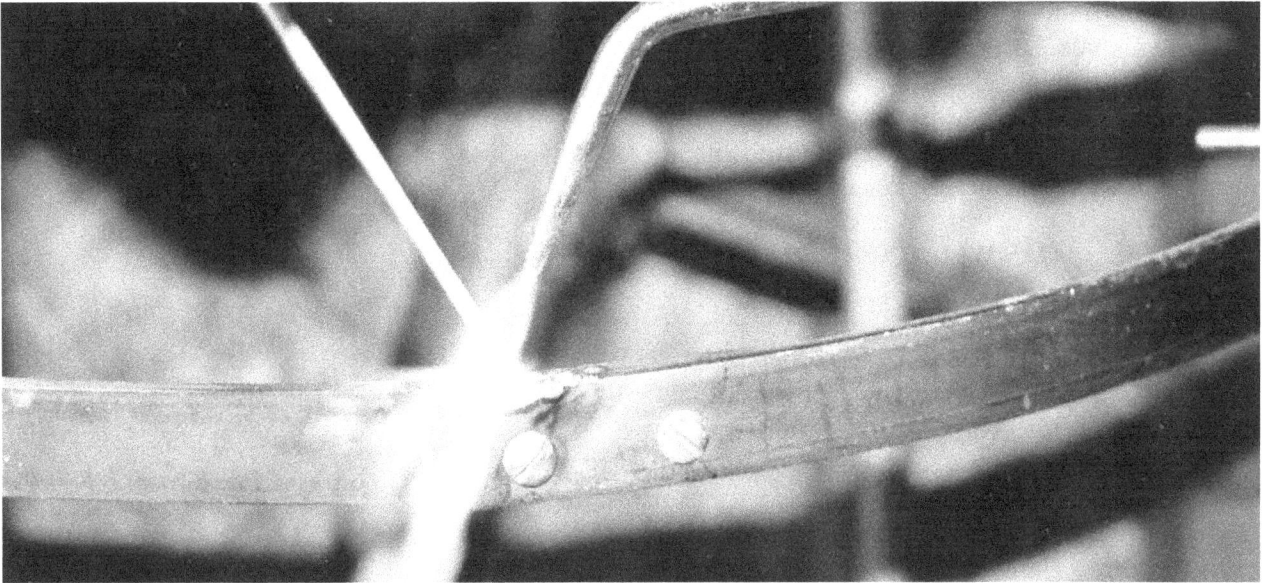

Brazing with an oxyacetylene torch.

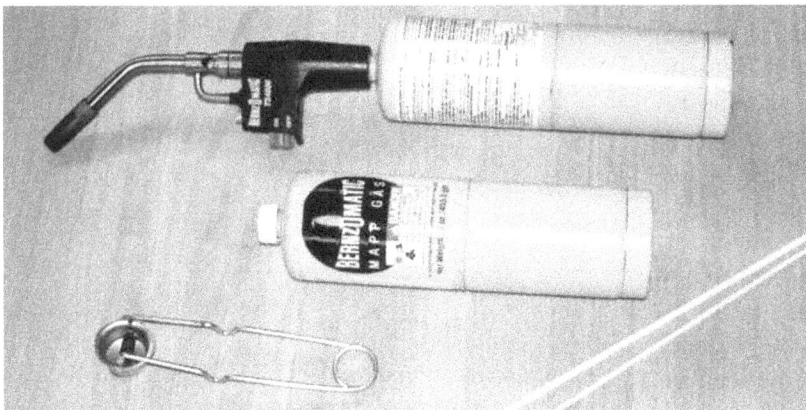

Numerous small braze jobs can be accomplished with an inexpensive MAPP gas torch, shown here with striker, flux-coated braze rods, and extra bottle.

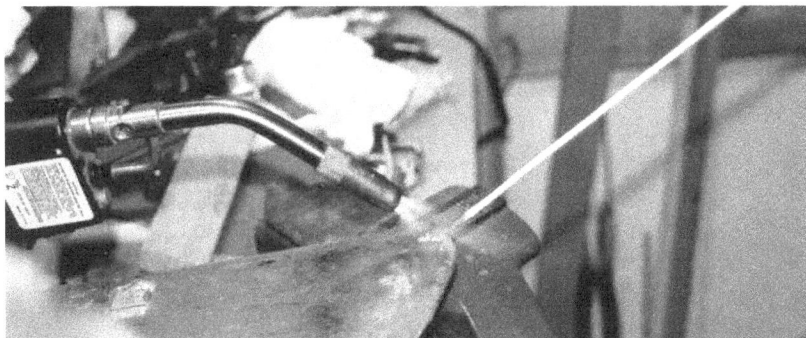

Brazing a crack in a shovel blade with MAPP gas.

while perfectly adequate for flame soldering, just doesn't throw enough heat for brazing.

Oxyacetylene welding torches have long been the traditional equipment for most brazing operations. However, I have managed to braze a number of lightweight seams and connections with a fairly inexpensive ($40) torch that uses MAPP gas, or liquefied petroleum gas. MAPP is a trade name for a Dow Chemical Company product, and small cylinders of this gas, as well as the easy-to-use BernzOmatic torches, are sold in every hardware store I have visited in recent years. Many of these torches even have a convenient trigger-activated, built-in lighter/striker, eliminating the need for a separate striker. This type of torch provides a cheap and easy way to accomplish brazing.

Even as strong as a good soft-soldered connection can be, properly brazed connections are considerably stronger. Remember, for the braze filler to reach all the surfaces properly and provide adequate adhesion, the base metals must be hot enough. I heat the base metals to a glowing red before adding the braze filler. I normally prefer the flux-coated rods (available at most hardware stores) for their convenience.

GAS WELDING

The most authoritative book I have ever seen on the subject of welding is *Welder's Handbook* by Richard Finch. In it, Finch recommends mastering gas welding before learning any other type of welding. Not only is a gas torch quite versatile, he points out, but perhaps more important to the beginning welder is the view that mastering heat control with a flame, as well as the basics of forming a puddle of molten metal, will enhance one's grasp of other techniques that rely on the same fundamental principles.

A gas torch is certainly *not* the easiest type of welding equipment to learn how to use (I would venture to say that MIG welding probably wins in that category nowadays), and melting and fusing metals with the flame of a torch is slower than electric arc welding. But a gas torch can be used for fuse-welding steel as well as for brazing, soldering, cutting, and simply heating sections of metal for heat-treating or forming operations, much the way one might use a small forge. You can't perform some of these tasks with a stick or MIG welder. Another distinct advantage of the torch, besides its versatility, is that it doesn't depend on an electric power source.

Oxyacetylene (oxygen + acetylene gas) is the most common gas welding combination. The torch equipment utilizes two separate tanks, or cylinders: one for acetylene gas and the other for oxygen under pressure. A complete outfit will include the tanks, hoses, regulator gauges, usually one welding and one

cutting torch body, plus an assortment of tips for different uses. You can buy a complete small starter kit, such as the Harris Port-A-Torch, including full

A small oxyacetylene torch outfit like this one is compact and economical.

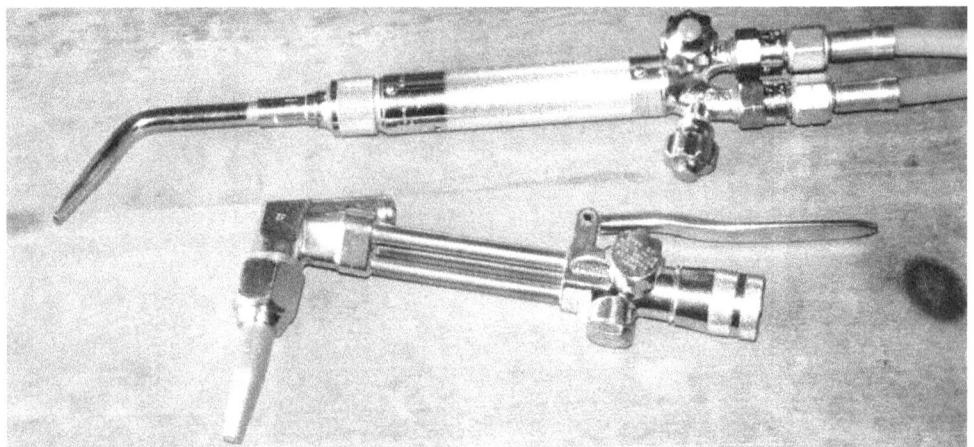

A complete torch kit will normally include a welding/brazing tip (top) and a cutting tip (bottom).

cylinders, for around $300 at the time of this writing, or you can spend $500 or more for professional-quality equipment. Either way, the beginner should study available literature on the subject and ideally take a welding class before connecting it all up and lighting the torch for the first time.

Welding rods for a gas torch used to weld steel are plain, mild-steel round rods of small diameter, commonly 1/16 to 1/8 inch, most often sold in 3-foot lengths. The best quality gas-welding rods are bare steel—they are not coated with any other type of material. The cheaper variety available at the local hardware store will usually be copper coated. There is no advantage I know of to using copper-coated rod, and some professional welders insist that the copper can actually interfere with a quality weld, in addition to creating a potential health hazard with the copper vapors. The copper coating merely eases the manufacturing of the rods.

Unlike braze or other types of welding rods, the rod for gas welding steel is used without flux. The flame fed by acetylene and oxygen, which typically burns at a temperature higher than 5,700°F (neutral flame temperature), is directed onto the base metals such that a molten puddle is formed, and the end of the welding rod is dipped into it as the filler metal is needed. The process is simple in concept, but it does take practice to perfect. Beginners tend to either fail to heat the metal enough or overheat and burn the metal.

Different sizes of oxygen and acetylene cylinders can be purchased or rented from a welding supply store, where they can also be refilled or replaced when emptied. Cylinders should be kept upright and secured so they can't fall over. Acetylene can be unstable in a cylinder that isn't standing upright, and a full oxygen bottle that falls from sufficient height to break off the valve becomes a dangerous rocket (oxygen is contained at pressures as high as 2,200 psi), so careful handling of these cylinders is imperative.

An oxyacetylene outfit has three sets of valves: the cylinder valves, the regulator valves, and the torch valves for both oxygen and acetylene. The hoses are color coded to minimize confusion; the acetylene hose will be red, and the oxygen will be either green or black. Also, the fittings for acetylene have left-hand threads and screw on counterclockwise, while oxygen fittings have right-hand threads and screw on clockwise.

I followed the recommendation in Finch's book and installed flashback arrestors on my gas welding hoses. Some of the more expensive oxyacetylene equipment is sold with arrestors built in. Flashback is a potentially disastrous condition where the torch flame burns back up the hoses and into the equipment, often producing a hair-raising squeal that lets you know what's happening. Reverse-flow check valves that minimize the chance of mixing gases in the hoses are also highly recommended.

Eye protection for gas welding is accomplished with dark welding goggles. These do not have to be as darkly shaded as lenses for arc welder helmets, because a torch flame is not nearly as bright and does not create ultraviolet light like an electric arc. Proper protective clothing for most welding activities

Flashback arrestors installed between torch body and hoses.

includes a welder's jacket, heavy denim long pants with no cuffs that could trap sparks, high-top leather work boots, and leather gloves. The object is to protect the eyes and the body from burns.

A torch should be ignited with a striker that generates sparks and never with an open flame. Most instructional welding books also recommend checking the equipment for leaks before lighting the torch. One method for doing this entails adjusting the regulator gauges for 20 lbs. oxygen and 10 lbs. acetylene with the cylinder valves open and the torch valves closed. Then close the cylinder valves and turn the adjusting screws on the regulator valves counterclockwise one turn. Observe the gauges for several minutes to see if the readings change. If the readings don't change, the system has no leaks. Another method is to apply an oil-free soapy solution to the equipment and watch for bubbles that would indicate leaks. Oil or grease should never be allowed to come in contact with any gas welding equipment.

It cannot be stressed enough that whenever working with heat and flames, one should always be very conscious of the potential hazards. Adequate ventilation in the work area; the ability to immediately extinguish any fires, including the torch flame; avoiding unintentional ignitions or combustions of shop materials or chemicals; and controlled, safe handling of the equipment are all critical considerations. Welding or torch cutting is best avoided on or around gas tanks, oil drums, or flammable material containers unless the welding operator is an experienced expert who specializes in this sort of thing.

You need to become familiar with several different flames when using an oxyacetylene torch. The first is the pure acetylene flame one sees immediately after lighting the torch. It will be a thick yellow flame that produces black soot. Right away, the oxygen valve should be opened to add oxygen to the flame. A gas-rich flame is called a carburizing or reducing flame, which throws a long, feathery, orange-white outer flame enveloping a light green inner flame that extends an inch or so beyond a light blue-white cone at the torch nozzle. This flame might be used for soldering and brazing. An oxygen-rich flame, called an oxidizing flame, burns hotter, and it will have an almost colorless to light blue feathery flame with a small white cone at the nozzle and no inner flame. It will make a loud

Igniting the torch the correct way—with a striker/torch igniter.

Acetylene-only flame—orange with black smoke.

Soft reducing flame with some oxygen added. The inner flame near the nozzle is light green.

hissing sound. The most commonly used flame in fuse welding is the neutral flame having equal oxygen and acetylene. It will have a long, feathery, whitish-bluish flame with a distinctive light blue cone and no inner flame. It won't have any loud hissing sound.

Cutting operations using a torch require more oxygen than gas to provide an oxidizing flame. When fuse welding with an oxyacetylene torch, the regulators would normally be adjusted between 3 and 5 psi for both the gas and oxygen; for cutting, 3 to 5 psi is normal for the acetylene, but the oxygen typically would be adjusted to about 15 psi for most cutting operations and slightly higher for the thickest material. As previously noted, the special cutting torch body and tips are required.

It is easy to think of the common welding methods as they apply to joining alloys of steel, but a number of aluminum alloys are commonly welded as well. Aluminum has a much lower melting temperature than steel (1,218°F to 1,271°F, depending on the alloy), so welding aluminum with a gas torch is most easily done using hydrogen instead of acetylene because of the oxy-hydrogen's lower flame temperature. Check with your local

welding supply store for Welco #120 welding rods and the best flux for welding aluminum. Hydrogen is not considered a suitable gas for welding steel.

MIG WELDING

I suggested earlier that MIG welding is possibly the easiest type of welding to learn, and I believe this is generally true. My dad had almost no prior welding experience when he purchased his MIG welder about 15 years ago, but within a very short time he had become quite proficient with it. Some of the repairs he has since made to broken gun parts using his MIG have been truly amazing, in my opinion. One example that comes to mind was an old double-barrel flintlock pistol with one of its side hammers missing a large portion of its top half. Dad managed to build up enough metal onto the existing section with his MIG welder to sculpt a completely restored flintlock hammer that very closely matched the original hammer on the opposite side.

The term MIG is an acronym for metal inert gas. This type of welding is also known as gas metal arc welding (GMAW), or sometimes just wire feed. As these names imply, the process involves the controlled feeding of a wire electrode (fed from a spool through a special nozzle) to the grounded work, where an electric arc melts the base metals together with the wire. To prevent oxidation in the molten metal, an inert gas such as CO_2 or sometimes argon with helium is delivered through the nozzle to surround the wire electrode being fed to the work and shield the arc from the atmosphere.

Unlike stick arc welded connections that would normally be cleared of the crusty surface slag with a chipping hammer after the welding, gas-shielded MIG welds are characteristically cleaner and without slag scale or very much spatter. Wire-feed welding can be done without the shielding gas, but the gas clearly enhances the process.

Flux-cored arc welding (FCAW) is a wire-feed process similar to MIG, except that with FCAW the wire contains flux in its core rather than using shielding gas to prevent oxidation.

MIG welding has become very popular with both hobbyists and professional welders because it works so well for numerous applications and is so easy to do. It also produces what I consider to be very nice looking welds most of the time.

Miller's Millermatic 90 MIG welder.

Gene Ballou demonstrating the MIG welding process. Note: I recommend wearing welding gloves.

TIG WELDING

Another specialized type of welding is called TIG (tungsten inert gas), or GTAW (gas tungsten-arc weld). When it first became popular in the 1940s, it was commonly referred to as Heliarc, which was the brand name of the TIG torches developed by the Linde Division of Union Carbide that used helium as the shielding gas. Helium has since been replaced mostly by argon and other gases in TIG welding.

TIG welding tends to be more precise and is better for smaller or intricate applications than either MIG or other arc welding methods, but it is generally considered more difficult to learn, and it is also a slower welding process—in this respect, it is similar to gas welding. The TIG torch uses a small, pointed, tungsten electrode to accurately direct the electric arc where needed. The arc is shielded with the gas, very similar to the MIG process, but a separate filler metal is added just as with oxyacetylene welding since the tungsten electrode is nonconsumable—the electrode is not melted in TIG welding.

ARC WELDING

The least sophisticated of the arc welding processes, correctly called shielded-metal arc welding (SMAW), or sometimes loosely called stick welding or scratch-start welding, is in many ways the simplest and certainly the oldest of the electric welding methods.

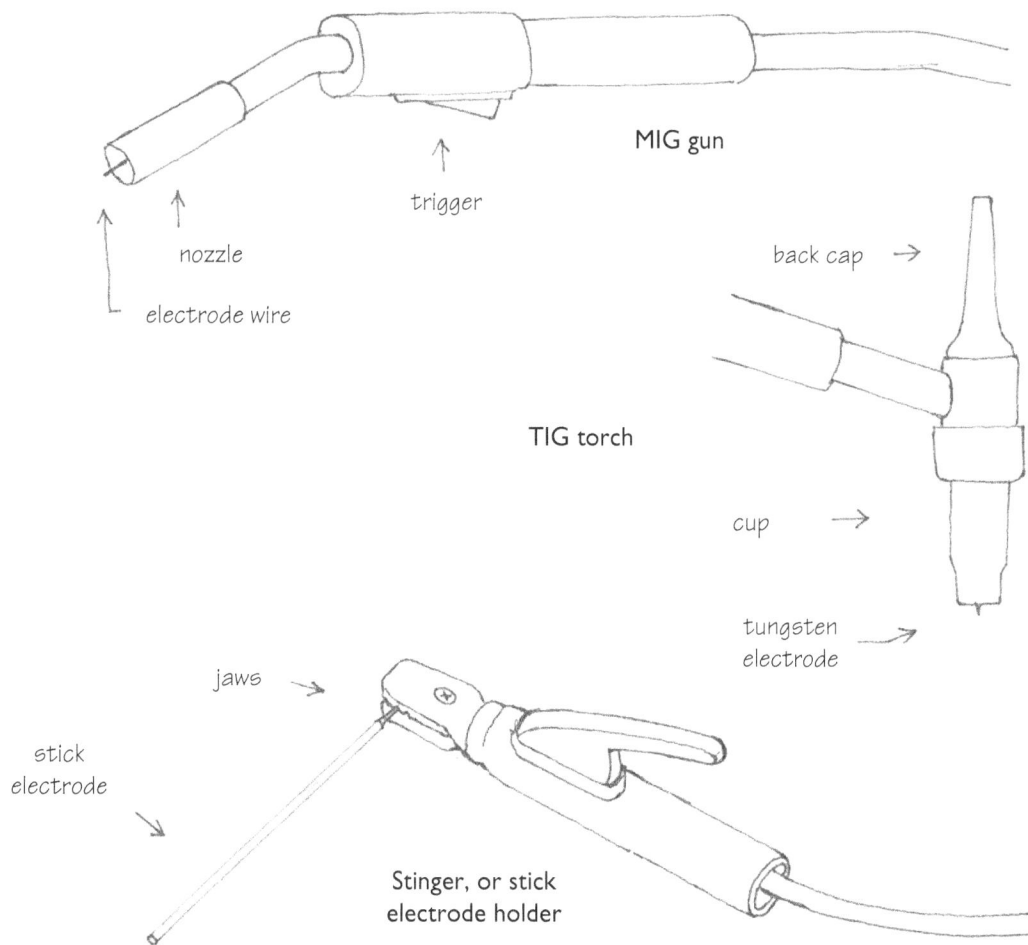

MIG gun

trigger

nozzle

electrode wire

back cap →

TIG torch

cup →

tungsten electrode →

jaws →

stick electrode

Stinger, or stick electrode holder

Several arc welder types.

A typical AC current arc welding machine consists primarily of iron-core transformers that convert the input current to the low-voltage/high-amperage electricity that provides the hot arcing needed for melting and fusing metal. These transformers are housed and protected inside a sheet metal case, usually with an electric fan or two to prevent the unit from overheating. Some of the circuit schematics for arc welders that I have seen are surprisingly simple. I have a tiny, inexpensive stick welder that runs on house current and utilizes only a single transformer to power the arc.

Besides the power cord, two cables extend from the machine: the work cable, or return lead cable that is attached to the grounding clamp, and the welding lead cable attached to the electrode holder (sometimes referred to as a stinger). In operation, the grounding clamp is fastened to the metal being welded (i.e., the base metal or workpiece), and a special flux-coated metal rod called a consumable electrode, which should be firmly held in the electrode holder, is scratched on the workpiece to start the arcing. The heat generated at the arc can be as high as 10,000°F—more than enough to liquefy any kind of metal you will ever weld.

It is vital that the equipment be grounded properly before turning on the machine and striking the arc. One should never allow any part of the body to make contact with the workpiece between the grounding clamp and the arcing electrode, where the current travels. When gas welding, one would be concerned mainly with control of flames, possible gas leaks, flashbacks, and pressurized cylinders; the big concerns with arc welding include flash burns, hostile light, hot sparks and molten metal, and especially electric shock (although the last hazard can be eliminated with a voltage reduction device, or VRD). The proper clothing for arc welding will be very much the same as with gas welding but should include a full-mask welder's helmet, having a lens with at least #10 or darker shade. (By contrast, an operator of an oxyacetylene torch might protect his eyes with goggles having #3, #4, or #5 shaded lenses.) You should also set up some type of barrier to shield the eyes of onlookers, pets, or farm animals from the arc welder's ultraviolet light.

The flux-coated, consumable electrodes come in various sizes and types for the different welding applications. Common designations like E6011, E6013, or E7018 make it easy to identify the type of electrode. The letter E indicates that it is an electrode. The first two digits show the tensile strength of the weld in thousands of pounds per square inch (E6011, for example, indicates 60,000 psi). The third digit defines the position in which the electrode can be used: 1 indicates all positions, 2 means flat or horizontal position only. The fourth digit identifies the composition of the electrode's flux coating and also the proper electrical current.

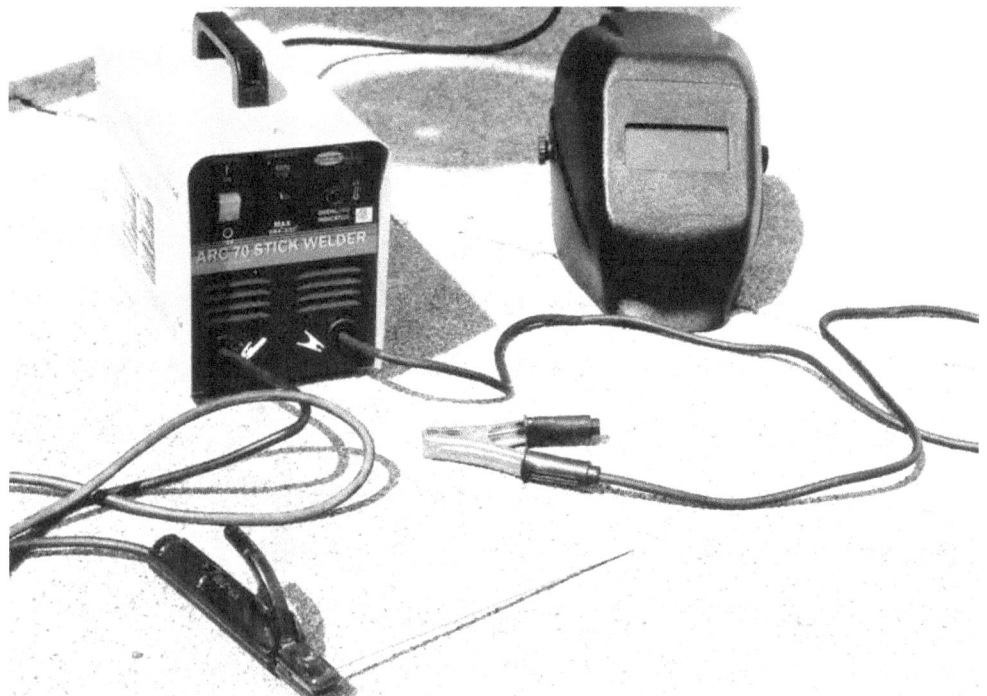

The smallest stick welders like this one cost only about $100, run off 120-volt house current, and can be a lot of fun to use for small welding projects.

For example, an E7018 electrode rod is coated with iron powder, low-hydrogen flux material (indicated by the 8) and is appropriate with either alternating or direct current (AC or DC). Electrodes come in sizes from 1/16-inch diameter (measuring wire diameter rather than the diameter of flux coating) to larger than 1/8 inch.

Again, the stick weld operator starts his arc by scratching the tip of the electrode on the work. The trick is holding the arc by maintaining the proper gap and running a consistent bead of molten metal. Occasionally the electrode will stick to the work and must be wiggled free. Unless an auto-darkening helmet is used, it can be a challenge starting the bead exactly where desired because the dark lens of the welder's helmet makes it next to impossible to see the work until the arcing starts. (A little portable quartz light can help here. It's bright enough to light up your work, and it won't blind you as long as you don't look right at it.) A common technique for producing a good weld bead is to run a progression of small, partially overlapping loops with the arc along the weld seam. You won't see how clean or messy the result is until you chip away the surface slag.

steel tubing

A good weld bead will usually look something like this.

Gaining any degree of proficiency with this takes some practice. Because the electrode is consumable, the process requires frequent changing of the welding rods in the electrode holder. Also note that the bare wire end of the electrode is held by the stinger.

Besides transformer-driven arc welders (commonly called buzz boxes because they make that noise when their power is on), there are arc welder designs that are powered by motor generators. These often produce DC electricity for welding, although you can find generator welders that work with AC. Generator welders have the obvious advantage of being able to operate off the grid, such as at a remote job site.

DC welding can be done in either of two polarity settings. Straight polarity (also called negative polarity) is where the electrode is electrically negative and the grounded workpiece is positive. The other setting is reverse polarity, where the electrode is positive and the work is negative. Straight polarity results in deeper weld penetration, because the workpiece gets hotter, whereas the electrode gets hotter (and more rapidly consumed) in reverse polarity. Reverse polarity is the more common setting in DC welding, because it tends to provide a steadier arc and makes the welding easier. This is not an issue with AC welding, where the polarity switches back and forth 120 times (60 cycles) a second.

The efficiency of an electric arc welding machine will be affected by its duty cycle. Basically, this refers to the duration a power supply can run without overheating. The duty cycle of an electric welding machine is the number of minutes the unit can operate at its peak performance during a 10-minute period. If your welder is rated with a duty cycle of 20 percent at its maximum amperage, it simply means that after two minutes of continuous operation at that level, the machine should be given a rest for eight minutes. Using the machine at lower amperage will increase its operational duty cycle.

Most of the standard-size and large electric welders require 220- or 240-volt current, limiting where they can be plugged in and used. Nowadays a number of small electric welders are available that plug into 120-volt house current. These are often suitable for small welding projects.

A Homemade Welding Machine

Instructions that explain in detail how to construct arc welders using transformers salvaged from discarded microwave ovens are provided on a number of Internet websites. Although this seems to be a popular makeshift project, I will explain how a

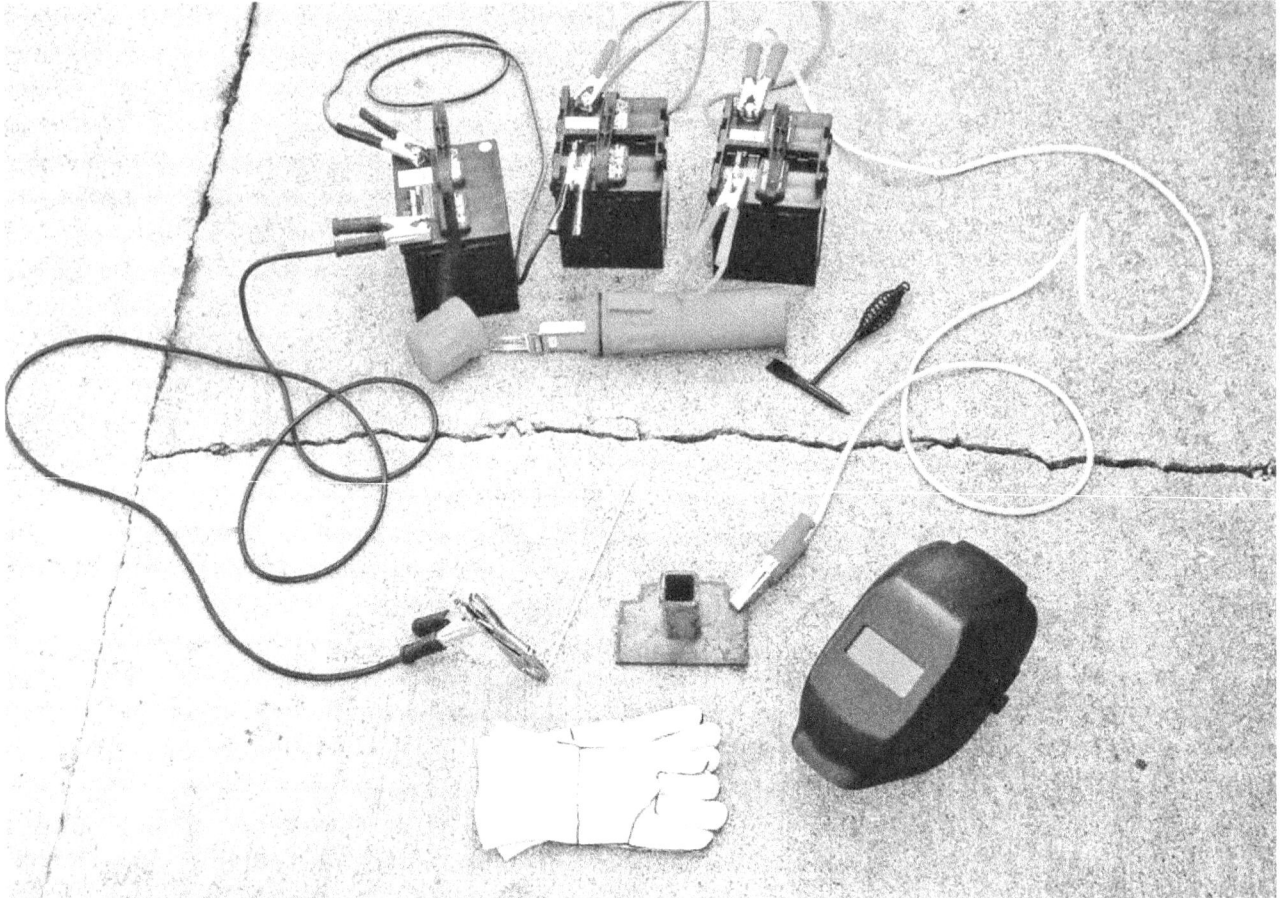

Everything needed for a quickie battery weld. Just below the batteries is an electrode container, sold in welding supply stores primarily for that purpose because the screw-on lid provides a good seal and keeps the stick electrodes dry. The T-shaped item to its right is a chipping hammer for chipping the glassy flux or slag off arc welds when the work is done.

simpler arrangement for quick weld repairs can be devised by almost anyone. It requires only several car batteries (it works best with three), two sets of jumper cables, a pair of locking pliers, and, of course, the consumable stick electrodes. Other than your welder's helmet, proper clothing, and welding gloves, these items are all you will need to make an effective DC stick welder, capable of welding 1/2-inch-thick steel.

The neat thing about this method is that you can do some welding in remote places with only the limited amount of gear mentioned above. I make no claims about how safe or dangerous this might be. The jumper leads can eventually get hot, and my guess is that overheated batteries from extensive, continuous welding could at some point create a hazard. I can only tell you that I have researched the

subject enough to learn how to make it work and have tried it out as I will explain here, and it worked surprisingly well for me without incident. Anyone else who attempts it does so at their own risk.

Some say that welding could be achieved using only two batteries (I haven't tried that yet), but to reliably strike and hold an arc for a good weld, you will want three 12-volt automotive batteries that still have enough charge left in them. They don't have to be any particular brand or size. You will be connecting them together in series, positive to negative, with your jumper cables.

Jumper cables are sold as pairs—the two leads will normally be joined together on their rubber covering to make them usable for jump-starting automobiles. Each lead has handy spring clamps at each end. You will need two sets of cables, and I

three 12-volt automotive batteries connected in series

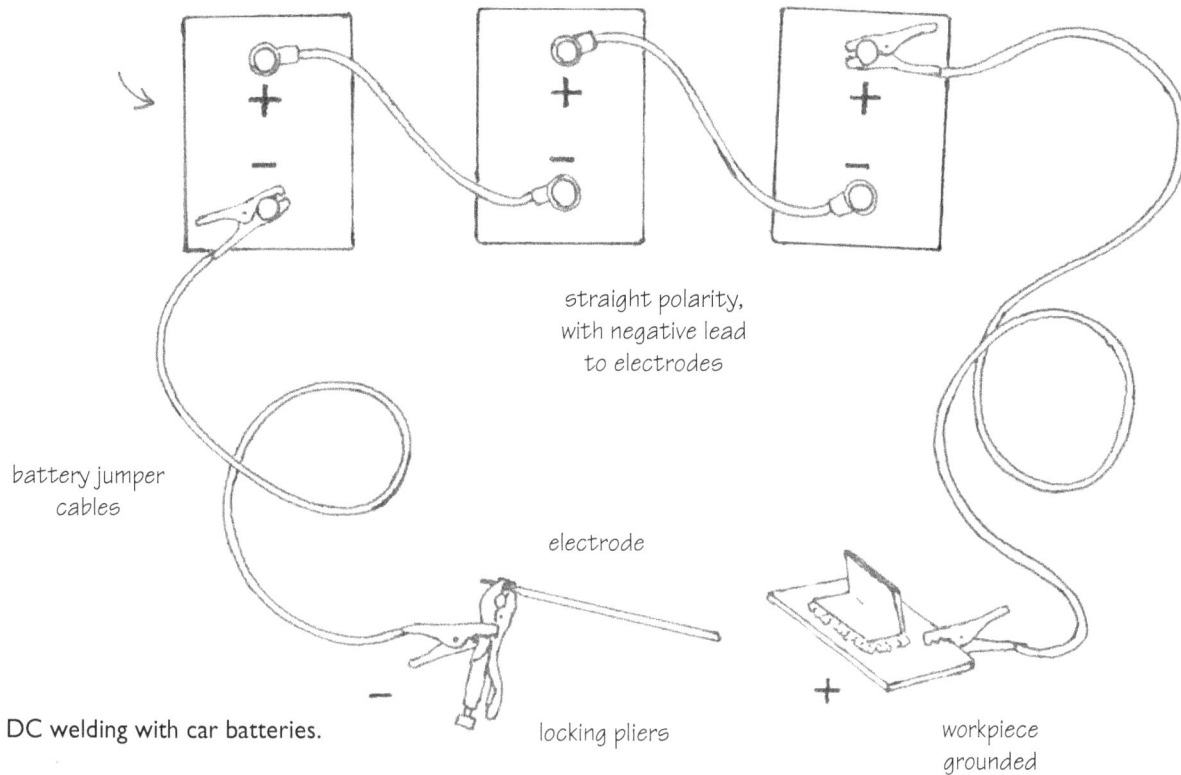

straight polarity,
with negative lead
to electrodes

battery jumper
cables

electrode

DC welding with car batteries.

locking pliers

workpiece
grounded

These thick pieces of steel were welded together using car batteries to power the arc.

would buy the heaviest-duty cables you can afford, because the smaller ones get warmer faster due to the increased resistance in smaller wires. You need to separate the leads so the two sets of cables become four individual cables. It is usually easy to just pull them apart. Two cables will be used to connect the terminals of the three batteries together in series, the third cable will be the ground lead that will clamp to the work, and the fourth will be clamped to the electrode holder—in this case locking pliers, as shown in the accompanying photos and illustration.

This is direct current, 36 volts, shown here set up with straight polarity. I used 1/8-inch E6013 electrodes in my experiment, and they worked great. It is a good idea to cover the batteries with a tarp to shield them from the sparks and hot spatter produced by the arcing, or at the very least execute the weld as far from the batteries as the leads will allow.

The obvious downside to battery welding is that it will drain the charge of the batteries. Adding a battery charger to the list of gear should extend the useful life of this setup to some extent.

WELD JOINTS

Anyone learning how to weld with any of the methods described in this chapter should become familiar with the different types of weld joints. A butt joint, which is a joining of the ends of two flat pieces butted together end-to-end, is a common type of connection in welding. Butt-welding thick pieces is usually accomplished best when the ends to be joined are first beveled to allow more area for the filler metal and provide deeper penetration. Avoid simple butt joints when soldering or brazing, because with those processes you are not actually melting the workpieces, so you won't end up with a sturdy connection. Whenever you need to solder or braze two pieces end-to-end, bridge them together with a third piece of metal to create a strap butt joint.

With most joints, it is easy to clamp the pieces together for the welding process, but this can be difficult with certain types of joints, such as T-joints using thin pieces of metal. Some method for propping up the vertical piece will be necessary to keep it in position until it is welded. Welding magnets are designed specifically for this purpose and come in a variety of configurations. With some of the more difficult joints, it might be practical to simply tack-weld the pieces at intervals to keep them in position before the full seam is welded.

FORGE WELDING

Basic blacksmithing techniques were covered in chapter 3. Now we will talk about how to use these skills to hammer weld two pieces of iron or steel together.

Forge welding was the first method ever used to weld two or more pieces of iron or steel together, and it is very

different from any other welding method. In this process, no filler metals are added to the base metals; instead, the base metals are heated and simply beaten together with hammer blows to form one more or less homogeneous piece. The pieces actually merge together where they are joined, and therefore forge welds lack the characteristic bead common to most other types of weld seams.

Forge welding can be tricky, because everything has to be just right for it to work properly. If you get the metal too hot, it will burn. If it isn't hot enough, the metal won't fuse together. If the surfaces aren't adequately fluxed or become contaminated with oxides or other impurities, they

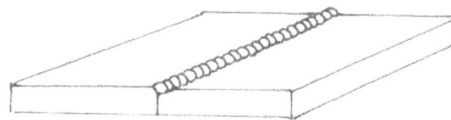
butt joint

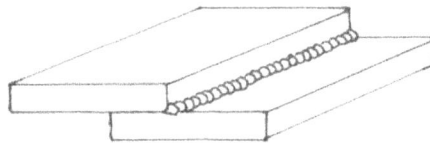
lap joint

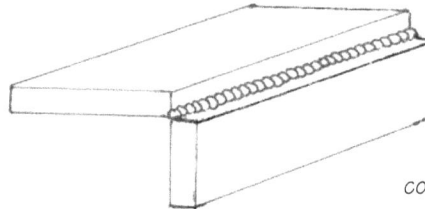
corner joint (outside corner shown here)

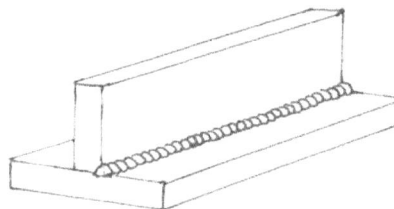
T-joint

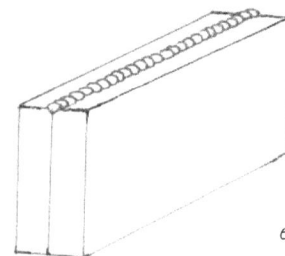
edge joint

The five common weld joints.

Sparks, flux particles, and globules of molten metal will splatter dramatically in every direction when glowing yellow steel is struck with a hammer, so eye protection, leather gloves, and a leather apron are essential whenever forge welding. Onlookers should also be kept at a safe distance.

Forge welding is normally accomplished in the following steps:

1. Heat the workpieces in the forge with the cleanest coke fire possible.
2. Add flux to the surfaces to be welded when scale begins to form—normally when the steel begins glowing a light cherry red.
3. Continue heating the steel until it turns a bright glowing yellow.
4. Move the workpieces quickly from the forge onto the anvil, keeping one piece directly over the other exactly as they are to be joined.
5. Pound the pieces together with usually one or two accurate hammer blows.

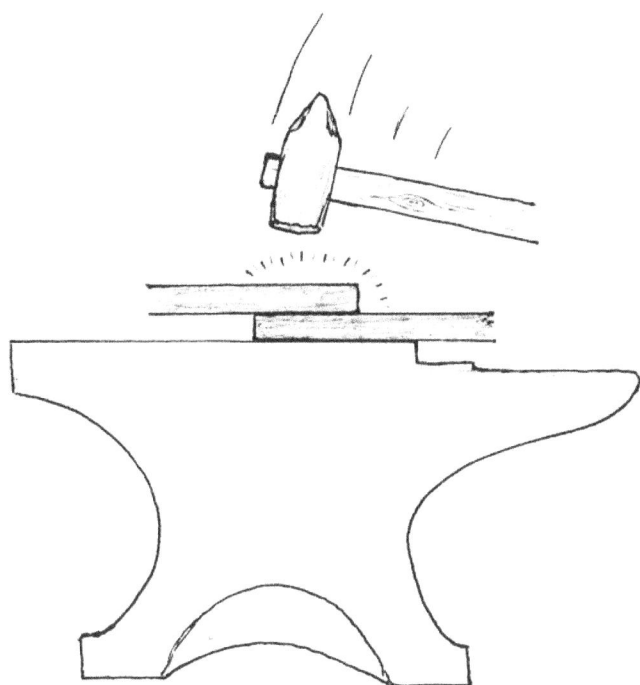

Forge welding heated iron over an anvil with hammer blows.

won't stick, no matter how hard they are persuaded with hammer blows.

Steel containing a lot of carbon presents a special challenge in forge welding. It is more easily overheated and ruined than is pure iron or low-carbon steel, and therefore it has a narrower heat range within which the welding can be accomplished. Plain carbon steel can be welded, but it takes enough practice and a thorough understanding of the process. Low-carbon mild steel is most commonly used nowadays. The old wrought iron that was once common for numerous applications is not very common now, but it was considered the easiest to forge weld because it contained almost no carbon.

Most forge welding is done at temperatures close to 2,000°F. Heating the material enough above this temperature—to the point where sparklers begin erupting from the surface and hissing sounds can be heard—will generally ruin any carbon steel. When you strike overheated steel with a hammer, it just crumbles to pieces. Blacksmiths typically describe the appearance of the ideal welding temperature as a buttery yellow, just before the white-hot range.

This sounds pretty simple, but a lot of things can go wrong that could spoil it for you. When the steel is hot enough to be welded, you will only have a brief window of time within which to move the pieces from the fire to the cold anvil and hammer them together, because the required welding heat fades fast. If the pieces remain in the hot fire a few seconds too long, they can easily be ruined. If your hammer blow isn't delivered straight down on the top piece, you might actually shove the pieces apart rather than together. The surfaces to be joined have to be clean enough. If you didn't get enough flux where it needed to be, the surfaces will resist welding together. I know firsthand about just how frustrating this process can be.

A popular practice with a lot of custom knife makers is to forge weld a stack of flat pieces of different steel alloys to produce a kind of laminated, Damascus-style work blank. Their usual method is to hold the individual pieces together with bindings of wire until welded, and this useful technique can be applied to simpler forge weld projects as well. It can save a lot of frustration trying to handle two hot pieces of steel, keeping them properly aligned and heated equally.

The most common flux used in forge welding is 20 Mule Team Borax. I have read about blacksmiths using iron filings, salt, and sand as flux, but to date I have only used borax. The flux combines with the oxides we see as scale forming on the surface of the heated steel that would impede the welding of the metal, and melts it away like a solvent.

CHAPTER 7

Things You Can Make Out of Other Things

T he modern makeshifter has a world full of raw materials at his disposal, as we learned in chapter 1, and sometimes it comes in the form of discarded junk that can be recycled or used to serve new, innovative purposes. In fact, a large percentage of the items I create in my home workshop are fabricated from other existing products rather than being devised entirely from raw materials. In some cases, it is more practical to modify or adapt existing things to meet your needs. The possibilities are infinite as to what types of things can be made from other things, limited only by the human imagination. Let's take a look at a few interesting ideas in this chapter.

COAT HANGERS

The common coat hanger is one of the most versatile products for makeshift projects. Coat hangers are cheap, widely available, found in almost every home in America, and routinely discarded whenever they bend out of their functional shape. Yet the gauge and strength of their wire make them uniquely suited for countless purposes.

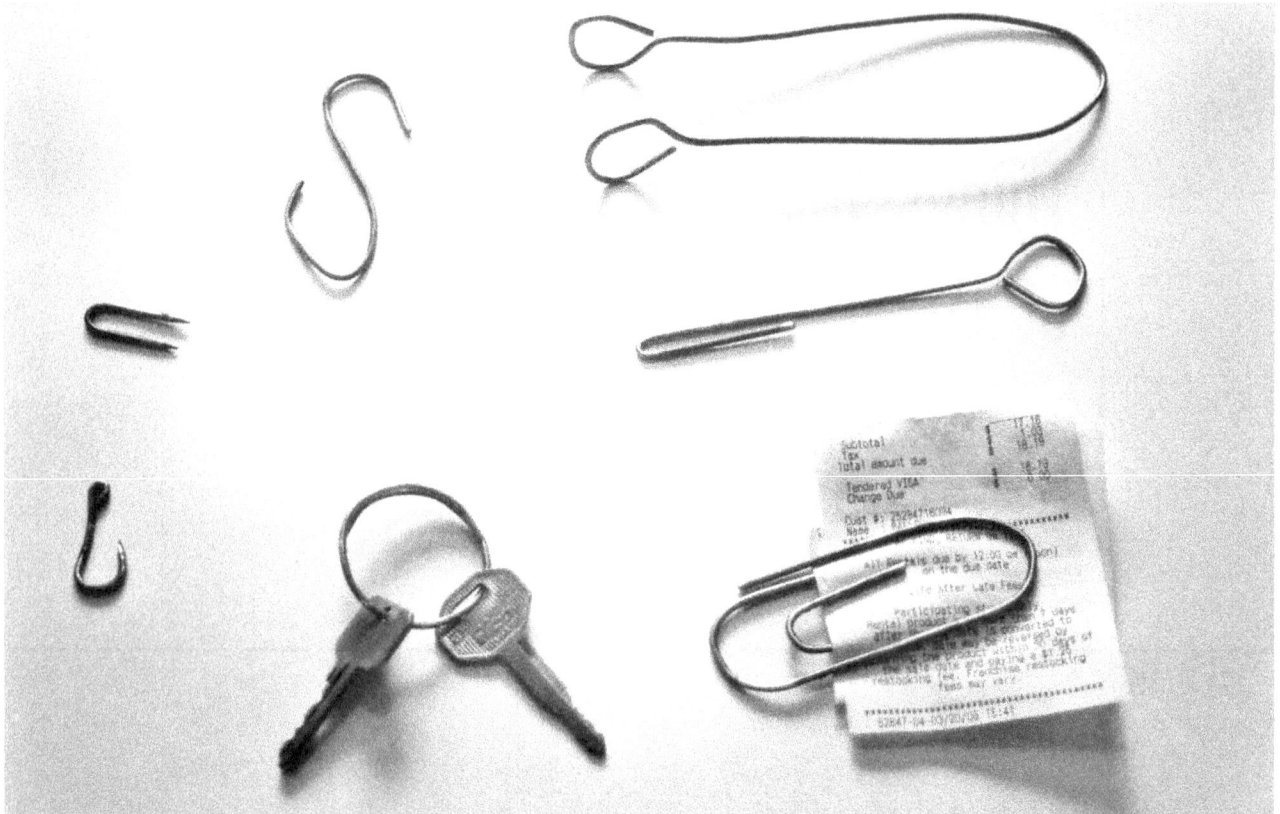

Coat hanger wire used here for (clockwise from left) makeshift fishhook, staple, S-hook, salad tongs, stir stick, large paperclip, and key ring.

I have used the wire from hangers to fashion grating in makeshift tin can stoves, bails for small buckets, a tool for unclogging a bathroom sink, a long-handled hook for recovering small items from narrow spaces, a frame for a butterfly or minnow net, grid bars in a small box trap, hinge pins for small doors, skewers for roasting marshmallows, staples, and pot holders, among other things. Others have used them as frames for paper-mâché projects, paintbrush drip hangers, and expedient TV antennas, for hanging potted plants, and to open locked car doors.

Coat hanger wires have been used for years as makeshift welding rod filler material by fabricators using oxyacetylene gas welders, being the right gauge for many projects and because they're cheap and widely available. However, this practice is generally not recommended because the paint on the wire can contaminate the weld and because the wire contains steel of unknown alloy.

Of course, coat hangers can be used as expedient, heavy-duty wire in a number of applications. I used wire from several coat hangers to wire up a loose board in my fence when all the other wire I had on hand proved not strong enough for the task.

The list of possible uses for coat hangers could probably fill a book. I like to keep some around the house for their versatility, even if they're not the greatest clothes-hanging devices ever invented.

COFFEE CANS

Metal coffee cans are similarly versatile. I'm a coffee drinker, and I hate throwing away good empty cans, so I always have coffee cans on hand for any makeshift use that comes to mind. I have attached a bail made from coat hanger wire to the rim of a coffee can to create a water bucket; cut a strip of metal from the side of one can, rolled it into

Clockwise from lower left: beer mug, barbecue, water pail, container for nails, water dipper, and cooking pan all made from coffee cans.

a handle, and soldered it to the side of another can to create a drinking mug; soldered a long, thin, flat strap of steel to a small can to form a dipper; converted cans to small barbecues, cook stoves, and camp heaters; and used a number of these handy disposable products as storage containers.

An interesting homemade candle lantern was described by Bruce Lamb in an article he wrote for *The Backwoodsman* magazine (November/December 2007 issue) titled "Old Time Wilderness Camping & Survival" that he calls a "bug." His description calls for cutting the top out of a tall 48-oz. juice can, but I discovered that a full-size metal coffee container will also work quite well, and the top is already open.

To make this coffee can lantern, cut or punch two slots to form an X in one side of the can, about halfway up the side near the middle. This can be done with the tip of a sharp knife blade, but I used a corner of a wood chisel's edge because it's sharp and

sturdy enough for the task. Push the center corners of this X inward to produce prong-like protrusions inside the can, upon which the base of a candle can be forced to hold it upright in use. This side will become the bottom of the lantern.

Next, punch or drill a cluster of holes into the opposite side from the X hole, which will allow venting above the burning candle. A long wire handle can be affixed to the base and the mouth of the can so it can be comfortably toted in its horizontal position. It might even be practical to somehow attach bent wires to the side that forms the new bottom so the lantern can be set on a table without rolling over. The shiny metal inside surface at the closed back end (the original bottom of the can) serves as a reflector for the candle light, which shines out the opening much like that of a flashlight. As Mr. Lamb explains, the burning candle in the can isn't easily blown out by the wind.

In researching possible uses for coffee cans, I

opening

vent holes
in top

wire handle

Bottom inside of can
acts as a reflector
mirror behind candle.

candle inside can

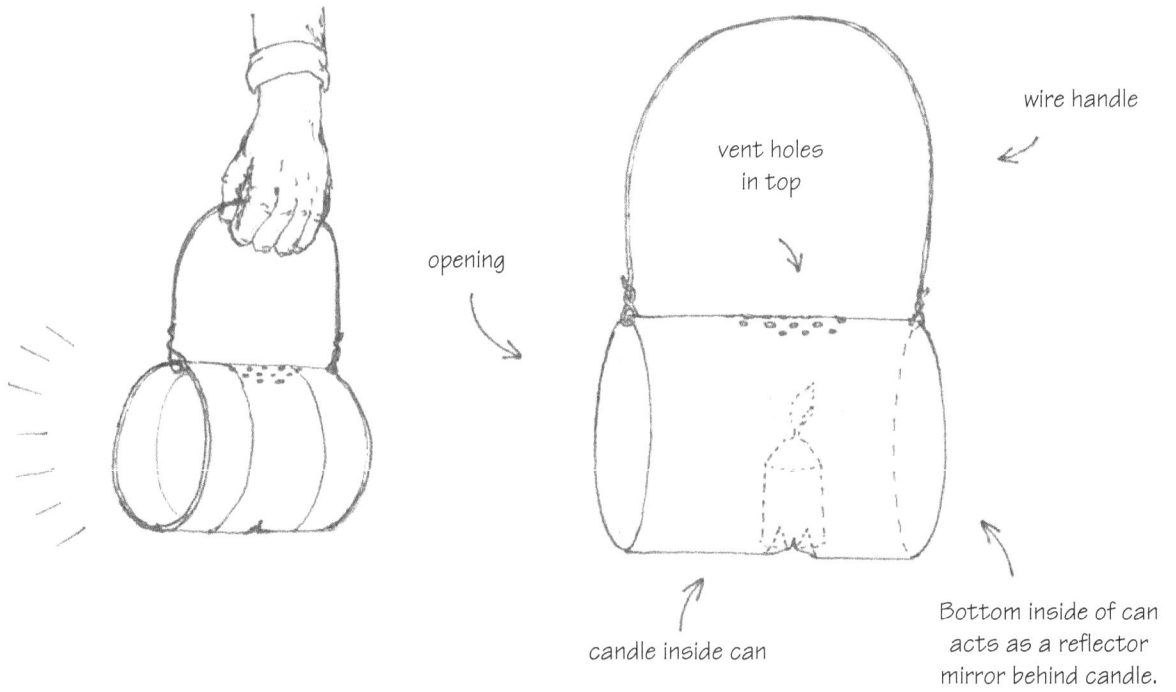

Coffee can lantern. The base of the candle is pressed down on the bent metal corners of the X slot.

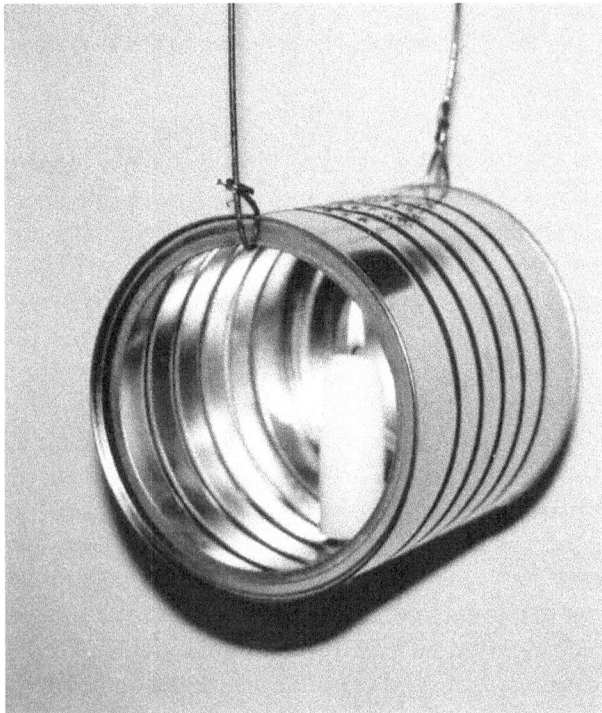

The operational coffee can candle lantern.

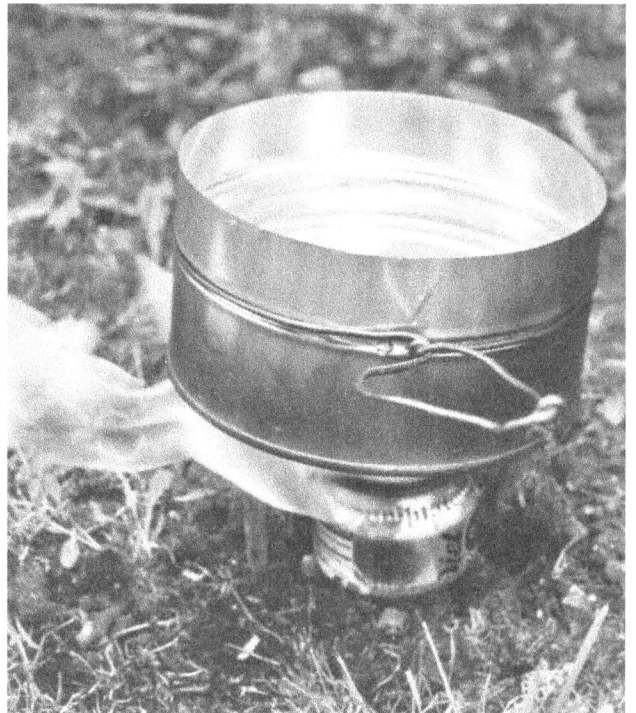

Boiling water in a coffee can pan.

discovered that some people have successfully turned them into toy drums, bird feeders, piggy banks, Wi-Fi antennas, pinhole cameras, and God only knows how many other things. In his classic book, *The Complete Modern Blacksmith*, Alexander Weygers describes using a coffee can as a small, makeshift forge, which he used to create the carving chisels he wanted in a remote environment.

WOODEN DOWELS

I use wooden dowels in more of my makeshift projects than perhaps any other single type of building material. In fact, I'm not sure I could remember every way in which I have used wooden dowels over the years, considering how frequently I've needed them.

I've made numerous tool handles from

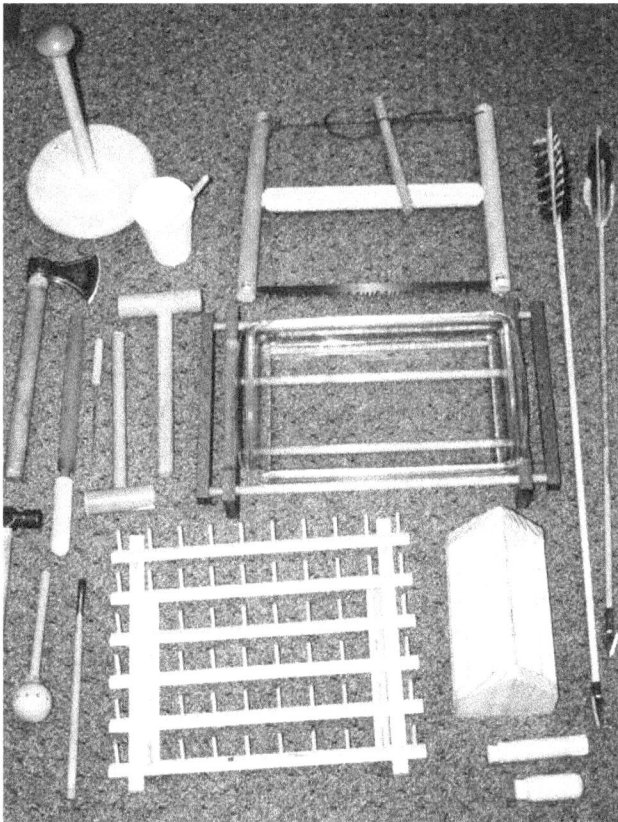

hardwood dowels, pegged wooden items together with dowels, and fashioned gun-cleaning ramrods, cross sticks for shooting, arrow shafts, hat rack pegs, and stir sticks from them. I've drilled holes into the ends of thick dowels to make tubular containers for such small items as matches, sewing needles, and fishhooks, using corks to cap the openings, and I've cut thin disks off hardwood dowels to make little wooden buttons. I have inserted medium-sized dowels perpendicularly into holes drilled through sections of larger dowels to create lightweight wooden mallets. A stout, 1 1/8-inch-diameter oak dowel several feet in length has served as a security stop inside one of my sliding glass doors for years.

When we were kids, we made whistles by inserting split sections of short, small-diameter dowels into holes we had drilled lengthwise into larger dowels, into which we had cut notches in the sides to create the necessary air openings. Flutes employ a similar design, except they are longer and

A multitude of makeshift products incorporating dowels in one way or another. Here we see tool handles, a paper towel rod, stir stick in a cup, wooden mallets, thread spools, bucksaw frame, dish rack, little tool-tote handle, tubular containers, and arrows.

Expedient dowel tripod supporting a tomato plant.

have a line of holes that can be blocked or unblocked as needed to obtain different musical tones.

I've seen pictures in books of birdcages that were constructed largely of wooden dowels. In years past, wheel spokes have been made of dowels, as have flagpoles, broomsticks, curtain rods, towel racks, chair legs, and wooden beads.

It is easy to make an expedient tripod rifle rest by lashing together a bundle of three dowels near one end with parachute cord or a bootlace. This can be folded up and stowed conveniently in a pack or shooting bag; when needed, the legs are simply spread out enough to form a rigid support upon which to rest the front end of the rifle. It can be made any length, depending on the desired height.

You will find sources for dowels virtually everywhere you look in a typical household. They can be scrounged from mop and broom handles, old tool handles, furniture (wooden chairs can be especially rich sources), kids' toys, and all sorts of other common items if you just take the time to look. Even a peeled twig from the yard could be pressed into service in a pinch.

Towel racks incorporating dowels are quite common.

Three dowels lashed together with cord make a functional makeshift tripod rifle rest.

FILE STEEL

Old, dull, or broken files shouldn't be discarded. They contain some of the hardest steel widely available, and as we observed in chapter 4, they can be used to make a variety of knives, edged tools like scrapers and chisels, and other items that require high hardness.

I have made a number of knives from files, and although they aren't ideally suited as prying tools because of their brittle nature, their ability to cut a wide variety of materials is really hard to beat. I might also note here that the most effective handmade flint strikers I have made and seen were merely carbon steel files with the teeth ground off. A sharp edge of flint struck against a smooth surface of hard file steel will normally produce a bright shower of hot sparks.

Some common household sources for dowels. There are almost 70 individual dowels in this photo—and that's *before* cutting them into smaller sections.

A section of plastic pipe with a threaded cap at both ends makes a convenient container for storing thin saw blades.

PLASTIC AND STEEL PIPES

Plumbing products of both plastic and steel serve a myriad of makeshift projects quite wonderfully. One of the best things about water pipes is the wide range of sizes and configurations available. There is usually some type of pipe available at the local hardware store to fill just about every need.

I use various sizes of plastic pipes as containers quite often. The neat thing about them is that they can be purchased with their ends already threaded for such attachments as end caps or couplings. This really makes life easy for the do-it-yourselfer. A plastic pipe capped at both ends makes an ideal container for storing things like drill bits or long, thin saw blades. Tom Forbes provides a number of additional ways to use plastic pipe in his books, *PVC Projects for the Outdoorsman* and *More PVC Projects for the Outdoorsman*, published by Paladin Press.

Steel water pipes lend themselves very well to a

multitude of purposes besides piping water. I used an assortment of pipe products to complete the stand of a makeshift forge (see photos in chapter 3). Where some type of rigid framework is needed for a makeshift contraption of one kind or another, steel pipes might be the most convenient materials to use for its creation. Having access to welding or brazing equipment can be helpful in the fabrication of such a frame, but I have discovered that steel pipes can very often be bolted together just as effectively.

Anyone familiar with the Department of the Army's TM 31-210, *Improvised Munitions Handbook*, is probably familiar with how steel water pipes can be used as expedient barrels for makeshift firearms. Operational pipe guns have been improvised many times by prison inmates, members of street gangs, and guerrilla fighters who lacked better equipment. Schedule 40 or thicker seamless steel pipe of various sizes might serve this purpose in a desperate situation. The best book I have ever seen that explains in detail how to build functional pipe guns is *Homemade Guns and Homemade Ammo* by Ronald B. Brown, available at the time of this writing from Paladin Press.

If pipes are to be welded or brazed, any greasy or oily surfaces should first be cleaned where they are to be joined, and if galvanized pipes are to be heated, one should be mindful of the toxic vapors. (If you're going to weld galvanized pipe, it's a good idea to remove the zinc first to improve the integrity of the weld. Hydrochloric acid does it in a flash.)

SAW BLADES

Saw blade steel is considered ideal for a myriad of purposes. Usually consisting of some variation of spring steel, it is hard enough to be suitable for a variety of cutting tools. The large circular saw blades used in lumber mills are a popular source of steel for custom knives, as are the old crosscut handsaws used by loggers. Rough cutting a knife blade's basic shape out of a large saw blade is

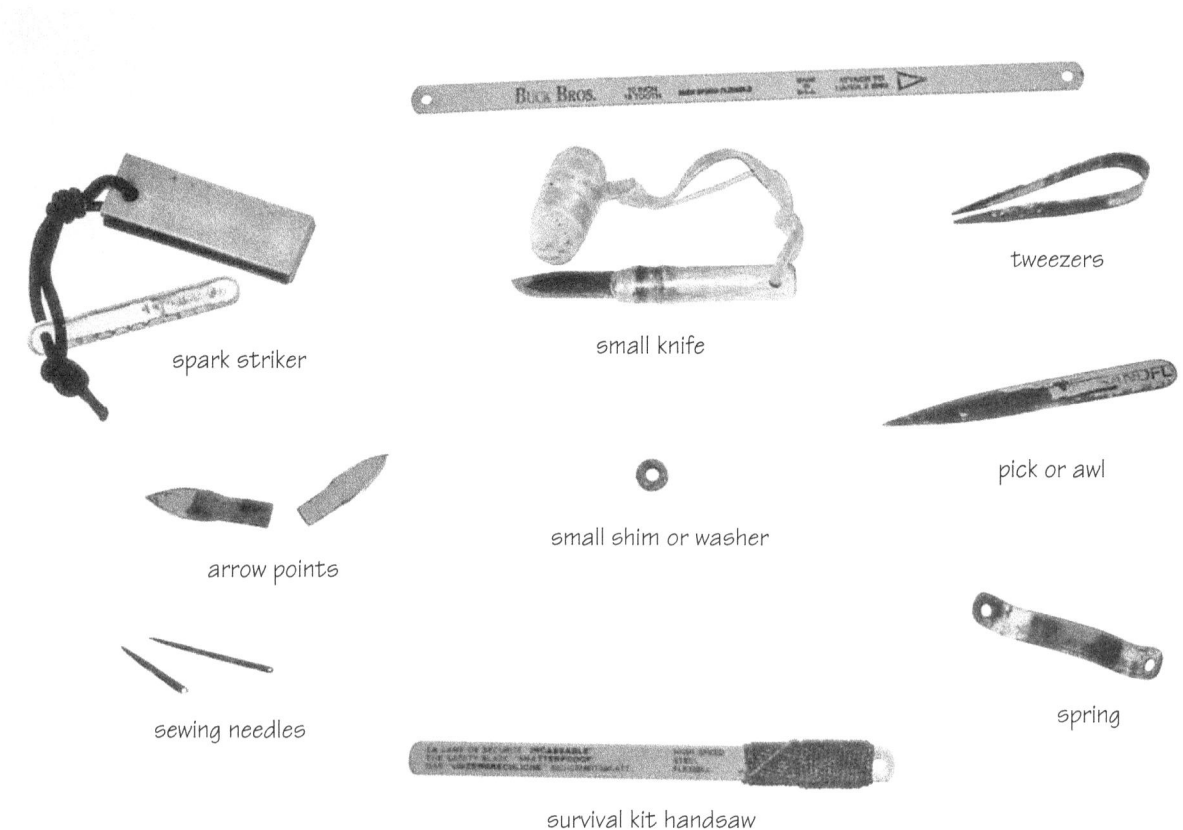

tweezers

spark striker

small knife

pick or awl

arrow points

small shim or washer

sewing needles

spring

survival kit handsaw

Things made from hacksaw blades.

usually accomplished with a cutting gas torch or a plasma cutter, but a high-speed rotary tool with a grinding disk can also be used to very slowly grind through the material along an outline of a knife shape drawn on the surface. This steel is simply too hard to effectively cut with a hacksaw, unless one possesses an excess of time, patience, and extra hacksaw blades, or unless the material is annealed first to soften it up.

Old saw blades are salvaged not only for practical purposes; they have been used in sculpture and other art projects for years. Saw blade art featuring creative scenes and images painted on the blades' surfaces has become fairly popular for decorating the walls of dens and restaurants.

The thin blades of hand hacksaws provide useful material for a number of purposes. I have used them to fabricate makeshift springs, small knife blades, spark strikers for cerium fire igniters, and other items that require thin spring steel. I created some of my favorite leather sewing needles out of hacksaw blades. Being so thin, they are very easy to stitch with. Other things that might be made out of hacksaw blades include tweezers, shims or flat washers, small arrow or dart points, flat bands, and lock-picking tools.

It is extremely easy to work with hacksaw blades. It is not too difficult to drill holes through the thin steel, and a blade can be broken wherever desired by bending it back and forth with pliers. They are also easy to shape quickly with a bench grinder or belt sander.

REBAR

Rebar is the common term for concrete reinforcement bar, widely used in masonry and foundation construction. Composed of various

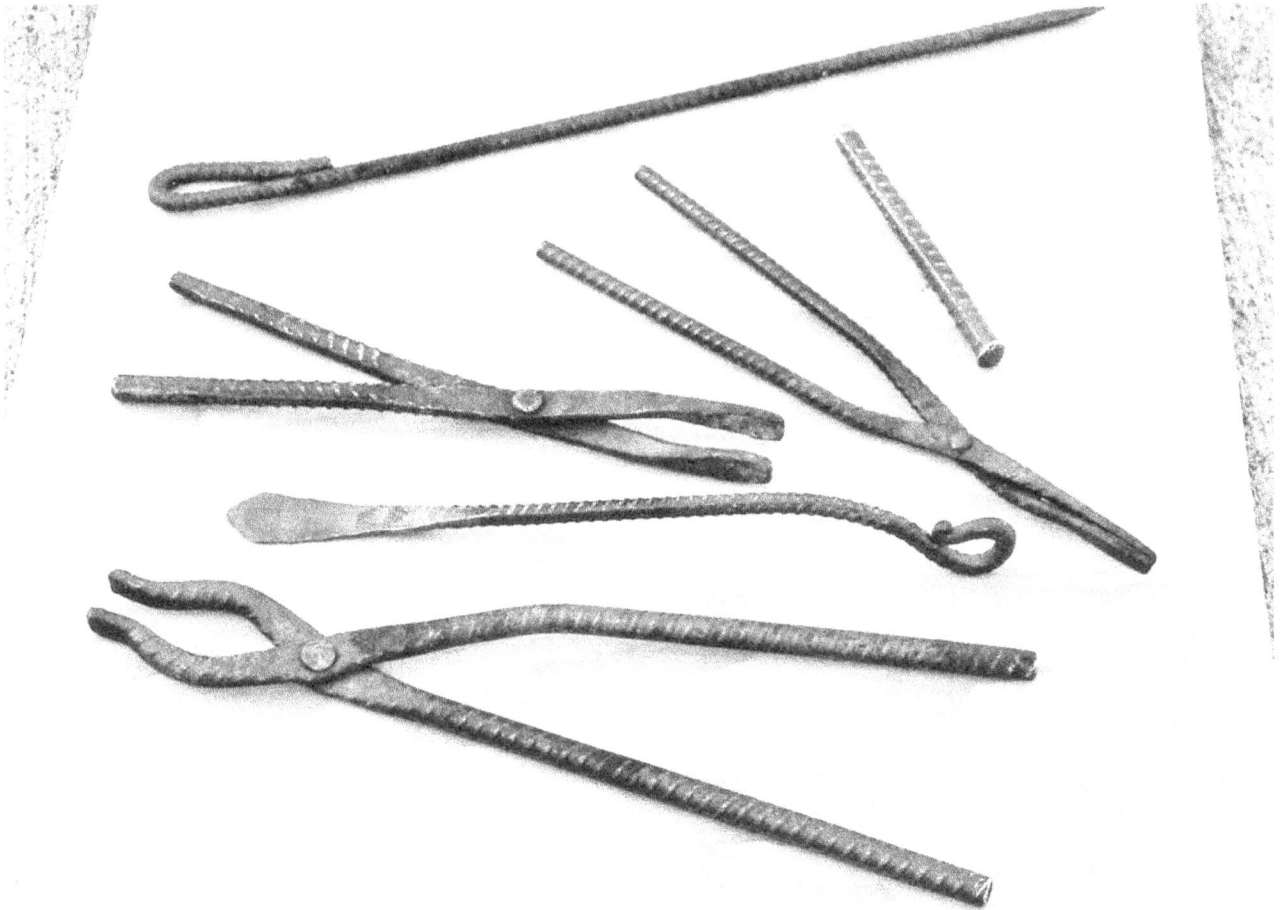

Miscellaneous tools made from rebar—three pairs of tongs, a digging tool for weeds, a punch, and a fire poker.

proportions of carbon steel (different grades are available), rebar comes in several different diameters and lengths. A hardware store in my area sells 3/8- and 1/2-inch-diameter sticks of rebar measuring 3 feet long and shorter, and they are quite a bit cheaper than the same size of plain mild steel rod sold at the same store. Builders typically get their rebar in much longer sections for foundation work. Let's consider how useful products can be fabricated out of common rebar.

I have discovered that, with the help of a forge, sections of rebar are ideal for creating pliers and blacksmith tongs, as shown in chapter 3. For a number of years, the grate in the bottom of my coal forge was merely a section of 1/2-inch rebar that I had coiled up to cover the opening, allowing air to pass between the coils but preventing chunks of coal from falling through.

Long sections of 3/8-inch rebar are not difficult to bend when heated, and even while they're cold it can be done using the appropriate jigs to facilitate good bending leverage. In fact, there are tools specifically for making it easier to bend and turn rebar, called hickey bars. There are several variations of hickey bars available, but a simple

design consists of a heavy steel bar for the handle, having a flat section at one end with stout prongs protruding from one or both sides that hook onto the rebar for bending.

A makeshift turning jig would not be too complicated to make. It could consist of several thick posts (using heavy lag screws, bolts, steel pins, spikes, or whatever you can find to make sturdy posts) either threaded into corresponding holes in a steel base plate secured to a solid stand, or pounded into the top of a tough tree stump, about 1 1/2 to 2 inches apart. You might even be able to find a notch in a tree that will serve the same purpose. You can also readily bend rebar just where you want to by putting it through two pieces of pipe (using the smallest size that will slip over it) and bending where the two come together. Just remember that you would never want to heat rebar for bending if it is to be used to reenforce concrete, because heating it might alter its structural capacity.

Things like shepherd's hooks for gardens, S hooks for hanging cast-iron pots, fire pokers, pot racks, large chain links, barrel hoops, triangle dinner bells, framework for table stands, grates for barbecues, cupboard door handles, small boat

Bending rebar with a rebar bender, also known as a hickey bar.

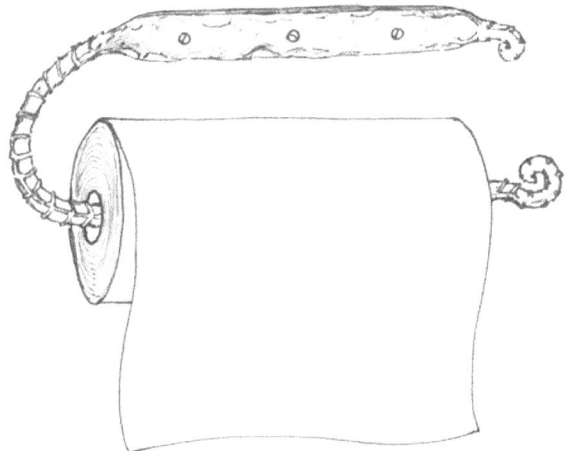

Paper towel holder made from bent rebar.

shepherd's hook

door handle

wall hook

S hook

towel ring

shelf bracket
decoration

root digger

tent stake

tie rod

pot stand

chain

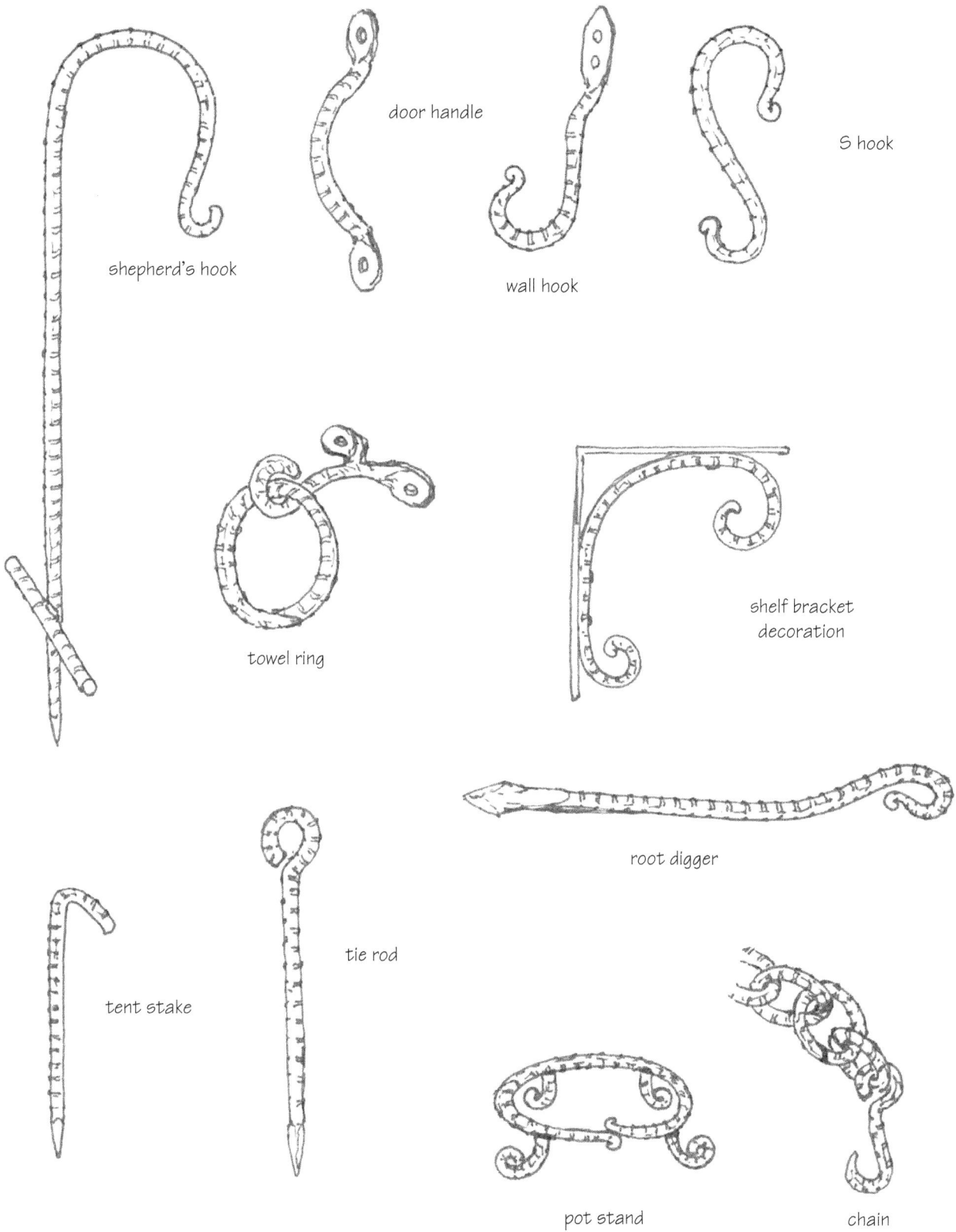

Forged rebar—some possibilities.

anchors, spikes, brackets, lantern hooks, towel rods and towel rings, shelf supports, fireplace andirons, wine racks, candle holders, tent stakes, and decorative scrolls to adorn metal gates, walls, and fences can all be fashioned out of rebar, to mention just some of the possibilities. I've also used pieces of rebar to create functional chisels and punches for my blacksmith shop.

If the characteristic ribs on the rebar constitute an annoyance, they can be removed with a grinding wheel or pounded out over an anvil. The bar can also be hack-sawn into sections of just about any desired length, heated in the forge, and then beaten into a squared, triangular, tapered, or flat shape, depending on the need.

Rebar rusts easily. This problem can usually be remedied by cleaning it up and painting it or by keeping its surface oiled and out of the weather.

NAILS

An assortment of common and specialty nails are sold at every hardware store—these are perhaps

civilization's most fundamental fasteners—and a surprising variety of makeshift products can be fashioned from them.

I created a useful pair of small pliers entirely from three nails: two large nails for the handles and jaws, and a smaller nail for the pivot pin. I have also created fishhooks and sewing needles from small, common nails.

The sewing needles were made by hammering one end to partially flatten a section for the eye so that a small hole could be drilled through it, elongating the eye with a round needle file, and tapering the other end of the crude needle to a point with my bench grinder. They are functional with certain leather stitching projects, although they are not the easiest needles to work with, in my experience.

The little fishhooks, on the other hand, really work well! I caught a trout for the frying pan using one baited with salmon eggs the first time I ever fished with a homemade hook. I heated the nails with a propane torch for bending and hammer shaping, drilled the holes for the eyes to attach the

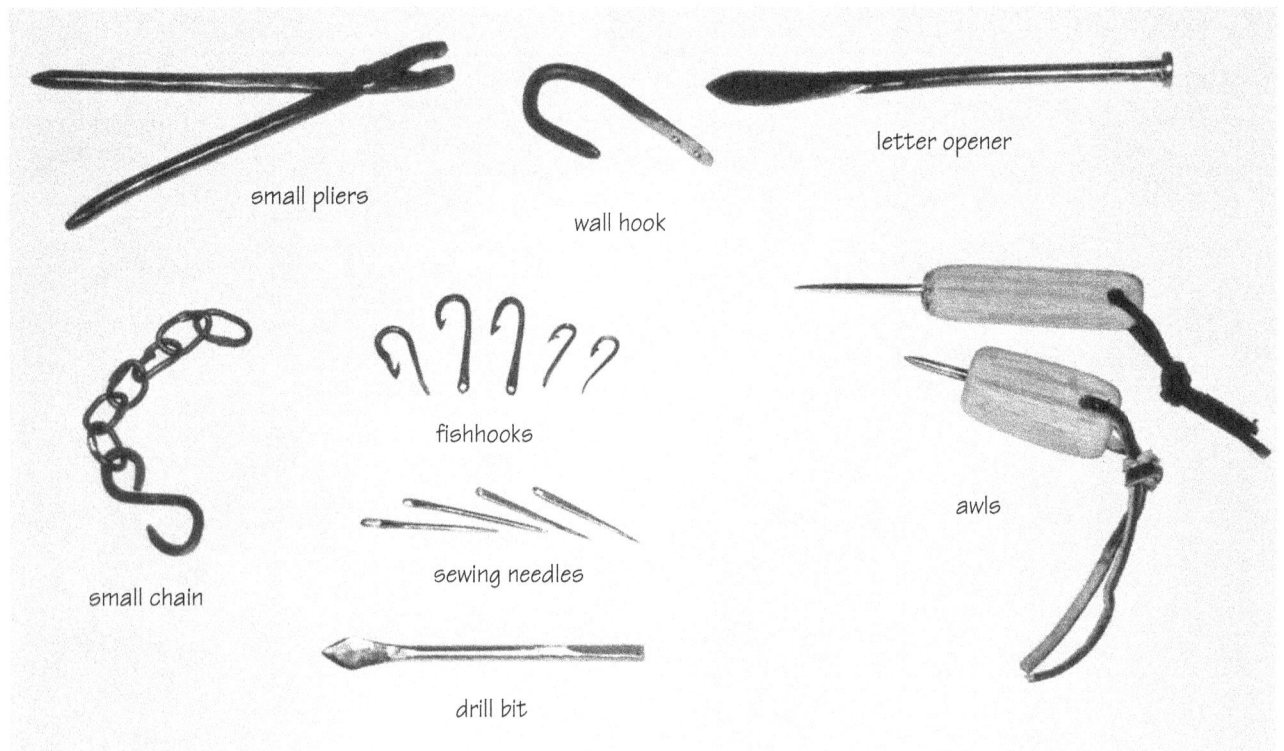

Some things made from nails.

fishing line, and filed the barbs. They look crude up close, but they are perfectly functional.

An even simpler improvised fishhook could be created by merely bending a small nail into the shape of a J (it already has a point on the hook end), and then tying on the fish line just below the head to secure it.

Awls are easy to make out of nails. The simplest way is to hammer a nail partway into whatever piece of wood is selected for a handle, and then grind or file the protruding section of nail to a tapered point. The chances of splitting the handle when inserting the nail can be reduced by predrilling with a slightly smaller diameter drill bit, but the nail should go in tight so it can't be pulled out easily.

In chapter 5, I noted how the shafts of common nails are ideally suited for solid rivets. Since most nails are considerably longer than average rivet length, multiple rivets can be cut from a single nail.

The purpose for which nails probably see the most use, aside from their primary role as fasteners, is as hanger pegs in walls for things like picture frames, mirrors, hats, guns, tools, and key chains. If you want to hang something on the wall, the easiest and quickest method is to partially hammer in a nail or two.

2 x 4 LUMBER

I once needed to climb up into my garage rafters during a remodeling project, and I didn't happen to have a ladder at the time. However, I did have a stack of used 2 x 4 framing studs at my disposal, so I proceeded to assemble my own expedient ladder from the lumber and assorted nails and screws. Less than an hour later, I was able to comfortably access the rafters of my garage.

Although much heavier than any conventional ladder purchased at a hardware store, my wooden ladder served me well for a number of years whenever I needed to climb onto the roof of my house. Lacking adequate space to keep it out of the weather, I left it outside, and it eventually rotted and became unusable. But whenever I think of that ladder, I am reminded of the versatile nature of ordinary 2 x 4s.

The rungs of a 2 x 4 ladder can be screwed or nailed flat to the top edges of the side boards, with a couple of reinforcement pieces secured to the top and bottom edges to keep the whole thing rigid (quick, easy, and similar to the way I did mine), or they can be cut to fit between the side boards and pinned or screwed into position from the outsides of the side boards. This second method is the better way to produce a better looking and sturdier ladder, but it also requires more care in the measuring and cutting. It would be ideal for building a ladder leading to a top bunk bed, a loft, or an attic because the result is more compact, and the rungs will form level steps with the ladder leaning at a fixed angle.

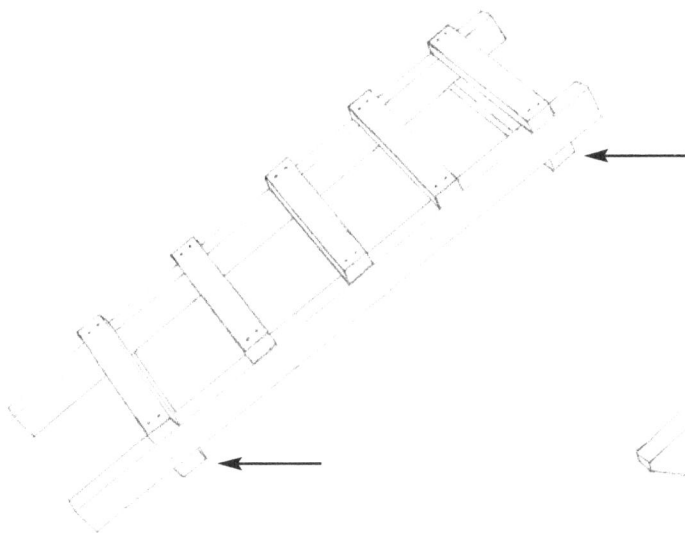

Quick and simple 2 x 4 ladder. Note the reinforcement pieces at the top and bottom.

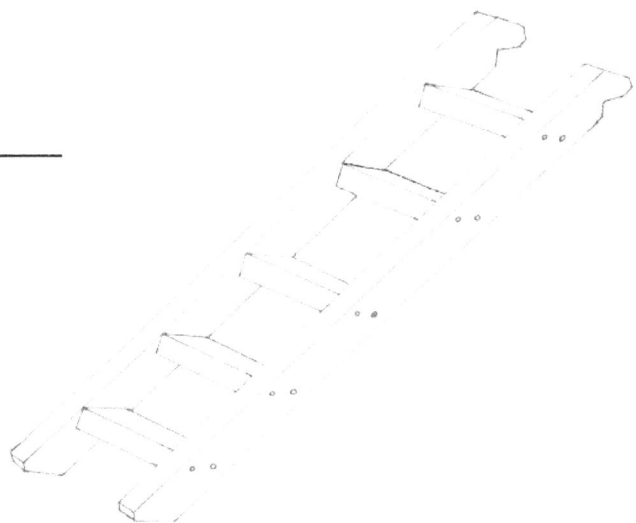

The better 2 x 4 ladder design, with rungs between the sides. Useful only at a fixed angle.

If I were to build another 2 x 4 ladder, I would attach the lumber using either 1/4-inch-diameter carriage bolts with corresponding nuts and flat washers, or large lag screws. This would provide increased security at the connections as well as make it easier to disassemble for storage or recycling the materials after the ladder fulfilled its useful service.

At present I have two wooden workbenches in my garage. I built one of them myself, and it contains a fair number of 2 x 4s along with other dimensional lumber. The other workbench was built by my dad almost 20 years ago, and other than the bolts that hold it together and one board of 1 x 6 material across the back of the bottom shelf, it consists entirely of 2 x 4 lumber. It is a very solid little bench.

I made several small, handy tool racks out of 2 x 4s. I drilled various sizes of holes into one and mounted it to the wall of my garage like a small shelf. It holds such things as punches, pencils, and small round files. I cut angled slots into a similarly mounted piece of 2 x 4 for hanging bastard files. This is an inexpensive way to keep your small tools handy.

I've seen shelving and shelf supports constructed of 2 x 4s that appeared to be extraordinarily rigid and secure, typically in someone's garage or pole barn. This size of lumber seems to be ideally suited for a myriad of heavy-duty brackets and wall mounts.

Serviceable park benches, patio tables, and chairs might be fashioned from 2 x 4 lumber, but the wood should be painted with several coats of varnish if it is to be left out in the weather for any period of time.

Sawhorses, sawbucks, and portable tool stands are commonly fabricated from 2 x 4 lumber. The frame of a tool cart or cabinet on wheels might be a practical way to use 2 x 4s. A small platform with

Workbench made almost entirely of 2 x 4s.

Handy tool holder made of a short section of a 2 x 4.

runners, called a stone boat, can be built out of 2 x 4s and used to drag heavy rocks over the ground. For crates, boxes, and wooden trunks, 2 x 4 lumber makes very sturdy building material.

Simple frame for a dirt sifter constructed of 2 x 4s.

For indoors, a surprisingly attractive 2 x 4 coffee table can be made with the appropriate stain finish. A bed frame of 2 x 4 lumber can also be a functional piece of furniture that is easy and cost-effective to build.

We refer to the subject of this discussion as 2 x 4 lumber, but the "two by four" is only a nominal designation. In fact, nowadays the boards measure closer to 1 1/2 inch thick by 3 1/2 inches wide. Apparently, at one time 2 x 4 lumber actually measured 2 inches by 4 inches.

This lumber is available in different lengths (usually at least 8 feet and longer), of several different varieties of wood, and of different quality grades. Framing studs aren't always pretty, but they are common and usually not too expensive compared with most other lumber.

One advantage to building with wooden 2 x 4s over things like rebar or other steel materials is that it requires only the most basic tools. No forge or welding equipment is needed. Almost anyone with limited skills, a claw hammer, a handsaw, maybe a tape measure, and a can of nails can create functional structures all day long with wooden boards.

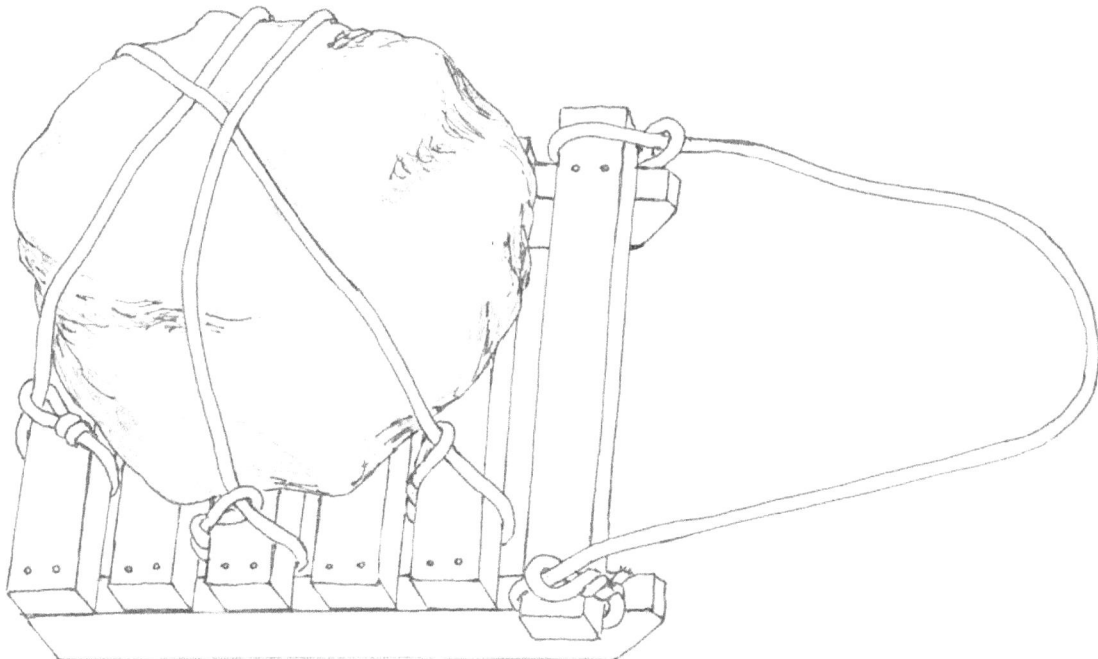

Stone boat made from 2 x 4s. Handy way to move heavy rocks over land.

THINGS MADE FROM CAR PARTS

The modern gasoline-powered automobile has to be one of the most versatile sources of potential building materials I can think of. A single motor vehicle comprises literally thousands of different parts, many of which could be used to make all sorts of useful things.

Assorted screws, nuts, bolts, washers, shims, pins, and other fasteners are used to hold engines and structural components together, and the electrical system is connected with generous amounts of insulated metal wire. Under the hood of any conventional car you will find pulleys, belts, rubber hoses, brackets, small springs, metal tubing, electric motors, and other components that might be usable in the fabrication of numerous other mechanical devices or inventions not necessarily automotive related, although car parts can be modified or recycled to serve auto-related purposes as well. A friend of mine recently showed me the air compressor he mounted under the hood of his Jeep, which he uses as a tire inflator while four-wheeling off the beaten path. He adapted it from an air-conditioning unit salvaged from another vehicle. He explained that this setup is not uncommon among off-road vehicle enthusiasts.

Lights and small light bulbs are found in various locations throughout a car's schematic. An important thing to remember is that the electrical system of a motor vehicle uses direct current rather than the alternating current you find in your home, and modern cars have 12-volt systems (50 years ago, standard automobile batteries were 6 volts). Hence, electrical devices stripped from cars normally will not be particularly easy to adapt for home use when plugged into the grid.

In chapter 6 we learned how car batteries could be used to power a makeshift arc welder, and below I'll talk about how 6-volt batteries can be fabricated into an improvised lantern. But charged batteries can be used to power other direct current applications besides welders or lights. It is useful to remember that the voltage increases (i.e., is added together) when batteries are connected *in series* (positive terminals to negative terminals, negative to positive), but the current (amperage) remains the same. Hence, two 12-volt batteries connected in series will give you 24 volts, four connected this way will give you 48 volts, and so on. On the other hand, if the batteries are connected *in parallel* (positive to positive, negative to negative), the voltage remains the same but the current increases.

Wires stripped from junked automobiles might be used to complete small electrical circuits or to make expedient field antennas, radio coils, makeshift clotheslines or guy wires for tents, and a variety of traps and snares, among numerous other things that require wire.

All cars contain various sizes of springs. Auto leaf springs are popular with custom knife makers looking for good quality steel that is long and wide enough for knife blades of all sizes. Heavy coil springs found in the suspension system also contain a considerable amount of excellent material. Someone with a forge can heat and straighten sections of a heavy coil spring and use the round bar for a multitude of other purposes, such as constructing chisels and punches. Endless smaller springs can also be fabricated from the same spring steel.

Side- and rear-view mirrors pulled from a car could become important items in an emergency survival situation, where signaling with a mirror might be the best way to attract the attention of

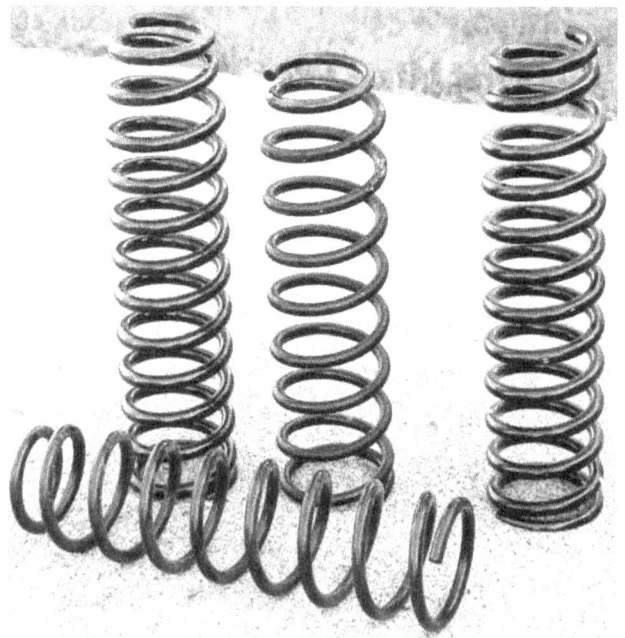

Heavy auto coil springs contain useful, tough round bar. You merely have to heat it in your forge and straighten it out to make it more usable.

rescuers. A car mirror might also be handy in a camp or remote cabin for shaving and other personal hygiene tasks.

Vinyl is commonly used in car seats, and pieces of this material can be used as an alternative to cowhide to fabricate all sorts of usable things, including wallets, arrow quivers, and knife sheaths. The vinyl is easy to cut with a sharp utility knife. Seat belts can be converted into short equipment straps or for other purposes requiring nylon webbing.

The average car body comprises an enormous amount of sheet metal. This could be cut into small pieces and used to construct all kinds of flat metal objects like small shovel or trowel blades and other garden tools, arrow points, dustpans, scrapers, trays, lightweight hinges, metal strapping, shims, and chimney flashing. The paint might need to be sanded off for some projects, but sheet metal is sheet metal. Don't forget that you can cut any sheet metal with your Dremel, using the heavy cutoff wheels.

I have heard about car hoods being removed, turned upside down, and used as sleds for carrying firewood by being towed behind snowmobiles with ropes. Utility trailers made out of old pickup truck beds also seem to be popular these days.

A thick, flat part of a car's cast-iron engine block would serve as a pretty good makeshift anvil if you have the equipment to lift it out of the engine compartment. Brake drums, especially the larger ones from trucks, have been really popular for building inexpensive bowl forges. These are just two examples of salvaging heavy-duty car metal for makeshift projects—considering the amount of usable scrap steel that can be pulled from junked cars, any wrecking yard ought to be like a candy store for a modern-day blacksmith or hobby metal tinkerer.

Makeshift Headlight Lantern

As an experiment, I wanted to find out how easy it would be to adapt a vehicle headlight for use as a portable hand-held lantern. I acquired a new halogen headlight at the local auto parts store, along with some insulated 14-gauge wire, alligator clips, and a neat little on/off toggle switch. The headlight unit had two connection prongs on the backside, so I figured powering the light would simply be a matter of connecting these prongs to the battery terminals with the wire leads.

Car headlights are designed to operate on 12-volt car battery power, but using a car battery for my lantern experiment would spoil the whole idea of a portable light. Instead, I tried using two smaller 6-volt lantern batteries I bought at the local hardware

Cast-iron brake drum waiting to be made into a small coal forge.

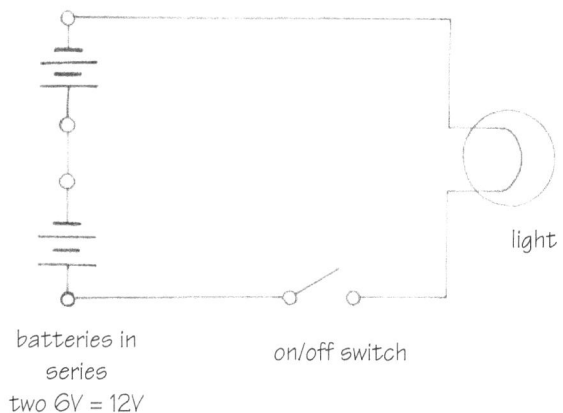

batteries in series
two 6V = 12V

on/off switch

light

Simple lantern schematic.

store, connecting them in series to get the desired 12 volts, and discovered that this works well. In fact, the headlight will shine even when connected to a single 6-volt lantern battery, but it doesn't appear nearly as bright as when powered by two batteries.

I fabricated the connection leads from the wires and alligator clips, wiring the switch into one of the leads. I then built a little platform out of wood, like an open-top box with sides, to keep everything together as a unit.

I also made a handy carry handle from plastic pipe components. I cut away a flat section along the vertical mounting pipe so I could bolt it directly to the box, drilled the holes for the bolts,

The basic components of the headlight lantern.

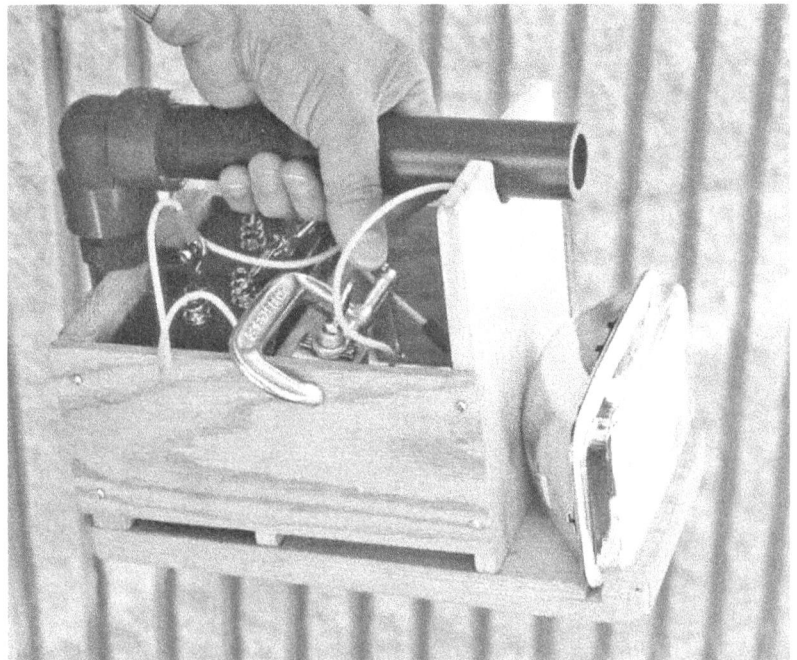

and attached this to the back wall of the platform. An elbow connection allows a length of pipe to be attached (or removed as needed) for the horizontal handle.

The toggle switch didn't come with any kind of mounting bracket, so until I eventually devise such a part, I simply have it secured temporarily with a C-clamp to one of the sideboards in an easy-to-reach position. The battery hold-down brackets (not shown in the accompanying photos, as these were installed later) were easily improvised out of 1/4-inch carriage bolts and fender washers. The bolts protrude vertically through holes in a wooden crosspiece and are secured in position across the front of the batteries, level with their tops. The outer edges of the fender washers hang over the tops of

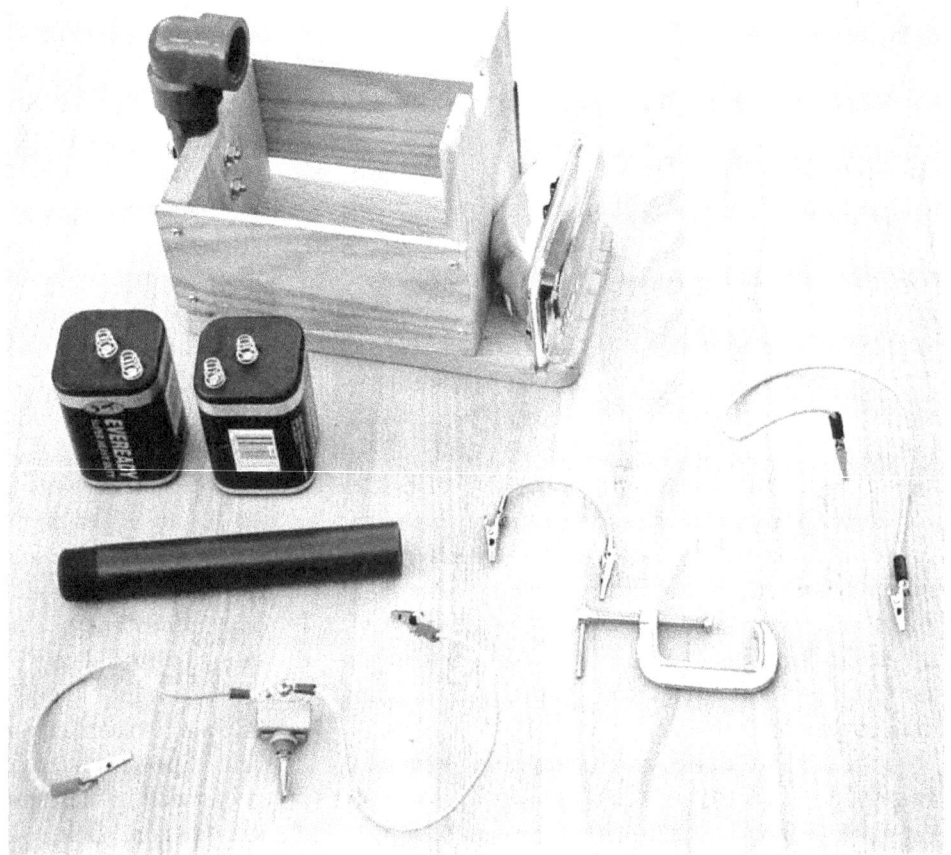

The headlight lantern assembled and operational.

the batteries so they can be clamped down with wing nuts.

While this makeshift lantern is heavier and bulkier than any standard flashlight, it is still very portable, completely functional, and provides a bright beam of light.

Homemade Sandals from Car Tires

Automobile tires have been used by resourceful individuals to sole shoes and for improvising sandals for years (most famously by the Viet Cong during the Vietnam War). Tire rubber is actually ideally suited for footwear, already having the appropriate tread ridges and grooves for traction and being rubbery enough to cushion the feet while at the same time providing an excellent protective barrier between the bottoms of the feet and the terrain.

I learned something the hard way about cutting up automobile tires. Tires with steel cable embedded in them—and apparently this includes the majority of tires on the road now—are incredibly difficult to cut. I tied into one with my hacksaw, thinking that a blade designed to cut through metal should make short work of the cabled tire. Well, I was wrong. After changing blades five times and

trying new blades having 32, 24, and finally 18 teeth per inch with no noticeable improvement to my struggle, I finally decided to go back to the drawing board and do more research to see how others cut their tires when making sandals.

The key is to select tires with no metal in them. Fortunately, there are still plenty of them around. A local junk dealer found a clean one for me in his pile of tires. If you don't have such help, check the printing on the sidewall—it will say what type of fiber reinforcements the tire contains.

I first removed a rectangular slab from the tire with just a hand crosscut saw; then I drew the outline for my sandal sole on the smooth side of the tire. The outline can be cut the hard and dangerous way with a utility knife, or a band saw or jigsaw can be employed to save time, sweat, and knife-slip injuries. My band saw did a nice job following the marker lines I had drawn. The thick rubber tends to bind and slow the blade periodically, but if you don't rush it, this is a good way to cut out tire rubber.

The sandal thongs, or straps for the feet, can be obtained in a number of ways. Normally available at most fabric stores, 1-inch-wide woven belt material is probably as close to perfect as you will find for this. Fabric stores also sell the little plastic buckles, or you can use metal double D-rings.

Cutting into an automobile tire. You want to avoid tires with steel cable embedded in them.

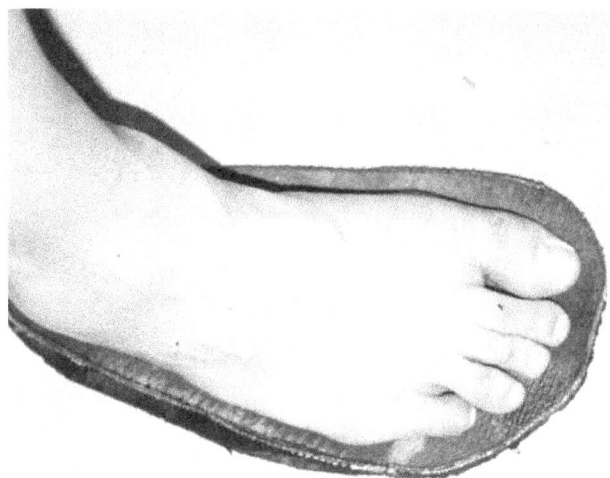

The rubber sole should be slightly larger than your foot. I cut the basic shape using my band saw.

The tread on the bottom of the sole.

The sole with the straps attached.

Give some forethought to a suitable way to attach the straps before cutting out the final shape of the soles. One design I saw in a magazine had tabs with slits in them protruding on both sides and at the back end to hold the straps. For my sandals, I simply used an X-Acto knife to cut slits, about 1/8- inch wide by 1-inch long, directly into the sole close to the edges and fed the strapping through the slits.

One of the best things about homemade sandals is that you can custom-design them in your own preferred style and make them the proper size for your own feet.

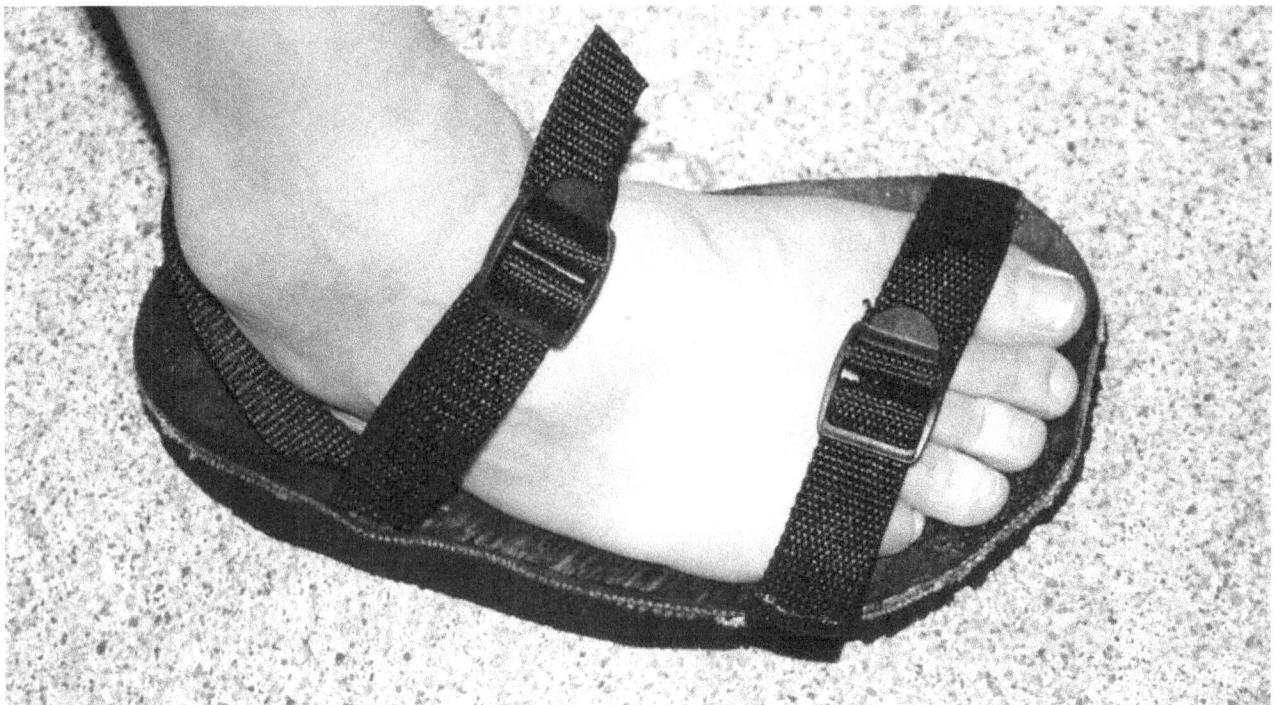

Testing the tire tread sandal.

A LIST OF MAKESHIFT SUBSTITUTES

Conventional Item	Possible Substitutions
Knife sharpening stone	Abrasive flat rock; terra cotta brick or flowerpot
Wrought or soft iron	Low-carbon mild steel
Hide glue	Gelatin powder boiled in water
Forging or heating coal	Charred wood; wood charcoal
Gunpowder	Crushed match heads (see *Homemade Guns and Homemade Ammo* in the Suggested Resources section)
Leather or cowhide	Soft vinyl or Naugahyde
Leather tanning oil or animal brain	Ivory soap; egg yolks; neatsfoot oil; 10W motor oil
Hard plastic	Rawhide when dry
Obsidian for edged weapons or stone tools	Untempered glass
Graphite pencil lead	Charred wood; pure lead
Lantern/lamp oil	Vegetable oil
Hand soap	Lard and wood ash mixture
Toothpaste	Baking soda
Shampoo	Vinegar
Coffee	Ground-roasted dandelion or chicory roots
Coffee filters	Paper towel; thin cotton cloth
Reading glasses	Pinhole aperture in paper or magnifying glass
Magnetic compass	Pocket watch or wristwatch (in northern hemisphere, point the hour hand toward the sun; halfway between the sun and 12:00 is south)
Winter mittens	Thick boot socks
Camper's frying pan	Garden spade or shovel blade
Small door hinges	Straps of thick leather or rawhide
Leather waist belt	Rope, ends tied together in front
Small backpack	Blue jeans with pant legs tied closed and used as shoulder straps, seat used as the bag
Small pup tent	Army rain poncho with bungee cords to string up a "poncho hooch" shelter between trees
Temporary lever or handle replacement	Vise-Grip locking pliers
Boot laces	Parachute cord
Tie-down rope	Telephone wire; bungee cords; cotton or nylon webbing; string of sturdy rags connected with knots
Canteen	Empty plastic jug; hollow gourd with cork stopper

CHAPTER 8

Practical Tips for the Craftsman or Handyman

A number of what I like to think of as makeshift procedural ideas will be discussed in this chapter. The goal is to make the execution of certain tasks as safe and successful as possible, given the sometimes unorthodox techniques we discuss in this book. You will learn some handy little tricks in this chapter that I hope will prove valuable in the future.

DRILL A STRAIGHT HOLE

Drilling a straight hole—especially a long, straight hole through a bar of steel, wooden dowel, or other material—can seem like an impossible challenge with any conventional drill machine. Drill bits have a tendency to drift off center during the procedure.

In the old days of rifle-barrel making, there was no way for gunsmiths to drill a long, straight hole through a bar of iron or steel. Instead, they would hammer weld the steel around a shaft used as a mandrel to form the tube. They would then ream out the bore to the desired dimensions before cutting the rifling gloves.

Bit guide for drilling a straight hole into the end of a pole.

The most reliable way to bore a straight hole through any material is to use a lathe to turn the object to be drilled, rather than turning the bit or cutting tool. This method keeps the hole centered and prevents a drifting bit.

Since a lathe may not be available to us for our drilling projects, in many instances we may have to resort to a less precise technique. My dad showed me an effective jig he devised for drilling a straight hole centered in the end of a wooden pole. It is essentially a coupling made from a section of plastic pipe that fits perfectly over the end of the dowel or pole to be drilled, with a guide for a steel bit (which he made with his metal lathe) secured into the other end of the coupling. This keeps the bit and the work in alignment for drilling a fairly short, straight hole centered in the end of a pole (in this case it was a flagpole).

Front-loading muskets and rifles required ramrods to push bullets down their barrels and for swabbing their bores to clean them. The long ramrods, made of either metal or wood, were normally carried with the weapons, housed in the fore-end section of the stock directly under the barrel. For this, a fairly long hole had to be drilled into the wood in the underside of the forearm, parallel with the barrel channel.

I watched this process accomplished in a video about handcrafting Colonial long rifles. The gunsmith used a long drill bit in conjunction with a hand brace. To keep the bit properly aligned as he turned the brace, he wrapped strips of cowhide at intervals around the stock fore end and over the shank of the bit lying in the ramrod groove he had chiseled for the forward part of the ramrod hole. This is another example of how a guide of sorts can be used to keep a bit aligned.

Sometimes, however, boring a perfectly straight, long hole is just not achievable with available tools. One very makeshift way around this problem is to drill as straight a hole as possible halfway through the workpiece from one end, and then repeat the process from the other end so that the two holes bored from opposite directions meet in the middle. This approach involves twice as much centering and aligning with the drill bit and workpiece, but it limits the bit-drifting problem to holes of only half the final length. Afterward, a long bit might be used from one end or the other to better align the two holes where they meet.

Another makeshift technique to achieve a reasonably straight hole is to adapt a trick from natives of the Amazon jungle for making their blowguns. They don't even try to drill a hole; rather, they split the pole, gouge out half the hole on each piece, and then glue it back together.

DRILL A SMOOTH, CLEAN HOLE

Boring a smooth hole through wood, metal, or other materials can also be tricky. Drill bits can grab, tear, split, and splinter a workpiece to the degree that the piece is either visually unattractive or unusable. Fortunately, you can take some steps to minimize these problems.

Soft mild steel and annealed high-carbon steel are normally easy enough to drill through. Attempting to drill into harder material, however, can be extremely frustrating. When drilling a hole into steel, I get my best results in the following manner.

First, select a sharp twist bit of appropriate diameter capable of drilling into metal. (Some bits are only suitable for drilling through softer materials like wood.) Make sure the drill press is geared to one of its slow–medium rpm speeds. (I seem to get better results with slower speeds for most of my metal drilling projects, but you might want to consult one of the published machinist charts showing recommended drill speeds.) Then secure the workpiece firmly in the drill press vise to minimize drift and vibration. After aligning the point of the bit in the exact center of the hole position on the piece (I often mark the spot with a center punch), begin drilling slowly. Remember to wear safety goggles and keep shirtsleeves and long hair clear of the turning bit.

Something like a small stiff-bristle brush is almost essential for periodically sweeping away the resulting metal chips or sharp, spiraling curlicues. You need to clear the workpiece of these tiny obstructions because they build up, interfering with a clean cut and making the job difficult to monitor closely. Applying drops of cutting oil to the turning bit enhances the operation by lubricating and minimizing the friction heat generated by the cutting of steel (machine oil will serve as an acceptable substitute).

I would describe my technique for drilling a smooth hole in steel as a sequence of steps. I usually get the hole in the workpiece started before adding the first drops of oil, just to make sure the bit starts where I want it. Then I back the bit out, sweep away the metal chips, give a few drops of oil to the turning bit, and proceed to drill into the piece a little deeper before backing the bit out again and repeating the sequence until the hole is made.

Drilling a clean, smooth hole through wood is a slightly different process. Using oil to reduce friction would not normally be appropriate with wood, unless you were drilling through some extremely hard type of ironwood, and even then I'm not sure oil would necessarily help the process. Also, you might have better luck with a higher rpm speed whenever drilling into wood.

One of the most important considerations when drilling holes completely through any piece of wood, or through most any other type of material for

that matter, is the bit's exit on the opposite side of the workpiece. The exit hole at the backside of the piece is where splintering, splitting, or chipping usually occurs.

The solution to this problem is to clamp or otherwise tightly secure solid material to the backside of the work. A backed or supported surface will tend to facilitate a smooth exit hole with a near perfect opening. The bit will cut through the workpiece and into the next piece as if both were one solid piece. This way you eliminate the problem of a drill bit splintering its way out of an unsupported exit hole.

CUT A STRAIGHT LINE

Two essentials for sawing any material along a straight line are to select the right type of saw for the task and use a sharp blade. With certain sawing operations, such as using a circular saw to trim off the end of a 2 x 4, a steady hand and skill with the tool might suffice to obtain satisfactory results. However, if you needed to make a long, straight cut down the full length of a long board (called "ripping" when cutting with the grain), such as if you have to convert a 2 x 6 into two 2 x 3s using only a handheld circular saw at a job site where you don't have access to a table saw, the task can become tricky even for a carpenter with a lot of skill.

The key to obtaining a long, straight cut in this scenario is to use a guide for the saw. Another straight board clamped, temporarily nailed, or otherwise fastened to the workpiece to keep the saw cutting along the desired path usually does the trick.

We can use various similar makeshift guides and stops not only to keep our tools aligned, but also to prevent a workpiece from moving. An electrically powered cutting tool like a spinning drill bit or a saw blade can very easily catch or grab the work and fling it hard and fast, possibly causing damage to the workpiece or to the craftsman or bystanders. Fixed stops and guides can really help a craftsman keep his processes controlled.

On a related topic, carpenters frequently have to take measurements in order to cut their boards to fit, yet I would bet that mistakes in measuring are probably the most common ones carpenters make. It is easy to do. The inches and fractions of inches can get confusing or hard to remember after awhile. The flexible tape measure can bow or be unknowingly held at an angle that results in an incorrect reading. Pencil marks can be thick and less than precise. I wish I had a dollar for every piece of wood I cut too short or too long because I misread the tape or forgot what it showed. It happens, and it can be frustrating when it does. The simple solution, and the popular advice of carpenters, is to *measure twice, cut once.* Good wisdom that, when followed, saves a lot of unnecessary cutting, wasted time, and wasted lumber.

CUT OUT A LARGE DIAMETER HOLE

There are different methods to cut large diameter holes in different kinds of materials. A circle the size of a compact disk cut out of plywood, for example, might be accomplished most practically using a coping saw with a deep enough throat in its frame to allow the blade to reach the full circumference. A small hole would first be drilled within the circle to allow the blade to be inserted before starting the cutting, and then it's just a matter of sawing along the perimeter of the large hole. The blade can be removed from the frame, inserted into the drilled starter hole, and then locked into the frame to saw out the inside of the main hole. This could also be done with a narrow-bladed compass saw or a jigsaw.

Smaller holes in wood that are still more than an inch in diameter are sometimes cut out using hole saws, Forstner bits, or adjustable bits when they are available. A hole saw is a cylindrical saw—something like a coiled saw blade—turned by a drill machine in the same way a conventional drill bit works for cutting out holes. A Forstner bit is a special type of bit for drilling flat-bottom holes in wood. Either of these tools is usually better

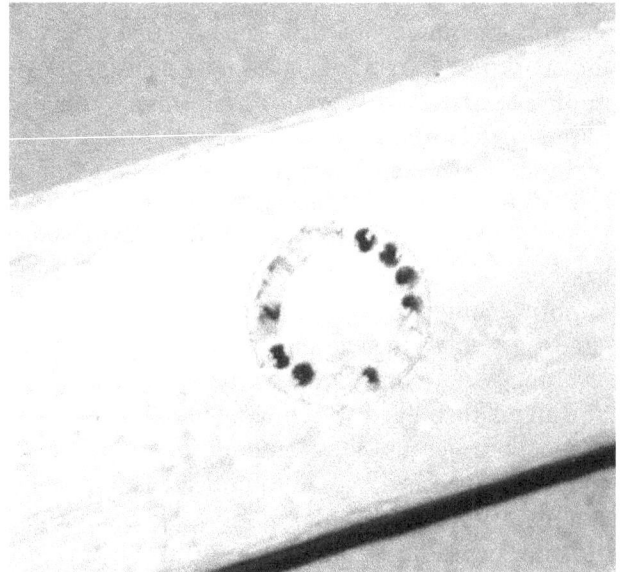

A series of small holes are drilled just inside the perimeter of the circle for the larger hole.

Filing out the inside of the hole using a half-round file.

The finished hole in the piece of wood.

suited for making larger diameter holes than are twist bits.

A technique I have employed on occasion to create a hole entails drilling a series of smaller holes just inside the border of the intended larger hole, all the way around and as close together as possible, to make material removal inside the circle easier.

One of my projects required a hole in a piece of wood to be 1 3/16-inch in diameter, but my largest twist bit was only 1 inch. To get the hole I needed, I first marked the border of the circle on the wood. Next, I drilled a string of small holes around the inside of the perimeter, as just described. Then I drilled out the majority of the center using my 1-inch-diameter twist bit, drilling halfway through the board from both sides to make the cleanest hole possible. I removed the thin material remaining between the small holes up to the inside perimeter of the large hole using both a rattail file and a wider half-round file, and finally I cleaned everything up with sandpaper. (A tubular sanding drum on a rotary tool can also be used to sand the inside edge of a hole.)

This same methodology is frequently applied to cutting large or odd-shaped holes in materials like steel. It's all about finding the most practical approach to removing the inner material by sawing, filing, grinding, or sanding, after first drilling a smaller hole or a series of smaller holes to make an opening large enough to allow files inside.

FIND THE CENTER OF A CIRCLE

Let's say you want to drill a hole into the center of the end of a round bar or cylindrical shaft. Some of us might be able to estimate the vicinity of the center of a circle fairly well by eyeballing it if we're careful, but that technique is far from perfect. What looks to be the center can end up being off to one side just a hair and just enough to mess everything up, only to be noticed after the drilling starts and it's too late to correct easily.

The easiest way to pinpoint the center of the circle is to box the circle with a square. Draw a square into which the circle fits perfectly, and then simply draw two lines across the square that connect the opposite corners. Assuming the circle is centered in the square, where the lines intersect will be the center of the circle.

MAKE A RIGHT ANGLE

Creating a right angle is as simple as swinging an arc with a compass from each end of a horizontal line, and then drawing a vertical line perpendicular to the horizontal line through the intersections of the

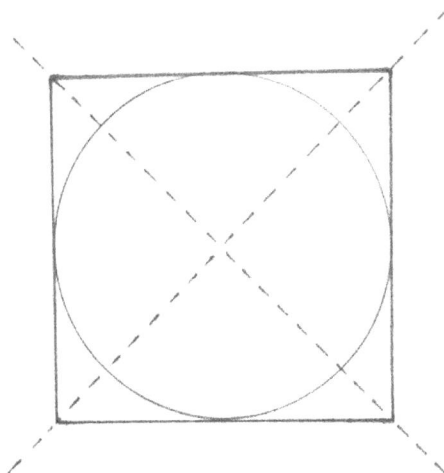

Finding the center of a circle.

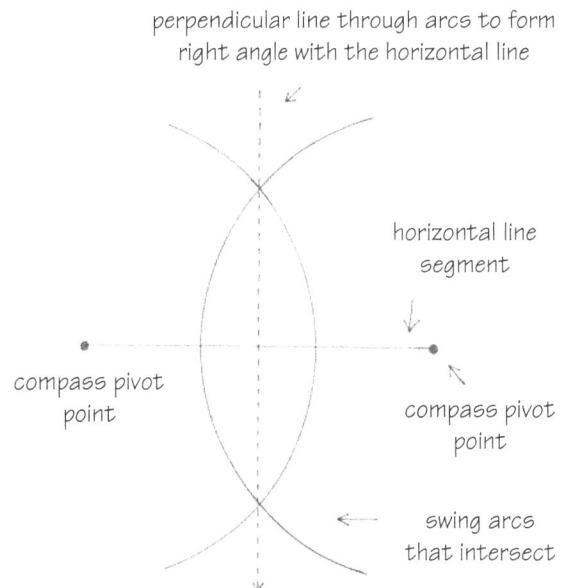

perpendicular line through arcs to form right angle with the horizontal line

horizontal line segment

compass pivot point

compass pivot point

swing arcs that intersect

Make a right angle.

semicircles of both arcs. Perpendicular lines form right angles.

LOOSEN A STUBBORN SCREW

Removing broken off or deformed screws using special screw extractor tools was addressed in chapter 5. There is another effective technique for loosening a rusted stuck or very stubborn screw if you have a drill press, a drill press vise, and a removable screwdriver tip that perfectly fits the slot of the screw head.

First, unplug the drill press to avoid accidentally turning on the motor at the worst possible moment. Next, tighten the selected screwdriver tip in the jaws of the chuck. Tighten the chuck on all sides with the chuck key to make sure the screwdriver tip won't slide up in the jaws under pressure.

Now secure the object with the stuck screw in the drill press vise, crank the table up, and make necessary adjustments to align the screwdriver tip with the slot in the screw head. When the tip fits into the slot as perfectly as possible, preferably with upward pressure on the screw head against the screwdriver tip, lock the table into position with the tightening nut.

At this point, an enormous amount of torque can be applied to the screw by simply turning the chuck—the screwdriver tip can't slip out of the screw's slot with everything tightened up like this. Slowly rotate the chuck by hand in the appropriate direction, using the chuck key in the chuck as a handle for leverage.

This method—preferably in conjunction with applying penetrating oil or a solvent to the screw head—will free up the majority of stubborn screws, but like every other makeshift approach, it won't always solve the problem. Screw slots can twist right out, and screws sometimes shear apart under the stress of heavy torque. If this approach doesn't turn the screw, you will probably have to drill or pull it out as described earlier.

CLEAN FILE TEETH

Anyone who has ever used a rasp or file knows how easy it is to clog up the spaces between the teeth. Dust and filings get trapped in a file and build up relatively fast, hindering the tool's ability to cut material to its full potential.

There are several techniques to clean files, and they vary in effectiveness. I found one source advising the application of WD-40 to the file to help lubricate the cutting action as well as to loosen up the gunk trapped between the teeth. This might be practical, but it is not my favorite method because the oil tends to attract dust particles. Another common trick is to scrape a piece of chalk across the teeth before using the file, which helps keep the filings from sticking to the tool.

A tool called a file card is very common for this purpose. It is a brush with very fine, stiff metal bristles that can scrape down between the teeth of even a fine-cut file and clear out much of the trapped material. I consider the file card or file brush an important maintenance tool in my own tool kit.

Another effective way to clean file teeth, and a method that is not as widely employed as it ought to be, considering how well it works, is to use a flat

Cleaning the crud out of a file using a flattened rifle casing.

scraper of soft brass to push the trapped crud out. The easiest approach is to simply squeeze shut the mouth of an empty brass rifle cartridge casing in the jaws of a vise or with a pair of pliers and use the flat edge as a scraper, pressing it against the face of the file and pushing it across the rows of teeth. The file teeth will cut little slots in the soft brass, allowing the small fingers that form between these slots to sink down into the grooves and essentially shovel the trapped material out. This is the most effective method I have ever used to thoroughly clean a file. It is only usable with files, however, and not with wood rasps.

PREVENT SPLIT BOARDS

Nailing boards together often results in split wood, especially when using large framing nails near the ends. I always found it difficult to avoid splitting studs whenever toe-nailing them to a bottom sill, for example, because the nail is so close to the end of the stud, where it is more prone to split. Small splits in the lumber present no major problems, other than the fact that they don't look very nice. Boards used in framing are commonly covered with wallboard anyway, hiding any unsightly splits.

This kind of splitting can be avoided almost entirely by predrilling the holes for the nails, using a slightly smaller drill bit so the nails fit tight. Cordless drills make this method very easy, although the extra time requirement makes the step impractical in some situations. (Where time is a critical factor, a nail gun will speed things up dramatically.)

Some years ago I heard about blunting the tips of the nails to minimize splitting. The nails are set on something solid, pointing upward, and a moderate strike straight down on the tip of the nail with a framing hammer blunts the point slightly. Care must be taken not to hit the point too hard, which can bend or buckle the nail.

The whole idea with this trick is that a sharply pointed nail wedges its way through wood, tending to split the wood apart, whereas a flat-nosed nail acts more like a punch or chisel that pushes the wood fibers out of the way. I discovered this actually does work to a degree.

PULL TIGHT NAILS

Nails are routinely pulled out of boards for one reason or another. Carpenters typically keep various claws and pry bars around for prying things apart and for pulling nails, but framing and claw hammers end up handling the task more often than not, mainly because they are almost always within close reach.

Big nails can be a hassle to pull from a board. You need to grip the stubborn nail securely, usually by its head if at all possible, and apply sufficient leverage to lift it from its tight seat. When a claw hammer alone just isn't adequate for the task, sometimes it helps to slide a block of wood under the head of the hammer to facilitate better leverage.

You may find yourself having to remove a nail that's been driven into a wall stud behind painted drywall, such as when rearranging pictures in a living area. In those situations, you can place a rubber computer mouse pad under the hammer to cushion the force of the prying and prevent marring the paint or denting the drywall.

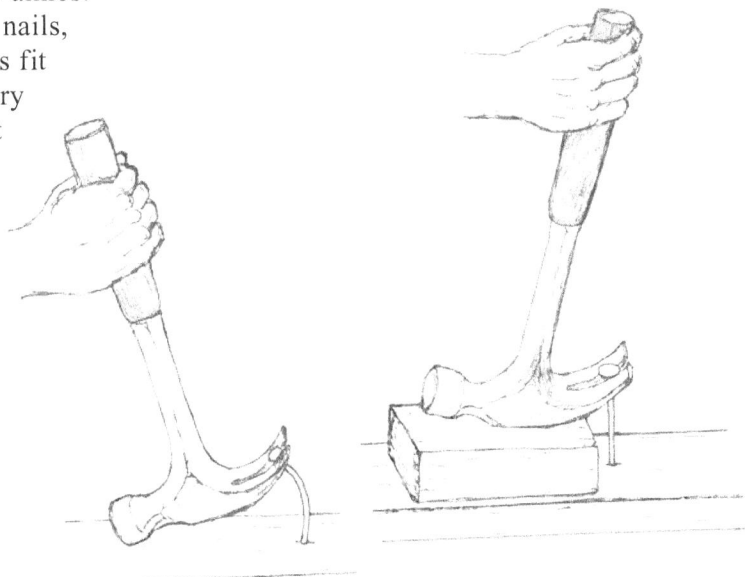

Poor leverage.

Pulling nails.

Block of wood under the hammer provides better leverage

PREVENT OVERHEATING SMALL METAL PARTS

Whenever soldering, welding, forging, or even grinding small pieces of steel, accidentally overheating and burning the metal is a common concern. Holding a small part to a fast-spinning grinding wheel generates a lot of friction, and the metal heats up very quickly. If care isn't taken, the part can easily be burned and ruined. Even if it doesn't burn, a tempered item, such as a spring, can quickly lose its proper temper. When the steel starts turning some shade of purple, brown, or blue, the colored area is generally no longer as good as it was before, even if it's not totally destroyed. This also goes for leaving small items in the forge too long. The smaller the piece of metal, the easier it is to ruin by overheating.

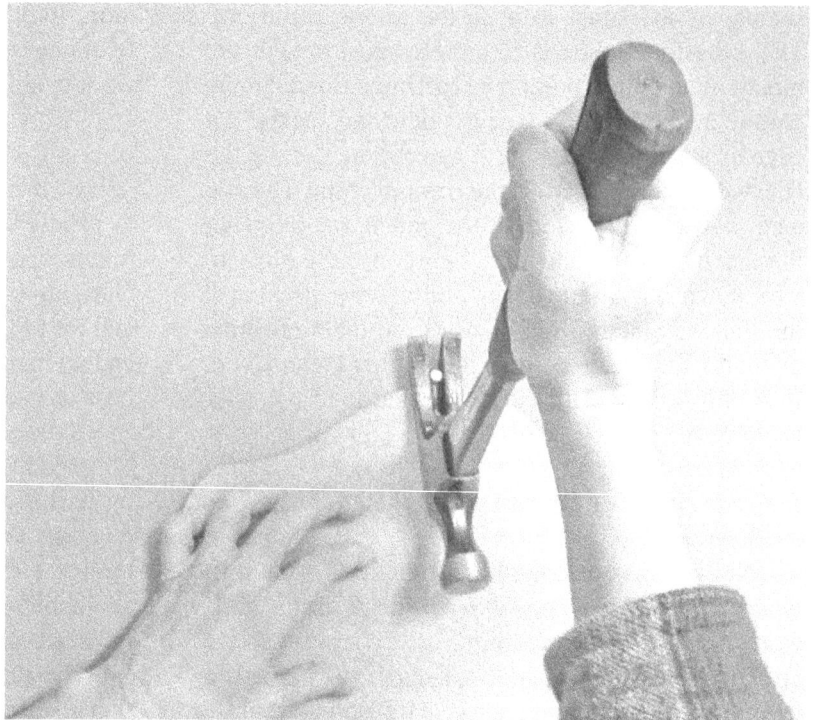

Pulling a nail out of a stud with the help of an ordinary computer mouse pad to protect the painted drywall.

There are ways to prevent or at least reduce this problem. Whenever grinding on a piece of metal, it is best to avoid pressing it hard against the spinning wheel. Whenever I rough-sharpen an edged tool on my bench grinder, I try to go slow and easy with the task so as not to build up too much heat too quickly. It also helps to dip the part in a can of water periodically to keep it cooled. I usually keep a coffee can half full of water close to my grinder for this purpose. I pay close attention to the thin areas, routinely looking for those dreaded colors in the steel.

There may come a time when you'll need to heat and form, or weld on, one end of a small spring. Control of the heat application is paramount under such conditions. You want some method for keeping the torch flame's heat concentrated in one small area without heating up the rest of the spring. There are several ways to accomplish this successfully.

If the piece to be heated is secured in a vise, the jaws of the vise can serve as a heat sink to draw much of the heat from the area making contact with the jaws. The key here is to clamp the item in the jaws with the maximum metal-to-metal contact, like a flat spring held flat in the vise, with only the small portion to be heated above the top of the jaws. The area between or below the jaws won't get nearly as hot.

Brass is a good conductor of heat, and a couple small pieces of sheet brass might be used to pad the steel vise jaws, to both protect the surfaces of the workpiece and dissipate a lot of the heat. This method can be used whenever the working temperature will not reach or exceed 1,700°F, which is the approximate melting point of brass.

Another technique often used for controlling heat transfer while soldering or brazing small metal items is to apply a heat control paste to the area you don't want to ruin by overheating. Brownells sells a special product for this purpose called Heat Stop, which will absorb a lot of heat wherever it is applied.

CREATE MAKESHIFT TOOL HANDLES

Small files are commonly sold without handles. Also, you might find good small tools at yard sales that are cheap because their handles are broken or missing. Fortunately, it is not difficult to shape and fit handles from sections of dowels and other wooden pieces. A good number of my own hand tools sport homemade handles, and these are more economical than, and work as well as, store-bought handles.

I discovered that those wooden eggs sometimes sold in arts and craft stores make comfortable handles for wood-carving chisels and small files. Smoothly sanded hardwood eggs the size of a chicken egg are ideal. The oval shape of the egg perfectly fits the palm of my hand. I fit them onto the tang of the tool by first drilling into the smaller end of the egg, using a bit the same diameter as the small end of the tang, to the depth equal to the length of the tang, and then drive them in with a rubber mallet. Epoxy can be poured into the hole first for added security.

Certain tiny tools, such as screwdriver tips and drill bits designed to be held in the jaws of a chuck in normal use, can be adapted for use by hand. T-shaped handles can be fabricated by cross-welding or brazing short sections of steel rod directly onto a small bit to create a tool that can be turned by hand. I made a handy little tool from two individual double-ended (Phillips head and flathead) screwdriver tips that I notched at their centers and brazed together into an X configuration. This produced a versatile and compact four-way screwdriver with its own integral T-handle.

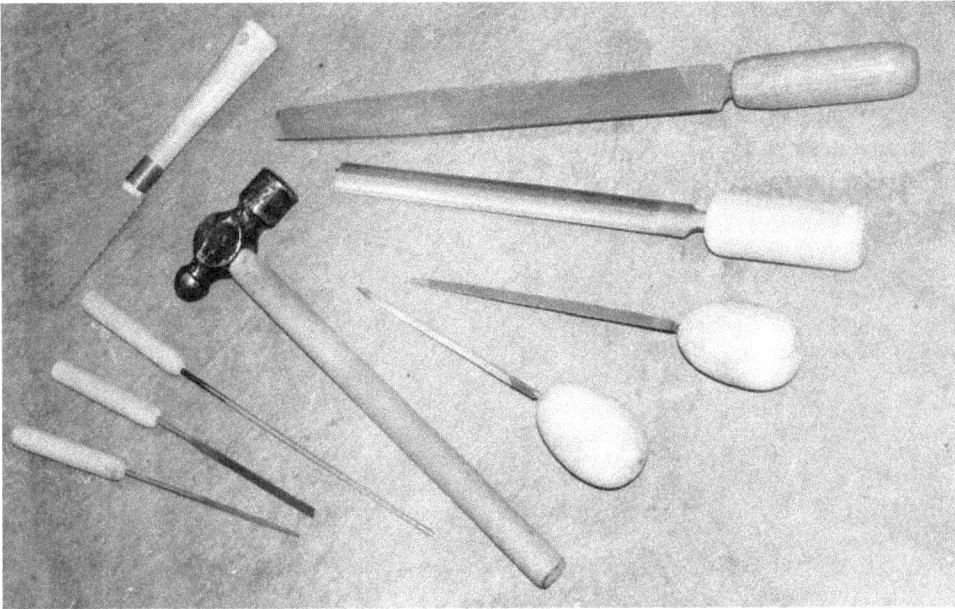

Some examples of functional makeshift tool handles.

Makeshift handles of bone and wood for three small, store-bought saw blades and one improvised blade (bottom). The blades are merely set into slots and secured in place with wrappings of cord and sometimes glue.

REMOVE RUST

Cleaning rusty tools, hardware, or old gun parts can be a chore with conventional methods involving solvents, sandpaper, or steel wool. I found an interesting method for removing rust I just had to try myself, called electrolysis. It works by suspending the rusty item in a bucket of water connected to a battery charger, where electric current draws the rust off the surface of the metal.

The first variation of this method I tried was the one detailed by David Leard in his article "404 Terrific Tech Tips" in *The Best of American Woodworker* magazine. Leard described using a metal bucket full of plain water, with a wooden stick set across the top. The rusty item is suspended in the water with string, and it should not be allowed to make direct contact with the metal bucket. The positive lead (red) from the battery charger is clamped to the rim of the bucket; the negative lead (black) is clamped directly to the rusty item in the water.

Leard noted that he usually lets it go for about

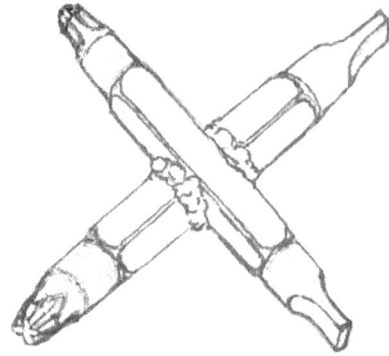

Two screwdriver tips notched and brazed together to form a handy four-way screwdriver.

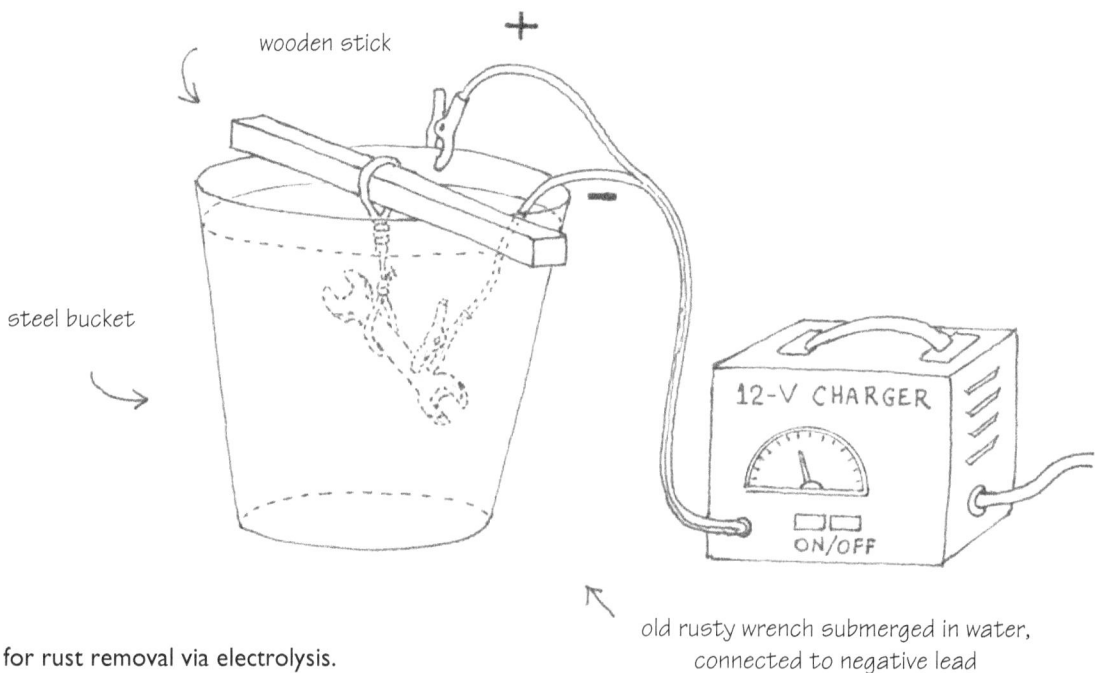

wooden stick

steel bucket

12-V CHARGER

ON/OFF

First method for rust removal via electrolysis.

old rusty wrench submerged in water, connected to negative lead

10 hours, but in my experiment with his version of the process, 10 hours was simply not enough. After more than 12 hours, I saw very little change in the amount of rust on the surface of the metal item.

Further research showed me how to make the process work a whole lot better. First of all, an alkaline solution known as an electrolyte should be added to the water to increase its conductivity. Although plain water will produce the same basic

reaction, it will do so much too slowly to be effective. Washing soda (sodium carbonate, Na_2CO_3, also known as soda ash)—*not* to be confused with baking soda—can serve as an electrolyte and is available in the laundry section of many supermarkets. (Arm & Hammer sells it under the brand name Super Washing Soda.) About one tablespoon per gallon of water is usually recommended, but a stronger solution will ensure

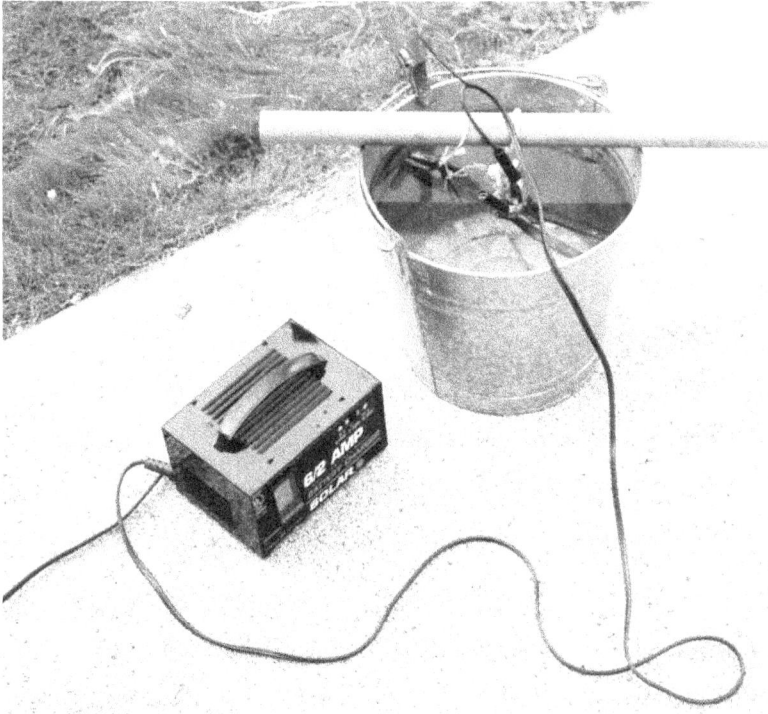

Cleaning rust off old pliers using a battery charger and a metal bucket full of water.

useful for this process, especially a galvanized bucket like I used, because the zinc could actually plate the cathode (i.e., the negative lead or clamp in contact with the part being cleaned), as occurs in electroplating. The better method calls for a plastic bucket, with a steel rod submerged in the solution to serve as the electrode to which the positive lead is clamped. I used a four-way lug nut wrench as an electrode in my second round of experimentation, and it worked quite well.

As far as I can tell, this appears to be a fairly safe process because it makes use of low-voltage current. Just be sure to avoid using any salts in conjunction with stainless steel containing chromium (chromium/salt mixtures are toxic), and do the work in a ventilated area. Also, be careful not to inadvertently substitute caustic soda (sodium hydroxide, also known as lye) for washing soda (sodium carbonate)

that there's enough in the water to act as an electrolyte to carry the current, and it may make things work faster.

I also discovered that a steel bucket is not very

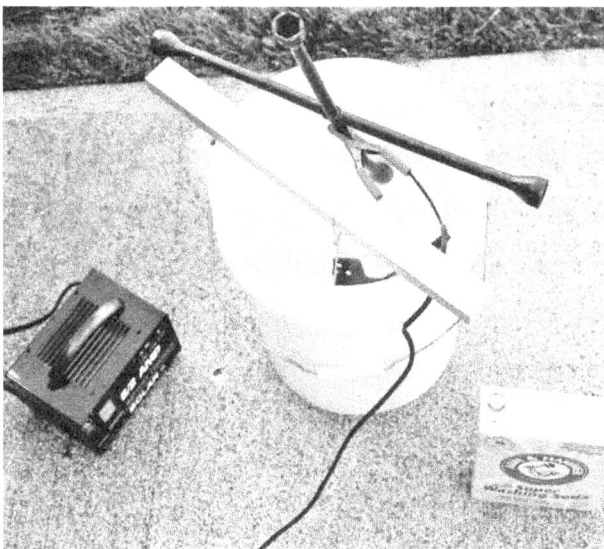

Electrolysis using a plastic bucket and washing soda as an electrolyte. The positive lead is clamped to a lug wrench, which serves as an electrode.

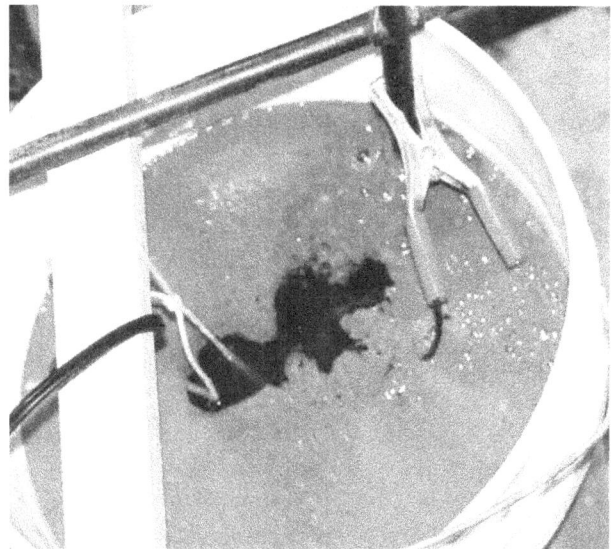

Much of the rust floats to the surface after 12 hours of electrolysis.

Rusted metal object before electrolysis.

Metal object after electrolysis, with most of the rust removed.

as the electrolyte. Caustic soda is extremely corrosive and can cause chemical burns and other serious injuries.

This second method removes rust very effectively if allowed to work for about 24 hours or more. Afterwards, the black residue on the item can be cleaned off with a stiff brush and soap and water before drying and lightly oiling.

The neat thing about this process is that you can be busy accomplishing other chores while your rusty metal parts are being cleaned without any attention.

MAKE YOUR TOOLS EASILY ACCESSIBLE

My dad has reminded me many times about the advantage of keeping tools where they are easy to find and easy to reach. Quite simply, if your tools are buried in a toolbox or in a bench drawer, hidden from view, it is too easy to forget about them, or you might simply avoid hunting for them when you're in a hurry. The tools hanging on the wall or stored where you can see them will probably be the tools you'll use the most.

You can buy or easily make little wooden shelves and modify them for use as tool holders. Simply drill holes of various sizes through the shelf, through which small tools with handles (like screwdrivers, punches, chisels, awls, and rattail files) can hang, or cut a series of parallel slots along the front edge for suspending flat files. It was previously noted how convenient sections of 2 x 4

can be in this application. The 2 x 4 makes a very solid little tool rack, and it can be mounted to the wall or a workbench with or without metal brackets.

In chapter 1, I mentioned that scraps of old leather can be rolled into tubes and screwed to a block of wood or directly to a wall or shelf to hang tools. I use this method for hanging pliers and wrenches in my blacksmith shop. This is also a great makeshift way to use old or worn-out leather belts.

A handy tool rack can be created simply by fastening a strip of wood or a narrow piece of steel horizontally to the exposed studs in a wall or to a bench frame so that pliers, tongs, and other long-handled tools can hang in a convenient location. I mounted several racks of this type in my blacksmith shop for hanging hammers and tongs.

Probably the most conventional method for hanging tools above a workbench in a shop, garage, or basement is with a pegboard and pegboard hooks. This is popular because it makes efficient use of available space, and the rack is very versatile. The hooks can be moved around as desired to rearrange the tools on the wall. Magnetic strips are also popular for hanging steel tools like chisels. Probably the quickest and cheapest way to hang tools for easy access is to simply hammer nails or staples into the wall. I hang a lot of my own tools on nails.

There are times when you or a family member will need to grab a common tool for some quick task, like hanging a picture or tightening up some screws. Rather than having to go to the basement,

These tools are easy to see and reach in this work area, making them especially convenient to find and use.

Tubes of old leather hold these tools where they are easy to see and reach when needed.

The tong rack in the background is merely a length of strap iron screwed to the wall studs.

Pegboard makes hanging tools on the wall easy and convenient.

garage, or wherever else the main work area is located to get what you need, it's convenient to have a selection of tools on hand in the living area of your home. Many people employ a kitchen drawer for this purpose, but a clear plastic tub stowed in a cabinet, an available cupboard shelf, or any number of other solutions work equally well.

CATEGORIZE MISCELLANEOUS HARDWARE

Any shop or work area worth spending time in while creating or repairing different things should be well stocked with assorted common hardware. Just about everyone who owns tools will also keep quantities of nails, screws, staples, nuts, bolts, washers, and other routinely needed items on hand. The more of this kind of thing you have in

An old, open-faced paper filer is used as a makeshift rack to keep a selection of common tools visible and handy in the household. Spackle, glue, duct tape, paracord, and an assortment of nails and other fasteners are stored nearby.

your garage or shop, the fewer trips you'll have to make to the local hardware store whenever you get into a project.

It is very common to find jars or cans containing quantities of nails, screws, or other useful hardware at garage sales, where the required investment typically is negligible. Accumulating this stuff is easy enough.

The big challenge then is in organizing your assortment of goodies so you can find exactly what you need when you need it. If you have to dump out the mixed nuts and bolts from a coffee can to search for a specific fastener, it can slow your progress down, assuming you will take the time out from your project to hunt for whatever you need in the first place. Sometimes it might seem easier to drop whatever you are doing and run to the hardware store, where you can buy exactly what you need.

The problem with that, besides the time it takes, is that new hardware items at retail prices can be expensive. It is better to keep stores of your own hardware on hand at all times.

There are different ways in which miscellaneous hardware can be organized for convenience. A workbench might have drawers, for example, where specific items can be stored. The front of the drawers can be labeled to identify what they contain.

For years, a common garage/shop storage system for especially small items, such as wood screws and washers, was to keep things in glass baby food jars, where they could be easily seen. Their metal lids were secured to an overhead shelf or wheel for convenient access. These were easy and inexpensive to make, and you'll still see them around occasionally. A modern upgrade would be to use plastic peanut butter jars. You can still see what's inside, and they don't break when you drop the jar full of screws onto the shop floor.

Nowadays, the most common storage system for this sort of thing seems to be those plastic bin or tray holders that can be mounted on a wall or stacked on a workbench. There are lots of different variations, but those with clear windows in front make it easy to identify the contents at a glance.

I use a combination of storage systems in my own shop that seems to expand as I accumulate more hardware. Jars full of nails and other fasteners crowd the shelves under my workbenches, and I keep small hardware in bin drawers.

Categorizing and sorting miscellaneous hardware in your shop calls for a convenient and well-labeled storage system. If you haven't already done so, it will take some careful planning. The photo on page 193 lists some of the common kinds of small hardware that I expect might be useful for categorization. It shouldn't be taken as an all-encompassing list, but merely an idea as to how miscellaneous hardware might be categorized in a shop for tinkering, repairing, and building makeshift products.

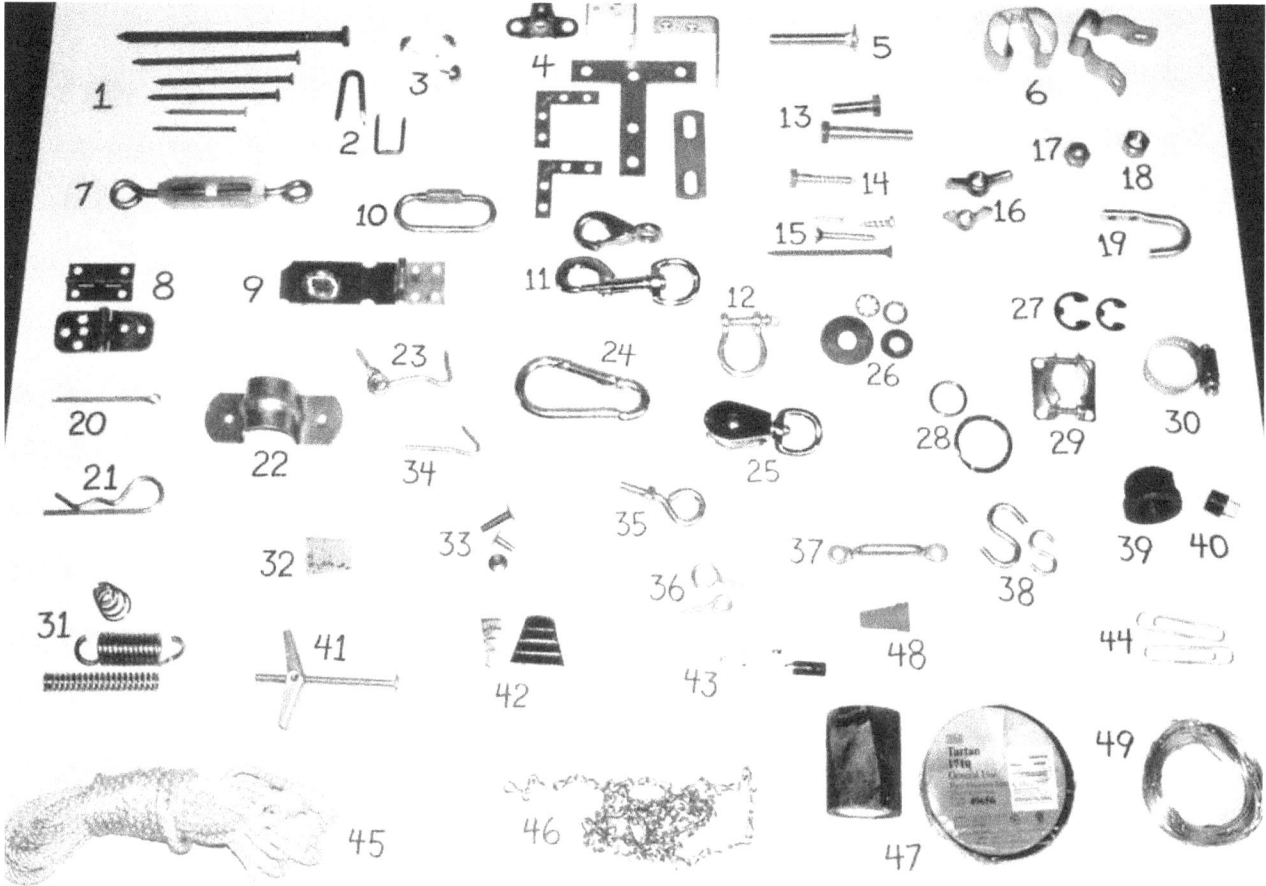

Miscellaneous hardware categorized by number:

1.	Assorted nails	18.	Hex nuts	35.	Eye bolts
2.	Staples	19.	Wall hooks	36.	Eye screws
3.	Tacks	20.	Cotter pins	37.	Pull handles
4.	Braces and brackets	21.	Hitch pin clips	38.	S hooks
5.	Carriage bolts	22.	Conduit mounting straps	39.	Pipe end caps
6.	Spring clips	23.	Hook-and-eye latches	40.	Pipe plugs
7.	Turnbuckles	24.	Snap links	41.	Toggle bolts
8.	Hinges	25.	Pulleys	42.	Handle wedges
9.	Hasp hinges	26.	Assorted washers	43.	Alligator clips
10.	Quick links	27.	E-clips/retaining clips	44.	Paper clips
11.	Snap hooks	28.	Split rings	45.	Nylon rope
12.	Anchor shackles	29.	Conduit clamp connectors	46.	Chain
13.	Common bolts	30.	Hose clamps	47.	Adhesive tapes
14.	Lag screws	31.	Assorted coil springs	48.	Wire nuts (electrical)
15.	Assorted wood screws	32.	Cork stoppers	49.	Brass wire
16.	Wing nuts	33.	Copper rivets		
17.	Cap nuts	34.	Screw hooks		

CHAPTER 9

Theorems and Formulas for Inventors and Builders

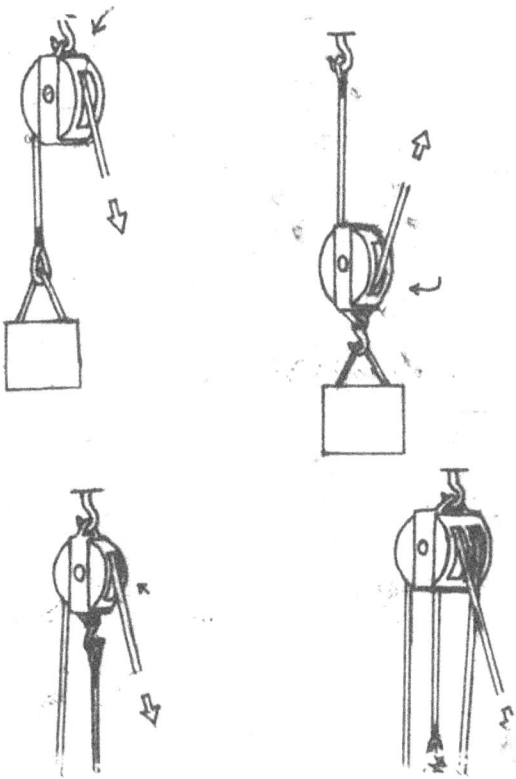

This chapter will provide the reader with valuable informational tools in the form of several essential theorems and formulas. If you found yourself isolated in any environment with limited gear and needed to improvise with makeshift contrivances, you would very likely want to know how to make important calculations and measurements applicable to your tasks at hand. The formulas in this chapter will help you do just that.

I know from experience that a person doesn't have to be a professional engineer or scientist to be able to productively apply formulas. Situational tasks will dictate the necessary calculations.

For example, if you were building a bowstring using B-50 Dacron cord rated at 35 pounds breaking strength, and you knew that the bow for which the string was being created had a 45-lb. pull at full draw, then using the common rule of thumb that a string should have four times the breaking strength of the draw weight of the bow,* you would discover

---

* This rule of thumb for determining the safe breaking strength of a bowstring for a given bow draw weight is described by Tim Baker in *The Traditional Bowyer's Bible, Volume Two*, in the chapter titled "Strings."

that you need a string with at least 180 pounds breaking strength. If you do the division, you can see that five strands of the 35-lb. Dacron cord would be very close to what you want, but six strands properly twisted and bound together would give you a generous margin of safety for your 45-lb. bowstring. This is an example of applying a very simple formula to a task at hand.

Throughout this book, I have used the term "mechanical advantage" to describe the advantage gained by using certain tools to apply force. Simple machines that provide a mechanical advantage include the lever, the wedge, the gear, and the screw, to name just a few. While it may not always be necessary to calculate the mechanical advantages of these items, it is certainly useful to know how, and we'll look at some examples of doing so in this chapter. It is more important to know how to effectively make and apply the devices that give us these useful advantages.

TEMPERATURE SCALE CONVERSIONS

Because a lot of creative makeshift projects require attention to varying temperatures (e.g., welding, soldering, forging, or heat-treating metal tools; boiling glues; firing clay), it is important to know the formulas for converting temperature scales.

People living in the United States are familiar with the Fahrenheit scale, but in many other countries and in the scientific community, the Celsius (what used to be called centigrade) scale is more common.

To convert from Fahrenheit (F) to Celsius (C), simply subtract 32 and divide by 1.8. For example, you might already know that water boils at 212°F. If you subtract 32 from 212, you get 180. If you then divide the 180 by 1.8, you end up with 100. Hence, you know that water boils at 100°C.

To convert from the Celsius scale to Fahrenheit, multiply by 1.8 and then add 32. Again using the temperature at which water boils as an example, you would take the 100°C and multiply it by 1.8 to get 180, and then add 32 to get 212°F.

It can be useful to practice these formulas with temperatures you already know to confirm your accuracy. It is common knowledge that water freezes at 32°F and at 0°C. If you do the math, it will confirm what you already know.

To keep things simple, you might wish to memorize the formulas as follows:

Fahrenheit to Celsius:
F − 32 ÷ 1.8 = C
Celsius to Fahrenheit:
C x 1.8 + 32 = F

Very simple formulas to remember, and very handy when you need them.

DETERMINING THE MECHANICAL ADVANTAGE OF PULLEYS, BLOCKS, AND TACKLES

Another example of how a simple formula might be especially useful under certain circumstances is the mechanical advantage ratio that applies to blocks and tackles, which is figured by counting the number of parts of rope leading to and from the movable block in a multiple-block, or tackle, arrangement. This could be an important formula for anyone who needs to lift heavy objects with rope and tackles, such as when building a log cabin or other large structure.

With this formula, we can quickly determine that with a block and tackle arrangement known as a gun tackle—where you have a movable block suspended with the object to be lifted and a second block fixed to an overhead structure so the direction of pull is down from the top block rather than up from the movable block—the theoretical mechanical advantage would be two, meaning that a 200-lb. weight would require only 100 pounds of pull on the rope, when there are two parts of rope to and from the suspended movable block. With a double pulley or double-sheave block fixed above a single-sheave block, as with a luff tackle, where three parts of rope lead to and from the movable block, a pull of 100 pounds could theoretically lift a 300-lb. weight.

Why are these "theoretical" advantages? Because a certain amount of applied force is lost through friction—but the amount of effort lost due to friction can be accounted for with a simple adjustment. By adding 10 percent of the load per sheave (i.e., the grooved wheel) in the tackle, we can make a rough adjustment for the friction.

Example: a luff tackle uses three sheaves. Let's say we want to lift a 400-lb. weight with this

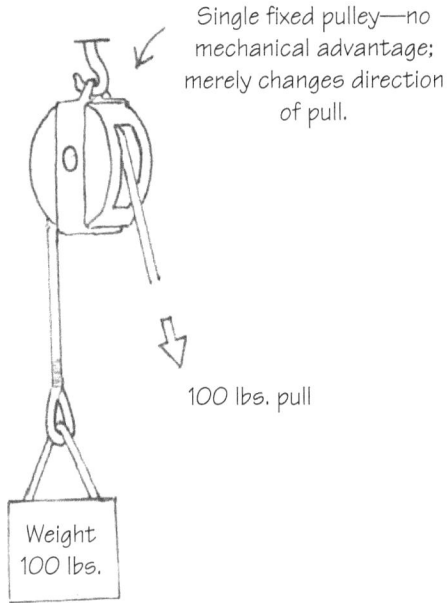

Single fixed pulley—no mechanical advantage; merely changes direction of pull.

100 lbs. pull

Weight 100 lbs.

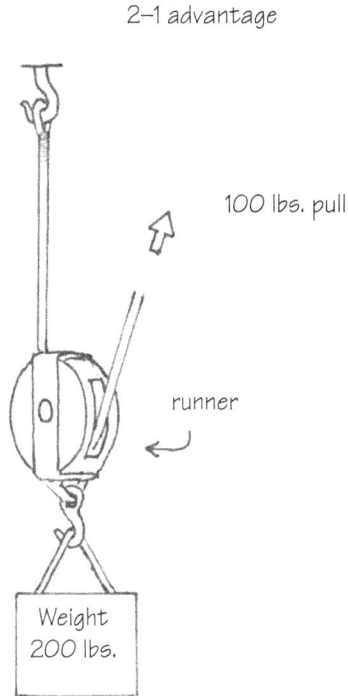

2–1 advantage

100 lbs. pull

runner

Weight 200 lbs.

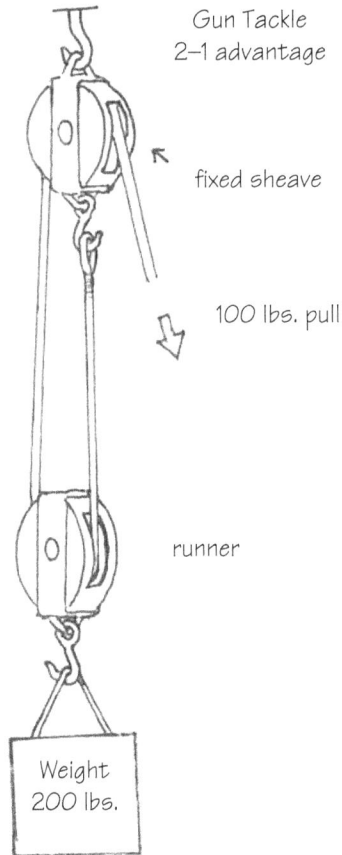

Gun Tackle 2–1 advantage

fixed sheave

100 lbs. pull

runner

Weight 200 lbs.

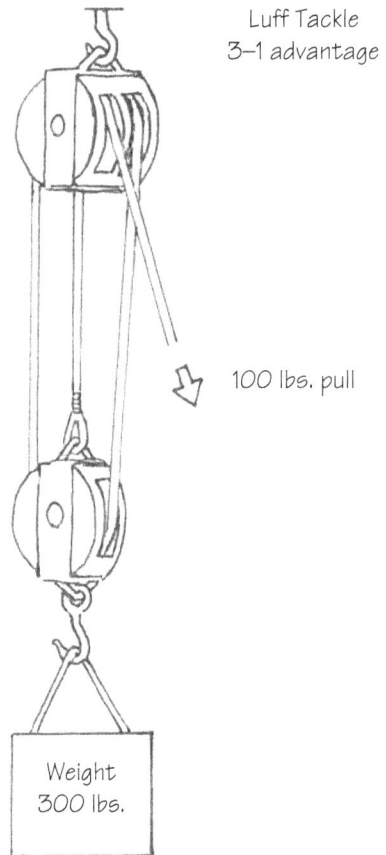

Luff Tackle 3–1 advantage

100 lbs. pull

Weight 300 lbs.

Pulleys.

arrangement. If we multiply the number of sheaves by 10 percent of the load weight (10 percent of 400 is 40, multiplied by 3 sheaves = 120), we discover that to account for loss of efficiency to friction, we should add 120 pounds to the total weight. So, while the theoretical mechanical advantage in this case requires about 133 pounds of force to lift the weight, we can see that the actual required force is roughly 173 pounds. (For a more thorough study of blocks and tackles, refer to U.S. Army manuals FM 55-501 and FM 55-17. Copies can be found online or through military surplus dealers.)

DETERMINING THE MECHANICAL ADVANTAGE OF A WEDGE

The wedge is a simple machine that is an example of an inclined plane. Wedges have a number of uses, one being the simple clamp device we studied in chapter 4. Wedges are also useful tools for splitting wood, holding doors open, and securing tool heads to wooden handles.

The formula for determining the mechanical advantage of a wedge is as follows: the mechanical advantage (MA) equals the length of either slope (S) divided by the thickness (T) of the large end, or MA = S/T. So, if we use a wedge that is 2 inches thick at the flat end opposite the tapered end, with its length on one of its slopes equal to 12 inches, we can see that the wedge will have a mechanical advantage of 6. In other words, 100 pounds of force at the thick end will provide 600 pounds of force outward along the inclined plane.

CALCULATING GEAR RATIOS

With an arrangement of two toothed gears of different diameters where one gear drives the other, it is a simple matter to determine the number of revolutions either of the gears will make for any given number of revolutions of the other gear.

Here is how it works. Let's say our machine has a large gear with 35 teeth driving a smaller gear with 15 teeth. And let's say that we want to determine how many revolutions the small gear makes for every six revolutions of the larger gear. In this example, we know the number of revolutions of one of the gears, as well as the number of teeth of both gears. The formula for this is to multiply the number of revolutions of the known gear by the number of teeth of the same gear, and then divide by the number of teeth of the other gear to find the number of revolutions it will make.

So, we know that our larger gear has 35 teeth and makes six revolutions, so 35 times 6 equals 210, divided by 15 (number of teeth of small gear) equals

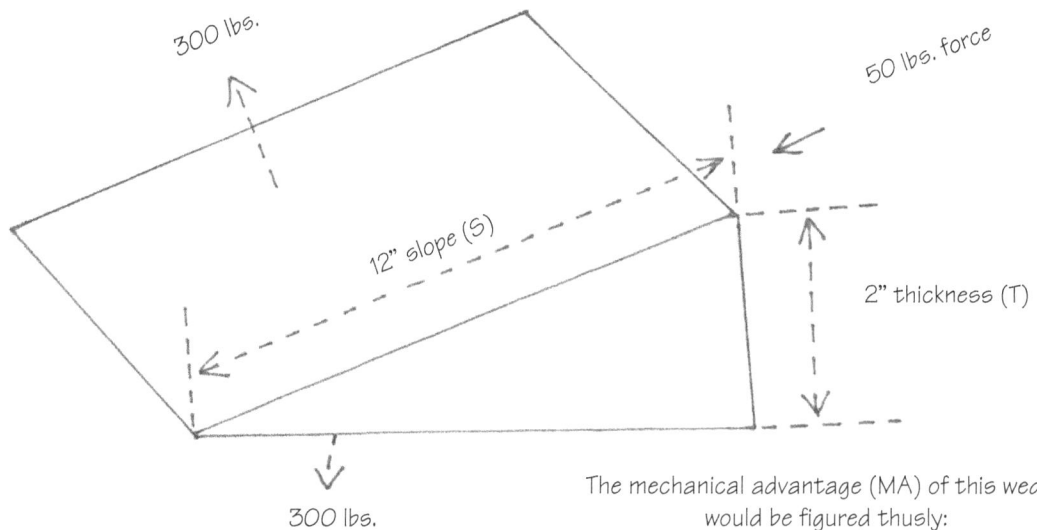

300 lbs.

12" slope (S)

50 lbs. force

2" thickness (T)

300 lbs.

The mechanical advantage (MA) of this wedge would be figured thusly:
MA = S/T
Or a mechanical advantage here of 6 (50 lbs. effort at the thick end will provide 300 lbs. force on slopes).

Wedge.

Find revolutions of gear B,
when gear A turns six revolutions:
35 x 6 = 210, then divide 210 by 15 = 14.
Gear B turns 14 revolutions.

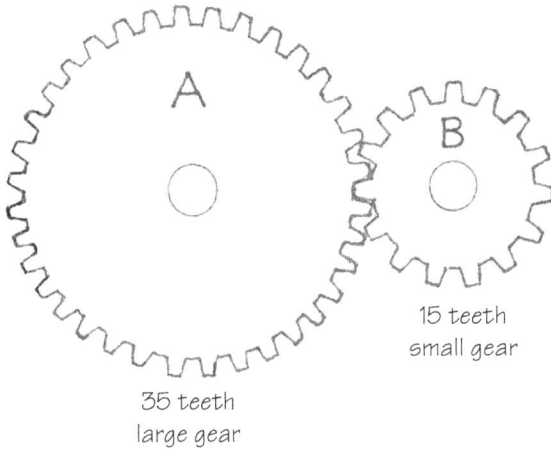

A

B

15 teeth
small gear

35 teeth
large gear

Also, if gear B turns 14 revolutions, then 14 x 15 = 210.
If we divide 210 by 35, we see that gear A turns
6 revolutions.

Gears.

14. Hence, we have determined that the small gear will turn 14 revolutions for every six revolutions of the larger gear.

To keep things simple, you might want to memorize the formula as follows: the unknown number of revolutions of gear B equals the number of revolutions of gear A times the number of teeth on gear A, divided by the number of teeth on gear B.

It is important to remember that this method for calculating gear ratios works either way—small gear to large gear or large gear to small gear, the formula remains exactly the same since we are dealing with the ratio of the number of teeth on the gears rather than the size of the wheels directly.

CALCULATING DIMENSIONS

Several simple geometric formulas pertaining to area, circumference, and volume might be worth memorizing for numerous practical applications. Area measurements could be particularly important when calculating how much paint or stain might be needed for a project. Circumference formulas are commonly used to measure articles of clothing or

thickness of rope. Being able to figure out the volume of a space would be helpful for such tasks as calculating how much fill rock is needed for a drainage trench.

Probably the simplest formulas are for calculating perimeter and circumference. Determining the perimeter of a square is as rudimentary as multiplying the length of one side by four. The perimeter of a rectangle can be quickly determined with this obvious and easy formula: length times two plus width times two. Some of you probably make these and similar calculations routinely without even thinking of them as geometric formulas.

Circles and spheres are measured using formulas containing the number represented by the 16th letter of the Greek alphabet, pi, which is the ratio of the circumference of a circle to its diameter (circumference over diameter) that is typically rounded to 3.14159 (or 3.1416). Hence, we can determine the circumference of a circle by simply multiplying the diameter by 3.1416.

The area of a circle can be determined by one of two formulas. If we multiply the square of the circle's radius by pi, or 3.1416 (the famous "pi r squared" formula, where "r" represents radius), we end up with the same number we would get by multiplying the square of the diameter by .7854.

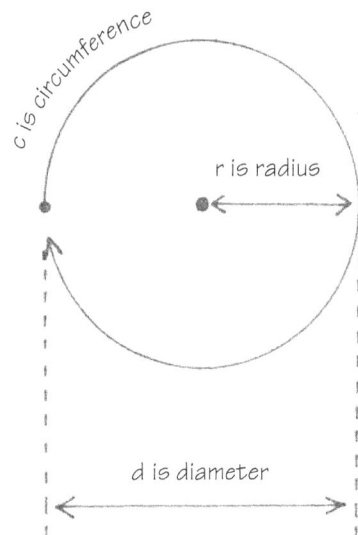

c is circumference

r is radius

d is diameter

Pi (symbol π) is the ratio of the circumference to diameter, or the number rounded to 3.1416.
$\pi = c/d$

Circle.

Example: a circle with a diameter of 4 feet has a radius of 2 feet. Two squared equals 4, times 3.1416 equals 12.57, and 4 squared equals 16, times .7854 also equals 12.57. So, we know that a circle having a diameter of 4 feet (radius of 2 feet) has an area of approximately 12 1/2 feet, if we round the numbers.

Finding the area of a square or rectangle is as simple as multiplying the height by the base, or the length by the width. In the case of a square, this is merely multiplying one side by itself, or "squaring" one side, since all sides are the same length.

The area of a triangle can be determined by multiplying the base by the height and then dividing by two. The surface area of a sphere (determining the land area of the Earth, for example) can be calculated by multiplying the square of the radius by pi (3.1416) and then multiplying by four.

Finding the volume of a body requires a bit more math, because volume is the space occupied by a solid figure, which is a three-dimensional object. The volume of a cube is obtained by raising the length of one side to the third power, or in other words the length of a side times itself, and then times itself again (one side "cubed"). The volume of a rectangular cube is obtained by multiplying the length by the width by the height.

The volume of a sphere can be obtained by multiplying the cube of the radius by pi (3.1416), and then multiplying by four and dividing by three. Likewise, the volume of a cylinder can be obtained by simply multiplying the square of the radius of the base by pi, and then multiplying that number by the height. This is a valuable formula for determining the volume of a barrel, canister, or other cylindrical container.

Finally, the volume of a cone can be calculated by simply multiplying the square of the radius of the base by 3.1416, then multiplying by the height and dividing by 3.

USING THE PYTHAGOREAN THEOREM

The Pythagorean theorem is definitely a valuable geometric formula to have in your repertoire. With it, you would always be able to determine, among other things, the length of any side of a right triangle, as long as you know the lengths of the other two sides.

I would paraphrase the theorem as follows: *the square of the hypotenuse of a right triangle is equal to the sum of the squares of the other two sides* (the hypotenuse being the side of a right triangle opposite the right angle).

Not only is this theorem used in graph charts, but it could also be useful for things like determining the amount of roofing material that will be needed on each side of a simple gabled or A-frame roof, given only the height from the rafter plate to the top of the center ridge, and the length and width of the building. We would divide the width of the building by two to obtain the longer leg of the triangle (or the shorter leg in the case of an A-frame house with a steep roof); the height of the ridge will form the other leg, and the rafter would be the hypotenuse for our purpose. The hypotenuse times the length of the building in this case will give you the area for one side of the roof.

An easy way to utilize the theorem for quick work is to simply remember "3, 4, 5." To check for square, measure 3 feet (or meters or whatever) down one leg and 4 of the same units down the other leg. If the distance between these two points is 5 units, then the two short legs are at a true 90 degrees. This trick is based on the Pythagorean theorem but is just an empirical way to do it without the math.

● ● ● ● ●

In this chapter, we have taken a look at some basic formulas that I believe can be useful to someone wanting to design and build a variety of makeshift products, and the value in memorizing them seems to me quite obvious. But this isn't supposed to be a math course, and the possible mathematical formulas one might learn and apply extends well beyond the scope of this book. I sincerely hope that your quest for practical calculating skills will continue, and that if this chapter has served merely to inspire further studies in this area, then I think an important task has been accomplished.

right triangle

c

hypotenuse

a

b

right angle: 90°

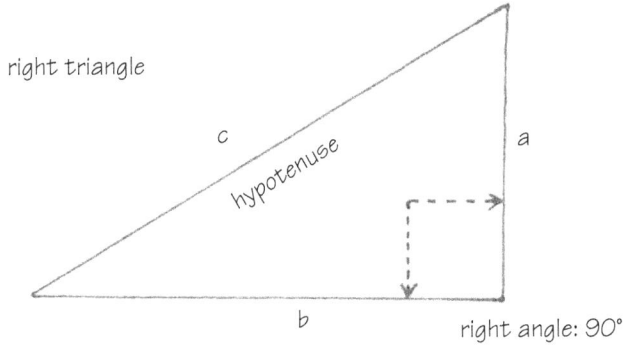

$a^2 + b^2 = c^2$
legs a and b form a right angle

Also:

$$\sqrt{a^2 + b^2} = c$$

Example:
If a = 5, and b = 12,
then c = 13

$a^2 = 25$, and $b^2 = 144$,
$(a^2 + b^2 = 169)$
then $c^2 = 169$

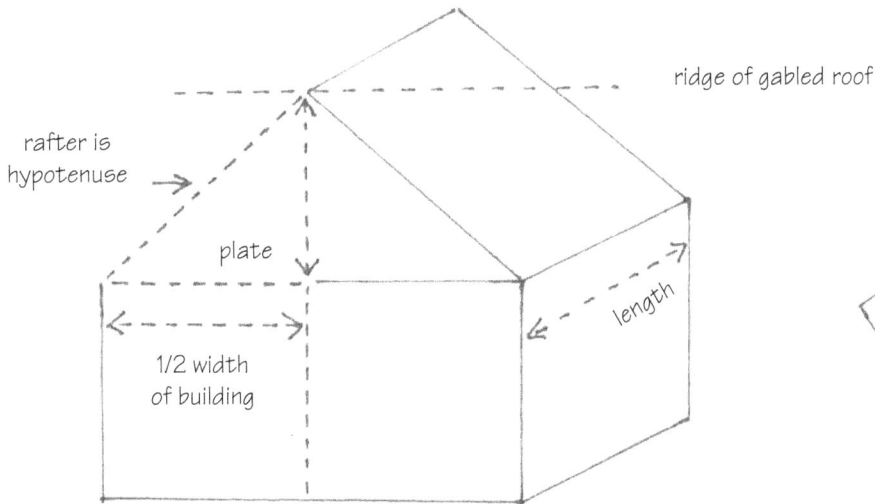

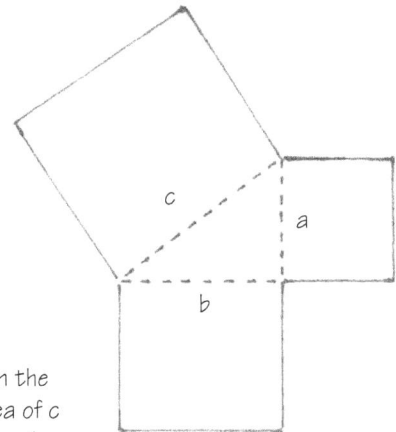

ridge of gabled roof

rafter is
hypotenuse

plate

length

1/2 width
of building

c

a

b

Squares built on the
triangle legs. Area of c
equals the sum of
squares a and b.

Pythagorean theorem.

Suggested Resources for Further Study

The following resources have been immensely helpful in my ongoing study of do-it-yourself skills. There are probably hundreds of similarly useful books, magazines, videos, and websites out there, but these are some of the ones I have turned to the most over the years. Of course, the Internet offers an entire universe of information to assist the makeshift craftsman, and I encourage you to use it as well when you need answers or direction for your projects.

OLD WORLD AND PRIMITIVE TECHNOLOGIES

- ***The Art of Flint Knapping**, Fourth Edition, by D.C. Waldorf (Branson, MO: Mound Builders Books, 1993)*
  An excellent work on stone tool technology, *The Art of Flint Knapping* contains plenty of clear illustrations by Valerie Waldorf that show the techniques broken down into stages for easy understanding. It also provides a useful discussion about heat-treating stone.

- ***Back to Basics: How to Learn and Enjoy Traditional American Skills,* Second Edition, by Reader's Digest (Pleasantville, NY: Reader's Digest Association, 1996)**

  The hardcover how-to books by Reader's Digest tend to contain high-quality, comprehensive, and easy-to-read instructional information, and the *Back to Basics* books are no exception. This 456-page classic contains an enormous volume of valuable information for traditional craftsmen, hobbyists, farmers, and homesteaders. In my view, no self-reliance library is complete without this book.

- ***Earth Knack: Stone Age Skills for the 21st Century* by Bart and Robin Blankenship (Layton, UT: Gibbs Smith, Publisher, 1996)**

  Earth Knack is a handy book for anyone wanting to learn about primitive basket weaving, flint knapping, cord making, and fabricating a variety of primitive tools and pottery. Includes an interesting section on how to create a center-seam boot moccasin. I have found the illustrations particularly helpful.

- ***Flintknapping: The Art of Making Stone Tools* by Paul Hellweg (Canoga Park, CA: Canyon Publishing Co., 1984)**

  This was the first book I ever studied about the art of knapping arrowheads and making stone tools. It is a useful little book that explains the techniques very well and includes black-and-white photos and clear illustrations sketched by Michael R. Seacord.

- ***Foxfire 5,* edited by Eliot Wigginton and his students (New York, NY: Anchor Books, Doubleday, 1975, 1976, 1977, 1978, 1979)**

  I have enjoyed the entire classic *Foxfire* series, but book number 5 tops my list. This volume contains lengthy chapters on iron making and blacksmithing, gun making, and bear hunting. I found the blacksmithing and gun-making chapters especially helpful during my research into low-tech tools and methods. All of the *Foxfire* books are famous for their lengthy interviews with some of the old-timers who mastered these skills in an era when educational resources weren't as vast as they are today.

- ***Primitive Technology: A Book of Earth Skills,* edited by David Wescott (Layton, UT: Gibbs Smith, Publisher, 1999)**

  Quite a number of authors contributed to this book, including David Wescott, Steve Watts, Errett Callahan, Paul Hellweg, and Jim Riggs, to name just a few. Put out by the Society of Primitive Technology, it is an excellent collection of articles describing primitive tools and other things made from natural materials like stone, bone, antler, and wood.

- ***The Traditional Bowyer's Bible, Volume Two* by G. Fred Asbell, Tim Baker, Paul Comstock, Dr. Bert Grayson, Jim Hamm, Al Herrin, Jay Massey, and Glenn Parker (New York, NY: The Lyons Press, 2000)**

  A brief reference was made in chapter 9 to Tim Baker's chapter about bowstrings, but this entire series provides worthwhile reading for anyone who works with woods, glues, sinew, and many other natural materials. They are, of course, especially helpful for anyone interested in primitive or traditional archery.

- ***Ultimate Guide to Wilderness Living: Surviving with Nothing but Your Bare Hands and What You Find in the Woods* by John McPherson and Geri McPherson (Berkeley, CA: Ulysses Press, 2008)**

  While the title might suggest this is essentially a wilderness survival book, I include it in this list of important resources for the makeshift hobbyist because it contains such an enormous volume of useful information about how to build things with natural materials. Basically a collection of the McPhersons' previous books published by Prairie Wolf throughout the late 1980s and early 1990s, it contains excellent information on bow and arrow making, basket weaving, wilderness cooking, and making primitive shelters, primitive clothing, and traps. The discussions about brain-tanning buckskins and making cordage are as complete and easy to follow as any you will find. With its hundreds of black-and-white photos, it is a great resource for any how-to library.

- ***The Woodwright's Shop: A Practical Guide to Traditional Woodcraft* by Roy Underhill (Chapel Hill, NC: The University of North Carolina Press, 1981)**
Some readers will be familiar with Roy Underhill's PBS television program of the same title. His 18th century-style wood- and iron-working shop makes use of only traditional tools, including a spring-pole reciprocating band saw, hand-turned flywheel wood lathe, manually powered grinding wheel, manual drill press, shaving horses, axes and adzes, and a blacksmith's forge. His craftsmanship with these old tools is amazing, and his processes are fun to watch. Definitely one of the most intriguing how-to books I have ever seen.

KNOTS AND CORDS

- ***The Book of Outdoor Knots* by Peter Owen (New York, NY: Lyons & Burford, 1993)**
This book cover a wide variety of practical, general-purpose knots. I especially like the big, clear, extremely easy-to-follow illustrations.

- ***The Klutz Book of Knots* by John Cassidy (Palo Alto, CA: Klutz Press, 1985)**
This spiral-bound workbook only covers 24 knots, but it is useful because it contains step-by-step diagrams and hard pages with holes to help the reader practice tying the knots. The copy I purchased new came with sections of different-color cord to practice with.

- ***The Morrow Guide to Knots* by Mario Bigon and Guido Regazzoni (New York, NY: Quill, 1981)**
A translation into English from its original Italian, this one covers a wide variety of knots and provides clear color photos of each. I found it especially useful in my study of net making.

- ***Practical Fishing Knots* by Mark Sosin and Lefty Kreh (New York, NY: Lyons & Burford, 1991)**
As its title suggests, this book explains knots commonly used for fishing. I think it is a very good reference for this, and it is one of the few knot books in my library to show the improved clinch knot, my favorite for tying line to a fishhook.

METALWORKING

- ***The Art of Blacksmithing*, Revised Edition, by Alex W. Bealer (Edison, NJ: Castle Books, 1976, reprinted 1996)**
While some of the material in this book might appear outdated as far as things like steel alloy designations are concerned, it still contains an enormous amount of forge-related information. The numerous illustrations helped me visualize the various traditional blacksmithing techniques, and Mr. Bealer's discussion of early thread-forming tools was particularly useful during my own experiments in this area.

- ***The Blacksmith's Craft: A Primer of Tools and Methods* by Charles McRaven (North Adams, MA: Storey Publishing, 2005)**
The first edition of this book was published in 1981, but the newer version is well updated. In addition to plenty of other valuable information, clear instructions are provided for building a coal forge out of an automotive brake drum. Discussions are well supported with black-and-white photos. I especially like the way McRaven explains things in a clear and generally nontechnical style. His writing reveals his many years of experience with hot metal, and much can be learned from this work.

- ***The Complete Metalsmith: An Illustrated Handbook*, Revised Edition by Tim McCreight (Worcester, MA: Davis Publications, 1991)**
A useful resource for anyone working with metals, precious stones, jewelry crafts, and even certain chemical processes such as photography and metal plating. Metal coloring, casting, soldering, and engraving are also covered. This handy spiral-bound book contains numerous tips, illustrations, data charts, shop recipes, and diagrams.

- ***The Complete Modern Blacksmith*** by Alexander G. Weygers (Berkley, CA: Ten Speed Press, 1997)
  A collection of several earlier books by Weygers, this book contains hundreds of realistic drawings by the author that illustrate the metalworking processes in impressive detail. It was Weygers' illustration of a process for file making that inspired my own experiments in this area. Anyone with an interest in tinkering with metal will love this book.

- ***The Master Bladesmith: Advanced Studies In Steel*** by Jim Hrisoulas (Boulder, CO: Paladin Press, 1991)
  This book, just like Jim Hrisoulas' earlier book, *The Complete Bladesmith*, provides in-depth instruction, exhaustively illustrated and photographed, about knife making and forge work, along with quite a bit of important information on steel and steel alloys, which will be particularly valuable to anyone working with steel. It also provides useful charts with lists of elements, drill bit sizes, tap and die thread sizes, chemical compounds, and weights and measures for quick reference. Both this book and his third in the series, *The Pattern-Welded Blade*, contain handy lists of the steel makeup of such common recycled items as old files, automobile axles, leaf springs, and sawmill blades. In my view, these books are all fantastic resources.

- ***Metallurgy Fundamentals*** by Daniel A. Brandt (South Holland, IL: The Goodheart-Willcox Company, 1992)
  Written like a textbook, this hardcover publication provides an easy-to-understand foundation in the science of metallurgy. Brandt does an excellent job of introducing the reader to the structural properties of steel and the characteristics of different alloys. This was the first book I studied when I initially became interested in metallurgy some years ago, and I have learned a great deal from it that has helped me with many of my projects in metal.

- ***Welder's Handbook: A Guide to Plasma Cutting, Oxyacetylene, Arc, MIG and TIG Welding*** by Richard Finch, S.A.E., A.W.S. (New York, NY: HP Books, 2007)

This is the most comprehensive book about welding I have ever seen. I used to carry a copy of the previous edition with me until I obtained this current edition. Now I keep the new book in my office at work and the older copy at home to ensure I will always have the information close at hand.

TECHNICAL INFORMATION

- ***Basic Machines and How They Work***, Revised Edition, by the Naval Education and Training Program Development Center (Mineola, NY: Dover Publications, 1994)
  It is important for the makeshift hobbyist to become familiar with simple machines, and this useful reference describes their basic principles and how they produce mechanical advantages. Among other things, it provides the formula for determining the mechanical advantage for blocks and tackles. This is a great little book that makes a number of seemingly complex mechanical principles very easy to understand.

- ***Carpenters and Builders Library No. 2***, Fourth Edition, by John E. Ball (Indianapolis, IN: Theodore Audel & Co., 1965, 1970, 1976)
  I purchased a copy of this hardcover math textbook for builders and engineers at a garage sale recently. It appears to be out of print now, although several online bookstores currently list used copies. I was never one to excel in mathematics in school, but I believe a book like this might have helped me understand certain mathematical concepts better. It shows applicable equations and formulas with workable examples. The geometry and trigonometry information is explained in such a way that I am actually able to understand it.

- ***Machinery's Handbook*** by Erik Oberg, Franklin D. Jones, Henry H. Ryffel, and Holbrook L. Horton (New York, NY: Industrial Press, Inc., 2008)
  The first edition was published in 1914; this is the 28th edition. All the recent versions are quite thick and contain a vast amount of information for mechanical engineers, machinists, draftsmen, toolmakers, millwrights, and other craftsmen. Often described as the

bible of metalworking and the mechanical industries, *Machinery's Handbook* is the single most comprehensive technical reference book of its kind that I am aware of.

- ***Workshop Formulas: Tips and Data*, Revised Edition, by Kenneth M. Swezey, updated by Robert Scharff (Danbury, CT: Popular Science Books, 1972, revised 1989)**
  Another formulas book, this one provides extensive information about wood stains, coatings, sealers, adhesives, cements, and concrete, as well as numerous calculations and conversions. It is a wonderful resource to have in any workshop.

OTHER BOOKS OF INTEREST

- ***Guerrilla Gunsmithing: Quick-and-Dirty Methods for Fixing Firearms in Desperate Times* by Ragnar Benson (Boulder, CO: Paladin Press, 2000)**
  This is a unique study of unconventional and expedient approaches to maintaining firearms. The text is well supported by black-and-white photos to help the reader visualize the methods described. Much of what is presented here is not found in other books about gunsmithing due to its particularly makeshift methodology.

- ***Homemade Guns and Homemade Ammo* by Ronald B. Brown (Boulder, CO: Paladin Press, 1986; originally published by Loompanics Unlimited)**
  A reference was made to this book in my discussion of makeshift pipe projects because it discusses simple improvised firearms made from steel pipe. Brown took the basic concept described in the Department of the Army's TM 31-210 on improvised munitions and went a bit further with his own experiments and detailed explanations. Contains plenty of clear illustrations and black-and-white photos.

- ***PVC Projects for the Outdoorsman: Building Shelters, Camping Gear, Weapons, and More Out of Plastic Pipe* by Tom Forbes (Boulder, CO: Paladin Press, 1999)**
  This is *the* book to study on the subject of constructing a number of practical projects with plastic pipe. Tom Forbes created a wonderful resource for makeshift hobbyists when he wrote this book. He followed up with *More PVC Projects for the Outdoorsman* in 2002.

- ***Sneaky Uses for Everyday Things* by Cy Timony (Kansas City, MO: Andrews McMeel Publishing, 2003)**
  This pocket-sized book is an interesting collection of truly unconventional makeshift projects, most of which are electronic in nature. For example, Mr. Timony describes how to improvise batteries using lemons. It was his instructions on how to make milk plastic that inspired my own research and experiments with that method. The illustrations are not particularly detailed, but they convey the basic ideas adequately. I found it to be an intriguing little book, and there have been two follow-ups: *Sneakier Uses for Everyday Things* (2005) and *Sneakiest Uses for Everyday Things* (2007).

ADDITIONAL RESOURCES

- **American Iron and Steel Institute (www.steel.org)**
  AISI is an organization dedicated to educating the public about the North American steel industry. Its website is a logical source for information about steel and the steel industry, with a glossary of related terminology, a question-and-answer page, and other useful features.

- **SAE International, formerly the Society of Automotive Engineers (www.sae.org)**
  This is "the premier membership society dedicated to advancing mobility engineering worldwide." This organization is described as "your one-stop resource for standards, developments, events, and technical information expertise used in designing, building, maintaining, and operating self-propelled vehicles for use on land or sea, in air or space."

- ***The Backwoodsman: The Magazine for the Twenty-First Century Frontiersman* (www.backwoodsmanmag.com)**
  This is my favorite magazine. It is published six

times a year, and its pages are always filled with how-to articles about such topics as boat building; log cabins; blacksmithing; guns and muzzleloaders; knives; slingshots; traps; camping; leather projects; old tools; treasure hunting; fishing; hermits, hobos, mountain men, and their lifestyles; wood carving; and anything else that might be of interest to its readership. Every issue provides a wealth of information for the makeshift hobbyist.

- **The Woodsmaster Survival Video Series (www.survival.com)**
  Excellent instruction is to be found in Ron and Karen Hoods' DVD series, with 25 volumes available as of this writing. These entertaining and educational how-to videos are well worth the money. If you want to find out how to construct primitive weapons, rig a makeshift forge with only discarded junk you find while out camping, or virtually anything else you might ever need to do to survive in the woods, these videos are really hard to beat.

www.ingramcontent.com/pod-product-compliance
Lightning Source LLC
Chambersburg PA
CBHW081359270326
41930CB00015B/3350